WHY NOT FREEDOM!

WHY NOT FREEDOM!

America's Revolt Against Big Government

James Ronald Kennedy
Walter Donald Kennedy

PELICAN PUBLISHING COMPANY
Gretna 1995

*The word "Pelican" and the depiction of a pelican are trademarks
of Pelican Publishing Company, Inc., and are registered
in the U.S. Patent and Trademark Office.*

Library of Congress Cataloging-in-Publication Data

Kennedy James Ronald.
    Why not freedom! : America's revolt against big government / James
    Ronald Kennedy, Walter Donald Kennedy.
        p.   cm.
    Includes bibliographical references (p.   -   ) and index.
    ISBN 1-56554-152-9 (alk. paper)
    1. Federal government—United States. 2. United States—Politics and
government—1993- 3. Decentralization in government—United States. 4.
United States—Social policy—1993- I. Kennedy, Walter Donald. II. Title.
JK325.K4 1995
320.473—dc20   95-16936
                                                                      CIP

Manufactured in the United States of America

Published by Pelican Publishing Company, Inc.
1101 Monroe Street, Gretna, Louisiana 70053

CONTENTS

III. THE PRESCRIPTION FOR THE CURE

IV. ADDENDA

Preface

The election held on November 8, 1994, will go down in history as the event in which America's middle class renounced the false god of liberalism. For more than four decades American liberalism has commanded the absolute obedience of everyone to its god—Big Government. The American public has been deluged with ever-increasing demands by liberals for more government-sponsored solutions for even the most mundane problems. These demands for more government solutions for every personal and societal short-coming have foisted on American society an element who have seemingly lost the ability to "fend for themselves." How long can any society exist when a large segment of that society no longer knows how to be or cares about being self-sufficient? This question of national moral character must be faced and answered.

Unfortunately, it will take more than one election to undo the severe damage done to constitutional government that these many years of liberalism have produced. The purpose of this book is to provide the average tax-paying, law-abiding, middle-class American an explanation of how he can help re-establish a political system that will safeguard individual liberties and personal property from an abusive Federal government. This abusive Big Government has shown itself resistant to efforts by even the most conservative Federal elected officials to bring it under control. The goal of this book will be to identify and describe the methods to be used to reduce and control the future growth of the god of liberalism, Big Government.

Many Americans have grown up never having heard about the principles of limited Federalism, State Sovereignty, and State's Rights. In an earlier time in our history, these principles were the central theme of our republic, yet they have suffered severely under the relentless attack of the liberal establishment. Most middle-class Americans believe in individual responsibility, yet for the past fifty years the Federal government has fostered a welfare society that has all but destroyed the work ethic that made us prosperous and free. Most middle-class Americans believe that religious principles help to create a virtuous society, yet for the past several decades the Federal government has fought to remove all acknowledgement of God from our public life. Most middle-class Americans do not want their children to be taught "alternate sexual lifestyles," yet recently the Federal government has promoted such teachings as "normal." Most middle-class Americans do not believe that gun registration will make our society safer from violent criminals, yet the Federal government has been actively engaged in passing such legislation. It should be obvious to even a casual observer that there is something very wrong with our country. When "our" Federal government can completely ignore the wishes of the middle class, when it can freely abuse its constitutional prerogatives, when it can totally ignore the limitations of a written constitution—something is wrong. The vote of November 8, 1994, demonstrated that the American people knew that something must be done about Big Government! *Why Not Freedom!* will provide concrete examples of just how illogical and uncaring the Federal government has become. Continue to read this book, and you will learn what can be done at the local level to rein in this abusive leviathan called the Federal government. We will not be satisfied with a temporary fix that will not solve the underlying problem. Such a makeshift solution will only give us a little breathing space while the enemies of liberty continue to forge the chains of our eventual total bondage. Instead, we will explain how to establish a system that will prevent the Federal government from ever again threatening our most precious liberties.

There are several important players in this current struggle—and make no mistake about it; this is a political struggle of gigantic proportions. The players consist of: (1) the middle-class taxpayers, (2) the liberal establishment, which includes government, media, and education establishments, and (3) the official political parties, both Democratic and Republican. As you read through this book, you will see examples of how all elements of the liberal establishment have worked to destroy middle-class values. You will also see that, while the Democratic party has been the leader in the struggle to enlarge government at the expense of the rights, property, and liberty of the middle class, the Republican party has also participated in the abuse of the middle class. If the middle class is to be made secure in its liberty and property, we must not rely upon a national party to protect these liberties and property. We must have a system that will transcend national political parties and the influence and power of the liberal establishment. You may be surprised to find out that such a system was at one time an acknowledged fact in America's political life. We will give you examples of how Americans, such as Thomas Jefferson and James Madison, in their day used this system to protect the individual liberties of citizens from an abusive Federal government! This same system is available to us today if we have the will to reassert our rights under the original Constitution of the United States of America.

In *The South Was Right!*,[1] it was demonstrated that the Southern people have traditionally maintained the proposition that the power of the Federal government, as an agent of the states, was limited by the Constitution, and that all power not delegated to the Federal government remained with "We the people" of the sovereign states. The unreconstructed leaders of the post-war South maintained the proposition that the loss of the War for Southern Independence changed the nature of the original government from a Republic of Republics, founded upon the free and unfettered consent of the governed, to its new and dangerous form of a centralized national (big) government. This new government that now claims to be the exclusive judge of the limits of its power is a different government from that established by our Forefathers, one created not upon the principle of consent but upon the principle of conquest. The South, since Appomattox, has been treated as a conquered nation. The resulting constitutional disaster, though, has not been confined only to the South. For example, children in Boston, Massachusetts, are victims of forced busing ordered by arrogant Federal judges. The ability of a Federal judge to assign pupils to local schools according to the color of their skin is one of many examples of the result of the victory of unbridled Federalism in 1865. Today, Americans from across the country are beginning to demand the right of their state governments to ignore unconstitutional Federal intrusions, such as unfunded Federal mandates. The time has come for Southerners to assume their rightful place as leaders in the struggle to restore our

1 James R. Kennedy and Walter D. Kennedy, *The South Was Right!* (Gretna, LA: Pelican Publishing Company, 1994).

country to the principles of the original Constitution. The time has come for all Americans—North, East, West, and South—to join together and renew the principles of the original Constitution. The time has come for middle-class Americans to rein in an abusive Federal government and return control of our country and our lives to "We the people" of the sovereign states. No one can better protect our "dearest rights" and liberty than "We the people" at the local level. We have had more than 130 years of experience to prove that Big Government does not provide adequate protection for our rights and liberty. It did not work in the former Soviet Union, and it has also been proven a failure in America. Men and women of America, the hour for change has arrived.

We will never regain our lost rights if we do not understand the parties to this conflict, realize that the problems we face are created by an unbridled Federal government, and acknowledge that there is a prescription for a cure, a prescription penned in 1787 called the original Constitution of these United States. By restoring its authority, "We the people" of the sovereign states will once again be safe from an abusive Federal government.

WHY NOT FREEDOM!

Introduction

What does it mean to be "free"? In the context of U.S. history, Americans are free from what? Too often groups demand freedom without ever defining what they want to be free of or what they want to be free to do. The word "freedom" is often used by politically correct pressure groups and "protected minorities" to mean "special privileges." For example, when a black[2] militant demands "freedom" for his people, often what he is demanding is the right to preferential treatment when it comes to job selection (quotas), or the right to force children to ride a school bus in order to achieve a prescribed racial mix (busing), or the right to have a certain percentage of public construction contracts reserved for minorities (set asides), or the right to lower the test scores of whites with an automatic increase in minority test scores (race norming). What kind of freedom would sanction discrimination against white people while allowing privileged status for non-whites? Is this really what freedom is all about? Is this what our Founding Fathers had in mind when they resolved to secede from the Colonial Union[3] with Great Britain and establish a new government based upon the principle of the consent of the governed?

Many of the early state constitutions of America report that "all

---

2 Throughout this book we will use the traditional words and phrases to describe common ideas. A "politically correct" vocabulary will not be used. For example, the use of "black" when referring to a specific ethnic group will be used instead of the current (1995) term "African American." Instead of using the cumbersome but politically correct "his/her" word glob, we will use the correct gender pronoun when gender is indicated and otherwise use the traditional male pronoun with the assumption that all educated persons will understand that it refers to all humanity, not just the male portion thereof.

3 The attitude of our Colonial Forefathers is summarized by the words of the Virginia Independence Convention of May, 1776: "*Resolved,* That the union that has hitherto subsisted between Great Britain and the American colonies is thereby totally dissolved, and that the inhabitants of this colony are discharged from any allegiance to the crown of Great Britain." Virginia Convention—Independence as cited in *Patrick Henry: Life, Correspondence, and Speeches,* William Wirt Henry, Ed. (1891, Harrisonburg, VA: Sprinkle Publications, 1993) I; 396.

men are born equally free." It was the belief of the early political thinkers of the various American states that men should stand equally before the law. This belief in "equality before the law" was in no way a statement of the latter-day liberal theory of abject human equality; rather it established as an early American principle that certain men were not given a divine right to rule over other men. Not only are all men to stand equally before the law, but each man, as part of his civic responsibility, must support the society of which he is a member by obeying its laws and otherwise being a productive member of that society.

One of the prerequisites of freedom is a sense of individual responsibility. This sense of individual responsibility will produce the following characteristics in a person: (1) the concept that the individual is responsible for his actions, (2) the concept that the individual must accept the consequences of those actions, and (3) the knowledge that the individual will not be allowed to shift his responsibility to society if he does not take care of his own needs. The concept of taking responsibility for one's action coupled with the knowledge that society is not going to "pull one's irons out of the fire" is the hallmark of a healthy and free society. An individual (or even a whole people) who by his own effort cannot provide for himself is not free. People in bondage, be they prisoners or slaves, look to others for their basic needs. Those who rely upon society for their support (food, shelter, health care, etc.) are not free men.

When the Federal government, through its welfare system, creates an entire class of welfare dependents, it has, by the nature of that system, reintroduced slavery in America. People who cannot or will not take care of themselves and who look to government to provide them their food, shelter, and other requirements for life have ceased to be free. A "non-freeman" is nothing less than a slave. The Federal government, under the control of the liberal Big Government faction, has created welfare slaves who faithfully do the bidding of their liberal masters during each election. Thus, the master (Big Government) feeds the slaves, and the slaves elect liberals who maintain the well-being of Big Government. At each election, the liberal establishment can count on thousands of voters who are locked into the system of voting the liberal ticket in order to get more federal subsidies, such as midnight basketball, as provided by President Clinton's crime bill, and to continue collecting their welfare payments, living in free housing, and enjoying other special privileges. Nowhere in the current system of welfare and other Federally sponsored social programs is there a plan to move these poor people from the welfare class into the economic middle class of productive, tax-paying, law-abiding citizens. The truth is that liberals don't want to lose their welfare clientele. If the poor were to advance economically into the middle class, the liberals would lose their guaranteed block of voters. Individuals in the middle class tend to resist tax-and-spend liberalism; therefore, liberals have no incentive to solve the welfare problem! More than forty years of Big Government liberal social programs such as welfare have led to the destruction of the sense of individual responsibility in a large segment of our population. Too many people today have the attitude that "somebody owes it to me." No longer willing to assume personal responsibility, such individuals become slaves to their welfare masters.

Under the current system of government, we the taxpayers, by way of taxation, are forcibly deprived of our private property (our tax dollars, i.e., our money) to pay for social programs enacted by the liberal-dominated government. These programs are, to a large extent, repayment to the welfare class for voting the "right" (usually Democratic) candidates into office. Through welfare and social programs, the liberal establishment has perfected the age-old technique of vote buying. Liberals don't use their money to buy votes; rather, through taxation, they use other people's money to buy votes. In each Southern election and in most urban Northern elections the liberal Democratic candidate can count on a huge block of social welfare votes. The candidate championing middle-class values such as limited government and low taxes must face the liberal block vote and overcome the anti-middle class, liberal news media in order to win an election.

This book has a special message for Southerners. It requires them to take a critical look at the reality of contemporary Southern politics. It challenges them to join with their Northern friends who are already in the field fighting for a return to the principles of the original Constitution. But the principles discussed in this book are still very relevant to all middle-class Americans. Hopefully, middle-class citizens from all across this land will join in this struggle to restore the original constitutional government. But, just like charity, political solutions must begin at home. The authors' home is the South, and it is to Southerners especially that we issue this call to take the lead in this most important struggle. This is a struggle waged by the middle class to regain control of our political destiny. It is a fight against entrenched establishments. It is a battle waged by the common people of this nation to get Uncle Sam off our backs and out of our pockets!

Why Not Freedom! looks at those hot issues that very few politicians are willing to talk about. Although middle-class Americans are concerned about these issues, the politically correct politicians of both parties are unwilling to discuss them. We want you, the reader, to know at the outset that we do not believe that Americans are as free today as our Forefathers were in the beginning of this country. We believe that radical and illegal changes were made in the original constitutional government of these United States. We believe that in order to regain our lost freedom we must return to the original form of constitutional government. We must have a society in which local control, State's Rights, and a limited Federal government constitute the norm. In *The South Was Right!*, we the authors defended the South's historical right of self-determination, the inalienable right of "We the people" of the sovereign states to be free. In each chapter of this book you will see that the problems besetting us today arise from an overly powerful Federal government against which "We the people" of the sovereign states are unable to protect our God-given liberties. The Federal government that invaded the South in 1861 is the same government that is currently invading our pocketbooks and our private lives. The Federal government that invaded the South in 1861 is now destroying the rights and liberties of middle-class Americans—North, South, East, and West. The problems faced by middle-class Americans today are proof that in 1861 *the South was right!*

SECTION I

THE PARTIES TO THE CONFLICT

INTRODUCTORY COMMENTS

In the next four chapters, we will identify the parties (participants) in the development of our current political situation which is proving itself so injurious to the freedom of middle-class Americans. In Chapter 1, we will look first at the historical development of the Federal government. We will demonstrate that the Federal government was established by the states to act as their agent in very limited and specified areas. We will offer specific historical examples of how in our early history the Federal government actually violated the Bill of Rights by denying its citizens the right of freedom of speech and freedom of the press. We will then provide an example of how two of the Founding Fathers assisted the states in responding to the unconstitutional Federal actions by calling for nullification of those actions. We will demonstrate how the division of powers among the executive (president), legislative (Congress), and judiciary (Federal courts) branches is not sufficient to protect the civil liberties of "We the people" of the sovereign states. We will show how all three branches of the Federal government actually worked together to enact and enforce unconstitutional laws and how it was the brave actions of the sovereign states that prevented the continuing violation of the civil liberties of early Americans.

In Chapter 2, we will look at another important participant—the American middle class. We will note that this most important part of our country's political fabric has been abandoned by those who control the Federal government—the same Federal government that today views the middle class as America's "cash-cow" to be milked, i.e., taxed, for the benefit of others! We will demonstrate how our Founding Fathers feared the actions of an abusive central government; therefore they ensured the maintenance of State's Rights to

19

act as the bulwark between "We the people" and a potentially abusive central government.

In Chapter 3, we will look at the liberal establishment. We will show how it is composed of many overlapping parts: (1) the media establishment that serves as liberalism's unofficial propaganda ministry, (2) an education establishment that endeavors to teach politically correct values that are usually in conflict with the values of the parents of middle-class children, and (3) a political establishment composed of the left-wing liberal politicians with their social welfare, block-voting clientele. This liberal establishment has been the controlling element of the Democratic party since the days of Franklin D. Roosevelt. It has used its influence and power to promote its love of big, tax-and-spend, centralized government and its radical social ideology. Nevertheless, the liberal establishment has exercised much influence, as we will demonstrate, in both major political parties.

In Chapter 4, we will discuss the national political parties. To the dismay of neo-conservatives and other party loyalists, we pronounce "a plague upon both your houses" in respect to both of the national political parties. We will demonstrate that, while the national Democratic party has been the open and acknowledged enemy of middle-class values, it has been the national Republican party that has been instrumental in promulgating and enforcing the social schemes of liberalism. We will note that, while the Democratic party supported forced busing, reverse discrimination, and quota civil rights legislation, it was the Republican party that actually forced these liberal schemes upon the middle class. Once again, we will point out that, regardless of which national political party is in control of the Congress, the Supreme Court, or the presidency—"We the people" of the sovereign states must rely upon the one bulwark that is the only true defender of our "dearest interests." Individual freedom, personal property, and constitutional government are best protected at the local level by those whose interest it is to safeguard their own liberty from the abuses of an aggressive Federal government.

We will complete Section I with an extensive summary in the form of questions and answers. These questions and answers will be drawn not only from the foregoing text, but also from numerous questions asked the authors by radio and television audiences. While engaged in these radio and television interviews, we have noted that many of the same questions, regardless of the area of the country, are repeatedly asked. We are hopeful that these questions can be addressed to your satisfaction.

CHAPTER 1

The Federal Government

The American middle class is currently undergoing a struggle to regain control of its political destiny. There are several important participants in this struggle: the middle class, the liberal establishment, and the national political parties. Each participant attempts to gain control of the Federal government and use the excessive power of that government to advance its particular political agenda. At present, the United States government has become the dispenser of political patronage and power. During the past fifty years, it has been heavily influenced or controlled by the left-of-center political elite. The Federal government has become the vehicle which the power elite, the people who are in the driver's seat, use to promote their left-wing liberal schemes. Unfortunately, the cost is borne by those who are not a part of the power elite or the political clientele of that elite. For many years, the liberal establishment has controlled the appropriation, via Congress, of patronage and power. The annual bill for this Federal pork barrel has been presented to the middle class via increased taxes, inflation, and unemployment.

This current overgrown, tax-and-spend Federal government is not the type of government that our Founding Fathers intended to establish when they drafted the Constitution of 1787.[4] To understand the radical change that has occurred, we must first understand the original design for the Federal government. To do this, we will answer the following questions: (1) Who formed the Federal government? (2) What was the purpose of the original Constitution? (3) Who has the authority to determine the constitutional limits of the Federal government's powers? and (4) What authority did the sovereign state retain in the newly formed Federal republic? The answers to these questions will help to identify the role of "We the people" in our struggle to regain control of our political destiny.

4 James R. Kennedy and Walter D. Kennedy, *The South Was Right!* (Gretna, LA: Pelican Publishing Company, 1994) 155-83.

The answer to the question "Who formed the Federal government?" can be found in the writings of a famous American statesman, John C. Calhoun of South Carolina. He tells us that "[O]urs is a system of governments, compounded of the separate governments of the several States composing the Union, and of one common government of all its members, called the Government of the United States. The former [the states] preceded the latter, which was created by their [the states'] agency."[5] From this we see that the sovereign states created the Federal government to be their agent and to perform only those duties that the states, acting on behalf of the people of their respective states, specifically delegated to their agent, the Federal government. Calhoun noted that the people of the states were careful to maintain their right to control any government that they created: "It [government, both Federal and state] has for its fundamental principle, the great cardinal maxim, that the people are the source of all power; that the governments of the several states and of the United States were created by them, and for them; that the powers conferred on them are not surrendered, but delegated; and as such, are held in trust, and not absolutely; and can be rightfully exercised only in furtherance of the objects for which they were delegated."[6] Alexander Hamilton, while supporting the ratification of the original Constitution, went so far as to declare that any acts of the Federal government not pursuant to the authority delegated to the Federal government by the states would be "merely acts of usurpation" and not deserving the authority of law.[7]

Not only did Calhoun, a Southerner, point out that the states created the Federal government, but many Northerners, such as William Rawle of Pennsylvania, also pointed this out. In his textbook on the Constitution, Rawle states that the formation of the Federal government ". . . was not the simple act of a homogeneous body of men, either large or small. It was to be the act of MANY INDEPENDENT STATES [emphasis added], . . . it was to be the act of the people of each state, and not the people at large."[8] Rawle describes who

5 John C. Calhoun, *The Works of John C. Calhoun* (New York, NY: D. Appleton and Company, 1844) I; 111.

6 Ibid, 112.

7 Alexander Hamilton, *The Federalist No. 33,* quoted in George W. Carey and James McClellan, *The Federalist: Student Edition* (Dubuque, IA: Kendall/Hunt Publishing Company, 1990) 161.

8 William Rawle, *A View of the Constitution of the United States: Secession as Taught at West Point,* Walter D. Kennedy and James R. Kennedy, Eds. (1825, Simsboro, LA: Old South Books, 1993) 31-32.

may alter or abolish the constitution under which a people live and how it can be done: "A moral power equal to and of the same nature with that which made, alone can destroy."[9] Thus, following the instruction of this early constitutional authority, once we understand who created the Federal government, we will see who has the right to change or destroy that government.

It is important to note that the Founding Fathers did not create an all-powerful national government. There were a few of the Founding Fathers who desired to form a strong central government similar to the British model from which the colonies had recently seceded.[10] At the Constitutional Convention of 1787, with a majority of delegates present, a motion was proposed to have the convention form a national government, but the resolution died without the benefit of even a second! It is important for Americans to realize that the Federal government of these United States was not designed to be a government of a nation-state, exercising ultimate authority over the people at the local level. The language of the Founding Fathers was very specific regarding the function of the Federal government and their determination to maintain the rights and liberties of "We the people" of the sovereign states. Having just experienced the terror of an all-powerful central government under the control of King George III, the Founding Fathers were determined to create a central government that could be controlled. The purpose they had in mind was to leave "We the people" a means to protect our most precious liberties should the central government, i.e., the Federal government, abuse its powers and infringe upon the people's liberties. The sovereign state then would serve as the final bulwark between "We the people" and an abusive and oppressive Federal government. Alexander Hamilton, even though he was an advocate of a strong, centralized Federal government, declared that "an entire consolidation of the States into one national sovereignty would imply an entire subordination of the parts; and whatever powers might remain in them would be altogether dependent on the general will. But as the plan of the convention [the Constitutional Convention of 1787] aims only at a partial union or consolidation, the State governments would clearly retain all right of sovereignty which they before had and which were not, by that act exclusively delegated to the United

9 Ibid, 31.

10 Kennedy and Kennedy, 219-35.

States."[11] Some may at this point ask, "What rights and sovereignty did the states have before the Constitution of 1787?" Prior to the ratification of the Constitution of 1787, the states were members of a union under the Articles of Confederation. Article II of the Articles of Confederation declared that "Each state retains its sovereignty, freedom, and independence, and every Power, Jurisdiction and right, which is not by this confederation expressly delegated to the United States, in Congress assembled." The states, prior to the ratification of the Constitution of 1787, were sovereign, free, and independent. These same attributes were retained when they seceded from the government created by the Articles of Confederation and then acceded to the new government formed by the Constitution of 1787. The states were and still should be the primary protector of "We the people" as was the intention of our Founding Fathers.

A point overlooked by many in the study of the United States Constitution is that the Federal Constitution is a composite of, or at least a reflection of, the better parts of the existing state constitutions. Yes, before we ever had a Federal constitution, the states had already provided for the "safety and happiness" of their people by establishing their own state constitutions. These early state constitutions were provided with a bill of rights or a declaration of rights composing the protection for what we would call today our civil liberties. These early state documents also provide us today with evidence of how the people in each state viewed themselves as a society. For instance, the constitution of the state of Massachusetts states that the citizens of that state were forming a government for themselves as ". . . a free, sovereign, and independent political body."[12] Nearly identical words as those used by Massachusetts were used by the other states that later ratified the Federal Constitution. Even as late as 1812, the people of Louisiana entered the Union with a constitution, approved by the United States Congress, which states that the people ". . . do mutually agree with each other to form ourselves into a free and independent state, by the name of the state of Louisiana."[13]

We have now seen that the states, acting in their sovereign capacity and through the instrument of the original Constitution, created

11 Alexander Hamilton, *The Federalist No. 32*, quoted in Carey and McClellan, 156.

12 Constitution State of Massachusetts, quoted in *The American's Guide to the Constitutions of the United States of America* (Trenton, NJ: Moore and Lake, 1813) 75.

13 Constitution State of Louisiana, quoted in *The American's Guide to the Constitutions of the United States of America*, 341.

the Federal government. We now must answer the question "What was the purpose of the original Constitution?" Many Americans have the mistaken idea that the Constitution, and especially the Bill of Rights that was added after ratification, grants specific rights to American citizens. This is an incorrect and dangerous idea. The Constitution is a compact between sovereign states whereby the states agree upon a mode of government among themselves and delegate certain and specific powers to their newly created agent—the Federal government. It can be thought of as a contract between the states. Each state must contribute (delegate) specific powers to the new creature, and, in return, each receives something of value. In the case of the thirteen original states, each state received protection of its borders, a free trade zone among the other states of the Union, and assurances of domestic tranquility (today we would probably use the term "law and order").

The Constitution was essentially a document establishing the limits of proper authority for the newly created Federal government. "We the people" of the sovereign states were already in possession of our rights and liberties. Therefore, it was not thought necessary or proper that the document creating the Federal government (the Constitution) should also attempt to codify all the rights and liberties belonging to "We the people" because these rights originated at the local level and belonged to the people even before the Federal government was created. For evidence of this, we again invite the skeptic to review the early constitutions of the original states. "We the people" had already provided for the protection of our rights and liberties at the local level. This, as Calhoun and Rawle have pointed out, is exactly where such power belongs. "We the people" created our respective states, and our states, acting as our agent, created the Federal government to be the agent of the states. In America, power and liberty originate with the people as members of a sovereign community or state; the Federal government is not the original dispenser of rights, liberty, or power.[14]

Calhoun declared that the Constitution was established to rule over the Federal government: "it was over the government which it created, and all its functionaries in their official character, and the individuals composing and inhabiting the several States, as far as they might come within the sphere of the powers delegated to the United States."

14 Rawle, 235.

He then noted that by careful examination and analysis he had demonstrated "conclusively, by arguments drawn from the act of ratification, and the constitution itself, that the several States of the Union, acting in their confederated character, ordained and established the constitution; that they ordained and established it for themselves, in the same character; that they ordained and established it for their welfare and safety, in the like character; that they established it as a compact between them, and not as a constitution over them; and that, as a compact, they are parties to it, in the same character. I [Calhoun] have thus established, conclusively, that these States, in ratifying the constitution, did not lose the confederated character which they possessed when they ratified it, as well as in all the preceding stages of their existence; but, on the contrary, still retained it to the full."[15]

The Constitution was not designed as a document by which the people of the sovereign states were to surrender their most precious liberties to the watchful care of a central government. In their ratification of the Constitution, states such as New York and Virginia specifically reserved the right to recall any or all powers delegated to the Federal government. New York and Virginia clearly stated that, should those powers granted to the Federal government by the states be used against the people of the sovereign states, the people of those states would recall (take back) that which they had granted.[16] By this very act, the sovereign states were making known to all future generations of Americans that the state retained the right to judge for itself whether the Federal government was living up to its end of the bargain. The states retained more than the right to judge whether the Federal government was acting in an unconstitutional manner; they also expressly reserved the right to withdraw from an abusive union should it become necessary to protect their most precious liberties. As Patrick Henry stated, "The first thing I have at heart is American *liberty*; the second thing is American Union."[17] John C. Calhoun would later reply to Andrew Jackson's words, "The Union, it must be preserved," by declaring, "The Union, next to our liberties most dear." Liberty is more important than the trappings

15 John C. Calhoun, *A Discourse on the Constitution and Government of the United States,* quoted in *The Works of John C. Calhoun,* I; 131.

16 Kennedy and Kennedy, 162.

17 Patrick Henry, quoted in William Wirt Henry, Ed., *Patrick Henry: Life, Correspondence, and Speeches* (1891, Harrisonburg, VA: Sprinkle Publications, 1993) III; 449.

of a government. To many modern Americans, this may seem a little radical, but remember the words of James Madison, ". . . the safety and happiness of society are the objects at which all political institutions must be sacrificed."[18] Madison, the faithful defender of the Constitution, makes it clear that the safety and happiness of society are to take precedence over any institution of government or even government itself. As Madison taught us, when a government becomes destructive to the ends for which it was established by a society, that society has the right and obligation to alter or if necessary to destroy that abusive government. Let us not forget that the American Revolution was in deed and in fact a radical departure from the idea that rights are a grant from government. In America, rights were seen as originating from the Creator, thus they were "unalienable." These rights come from God to the people who then form themselves into societies that form governments. The government in the American historical context is the servant of the people of a society (a sovereign state) and not a master to rule over the people.

The sovereign state was to be the final means by which "We the people" could protect ourselves from the abuse of the powers granted to the newly created Federal government. If the Federal government should attempt to infringe upon the right of free speech, which the Bill of Rights specifically prohibited it from doing, then the people could appeal to the sovereign authority of their state to protect them. Hamilton admitted that, if the Federal government attempted to encroach upon the rights of the states, "[W]e may safely rely on the disposition of the State legislatures to erect barriers against the encroachments of the national authority."[19] In another place, Hamilton states, "[I]t may safely be received as an axiom in our political system, that the State governments will, in all possible contingencies, afford complete security against invasions of the public liberty by the national authority."[20] You may be asking yourself where has the power of the sovereign state been when your children were ordered by a Federal judge to be bused across town, or when you were the victim of Federally enforced reverse discrimination and quotas, or when your state raised your taxes to pay for unfunded Federal mandates? Your inquiry deserves an answer.

18 James Madison, *The Federalist No. 43,* quoted in Carey and McClellan, 228.

19 Alexander Hamilton, *The Federalist No. 85,* quoted in Carey and McClellan, 285.

20 Alexander Hamilton, *The Federalist No. 28,* quoted in Carey and McClellan, 141.

According to Supreme Court Justice Salmon P. Chase, "State Sovereignty died at Appomattox." This simple observation explains why Southerners should refuse to accept the outcome of the War for Southern Independence as the final judgment regarding their rights under the current Federal government. The massed weight of bloody bayonets cannot legitimately change principles of constitutional government. The change from a Republic of Republics composed of sovereign states and a constitutionally limited Federal government to a centrally controlled national government having sole discretion as to the limits of its powers was not brought about through a democratic, and certainly not a constitutional, process. It was created not at the ballot box or by the free and unfettered consent of "We the people" but as a result of the moral suasion of bloody bayonets! The original Federal government was based upon the principle of consent, whereas the present Federal government is based upon the principle of conquest.[21] Note that James Kent in his *Commentaries on American Laws* sets forth the manner by which the Federal Union was to be maintained: ". . . for on the concurrence and good will of the parts, the stability of the whole depends."[22]According to Kent, it is concurrence and good will, not bayonets, that should hold the Union together.

The Federal government that arose from the ashes of the War for Southern Independence has become a tool of the politically correct, liberal establishment to force an unwilling middle class to accept its left-wing social schemes. It is important to note that the evil that the central government is now capable of doing to the middle class is not limited to Southerners. The monstrous central government in Washington, D.C., is now riding roughshod over the most precious liberties of all Americans (notwithstanding their accent). The question of State's Rights and limited Federal government is no longer strictly "a Southern thing"; it is now, as it was in the early days of this Republic, an American issue. As we will demonstrate in Section II of this book, "The Problems Facing Middle-Class America," this new Federal government has grown to the point of total disdain for "We the people" of the sovereign states, regardless of where in America we live—North, South, East, or West.

21 Kennedy and Kennedy, 155-83.

22 James Kent, *Commentaries on American Laws* (1826, New York, NY: Da Capo Press, 1971) I; 369.

John C. Calhoun taught that government had within it the propensity to abuse its legitimate powers for the benefit of those who control the government. This is due to man's natural tendency to be more concerned about himself than about society at large. Thus, according to Calhoun, if a group of people could gain control of a government, they could use the police powers of that government for their own purposes. The police power of a government could be used to take away the property of those who have no government to protect their rights and property (for example, this could include those who do not belong to one of the liberal elite's clientele politically referred to as a "protected minority"). Patrick Henry warned the South about the danger inherent in the proposed Federal government. He foresaw the time when the commercial interests of the North would use their numerical majority to control Congress and thus enact protective tariffs and other revenue bills. Once this happened, according to Henry and others, the Southern states, being agricultural rather than commercial, would be forced to pay the larger portion of the expense of the Federal government even though the South would be the smaller section.[23] Henry did not object so much to the nature of the partnership into which his state was about to enter as to the nature of the partners with whom she was about to contract. He saw the two sections, North and South, as dissimilar, with antagonistic interests: "[I] am sure that the dangers of this system are real, when those who have no similar interests with the people of this country [Virginia] are to legislate for us—when our dearest interests are to be left in the hands of those whose advantage it will be to infringe them."[24]

When the Southern states exercised their constitutional right to secede from the Union,[25] Abraham Lincoln was asked why the North should not simply allow the Southern states to go their way. His response on three separate occasions was, "Let the South go? Let

---

[23] By the early 1800s Patrick Henry's prediction had become reality for the South. Senator Benton declared that the states of Virginia, North Carolina, South Carolina, and Georgia were supplying 75% of the revenues required by the Federal government. A larger percentage of these Southern taxes were being used by the Northern-controlled Congress to finance "internal improvements" in the North. See Kennedy and Kennedy, 43.

[24] Patrick Henry, quoted in Raphael Semmes, *Memoirs of Service Afloat* (1868, Secaucus, NJ: The Blue and Gray Press, 1987) preface.

[25] Rawle, 234-42.

the South go! Where then shall we gain our revenues?"[26] The South seceded in 1861 because she foresaw the day when her "dearest interests" would be completely controlled by those whose advantage it would be to infringe upon the liberties of the Southern people. Since the loss of the War for Southern Independence, the "dearest interests" of every American have been in the hands of those who control the Federal government.

26 Abraham Lincoln, quoted in Kennedy and Kennedy, 50.

CHAPTER 2

The American Middle Class

The second key player in our political struggle is the American middle class. The middle class is a large, unorganized, and difficult to define group. Many people attempt to define the middle class strictly along economic lines. For the purposes of our discussions, we will define the middle class economically as well as culturally, that is, a group that supports certain general cultural values.

As far as the Federal government is concerned, the middle class is where tax revenues are to be found. During the 1986 tax reform debate, a poll disclosed that most Americans did not believe the tax reform would help them. A large majority believed that the tax reform would either increase their taxes or do nothing to reduce their tax burden. The Federal government acquires 76% of its tax revenues from the middle class. The people of this class know that any time the government talks about tax reform what it is really doing is trying to find new ways to get more money from its middle-class "cash-cow."

Anyone who acquires the principal part of his income from wages and salaries (as opposed to investments) belongs to the middle class. The wage and salary property of the middle class is taken by the government to finance programs that provide little real benefit to the citizens who are forced to pay the taxes. Working men and women live off the money they earn from their labor. They do not live off investment income or accumulated capital. Their wage and salary property is the primary means (in most cases, the only means) by which they maintain their living standard. By taxing the working man's labor to pay for pork-barrel social programs aimed at liberal clientele, the Federal government is depriving the middle class of a large percentage of the only means it has to support itself. Middle-class tax revenues are then spent on government programs for which the average middle-class taxpayer would not voluntarily spend his

33

money. This group includes retired workers. While retired workers were part of the work force, their wages were pilfered by the government tax collector who took what he wanted and left them to figure out how to pay for their family's day-to-day living expenses and make adequate plans for retirement (not too different from the way the Lord of the Manor treated his serfs during the Dark Ages). The middle class is composed of all working and retired Americans. They are the people who finance government through the taxes assessed upon their labor; they obey its laws; their sons and daughters make up the largest percentage of those who fight to protect this country when it is threatened by external enemies. The middle class is America, and for too long its values and rights have been ignored or, worse, abused by the political establishment that controls the Federal government.

The American middle class can also be described in terms of cultural values. Essentially, the middle class places a high premium on values such as individual responsibility. The middle class generally adheres to traditional moral and ethical values based on the teachings of the Old or New Testaments. There is also a strong sense of family and a high regard for the role of the traditional family, especially for the role of the family in molding the lives of children. In a modern world which declares that there are no moral absolutes, no right and wrong, the middle class has resisted the temptation to abandon its traditional values and the "faith of our fathers." The middle-class family is more likely to attend religious services on a regular basis, more likely to look to Holy Scriptures as a source of moral and ethical guidance, and more likely to reject social doctrines that promote public acceptance of lifestyles that have traditionally been viewed as perverted and socially unacceptable. This is not to imply that the middle class is composed exclusively of puritans or religious zealots. Yet, even those members of the middle class who do not attend church or synagogue still accept and incorporate cultural values that are based upon orthodox religious teachings. The average middle-class individual has no problem accepting the fact that crime is wrong and should be punished; no problem with the concept that those who are capable of working but refuse to do so should not eat; that government should not provide an incentive for welfare mothers to have more illegitimate children; and that capital punishment is necessary for criminals convicted of heinous crimes.

Culturally, middle-class Americans can be described as law-abiding, honest, hard-working men and women who expect everyone else to act likewise. To the liberal establishment, the middle class is composed of a bunch of uncultured ignoramuses who inhabit America's archaic "fly-over" country.

America's liberal establishment, the political parties, and the Federal government have all abandoned the middle class. The social and political values of the middle class have been under consistent attack for the past fifty years. Members of the Reverend Jesse Jackson's Rainbow Coalition can look to various departments of the Federal government to protect and promote their interests. Yet, who can the middle class look to for protection and promotion of its cultural values? Organized homosexuals such as The Gay Liberation Front or Queer Nation have found many willing defenders in the liberal media. Yet, where are the mainstream media defenders of middle-class values? As president, George Bush, a Republican, signed America's most extensive affirmative action civil rights bill even after he had labeled it a quota bill. What legislation did the Republican party sponsor to restrict anti-middle class reverse discrimination? The answer is simple; the Republican party, just like the liberal establishment and the Federal government, can and often has abandoned the middle class.

When Thomas Jefferson was inaugurated as president, he declared that the Federal government should be ". . . a frugal government that does not take from the worker the bread he has earned." Jefferson saw the Federal government as an umpire to assure fairness but not as a player to participate in organizing, directing, and controlling American society. Jefferson and most of the Founding Fathers foresaw the dangers of an intrusive, meddling, central government that did not respect the citizen's liberties, rights, and property.

As amazing as it may sound to modern Americans, it was only nine short years after the constitutional convention that produced the original Constitution of 1789 when the Federal government began to act as an intrusive and oppressive central government. At that time, the Federal government began to infringe upon the right of freedom of expression, freedom of speech, and freedom of the press under the Alien and Sedition Laws. Congress, despite the prohibitions of the Bill of Rights, passed a law forbidding criticism of Federal policies or officials![27] Private citizens were brought before United States Supreme Court justices, fined, and thrown in jail for violation of this unconstitutional law. What recourse did the people have when the Federal Congress, the Federal president, and the Federal Supreme Court all agreed that this affront to American civil liberties and blatant violation of the Bill of Rights was within the powers of the Federal government?

The Founding Fathers had a very efficient safeguard against such unwarranted oppression of American citizens' civil liberties. Not only did they establish a system of checks and balances within the Federal government but, just in case the checks and balances within the Federal government did not work, they established a system of coordinate governments—Federal and state—sometimes referred to as a Republic of Republics.[28] The sovereign state retained all rights not specifically delegated to the Federal government. Therefore, it is the state's responsibility to protect its citizens should the Federal government overreach its authority and oppress the civil liberties of any of its citizens. The framers of the Constitution accepted the likelihood of Federal usurpation of power as a real possibility. Hamilton declared that "It may safely be received as an axiom in our political system, that the State governments will, in all possible contingencies, afford complete security against invasions of the public liberty by the national authority."[29] During the debate whether to ratify the proposed Constitution, the anti-Federalists charged that the Supreme Court proposed under the new Constitution would have the power to hear suits against a state. Most early Americans viewed this as an unacceptable infringement of state sovereignty. The Federalists, those who supported the ratification of the Constitution, countered with the argument that such an overreach of Federal authority was unthinkable because as Hamilton noted, "I hope that no gentleman will think that a State will be called at the bar of the

---

27 See the discussion of the Alien and Sedition Acts, and the Kentucky and Virginia Resolutions of 1798, quoted in James R. Kennedy and Walter D. Kennedy, *The South Was Right!* (Gretna, LA: Pelican Publishing Company, 1994) 164, 190, 192, 230.

28 William Rawle, *A View of the Constitution of the United States: Secession as Taught at West Point,* Walter D. Kennedy and James R. Kennedy, Eds. (1825, Simsboro, LA: Old South Books, 1991) 40-42.

29 Alexander Hamilton, *The Federalist No. 28,* quoted in George W. Carey and James McClellan, *The Federalist: Student Edition* (Dubuque, IA: Kendall/Hunt Publishing Company, 1990) 141.

Federal court . . . . It is not rational to suppose that the sovereign power should be dragged before a court."[30]

No one at the time of the ratification of the Federal Constitution knew how soon all of the debate about the Supreme Court's unwarranted power would be put to the test. Shortly after the ratification of the Constitution, the United States Supreme Court attempted to order the sovereign state of Georgia to appear before the United States Supreme Court and defend itself against a suit brought by a private citizen residing in another state. The sovereign state of Georgia refused to acknowledge the authority of the Federal government's courts. Prior to ratifying the new Constitution, the states had been assured by the Federalists that the sovereign states would not be under the threat of Federal suits by private citizens. In the *Federalist Papers* Hamilton declared, "It is inherent in the nature of sovereignty not to be amenable to the suit of an individual *without its* [the sovereign state's] *consent* . . . exemption [from suits by private citizens] as one of the attributes of sovereignty, is now enjoyed by the government of every State in the Union."[31] Even Hamilton, the ardent proponent of a strong central Federal government, admitted that, if the Federal government infringed upon the liberties and rights of the states, then the states would have the authority and duty to protect "State's Rights." Hamilton stated, "We may safely rely on the disposition of the State legislatures to erect barriers against the encroachments of the national authority."[32]

The state of Georgia declared that to submit to the jurisdiction of the Federal court would be to destroy the "retained sovereignty of the State." The Federal Supreme Court issued an order commanding the state of Georgia to submit to the authority of the Federal government. The Georgia legislature passed a bill declaring that any Federal agent attempting to enforce the Federal government's order within the sovereign state of Georgia should ". . . suffer death, without benefit of clergy, by being hanged."[33] The refusal of Georgia to comply with the unconstitutional Federal court order was instrumental in compelling the sovereign states to adopt the Eleventh

30 Alexander Hamilton, as quoted in Kennedy and Kennedy, 229.

31 Alexander Hamilton, *The Federalist No. 81*, quoted in Carey and McClellan, 420.

32 Alexander Hamilton, *The Federalist No. 85*, quoted in Carey and McClellan, 453.

33 Kennedy and Kennedy, 229-30.

Amendment, thereby settling the issue. The Georgia case illustrates
the proper function of the sovereign state. It was the function con-
templated by the Founding Fathers. They intended the sovereign
state to provide the final and ultimate protection for the "dearest
interests" of "We the people." The Virginia and Kentucky legislatures
of 1798 acted in a similar manner when faced by the threat of the
Federal government running amok over the civil liberties of their citizens. They interposed their sovereign authority between an abusive
Federal government and the "dearest interests" of their citizens,
thereby performing the vital task of defending the "dearest interests"
of their people. As can be seen, this is indeed a most vital function
of a sovereign state in this Republic of Republics. With the loss of this
function of a sovereign state, citizens of the United States stand alone
and powerless before a gigantic bureaucratic monster, the Federal
government.

The middle class who make up the largest part of "We the people" of the sovereign states have only one mechanism by which we
can protect our liberties from an abusive Federal government. The
sovereign authority of the state is, or should be, the ultimate
defender of our "dearest interests," that is, our rights and liberties
under the original Constitution. People at the local level have a better opportunity to influence local government and, therefore, a better chance to correct any problems that may exist and a surer means
of protecting their civil liberties. The sovereign state is the primary
means that "We the people" can rely upon to protect ourselves from
unconstitutional Federal intrusions, such as unfunded Federal mandates, reverse discrimination, and busing. As John C. Calhoun
declared, a good government

> . . . will furnish the ruled with the means of resisting success-
> fully this tendency on the part of the rulers to oppression and
> abuse. Power can only be resisted by power, and tendency by ten-
> dency. Those who exercise power and those subject to its exer-
> cise, the rulers and the ruled, stand in antagonistic relations to
> each other. The same constitution of our nature which leads
> rulers to oppress the ruled, regardless of the object for which
> government is ordained, will, with equal strength, lead the ruled
> to resist, when possessed of the means of making peaceable and
> effective resistance.[34]

34 John C. Calhoun, *The Works of John C. Calhoun* (New York, NY: D. Appleton and Company,
1844) I; 12.

As Calhoun so correctly noted, power can only be resisted by power. Only an authority higher than the Federal government can overrule an oppressive Federal government. "We the people" acting through our agent, the sovereign state, are the ultimate judge of the limits of Federal authority. Our Founding Fathers were confident that the sovereign states would always be ready and able to defend our "dearest interests": "I am unable to conceive that the State legislatures, which must feel so many motives to watch, and which possess so many means of counteracting, the federal legislature, would fail either to detect or to defeat a conspiracy of the latter [Federal government] against the liberties of their [citizens of the state] common constituents."[35] State's Rights and State Sovereignty are the indispensable ingredients for the protection of American civil liberties. Herein lies the only power consistently available to the middle class to protect our "dearest interests" against an intrusive and oppressive Federal government.

35 James Madison, *The Federalist No. 55,* quoted in Carey and McClellan, 288.

CHAPTER 3

The Liberal Establishment

The third participant in the current conflict between Big Government and the liberties of the middle class is the liberal establishment. A political establishment is a group that shares a common political agenda. The liberal establishment in America is composed of four elements: (1) the Washington, D.C., political establishment, with its attendant bureaucracy that runs the government, (2) the tax-consuming welfare clientele of the political establishment, (3) the left-of-center media who serve as the non-elected propaganda ministry of the liberal establishment and, (4) the politically correct education establishment.

As we have already demonstrated, the United States as established by the Constitution of 1787 was designed as a Republic of Republics, with a Federal government of limited and specific powers, the residual power being held by individual sovereign states. Under this system of coordinate state-Federal governments, the Federal government was supreme in those specific areas delegated to it. As long as the people of a sovereign state chose to remain in the Union, and as long as acts of the Federal government were pursuant to the Constitution, that is, acts that flowed from a delegated power granted to the Federal government by the states, its authority in those areas was supreme.[36] All powers not specifically delegated to the Federal government by the states remained securely within the purview of the states to be exercised at the pleasure of the people thereof, and, in the areas of retained powers, the state was supreme.[37]

The Federal government was changed from a Republic of

---

36 Alexander Hamilton, *The Federalist No. 33,* quoted in George W. Carey and James McClellan, *The Federalist: Student Edition* (Dubuque, IA: Kendall/Hunt Publishing Company, 1990) 61.

37 The Tenth Amendment of the United States Constitution reads as follows: *The powers not delegated to the United States by the Constitution, nor prohibited by it to the States, are reserved to the States respectively, or to the people.*

Republics to a centralized Federal empire as a result of the War for Southern Independence. "State Sovereignty died at Appomattox," according to Supreme Court Justice Salmon P. Chase. According to this theory of centralized Federalism, Gen. Robert E. Lee surrendered not only the Army of Northern Virginia but the Tenth Amendment as well! Perhaps this is why General Lee a few months before his death declared, "Had I known what those people intended to do with their victory, there never would have been a surrender at Appomattox. No, I would have preferred to have died leading my brave men, my sword in this right hand!"[38]

There existed an uneasy truce between the forces of radical centralism in Washington, D.C., and the Southern middle class from the end of Reconstruction to the election of Franklin D. Roosevelt.[39] It was during the Roosevelt administration that the forces of contemporary liberalism gained control of the new and powerful centralized Federal government. The remnants of the original Constitution stood in the way of Roosevelt's social programs. He declared war upon it by packing the Supreme Court with judges who would be more likely to overrule the limitations of the Constitution and, by way of loose construction, enlarge the powers of the Federal government. The loss of the War for Southern Independence resulted in the destruction of the sovereign state as a bulwark between the citizen and an oppressive Federal government. This, coupled with the effects of an increasingly socially activist Supreme Court, gave Roosevelt's new liberal establishment the perfect tool to use to enforce liberalism's new social vision of America. The New Deal liberal elite sought to create a centrally controlled, Federally regulated, socialized America. A Federal government without the restraints of the original Constitution and draped with the trappings of legality became liberalism's main weapon to use against the conservative middle class—North, South, East, and West. It would be thirty years before the emerging middle class would begin to feel the yoke of governmental bondage that the liberal establishment devised for them in the late 1930s.

The liberal media, another element of the liberal establishment, have served as the liberal establishment's leftist, anti-middle class

---

38 Robert E. Lee, quoted in James R. Kennedy and Walter D. Kennedy, *The South Was Right!* (Gretna, LA: Pelican Publishing Company, 1994) 42-43.

39 Kennedy and Kennedy, 237-45.

ministry of propaganda. In 1976 polls demonstrated that journalists as a group were far more liberal than the population as a whole. The media's top management was more liberal than any other segment of the media. The Public Broadcasting System was described by one gleeful liberal as being so far to the left as "to make conservatives' blood boil."[40] The media have, until recently, had the ability to ostracize anyone so foolish as to take a public stand in opposition to the liberal, politically correct party line. If a public figure came out in opposition to quotas and reverse discrimination, the liberal media would silence him by branding him as a "racist." This technique of character assassination would both destroy the advocates of middle-class values and (more importantly) intimidate others, thereby preventing them from raising their voices against some pet liberal social program (liberalism's monopoly in the market place of ideas has a chilling effect on conservative free expression). While the liberal media were busy attacking those who defended middle-class values, the education establishment was doing its part to undermine the social values of middle-class children.

In the early 1960s, the education establishment began to acquire more and more of its operating funds either directly or indirectly from sources other than the local community. This financing scheme had the effect of freeing the education establishment from the local population and allowing educators to treat the local population as adversaries rather than as their employers. Education professionals began to act as if they had the right and duty to teach, not according to the values of the parents, but, according to the educators' politically correct values—values that were usually in opposition to those held by the local community. The education establishment has been primarily responsible for the development of liberalism's social agenda. Almost all liberal programs can be traced back to the universities, especially the social sciences sections of those universities.

> The social scientist, however, does not hesitate to invent both what the consumer has to desire done and a program to do it: both the goal and the means. Not only busing, but integration, radiated as a goal out of the universities into the media, as did the idea that crime could be controlled by social programs

40 Robert Whitaker, *A Plague on Both Your Houses* (Washington—NY: Robert B. Luce, Inc., 1976) 83.

rather than by swift and sure punishment. Programs which are now what we call liberal, from democratic socialism to Keynesian economics, from American guilt complexes about our history and culture to a centrally planned, ecologically based economy, all these concepts, as programs, came from the university . . . the day the new establishment [liberalism] admits that programs are doing more harm than good is the day most of the education-welfare complex goes out of business. The sale of social goals and social plans to fulfill the goals is therefore vitally necessary to liberalism. . . . New programs and expansion of old programs to employ the hundreds of thousands being graduated is an immediate necessity for academia. . . . It is essential to academic and new establishment interests in general that every crisis be exploited for the manufacture and sale of social goals and plans. . . . American workers, however, pay a major portion of their incomes for programs based on the success of the education-welfare complex in convincing them, by words, that these programs are needed. . . . To obtain a poverty program, new establishment forces must convince people they need to feed the hungry rather than buy a second car. Those administering these morality plays never receive less than five-figure salaries, and the taxpayers know it, so such taxpayers must not be allowed to dwell upon such facts. Families must be willing to have two instead of three children in the United States so that a program, again administered by upper-middle professionals paid accordingly, can feed the masses in India. . . . When the public shows signs of serious questioning, it can either be ignored or made to feel guilty. . . . Any serious dissident, anyone having a disagreement with the assumptions and aims and established truths of the new establishment [liberalism] will find any career in television, news, publishing, academia or in any other field related to verbalization of ideas an impossible route to follow.[41]

The liberal establishment consists of a cozy alliance between the Washington political establishment, kept in power to a large extent by the voting block of its social welfare clientele; the education establishment, which now looks to Washington's political establishment for its financial support; and the media, who act as the high priests of liberal ideology. The high priest offers a warm feeling to all adherents

41 Ibid, 86, 87, 89, 90, 91.

who need to feel good about themselves because they "care" so much about humanity. On the other hand, the electronic high priest of liberalism can effectively pronounce damnation upon anyone who dares to question liberalism's politically correct ideology. Such heretics are usually efficiently branded by the liberal media as "racists," "right wing extremists," "homophobes," or "insensitive buffoons."

CHAPTER 4

The National Political Parties

At first glance it may seem strange to lump both the Democratic and the Republican parties together by identifying them collectively as the fourth player in the middle class's struggle to regain control of its political destiny. Yet, when considering how both political parties have, at one time or another, abandoned the middle class, then it becomes more apparent that neither national political party consistently defends and promotes those cultural, social, and political values held by the middle class. Both national parties are captive to pre-existing political establishments.

America's political system has been described as being egg-shaped. At one end is a small but dominant Republican elite representing Big Money, industrialists, and the military. President Dwight D. Eisenhower referred to it as the "military industrial complex," all of whom can be and are consumers of large quantities of middle-class tax dollars. At the other end is another elite group that represents the interests of the liberal establishment and the "protected minorities" who make up liberalism's clientele. The "protected minorities" are also large consumers of middle-class tax dollars. The Republicans protect the interests of Big Money, while the Democrats protect their ideological vision and the interests of liberalism's "protected minorities" clientele. "But where," you may ask, "is the middle class?" We are caught in the middle, with pressure coming in toward us from both ends and, as of yet, with no means to protect our interests. In a phrase, we have been abandoned!

The Republican party has traditionally been the defender of Big Money. The GOP has been more concerned about protecting the financial resources of the upper 2-3% of America's wealthy and less concerned about middle-class social issues such as reverse discrimination and busing. In Chapters 5 through 24, we will provide numerous examples of how both the national Republican party and the national Democratic party have abandoned middle-class voters while kowtowing to the demands of "protected minorities" and other left-wing constituency groups. In short, the national Republicans have given the middle class useless rhetoric while surrendering to the demands of liberal pressure groups. One national Republican leader told a group of civil rights leaders, "Watch what we do, not what we say."[42] The intentional betrayal of America's middle class by the "conservative" national Republican party in many ways is far more deplorable that the vicious assaults launched against it by the liberal national Democratic party.

During the 1968 presidential elections, Gov. George Wallace championed the pressing middle-class issue of busing and crime control (he referred to it as "law and order"). As usual, the national Republican party was ignoring these middle-class issues, while the liberal Democratic party was actively promoting forced busing and other social programs such as prison reform that lead to early release for convicted criminals. The Republican party was assumed to be the champion of the conservative middle class, while the Democratic party was known to be vigorously pursuing its liberal agenda. Polling data demonstrated that a majority of Americans, not just Southerners, were opposed to forced busing, yet the Republicans continued to ignore the issue. It was not until after George Wallace began to win substantial support from Northern voters that the Republicans began to give lip service to these issues. When the Republican leaders realized that Wallace's third-party campaign would draw many of the middle-class votes away from the Republican candidate, they adopted some of Wallace's rhetoric but none of his commitment to these middle-class issues. It was the prospect of losing middle-class votes to Wallace's third-party campaign that forced the Republican party to "pretend" to be concerned about those social issues affecting the middle class. Nixon's attorney general had already told the civil rights leaders not to worry about what Nixon would say about these issues. In politics, actions speak louder than words!

The national Republicans kept their word to the civil rights community even though they broke their word to millions of middle-class citizens who voted for what they thought would be an anti-busing,

---

42 Attorney General-Designate John N. Mitchell explaining prospective Nixon administration civil rights policies to thirty Southern black leaders (1968), quoted in William J. Quirk and R. Randall Bridwell, *Abandoned: The Betrayal of the American Middle Class Since World War II* (Lanham, MD: Madison Books, 1992) 201.

law-and-order, conservative, pro-middle class president. It was Nixon, a "conservative" Republican, who gave America affirmative action, quotas, busing, and intrusive Federal regulations such as OSHA. It was also under this Republican president that the stage was set for the greatest rip-off of middle-class citizens in American history: the Savings and Loan failures and subsequent bailouts (using middle-class tax monies of course!).[43] Why would the national Republican party, the party that claimed to represent the middle class, be so hesitant to champion these burning middle-class issues?

Historically, the Republican party has not been a party of the people. After their victory over the South in 1865, the Radical Republicans set about to reshape the Federal government over which they exercised exclusive control. They invested the Federal government with new and unconstitutional powers which allowed it to exercise dominant authority over the states.[44] The weakened Democratic party was the only political opposition to the Radical Republicans and their Northern industrial clientele.

From 1864 to 1884, all the Republicans had to do to assure victory in elections was to wave the "bloody shirt" by claiming that the Democratic party was the party of secession. With this emotional appeal, they could gain the votes of the Western states that were necessary to maintain Republican control of the Federal government and enforce the high protective tariffs demanded by the emerging Northern industrialists. As a result, the East began to control American elections. The East, in turn, was controlled politically by the new industrial complex, a capitalist aristocracy that had grown rich as a reward for their efforts in turning out the material necessary to equip the Northern army during its invasion of the Confederate States of America. The fifty years following the War for Southern Independence were a new era for America. It was the first time that our country had ever been controlled by industrial wealth. This was the age of men such as Rockefeller, Ford, Mellon, and Scranton. Capitalists worth millions began to exert control over America's political destiny. The capitalists, given a free hand, enjoyed a cozy relationship with the government that netted them a high tariff to subsidize domestic industry (their own), gave vast

43 Quirk and Bridwell, 153-89.

44 James R. Kennedy and Walter D. Kennedy, *The South Was Right!* (Gretna, LA: Pelican Publishing Company, 1994) 166-83.

tracts of ground to railroads to subsidize their expansion, and instituted strike-breaking.[45]

The industrial establishment, protected politically by the Republican party, was overthrown at last by Franklin D. Roosevelt's New Deal Democratic party which was radically different from the traditional conservative Democratic party, the party of the Solid South. The new liberal establishment that replaced the old industrial establishment did not dismantle the machinery of centralized Federalism created by the Radical Republicans, but, instead, seized it and began using it to enforce their liberal, New Deal vision of social progress. FDR's New Deal Democratic party has evolved into the current politically correct, liberal Democratic party, a party that represents the values of Jesse Jackson's Rainbow Coalition much more than the values of the average, middle-class American citizen.

Since the era of the New Deal, the national Republican party has been fighting a rearguard action as it attempts to protect the interests of Big Money. But, as every good politician knows, money alone is not enough to win elections. Therefore, the Republican party has been forced to seek votes from the middle class and even from liberalism's primary clientele, the "protected minorities." During the time of Roosevelt's New Deal, the Democratic party made an intentional ideological shift to the left. This move away from middle-class values and toward radical, leftist social theory was antagonistic to middle-class interests. This antagonism was not recognized initially. It took several decades of radical, liberal Democratic control of the Federal government and the resultant social programs before the middle class began to recognize the dangers posed by this new liberal establishment. The Solid South was the last middle-class area to break with the Democratic party. This was due to a large extent to the lingering legacy of the collective Southern memory of Radical (Republican) Reconstruction.

The Democratic party's move toward radical liberalism left the middle-class with no place to go except to the only opposition party—the Republican party. The leadership of the Republican party was well aware of this fact. They knew that the middle class would not vote for radical liberalism. They knew that with a two-party system, one leftist liberal and the other tentatively conservative, the middle

45 Robert W. Whitaker, *A Plague on Both Your Houses* (Washington—NY: Robert B. Luce, Inc., 1976) 53.

class would be forced to vote for the "conservative" party candidate. Because the Republicans knew that they had a lock on middle-class voters, they were left free to pursue "the last vote."

"The last-vote" concept explains why the Republican party felt free to give conservative middle-class voters empty rhetoric while at the same time caving in to the demands of liberalism's "protected minorities." The tendency of national political parties to use minority voters at the expense of middle-class voters has been noted by other authors.

> The real [Republican] policy advocated quotas even though the majority of the middle class were opposed to quotas, and carried the social agenda of the [Democratic] Johnson Revolution even farther than Johnson had. That's why John Mitchell said "Watch what we do, not what we say." The 1969 Philadelphia Plan was the first mandated racial quota program—Lyndon Johnson had not dared to attempt this. John Mitchell [a Republican], on September 22, 1969, wrote an opinion, as attorney general, to the secretary of labor, supporting the legality of the Philadelphia Plan. The plan as followed by Secretary of Labor Order 4, 35 Fed. Reg. 2586 (1970), which mandated quotas for all federal contracts and federally assisted jobs. . . . For a generation [since these Republican actions] hiring and promoting in large corporations has been done on a racial basis. Higher education followed suit. Yale Law School, beginning in 1971, reserved 10 percent of its entering class for black students. Nixon and Mitchell fastened quotas on American society.[46]

So, again, we ask, why would a "conservative" Republican party force Americans to endure the discrimination of quotas? Again, we answer, "the last vote."

> The conservatives had no place to go, they had to vote for you. So give them some rhetoric to keep them happy. Push your real policies for the last vote. Where is the last vote? It is right next to the Democratic position on any issue. So you adopt *actual* policies which get as close to the Democrats as you possibly can.[47]

In the 1972 elections, the Republican party increased its margin of victory by fifteen million votes. This increase was achieved even

46 Quirk and Bridwell, 211.

47 Ibid, 212.

though the Republicans had failed to deliver the relief they had promised to the middle class in 1968 on issues such as busing, law and order, prayer in the schools, welfare reform, and a halt to the expansion of government spending. In 1972, the national political parties gave the middle class the choice between a card-carrying liberal, George McGovern, and a man who claimed to represent middle-class values, Richard Nixon. But Nixon is not the only Republican president to follow the dictates of the "last vote."

When it came time to allow the unconstitutional, punitive, South-only Voting Rights Act to expire, President Ronald Reagan cheerfully signed its renewal, even though it would continue to allow the Federal government to infringe upon the right of the sovereign states to establish legitimate, non-arbitrary voting qualifications. The right of the people of the sovereign state to define voter qualifications has been defended by Americans, North and South. This issue is not just a Southern issue, as can be seen from the words of a resolution by the state of New Jersey complaining about the unconstitutional actions of the Federal government in its efforts to enact the Fourteenth Amendment:

> . . . this section was intended to transfer to Congress the whole control of the right of suffrage in the State, and to deprive the State of a free representation by destroying the power of regulating suffrage within its own limits, a power which they have never been willing to surrender to the general [Federal] government, and which was reserved to the States as the fundamental principle on which the Constitution itself was constructed—principles of self-government.[48]

President George Bush established the benchmark for the practical application of the "last-vote" theory. In 1991, he and his Republican party claimed to oppose reverse discrimination, affirmative action, and quotas. While the 1991 Civil Rights Bill was making its way through Congress, Bush described it as "a quota bill." Nevertheless, it was with the assistance of Republicans and with the signature of Republican President Bush that this quota bill was made law.

For two and a half decades the Republicans had promised middle-class Americans a more conservative Supreme Court if the middle class would elect Republican presidents. It appeared that this was

48 Joint Resolutions, No. 1, State of New Jersey, quoted in Kennedy and Kennedy, 373.

coming to pass. The moderate Supreme Court had severely limited the Federal government's ability to enforce certain affirmative action and quota regulations. Yet, the 1991 Civil Rights Bill was specifically designed to overrule the Supreme Court's anti-affirmative action decisions. Even though he had declared it to be a quota bill, President Bush signed the bill into law. By signing the 1991 Civil Rights Bill, Bush overruled the conservative (really moderate) Supreme Court the Republicans had been promising the middle class for more than twenty-five years. What the Republicans gave the middle class with one hand (a moderate Supreme Court), they took away with the other hand (by signing the 1991 Civil Rights Bill)!

After the 1988 election, the late Lee Atwater, chairman of the Republican National Committee, made a deliberate decision to pursue "black votes." His plan was not one based upon converting black voters to conservatism, but it was based upon the "last-vote" theory. This is an example of how the middle class is abandoned by the so-called conservative Republican party. The GOP has been more concerned with recruiting black voters than it has been with promoting middle-class values and issues. By kowtowing to liberal social welfare objectives, the Republicans are deserting the middle class for those who systematically loot the resources of the middle class through taxation. The signing of an anti-middle class quota bill by President Bush is an example of Lee Atwater's plan in action.

During a convention of Young Republicans in Nashville, several Southern delegates placed Confederate flags on their tables. Lee Atwater, even though he was a Southerner, insulted the delegates and all Southerners in general by declaring that Southerners should keep the symbols of their Southern Heritage at home—hidden in the closet one would suspect. Other ethnic and cultural groups have not been censured in such a manner by the Republican party. Can anyone imagine a Republican official telling American Indians, hispanic Americans, or black Americans to leave their most sacred cultural symbols at home? Apparently the Republican party is more concerned about power than it is about protecting the interests and values of the middle class, especially the Southern middle class.

The "last-vote" theory will work only if the middle class has "no place to go." When the national Democratic party offers radical liberalism, then the middle class has no alternative but to support the Republican candidate. It is only when a third party has offered the middle class an alternative that the Republican party has been forced to give attention to issues affecting the middle class. In 1968 and 1972, the threat of George Wallace's third party forced Richard Nixon to talk about busing, crime, government spending, and taxes. Of course, all the middle class got was talk; the civil rights lobbyists got the action. By the time the 1992 election arrived, the Republican party had so betrayed the middle class that Bush could not count upon the automatic support of this conservative group. Ross Perot's third-party campaign gave many middle-class voters the alternative they wanted—someone to vote for who was not an extreme liberal, not a part of the political establishment, and someone who had not lied to them ("read my lips, no new taxes"). The result of George Wallace's third-party campaign was to force Nixon to the right, at least with his rhetoric. The result of Perot's third-party campaign was the election of an extreme left-wing liberal as president. Third-party efforts are very seldom successful.

What is the role of political parties relative to the middle class? Political parties tend to become captives of specific interest groups. The Republican party has always been the handmaiden of Northern industrialists and Big Money. The Democratic party since the days of FDR's New Deal has served the interests of liberalism. The middle class is trapped somewhere between these two elitist and well-organized special-interest groups. Why would the national Democratic party nominate a radical liberal as their presidential candidate when polling data had demonstrated that the majority of Americans did not approve of his ideological vision? The answer is that the special-interest groups control the party and will not allow the middle class to participate in a meaningful way in the selection of a candidate. Southern conservative Democrats still remember the night the liberals threw them out of their Democratic party and replaced them with the likes of the so-called Freedom Democratic Party! So much for the liberal Democratic party. Why then would the "conservative" Republican party push through anti-middle class social programs such as affirmative action, intrusive EPA and OSHA bureaucracies, and the 1991 Civil Rights Bill? The answer again is that special interests are in control. The financial conservatives of Big Money and Wall Street are more concerned about fiscal policy than they are about social policy. Therefore, they are willing to sacrifice middle-class social issues, such as quotas, if it allows them to win the "last vote" and thereby gain control of the Federal government. The Republican party will provide the conservative middle class with plenty of hot rhetoric, but in the final analysis the "protected minorities" know that all they need to do is to remember the promise of Nixon's attorney general: "Watch what we do, not what we say."

It is still very important for conservative middle-class voters to be actively involved in local political party activities. Currently, the only party that even approaches conservative middle-class views is the Republican party. Conservatives must continue to promote their social agenda through the elections of conservative candidates at all levels. But, a word of warning. The middle class cannot rely upon party politics to defend its "dearest interests." It cannot expect any political party to be the final defender of its rights and liberty. While at times it may prove a useful tool, party politics alone can never be trusted with the responsibility of defending American liberty under the Constitution.

Third parties can also be an effective tool for the middle class to use to defend its interests, rights, and liberties. Sectional political associations can also be used to influence national legislation. There are numerous political tools available for the middle class to use to protect its interests. The important thing is to remember that, even if Congress is controlled by a "conservative" Republican party, even if we elect a conservative Republican president, even if we have a conservative United States Supreme Court, all of these great political victories are not sufficient to assure the protection of our "dearest interests." The ultimate protector of American civil liberties in our constitutional republic is the sovereign authority of "We the people" of the sovereign state. Liberty and freedom are best protected at the local level. Therefore, our "dearest interests," our constitutional rights and civil liberties, will never be safe until we re-establish the authority of the sovereign state. The state is the final bulwark between the people and an abusive federal government.

SUMMARY OF SECTION I
Questions and Answers

While doing television and radio interviews, the authors have noticed that many of the same questions are being asked by different people from various sections of the country. We have taken those questions most commonly asked about the nature of the original constitutional republic that would pertain to the issues discussed in Section I and used them as a summary of the material discussed.

Q. You keep talking about the original constitutional government. Don't you know that times have changed? Do you really think our society can afford to go back to the way things were when the Constitution was ratified?

A. While it is true that time changes things, and no doubt we do enjoy technological innovations that our Founding Fathers could not have imagined, we are not discussing technology. What we are concerned about is the same thing our Founding Fathers were concerned about. They were concerned about a central government abusing its powers to the detriment of the people. They sought to establish a system by which "We the people" at the local level could enjoy the benefits of a Federal Union while maintaining a system by which we could protect our "dearest interests" if those interests were invaded by an intrusive Federal government. If circumstances changed, the people acting through their sovereign states could amend the Federal Constitution as necessary. Our concern is that the Federal Union has been altered by unconstitutional methods, enlarging the powers of the Federal government to the detriment of the liberties and freedom of the people. It also should be noted that the very document that announced to the world the independence of these states describes certain rights as "unalienable." According to the Declaration of Independence, these rights are given to man by a Divine Creator. Therefore, time has no meaning as far as the exercise of our God-given rights are concerned. Whether it is 1776, 1995, or 2076, these rights are ours and cannot be legally denied to us.

Q. You say that there has been a drastic change in the nature of the Federal government. In what ways is the Federal government today different from the so-called original Federal government, and was not this change a natural "evolving" process?

A. With a reading of *The Federalist* and *Anti-Federalist Papers,* and the accounts of the various state conventions which ratified the Constitution, one is left with the impression of what type of central government the founders of this republic desired. They envisioned a very limited government in which authority is granted by the states to a central government with the remainder of authority to govern remaining in the hands of the people of the various states. These states were to be free to act in every area that they had not freely delegated to the Federal government. These states were the ones which had fought the British, established sound systems of government with protection for civil liberties, and confederated with other states for their mutual protection. Today, the states exist as mere appendages of the Federal government. The states are not allowed to intervene to protect the rights and property of their citizens when molested by an abusive Federal government. In reality, the whole system as envisioned by the Founding Fathers has been turned upside down. In the beginning, "We the people" of the states formed our state governments; those state governments and conventions formed the Federal government. Power naturally flowed from the people to the state, then to the Federal government. Today, all power resides in Washington, D.C. From time to time, some minor cosmetic changes are allowed, such as when the middle class becomes too excited about the level of Federal abuse they are suffering, but *the apparatus for that abuse* remains in place at all times. If modern America were visited by the Founding Fathers, they would find their world turned upside down.

One of the reasons our Founding Fathers demanded a written constitution rather than an unwritten constitution, as seen in Great Britain, was to prevent an insidious change in the nature of government. They had experienced firsthand the result of the so-called evolution of constitutional power at the hands of King George III and his ministers. Note that, even before the United States Constitution was written, each state had already established the principle of a written document for the government of America. "Unalienable" rights do not evolve or devolve. That is why early Americans demanded a written constitution as opposed to the unwritten constitution of Great Britain. If changes were needed, then the people would be the ones to initiate and ratify those changes, not some mystical, hidden force of social evolution. Good constitutions do not evolve; they are made and retained by men and women who love freedom more than any institution of government.

Q. How has the change from the original Federal government to the current Federal government affected me and my family?

A. The Federal government was established according to Thomas Jefferson to be ". . . a frugal government that does not take from the laborer the fruit of his labor." In 1948, 23% of a family's income was subject to Federal income and social security taxes. In 1990, over 70% of a family's income was subject to Federal income and social security taxes. Under the 1986 tax code, a wealthy person could deduct all the interest on two homes valued at $500,000 each. Yet, the same tax code deprived middle-class taxpayers the interest on a college loan, the interest on an automobile loan, or the interest on credit cards. We find it hard to believe that the Founding Fathers would have tolerated such discrimination against working people. It does not take a rocket scientist to figure out that the Federal government is out of control.

Q. You keep referring to and quoting John C. Calhoun. This man was a defender of slavery! How can you justify such an institution?

A. As faithful believers in civil liberties, we have never defended the institution of slavery, but we do insist upon telling the whole truth about this institution as opposed to the liberal media's attempt to slander everything Southern because of slavery. Vice President and later Senator John C. Calhoun was one of America's leading political and constitutional theorists. His efforts were directed at defending the numerical minority of the agricultural South against the numerical majority of the industrial North. In Calhoun's day, the numerical majority of the North controlled both Houses of Congress. The numerical majority used the Federal government to force the South to purchase their industrial products instead of the less expensive European imports. Calhoun fought to defend the principles of State's Rights, State Sovereignty, and limited Federalism. These were the tools left to all Americans by our Founding Fathers to be used to defend our "dearest interests" against an oppressive Federal government. As to your accusations regarding slavery, we recommend that you read Chapters 2 and 3 of our book, *The South Was Right!* if you want to find out who was responsible for the nefarious slave trade and other issues concerning slavery in America. It is no more logical to condemn the South for slavery than it is to condemn the colonies for the slavery that existed during the Revolutionary War. Before indulging in self-righteous congratulations, non-Southerners should remember that the thirteen stripes on the United States flag represent thirteen original colonies, all of which had laws permitting slavery and many of which (Northern states) were active participants in the slave trade. We must remember that the first colony to legalize slavery was the northern colony of Massachusetts and the first colony that attempted to forbid the slave trade was the Southern colony of Virginia. If we refuse to honor Calhoun because he was a slaveholder, then we must also condemn men such as Washington, Jefferson, and most of the early presidents of the United States. Americans should realize that the institution of slavery existed throughout the world during the eighteenth and nineteenth centuries. As a matter of fact, more slaves were held outside of America during that time than were ever held within the United States. The hand-wringing and guilt trip that most liberals are so accustomed to putting on the middle class because of the issue of slavery is not done out of a desire to foster better treatment of the descendants of former slaves; rather it is used to divide Americans. As with other social issues of its day, slavery would have been, and in many cases was already being, addressed by the people of each state. Every civilization up until that time had to deal with the issue of slavery; very few had to resort to bloodshed to end the institution.

Q. What do you mean when you describe America's political society as being egg-shaped?

A. What we mean is that at both ends you will find a small but effective group of elitists. They control their respective parties. On one end, you have the liberal establishment with its supporters in the press, the educational community, and the welfare, quasi-welfare block vote. On the other end, you have the forces of Big Money, a small group of Americans who make up no more than 2-3% of our total population. Big Money has no allegiance to a particular country. It will move its resources wherever it can turn the best profit. Big money has no fear of liberal social programs. No need to worry about busing—the very idea that *their* children would attend a public school is ridiculous and insulting! No need to worry about quotas.

Such problems are the concerns of the plebeians, the lower classes; after all, why worry about their rumblings and complaints—let them eat cake! The liberal establishment that dethroned Big Money has controlled the Democratic party since the days of FDR. The Republican party has always been the handmaiden of the monied establishment. The Republican party was dethroned by the Democratic liberal establishment. Since the mid-1930s, the Republican party has made appeals to the middle class in order to regain political power. While it may "talk" about middle-class issues, and it may act the part of a conservative during elections, the Republican party's only consistent conservative agenda has been fiscally conservative— helping Big Business. Where does that leave the middle class? It leaves them in the middle, squeezed from both ends with no one to protect their "dearest interests" consistently.

Q. You make the statement that the South had a right to secede from the Union in 1861; even if it did, aren't you just reopening an old wound that is better off healed?

A. Indeed, the authors believe that the Southern states had a right to secede from the Union in 1861, but the Southern states did not have this right because they were Southern states, they had this right because they were American states. It is because the South lost the War that the Federal government has been enabled to grow at an unparalleled rate over the last 130 years. This radical growth of the power of the central government has been realized at the expense of the rights and liberties of "We the people" at the local level. If we are ever to regain our lost rights, we must face the fact that the Federal government has become a tyrannical force that no one is now capable of controlling. Southerners may have lost the War, but all Americans suffer the consequences of that loss. An alcoholic individual will never become a sober person until he admits that alcohol is his problem. If Americans refuse to admit that the Federal government is out of control, we will never be able to apply the proper remedies to get it under control and, more importantly, keep it under our control. As far as opening a healed wound, please remember that the passage of time never negates an act of aggression, whether it be rape, murder, or the invasion and conquest of a people.

Q. You often refer to "We the people." Does not this term as seen in the preamble of our Constitution prove that the Constitution was created by the people of America, and not, as you say, by the states?

A. You are correct; the term "We the people" does appear in the preamble of the United States Constitution. As a matter of fact, they are the first three words of the preamble. Please note that this is the preamble and not the body of the Constitution. This has a very important meaning in law because, as the United States Supreme Court ruled in *Jacobs v. Massachusetts,* the words of a preamble can only give an indication of what is in the body of a document; never are they to contravene or go against any article of that document. Thus, we see in Article VII of the Constitution who is to ratify the Constitution, that is, the states. Not only does Article VII tell us who will ratify, but it also tells us how many must ratify the Constitution to bring it into being. In Article VII, we see that the Constitution would be established "between the states so ratifying the same" when the number of states so ratifying reached nine. But note, this only established the Federal government among those states, not among those who had not ratified the Constitution. "We the people" of each state had the right to decide for ourselves, each state independent of other states, group of states, or people. The ratifying of the Constitution was an act of states, not of people in the aggregate. The people of each state acting for themselves only and constrained by no other force other than their will formed the Federal government. This is the true meaning of the "We the people" clause in the preamble. It was the sovereign will of the people of a sovereign community, i.e., state, that was doing the ratifying. When the preamble was first written and placed in the Constitution, instead of "We the People," it had stated "We the People of the States of" and had named the thirteen states. But since no one knew if all thirteen states would ratify or even which nine might ratify the Constitution, a change had to be made in the preamble. The change that was made and agreed upon by even the most staunch State's Rights men at the Constitutional Convention simply left off the name of the states and stated only "We the People." Everyone at the convention knew that "We the People" meant "We the People of the States." No other means of ratification were ever discussed other than ratification by the states. The only discussion was how the ratification was to be done by the states, that is, in their primary capacity as a convention or under their secondary capacity by the state legislature. Again, even the most ardent State's Rights man at the convention, George Mason, desired ratification by state convention.

Q. You state that according to the Declaration of Independence the people have the right and obligation to change any government that does not meet their needs or desires. Rather than being a call to destroy the government of the United States, don't you think this means that we the people have the right to vote out any elected official, and don't we have that right? We don't need to secede to change our government, do we?

A. The words of the Declaration of Independence are bold and revolutionary. Yes, we do have the right to vote and thereby change our elected officials; this is the primary line of defense for our freedoms, but that is not the only defense of those freedoms. If elections would do the job of giving and withdrawing our consent to a government, our Colonial Forefathers would have demanded such. When our Forefathers wrote the Declaration of Independence, they were not asking for permission to vote in any English election nor were they asking for representation in the British Parliament. The colonial Americans acting within their sovereign communities asserted the inalienable right of a people of a sovereign community to change the type of government, not just the elected men of a government. There are some very good reasons why this right is so important to a free people. What if the people's representatives were not recognized by the central government, or if those elected were corrupt? Under those circumstances, the civil liberties of the people would be held hostage to the corrupt government. Would the people under those circumstances be helpless? Not according to John Locke, James Madison, Thomas Jefferson, and many other philosophers of free governments. Remember the words of Locke: "Men can never be secure from Tyranny, if there be no means to escape it. . . ." Secession, i.e., withdrawing our consent from a tyrannical government, is our means of escaping tyranny. It is abundantly clear that at some point in time, "We the people," in defense of our freedoms, may have to go beyond casting votes.

THE PROBLEMS FACING MIDDLE-CLASS AMERICA

INTRODUCTORY COMMENTS

For more than fifty years, the liberal establishment has used the police power of the Federal government to force its left-wing agenda upon middle-class Americans. In Section II, we will document numerous examples of *abusive* Federal acts. In this section, specific examples of *intrusive* Federalism are cited. We demonstrate the illogical effects of affirmative action, quotas, and race norming. We review the disastrous results of a generation of Federal court-ordered busing. In chapter after chapter, we explore liberalism's flagrant disregard for the social values of America's middle class. Each chapter in this section represents another area in our lives that has been invaded by the Federal government; gun control, crime, high taxes, oppressive regulations, trillions of dollars of Federal debt, attacks against Western civilization and its history, HUD's invasion of peaceful neighborhoods, socialized medicine, and much more are documented. We demonstrate how the Federal government is being used to enforce anti-middle class laws, policies, and social engineering schemes.

Throughout Section II, we cite case histories that demonstrate how oppressive this once free country has become. These examples demonstrate why "We the people" of the sovereign state must once again reassert our right to govern ourselves at the local level and to maintain control of our political destiny. In this section, you will see how dangerous it is to allow the Federal government to be the sole judge of the limit of its powers. Through these examples, you will see why it is necessary for "We the people" of the sovereign state to regain our proper authority to limit unwarranted and unconstitutional Federal intrusion upon our inalienable rights. You will also see that both political parties are responsible for the creation and empowerment of an abusive Federal government. This section will show you the symptoms of a society that suffers from a centralized government, one that no longer recognizes the right of "We the people" of the sovereign states to control our own political destiny, one that no longer honors the American principle that "We the people" deserve to live under a government ordered upon the free and unfettered consent of the governed.

CHAPTER 5

Instead of an All-Powerful and Intrusive Federal Government— Why Not Freedom!

Our liberty is perishing beneath the constant growth of governmental power. Today, for example, Americans must obey thirty times as many laws as Americans at the turn of the century had to obey. Federal bureaucrats publish an average of two hundred pages of regulations, edicts, and guidelines each working day in the *Federal Register*—rules that have the power of law that any citizen could be sent to prison for violating! Have you read your *Federal Register* today? Yet, are the streets of modern America safer than the streets of thirty years ago? Do Americans enjoy more security for their hard-earned private property than Americans of thirty years ago? Does the average American feel that government is working for his benefit or for the benefit of government? Sober reflection upon these questions should be enough to make any thinking person realize that something of immense proportion has gone wrong with the great American experiment in government "by and for the people," i.e., free government.

Non-elected Federal agents now exert vast arbitrary power over the daily lives of American citizens. For example, bureaucrats of the Equal Employment Opportunity Commission assessed almost $150,000 of fines against an Illinois small businessman because he did not employ 8.45% blacks. Non-elected Federal agricultural bureaucrats have prohibited Arizona farmers from selling nearly one-half of their produce to other Americans. Remember, these otherwise law-abiding Americans are subject to the capricious action of non-elected bureaucrats who act as police, prosecutor, jury, and judge in all cases brought before them. In this medieval-like judicial system, everyone brought before this court is guilty until proven innocent.

Our First Amendment rights of free speech and press have also come under attack. Recently, a chain of twenty-five California newspapers was sent into bankruptcy as a result of a government-financed lawsuit over a classified housing ad that allegedly violated anti-discrimination provisions of the Federal Fair Housing Act. The ad in question specified "adults only"; what a crime! The Federal thought police cared not in the least for the middle-class families of workers who were left unemployed by the closing of these papers. The liberal establishment is now the criminal, the private citizen its defenseless victim!

The Federal government's relentless attack against private property has continued since the early days of the 1960s when it was "discovered" that the Constitution granted the government the right to force private business to provide services to everyone regardless of the private property owner's desires. Federal bureaucrats now enforce laws that virtually abrogate personal use of private property:

* A citizen of the sovereign state of Michigan unloaded several truck loads of dirt in his backyard. The Federal government took him to court charging him with violating the Federal Clean Water Act.[49]

* In Florida a father and his son were charged with criminal activities against the environment, tried, and sentenced to twenty-one months in a Federal prison. Their crime consisted of filling a small lot, owned by the father, with sand.[50]

* A public school district in the state of Oregon found out that it could be a Federal crime to build a baseball field for its students![51]

* According to Nevada's representative, James Hayes, "In Nevada, [subdivision] developments in the midst of cactus and parched earth are now being classified as 'wetlands'. . . ."[52]

The question we ask you is this: Do you have more freedom today than Americans had fifty years ago? Fifty years ago, were Americans faced with

* Working six months every year just to pay the cost of taxes and government regulations—we have become tax serfs to Uncle Sam.

* The glancing geese theory of constitutional law? That is, the loss of private property rights that occurs if a flight of geese should

---

49 Carrier Dowling, "Dumping on Wetlands in Yard Gets Man 2-Month Sentence," *Detroit News*, December 10, 1991.

50 Tom Bethell, "Property and Tyranny," *The American Spectator*, August 1994, 16.

51 Paul D. Kamenar, "The Federal Government Flunks Test for Regulating Wetlands on Oregon School District Property," *Washington Legal Foundation*, October 23, 1992.

52 *Congressional Record*, March 8, 1991, E843.

glance down, spy a body of water, and think about landing in it. In that case, the property becomes part of interstate commerce, and, therefore, comes under the regulation of the Federal government's Wet Lands Act. This means that the rightful owner cannot use his private property without first obtaining Federal permission.

* Forced busing to meet racial quotas?
* Reverse discrimination?
* Gun control?
* Anti-middle class, liberal, Big Government media?
* Cultural Genocide? By this we mean the relentless attack upon all aspects of Western, i.e., European, culture from Columbus and the Pilgrims to the demand for the removal and destruction of all symbols of Southern culture such as the Confederate flag, Confederate monuments, and Southern history.

Are Americans free, or are they vassals of a centralized Big Government? We submit to you that contemporary Americans are not as free as they have been led to believe. Contemporary Americans merely exercise "rights" at the discretion of the Federal government. It is the Federal government, *not* the average American, that decides how much freedom is allowed to be exercised and when that freedom may be withdrawn. The right to own a gun; the right to send children to a school of the parent's choice; the right to hire, fire, or promote an employee; even such mundane things as the right to set the appropriate speed limits on highways, are all "allowed" at the pleasure of the Federal government.

A fundamental law of political science states that "those who have the power to make also have the power to unmake." If Americans allow the Federal government to be the dispenser of their civil liberties, then the people are only as free as the Federal government deems appropriate. This is one of the great dangers facing Americans today as they elect more "conservatives" at the Federal level. To see lasting and permanent results, elected conservatives must do more than just dismantle an overgrown Big Government. Conservatives must put into place, or more correctly reintroduce, those measures which will give "We the people" of the sovereign states the tools necessary to protect our "dearest interests." In other words, it is not enough to put Big Government on a diet. "We the people," at the local level, must be given the means of controlling Big Government's access to our inherent liberties.

If the newly elected "conservative" Congress does no more than reduce the size of government, it will be a failure. Why? Look around you. How many times have you seen people go on a diet and lose weight, only to regain it at a later time? We all have seen it happen. Governmental growth is no different. Reduction of the size and intrusiveness of the Federal government is laudable, *but doomed to failure in the long run.* Conservatives must not settle for a short-term victory over Big Government. Politicians who offer to merely cut government down in size, *without* providing "We the people" of the sovereign states the means of keeping governmental size reduced, are not giving the middle class the protection we deserve.

What would our Colonial (and in the case of Southerners, our Colonial and Confederate) Forefathers do if they were here today and were faced with the unbridled force of an all-powerful Federal government? Would they mind their own business? Would they refrain from making controversial speeches or writing politically incorrect books? Would they be afraid to challenge the liberal media, the liberal education establishment, or the liberal political system? We don't know for sure what the answers to these questions are, but we can and must answer a far greater and more important question: What are Americans today going to do about the loss of their rights and liberties? Shall "We the people" remain docile and complacent while the centralized bureaucracy of the Federal government continues to threaten and destroy our rights as free citizens, or shall we, as a people, initiate a revolution that will return America to the principles of the original Constitution? Is America inhabited by a generation that will allow the destruction of American liberty, or are they the generation that will restore those great American principles of State Sovereignty, State's Rights, limited Federalism, and individual responsibility?

Some may despair and say that one man or woman cannot fight the Federal government. Really? We recall that one man wrote the Declaration of Independence, one man cried "Give me liberty or give me death," and one man fired the shot heard around the world. One man, Mahatma Gandhi, brought the entire British Empire to its knees. Yes, one man or one woman can do a lot!

You and I are the children (through blood and spirit) of such men as George Washington, Patrick Henry, John Hancock, Samuel Adams, James Madison, Thomas Jefferson, and George Mason. All

Americans, regardless of what section of this land we call home, are the inheritors of the legacy of men such as General Robert E. Lee, President Jefferson Davis, Gen. "Stonewall" Jackson, and Vice President and Senator John C. Calhoun. If freedom is such a wonderful commodity, and it is, isn't it past time for us to begin the struggle to reclaim it? Isn't it time for modern-day, middle-class freedom fighters to declare to the world that the Federal government must return to the principles of the original Constitution, to the principles of limited government, State's Rights, and individual responsibility, or else face the united voice of the American people as they declare that the South—and who knows how many other states, North, East, and West—shall rise again?

Instead of a big intrusive Federal Government—Why Not Freedom!

SUMMARY

Questions and Answers

Q. You make the statement that Americans are not really a free people. When I look around the world today, I don't see any people with more freedom than Americans. Don't you think you are just over-reacting? Aren't you just using this scare tactic to promote your brand of conservatism?

A. If you were told by your physician that you have cancer, but you should be thankful because it will take longer for the disease to kill you than most other patients, would this give you much reason to celebrate? The only cause to celebrate is in the fact that you will have a longer period of time to fight and hopefully defeat the malignancy. The same is true with the loss of our freedoms as Americans. Just because we still have more freedoms than most other people of the world does not mean that we can go about our lives as if nothing is wrong in America. Our body politic is in danger of dying from a deadly disease, i.e., the cancer of Big Government. We must pool our resources to fight this malignancy and recover our healthy, i.e., free, status. Americans today are satisfied with the few freedoms we are allowed to exercise, but the Americans of yesterday revolted when the British king infringed upon but a few of their freedoms. We must do more than merely attempt to hold on to what we have; we must recover our lost freedoms. As Thomas Jefferson is said to have declared, "Eternal vigilance is the price of liberty." To be "eternally vigilant" is not equivalent to using "scare tactics" in the defense of freedom.

CHAPTER 6

Instead of Racial Quotas and Reverse Discrimination—Why Not Freedom!

Southerners who were born in the late 1940s to the early 1950s have witnessed a social change unprecedented in history. The white South changed from an active insistence that the limited force of state government be used to enforce social conditions of segregation to an active insistence that government be color blind and treat everyone equally regardless of skin color. In the same period, the leadership of the black community changed from demanding that government be color blind and treat everyone equally to demanding that the unlimited force of Federal government be used to ensure preferential treatment for special minorities. We have seen the various elements of society make a 180-degree turn from denying equal opportunity to all citizens to endorsing equal opportunity for all, and from demanding equality before the law to the now current, politically correct, theme of special treatment and privileges for some citizens based solely on skin color. The primary difference is that yesterday black Americans were denied equal opportunity, whereas today white Americans are denied equal opportunity. Formerly, the limited power of state government was used to deny equality to black Americans, whereas today the unlimited force of Federal government is used to deny equality to white Americans.

The insistence on preferential treatment has been carried on under many banners—affirmative action, minority set-asides, race norming, and quotas, just to name a few. In all cases, the Federal government has renounced its former insistence on equal opportunity in favor of its new rule of equality of results. To put it simply, if your community does not have the same percentage representation by race in all areas of communal life, then it is guilty of discrimination and is punishable by Federal mandate. In other words, the Federal government has changed social relations into a numbers game. For example, if your community has 30% hispanic citizens, then it should have a work force comprised of 30% hispanics. Under this system, race is not neutral, it is all important; in fact, it is more important than merit. Good work history, good training, and good experience no longer matter; if the work force does not reflect 30% hispanics, then there is no need for non-hispanics to apply, even if they are better qualified! All that matters to the Federal government is skin color and numbers.

The Federal government has accepted the assertion that statistical disparities represent moral inequities and are caused by evil people in society actively engaged in discrimination. The Federal government claims that it has been empowered with the ability to measure discrimination mathematically. It assumes that any time a "protected minority" is not proportionally represented in the work force, the classroom, a government agency, etc., the cause is illegal discrimination. Therefore, it has a right to force citizens to correct this presumed evil. Can anyone imagine that the Founding Fathers intended to give such intrusive and pervasive power to the central government?

Even if the Federal government had constitutional authority to correct what it perceives as social discrimination, would such social engineering be necessary? Throughout history many groups have been discriminated against, and they still produced a higher income or educational level than those doing the discriminating. The Chinese were discriminated against in Malaysia, Vietnam, Indonesia, and Thailand, but the Chinese own the greater portion of investments in key industries in these countries. Did discrimination produce second-class citizens? In Malaysia, discrimination against the Chinese was written into the constitution, and the use of quotas in favor of Malaysians was required by law. Yet, the Chinese still produced a standard of living twice that of the average Malaysian. In the United States, the Japanese were historically subjected to discrimination. Yet, by 1959 Japanese-Americans had equaled the income level of white Americans and by 1969 were earning 33% more than the average white American.[53] The modern liberal is very selective with his compassion for victims of perceived discrimination. Even though Japanese-Americans earn 33% more income than the average middle-class white person, there is no hue and cry by liberals to institute social

53 Thomas Sowell, *Civil Rights: Rhetoric or Reality?* (New York, NY: William Morrow and Company, 1984) 21.

programs to bring white American income up to the level of our Japanese fellow citizens (nor do we advocate such an absurd scheme). Where is the liberal justification for quotas and reverse discrimination to assure equality of outcome for middle-class white Americans? Of course, the truth is that a successful individual, regardless of what color he may be, does not have to apologize for his success. Part of the middle-class work ethic is to work hard and succeed; the middle class is not prone to get angry if someone is successful. All the middle class asks for is that no governmental assistance or hinderance be used to assure the outcome. In short "We the people" expect a color-blind government that promotes a society of equality for all but special privileges for none.

Liberals have perverted the original concept of equality of opportunity into their current doctrine of equality of result, or equality by the numbers, which means quotas. Liberals will congratulate themselves for their "compassion" and sense of "caring" when questioned about their social engineering schemes. Apparently, they think of themselves as more enlightened and humane than the less intellectually astute middle-class citizen. Yet, when we look at this century's most well-known humanitarian, Mahatma Gandhi, we find a man who is at odds with modern liberalism's love affair with reverse discrimination. When Gandhi, a Hindu, was pressed by certain Moslems to reserve a specific number of jobs for minorities regardless of their qualifications, Gandhi objected and declared, "For administration to be efficient it must be in the hands of the fittest. There should be no favoritism . . . those who aspire to occupy responsible posts in the government of the country can only do so if they pass the required test."[54] Minority set-asides and quotas are not the "enlightened" thing to do, as demonstrated by Gandhi. John C. Calhoun of South Carolina declared a hundred years earlier, ". . . to go further, and make equality of condition essential to liberty, would be to destroy both liberty and progress. . . ."[55]

Liberals refuse to recognize that arbitrary discrimination, even in the name of doing good, leads to resentment as better qualified members are barred from entry into the market place. When people

---

54 Mahatma Gandhi, quoted in Louis Fischer, *The Life of Mahatma Gandhi* (New York, NY: Harper and Row, 1983) 220.

55 John C. Calhoun, *The Works of John C. Calhoun* (New York, NY: D. Appleton and Company, 1844) I; 56-57.

are denied such opportunity, resentment builds, and hatred encourages strife. Instead of improving relations among ethnic and cultural groups, the Federal government has made relations worse. Americans in general and Southerners in particular must continue to insist on equality of opportunity, equality for all, but special privileges for none! Those who aspire to and are elected to public office must be held to the principle of equality before the law. Upon this high moral ground, the middle class can successfully defend its place as guardian of American freedom. Upon this high moral ground, a society can be and is being built that will see the advancement of the skills of each individual and collectively the greater advancement of our society.

The middle class has looked to the Republican party as the advocate of our values and the defender of our rights. In the area of quotas, as in many other areas, the Republican party has betrayed us. For example, the 1991 Civil Rights Act was declared by the Bush administration to be a quota bill. The liberal media waged a tireless campaign to label those who opposed the act as being soft on racism or even racist. The GOP could not stand the pressure from the liberal establishment. At last, the so-called conservative Republican president signed the worse quota bill in history into law without even a word of apology to the middle class.

It should be plain to everyone that we cannot continue to rely upon "conservative" Federal politicians to protect our rights. Every time the Federal government increases its power to regulate our society and our lives, it does so at the expense of our personal liberty. We must regain control of our political destiny. We must gain the means to protect our individual freedom. Currently the private citizen stands defenseless against an all-powerful Federal government. He has no way to protect himself from an abusive and intrusive Federal government, agency, or bureaucrat. The only effective balance against an oppressive Federal government is the sovereign state. In Chapters 26 and 27 we will discuss how "We the people" of the sovereign states may legally regain control of this out-of-control Federal government and thereby protect our liberties.

For too many years, an oppressive, politically correct, liberal establishment has used the police power of the Federal government to deny equal opportunity to white middle-class Americans—all done, of course, under the pretext of "helping" the disadvantaged. The

American Federal government has become the world's most assertive proponent of a race- and color-conscious society. All across America, North, South, East, and West, middle-class citizens have adopted the principle of a color-blind society—equality of opportunity for all, special privileges for none. Unfortunately for the middle class, "its" Federal government, now held captive by special interest, has been out of step with the rest of America. As a society, we must now find a means by which we can prevent the Federal government from continuing to ignore our desire for a color-blind society. Members of America's middle class must establish the political mechanism to ensure that the Federal government will never again be allowed to use its police powers to discriminate against any segment of the population. As of now, the question we all must face is: "Instead of Federally enforced quotas and reverse discrimination—Why Not Freedom!"

SUMMARY
Questions and Answers

Q. How can we be assured that people who have been discriminated against will receive the help they need to overcome that discrimination if the Federal government does not help?

A. When talking about various forms of discrimination, we often forget that this is something that has been going on throughout history. Discrimination was not invented by twentieth-century Americans. Why is it that, in the latter part of this century, liberals for some unforeseen reason think that people cannot overcome obstacles without government assistance? Have liberals all of a sudden adopted the old segregationist view that current minorities are weaker than and intellectually inferior to other people in society and, therefore, must have help from government to become equal to the rest of society? The truth is that in a free society all members are encouraged to be the best that they can and to overcome obstacles that men of lesser societies could not overcome. What is needed is the freedom of action and the courage to act, not government-sponsored handouts. Each new group of immigrants to this country has had to overcome some form of discrimination and otherwise adjust to American society. To say at this late date that only with government rules and regulation can justice be found in America is to make a mockery of the achievements of all Americans.

Q. In an effort to improve the quality of life of many minorities, our government has found it necessary to offer preferred status to certain groups that have suffered discrimination. Only a very small number of white people have lost jobs or been denied jobs as a result. Why should we allow this small number of people to cause the government to cease helping minorities to overcome discrimination?

A. It may be true that only a small number of non-minority workers have been refused a job because of reverse discrimination. The problem with reverse discrimination in hiring practices is that everyone who is affected by it feels that "if it had not been for discrimination against me, I would have gotten that job." Therefore, the net effect on society is a gross increase of ill will toward those who receive a job because of their minority status. It should also be remembered that in addition to the white male who is directly harmed by reverse discrimination, there is also his family who suffer. Also, many non-white people who acquire jobs because they are truly qualified are unfairly lumped into a category with those who have their jobs not because of merit but because of their minority status. So, as you can see, this causes an increase in resentment for non-whites and a decrease in appreciation for the honest achievements of qualified and competent minorities. All of which is being done under the pretext of improving race relations.

CHAPTER 7

Instead of Gun Control— Why Not Freedom!

The paradox of modern liberalism's attitude toward crime and the law-abiding citizen is nowhere more pronounced than in the realm of the right to keep and bear arms. Strange as it may seem, at a time when this country is awash in crime, the Federal government's primary method of attacking crime is to infringe upon the constitutional right of the law-abiding citizen to keep and bear arms! At a time when crime often goes unpunished, the lawful citizen is having his constitutional right to keep and bear arms violated by the Federal government. From 1973 to 1991, 36.6 million Americans were injured as a result of violent crime. Six million Americans were seriously injured by criminals! One in four households in America is victimized by crime each year. In 1991, an estimated $19.1 billion was lost to criminal activity. Yet, the Federal government's reaction is to initiate actions that will eventually lead to the confiscation of all firearms from law-abiding citizens—the Second Amendment of the Constitution be damned!

The liberal establishment uses its control of the media to advance its propaganda line that guns cause crime. According to liberal philosophy, the individual is not responsible: an inanimate object, a gun, is at fault for gun-related crime. The object in this case, a gun, is to be scorned and punished, not the individual. When liberals talk about gun control, what they are really talking about is people control. Specifically, they are talking about controlling law-abiding, middle-class citizens! As we all know, they are not talking about controlling criminals, because criminals by definition do not obey the law and, therefore, will not obey liberal gun-control laws. The use of the power of the Federal government to infringe upon the citizen's constitutional right to keep and bear arms is a frightening warning to all Americans. Emboldened by the success of their attack upon your constitutional rights, the liberal establishment now feels free to exercise more control over you at its pleasure. Regardless of what the Constitution may say, your rights and liberties are now enjoyed only so long as it pleases the liberal politicians in Washington. As has been pointed out in earlier sections of this book, the Bill of Rights was established by the sovereign states to prevent the Federal government from intruding into your rights. Today, the Federal government has abrogated your rights that were protected by the Second, Ninth, and Tenth Amendments. To a lesser extent, rights protected under other amendments of the Bill of Rights have also been attacked by the politically correct forces that control the Federal government. If Americans lose part of their freedom to a centralized Federal government, it only remains a matter of time before the remainder is taken from them. This is why it is important not only for gun owners but also for all Americans to become alarmed at the usurpation of our Second Amendment rights.

The right of Americans to keep and bear arms was recognized early in our history. James Madison, the Father of the Constitution, declared that tyrants were "afraid to trust the people with arms" and praised our country because of "the advantage of being armed, which the Americans possess over the people of almost every other nation."[56] The Second Amendment protecting our right to keep and bear arms was described as necessary so that "the Constitution be never construed to prevent the people who are peaceable citizens from keeping their own arms."[57] That great Southerner, Patrick Henry, declared that "The great objective is that every man be armed."[58]

The right of citizens to keep and bear arms was also recognized after the end of our war with the British Empire. The writings of the early Americans who were debating the adoption of the Constitution demonstrate why maintaining the right to bear arms is important for a free people. "That the people have a right to bear arms for the defense of themselves and their own state, or the United States . . . and no law shall be passed for disarming the people or any of

56 James Madison, *The Federalist No. 46*, quoted in George W. Carey and James McCellan, *The Federalist: Student Edition* (Dubuque, IA: Kendall/Hunt Publishing Company, 1990) 244.

57 Don Kates, "Handgun Prohibition and the Original Meaning of the Second Amendment," *82 Michigan Law Review* (1983), 203-24.

58 Patrick Henry, quoted in Wayne LaPierre, *Guns, Crime, and Freedom* (Washington, DC: Regnery Publishing, Inc., 1994) 16-17.

them. . . ."[59] Free people have the right of self-protection. An early constitutional scholar recognized the importance of firearms in the hands of free men. The first textbook on the Constitution used at West Point was written by William Rawle in 1825. He was very clear and to the point regarding the protection afforded by the Second Amendment: "The prohibition is general. No clause in the constitution could by any rule of construction be conceived to give to congress a power to disarm the people." Rawle warns us that ". . . the prevention of popular insurrections and resistance to government by disarming the people, is oftener meant than avowed by [those who would restrict gun ownership]."[60]

The liberal establishment (which includes such varied groups as the media, the education establishment, and the government) tells us that the Second Amendment protection is meant only for the militia. Therefore, according to liberals, the only people protected by the Second Amendment would be National Guardsmen. They make this absurd claim without ever defining what was meant by "the militia." George Mason, the co-author of the Second Amendment, described the militia thusly: ". . . a well regulated Militia, composed of the Gentlemen, Freeholders, and other Freemen was necessary to protect our ancient laws and liberty from the standing army. . . ."[61] It is clear that he was not referring to a standing military organization such as the National Guard but to free citizens—in short, the people who possess their own weapons. Thomas Jefferson wrote into the Virginia Constitution that ". . . no free man shall be debarred the use of arms within his own land." George Mason left no doubt why it is important to maintain the citizen's right to keep and bear arms: "To disarm the people [is] the best and most effectual way to enslave them." Contemporary Americans need to be reminded that it was Britain's attempt to disarm the Colonists that led to the battle at Lexington. Our Colonial Forefathers did not insist upon the Second Amendment so that modern-day Americans would be free to go duck hunting. Hobbies such as hunting and target shooting had

59 *The Anti-Federalist: The Address and Reasons of Dissent of the Minority of the Convention of Pennsylvania To Their Constituents*, Herbert J. Storing, Ed. (Chicago and London: The University of Chicago Press, 1992) 207.

60 William Rawle, *A View of the Constitution of the United States: Secession as Taught at West Point*, Walter D. Kennedy and James R. Kennedy, Eds. (1825, Simsboro, LA: Old South Books, 1991) 110.

61 George Mason, quoted in LaPierre, 5.

very little to do with the adoption of the Second Amendment; defending our civil liberties against tyrants was the primary motivating factor. Tyrants will not tolerate an armed people!

The value of private arms in the hands of free men was well proven during the Revolutionary War with Great Britain. One British politician noted that the American people were dangerous because ". . . with principles of right in their minds and hearts, and with arms in their hands [Americans were determined] to assert those principles."[62] The British Empire knew the dangers posed by armed free men and attempted their own version of "assault weapons" control, an attempt that lead to the Battle of Lexington and the "shot heard around the world."

> On October 19, 1774, Lord Dartmouth, in a circular letter to the Colonial Governors, informed them that the King, by an order in Council, had prohibited the exportation from Great Britain of gun powder; or any sort of arms or ammunition, and his Lordship required the Governors to prevent the importation of the prohibited articles into the several colonies. Not content with preventing the purchase by the colonies of the munitions of war, the next move was to seize and carry away, or destroy, the ammunition already in their possession.[63]

Patrick Henry, as usual, saw to the core of the issue. He told his fellow Virginians that the issue of American independence would not become a burning issue in the hearts of Americans because of the tax on tea and other such provocations:

> But tell them of the robbery of the magazine, and that the next step will be to disarm them, and they will be then ready to fly to arms to defend themselves.[64]

During the War for Southern Independence, the people of New Orleans found out what it was like to live under the heel of a tyrant. After the occupation of New Orleans by Federal forces under the command of Gen. Benjamin "Beast" Butler, the city was placed under marshall law. The agents of marshall law were so oppressive that they even hanged a young man because he pulled down the invader's

---

62 Chatham, Member of Parliament, quoted in William Wirt Henry, Ed., *Patrick Henry: Life, Correspondence, and Speeches* (1891, Harrisonburg, VA: Sprinkle Publications, 1993) I; 272.

63 Henry, 276.

64 Ibid, 279.

flag *before* the city had formally surrendered. All civil liberties were restricted, including freedom of religion, freedom of speech, and freedom of assembly; and, of course, an order was given by Butler to confiscate all guns held by private citizens.[65] During Butler's reign of terror, millions of dollars of private property were stolen (confiscated from "rebels") from the people of Louisiana and sent back up North (thieves have always known that it is much safer to rob disarmed citizens). Any country that has been invaded understands how important it is to have free men who possess and know how to use firearms. Tyrants also recognize the danger and act accordingly.

Adolph Hitler, the archetypical tyrant of the twentieth century, was a believer in gun control. In 1938, Hitler signed a Nazi gun-control law for the Federal government of Germany. This was done after he had consolidated all power from the German states into a strong central government. His gun-control law required police permission to own a pistol. All firearms were required to be registered. Those who wanted to "keep and bear" arms were instructed to join the army. The Nazis also enacted special gun-control laws for "politically incorrect" individuals. Shortly thereafter, the gas chambers began working overtime. No guns—no resistance. Firearms registration lists were used by the Nazi SS to collect weapons from political enemies and occasionally to collect the owner as well. Once again, just so you will understand our point, TYRANTS DO NOT LIKE ARMED CITIZENS. We must not allow any government to infringe upon our right to keep and bear arms.

How can "We the people" protect our Second Amendment rights? The same way we can protect all of our rights and liberties. We must have a counterbalance to the Federal government. As Madison declared,

> . . . the State governments, with the people on their side, would be able to repel the danger [of an oppressive Federal government]. . . . Besides the advantage of being armed, which the Americans possess over the people of almost every other nation, the existence of subordinate governments [sovereign states], to which the people are attached, and by which the militia officers are appointed, forms a barrier against the enterprises of ambition. . . .[66]

65 John D. Winters, *The Civil War in Louisiana* (Baton Rouge, LA: Louisiana State University Press, 1963) 136.

66 James Madison, *The Federalist No. 46,* quoted in Carey and McClellan, 244.

When the rights and liberties of "We the people" of the sovereign states are infringed upon by an abusive Federal government, it is the duty of the sovereign state to be the protector of our rights and liberties, just as our Founding Fathers intended. When the Federal government attempts to force a local sheriff to enforce unconstitutional gun-control laws, then it is the duty of the sovereign state to stand between the local official and the unwarranted Federal actions. Our Founding Fathers knew that a private citizen would not have the resources to fight the Federal government. They left that responsibility to the sovereign state.

We must not rely upon the good luck of having elected a "conservative" Congress as the only means to protect our rights and liberties. We must not rely upon the chance of having elected a "conservative" president who (we hope) will veto laws that infringe upon our Second Amendment rights. We cannot entrust our constitutional liberties to the interpretations of a "conservative" Supreme Court. No! Freedom and liberty are best served and protected at the local level by "We the people" of the sovereign state. Americans must recall Patrick Henry's warning that we must not allow people in a faraway government to have control of "our dearest interests." A government powerful enough to disarm law-abiding citizens is evil enough to trample upon their remaining liberty. Instead of unconstitutional gun-control laws—Why Not Freedom!

SUMMARY
Questions and Answers

Q. Guns have always frightened me. Why should I want to assist anyone in keeping guns in our society?

A. You are at liberty to make your decision whether you will own a gun. That is your right as a free person. No one, especially the Federal government, should be given the authority to make you own a gun. On the other hand, if you, being a free person, decide to own a gun, the Federal government, according to our Federal Constitution, should not stand in your way. If you are not willing to help defend your fellow citizens' right to keep and bear arms, then right of gun ownership alone with other precious liberties will slowly be eroded away. Remember that freedom is not divisible. If one area of our freedoms is diminished, then the total amount of our freedom is diminished. Freedom is like a ball of wax. If you take away any of the wax, then the ball gets smaller. If the Federal government is allowed to take away one right protected in the Bill of Rights, then we have implicitly authorized the process by which the Federal government may take away any other right protected by the Bill of Rights. Just because you do not utilize a freedom does not negate your responsibility to your fellow citizens to assist them in protecting that right. After all, they are the citizens whom you will call upon to come to your aid when one of your freedoms comes under attack.

Q. The liberal establishment has recently (November 8, 1994) been handed a defeat at the ballot box. With more conservative members in control of Congress, why are you so worried about what liberals are going to do now that they are out of power? Aren't you over-reacting?

A. Surely everyone who believes in the ideas of conservatism feels better when conservatives are in control of the Federal government. But what happens when conservatives lose control of the Federal government? How will we at the local level protect ourselves, our property, and our "dearest interests" when the Federal government once again becomes an instrument in the hands of those who would destroy those interests? The answer is simple: we can never be secure in our freedom until we dismantle the apparatus that has grown up in Washington, D.C., which is responsible for the loss of so much freedom. Conservatism is good, but it cannot give "We the people" the protection that our original constitutional republic gave us. Regardless of how many conservatives are currently in Washington, D.C., they can never give us, at the local level, a means to place a check upon the abuse of Federal power. "We the people" of the sovereign state will never be safe from an abusive Federal government until we have the clear and undivided attention of OUR agents in Washington, until they understand that "We the people" of the sovereign states hold ultimate power and if necessary will use that power to nullify any intrusion upon our "dearest interests." One point often overlooked by conservatives is that, even under the control of conservatives, the Federal government can be misused. We must always remember that, if a power is given to a group of people, that power can and at some point will be misused. "We the people" must have

the means to protect our liberties from an abusive Federal government regardless of who controls it. One cannot logically expect that
the means to protect ourselves from an abusive Federal government
will come from the Federal government itself—even though today
that government may be controlled by "conservatives." Free men
must insist upon the means to protect their own liberties. To rely
upon the good will of faraway officials, intoxicated by the arrogance
of power, is to rely upon false hope. Liberty is never maintained by
irrationally clinging to such delusion. We must rely upon ourselves.
We must insist upon the tools necessary to protect our "dearest interests." "We the people" of the sovereign states are the last and best
hope for the preservation of true liberty.

CHAPTER 8

Instead of Forced Busing—
Why Not Freedom!

In 1896, the United States Supreme Court officially sanctioned the policy of "separate but equal" and thereby established racial segregation as the official policy of the United States of America.[67] This policy would be codified into law (de jure segregation) in more than twenty-six states, mostly those states with large black populations and enforced by local customs (de facto segregation) in those states with relatively small black populations. This American policy would continue until the United States Supreme Court reversed its prior decision in 1954.[68] Because of its relatively large black population, the South became the primary target of this change in social policy. In the United States, the social change, referred to as racial integration, was supported inversely to the percentage of black population; that is, the general public tended to support the concept of racial integration more in those states with the smallest number of black citizens. Racial integration was generally supported in those Northern states with small black populations and generally resisted in Southern states with large black populations. To the average white Southerner this appeared to be a rather hypocritical stance. The people of the North were attempting to force a radical change in social conditions, yet Northerners to a large extent would not be forced to live with these radical changes. Dire predictions were made by Southern people of what would transpire if the policy of racial integration were implemented. Many Southerners predicted integration would lead to a destruction of moral standards, a decreased educational level, an increased illegitimacy rate, increased violence in schools, and loss of local control of schools. Regardless of the cause, the dire predictions made by many Southerners have been realized. As of

67 *Plessy v. Ferguson,* 163 U.S. 537 (1896).

68 *Brown v. Board of Education of Topeka,* 347 U.S. 482 (1954).

1994, approximately twelve hundred school districts are under Federal court-ordered desegregation plans.[69]

On the bright side, many Southern libertarians, who opposed the use of government force to obtain social ends, celebrated the opportunity to end the era of government-enforced segregation. For several decades after the 1954 decision, the thinking of Southerners about this issue evolved from support for government-enforced segregation to opposition to either government-enforced segregation or integration. This has been a remarkable political and philosophical evolution. In 1950, the majority of white Southerners supported the concept of inequality before the law, permitting special treatment in favor of white Southerners by state government. By 1980, the majority of white Southerners had changed their political philosophy to support the idea of a color-blind society more in keeping with the old Jeffersonian idea of equality before the law without the use of governmental force. A common phrase from that time stated "equal rights for all, special privileges for none" and summed up the feelings of most Southerners.

Unfortunately, while the white South was reorganizing its expectations for its society to fit the model of contemporary equality, the black South (or at least its self-appointed leadership) was assuming a position opposite its original concept of social equality. The 1954 decision required the rejection of enforced segregation in favor of a society in which the individual was allowed freedom of choice. Under this system, so it was taught, American society was to evolve into a color-blind society. Parents would select the school to which they would send their children based not upon color of skin but upon the parents' understanding of what was best for their children. No longer would the state make pupil assignment according to race or color of skin. Under the new system of public education, parents would be the sole determining agent as to where their children would go to school.

From 1896 until the 1954 school desegregation decision, the liberal establishment demanded freedom of choice in education. Yet, after less than ten years of freedom of choice in education, liberals ceased being satisfied with this system. The liberal establishment that once fought against the use of state-sponsored force and racial identity in student assignment to school, suddenly changed and began a

69 *The Wall Street Journal,* December 21, 1994, A19.

nationwide campaign to force schools to take students solely on the basis of race.

In 1966, the United States Supreme Court reintroduced race and governmental force into the assignment of pupils to public schools. The infamous busing decisions would demonstrate to all Americans in general and to Southerners in particular just how powerful and oppressive the Federal Government can be. Busing is nothing less than the naked force of the liberal establishment unleashed against the middle-class citizens of America—especially the American South! It must be remembered that the horror of having one's children bused out of an established community into an unknown environment, surrounded by strangers, is in direct proportion to the number of minority citizens within a city and/or state. All across the South and in numerous Northern urban centers, the cry arose to "the powers that be" in Washington, D.C., to relent and allow parents the privilege (in actuality it is an inalienable right) of sending their children to neighborhood schools. In petitions, protest meetings, letters to editors, and letters to elected officials, American citizens attempted to persuade their government to allow them to exercise this most basic of freedoms—the freedom to choose the school to which they would entrust their most precious objects of love, their children.

The Federal government's reply to the middle class's protest about the loss of control of the education of their children left no doubt as to the new relationship between the citizen and the government. American citizens had become the subjects of an all-powerful central government. Today, the Federal government acts as if it owns the nation's children. Our children have become helpless pawns in various liberal schemes and numerous social experiments. Parents have been forced to stand aside and watch as their children are used by faceless authority figures attempting to implement an untested and unproven liberal social experiment. The children of the middle class have learned by cruel experience that their parents are powerless against the government. Parents can do nothing to protect their children from an all-powerful Federal government. Although, to a small extent, the system of forced busing has diminished outside of the South, in the South an entire generation or more of Southern students have been robbed of the right to attend neighborhood schools, robbed of the pleasure of a safe education in familiar surroundings, robbed of their freedom of choice by a callous, uncaring Federal government. In virtually every school district of the South, and in many Northern urban school districts, students have learned first hand that their "rights" are enjoyed at the pleasure and discretion of the Federal government. They have also learned by first-hand experience that the protected minorities' rights are more important than their rights. Southern and many Northern students know first hand that they are second-class citizens. How and why was this social experiment, using middle-class children as guinea pigs, forced upon America's children?

The Federal courts based their 1966 busing decision on the work of Dr. James P. Coleman. His untested thesis insisted that the only way to bring about racial integration was to remove the parents' right to make the choice of where their children would be educated and have the Federal government make pupil assignment according to color of skin. After a decade of "forcing" parents to send their children to schools in strange neighborhoods, the weak support for busing has evaporated. Even black parents no longer support the concept. Yet, the Federal government continues its campaign of forced pupil assignment—based upon the criteria of skin color. Even Dr. Coleman became disenchanted with his original recommendation. No matter though, the Federal courts and the Department of Civil Rights maintain their oppressive stranglehold over local schools.

The resistance to busing was not limited to the South. Northern urban centers also felt the heavy yoke of the Federal Supreme Court. In Boston, Massachusetts, protests, fights, and boycotts greeted Federal Judge Garrity's busing order. The parents' complaints were not that blacks would be attending white schools, but that the Federal government had, without constitutional authority, denied parents the right to choose the best school for their children. The Federal government had, in effect, seized children and made decisions as to the education of those children—decisions that heretofore were the sole and exclusive domain of parents. Judge Garrity is an example of the hypocrisy of the elitist, liberal establishment that issued the Boston busing court order. Yet, his grandchildren did not attend public schools but were safely enrolled in a private school. Massachusetts Senator Ted Kennedy, another great champion of liberal busing programs across the country, sent his children to private schools. Thus, those who were instrumental in forcing the middle class to bus its children were themselves insulated from the disastrous results of their liberal folly! Even in the 1990s, we find out that the greatest liberal of all time, Bill Clinton, sends his child, not to the fine public schools of Washington, D.C., but to a private school!

The middle class has paid and continues to pay an enormous price for this failed system of liberal social experimentation. The system of busing has destroyed the close connection between parents and their local schools. This, in addition to other liberal policies, has driven a wedge between educators and parents. Once it was a simple matter to pass a school bond issue or tax increase. Today, the education system more often than not is seen to be at odds with the values of the middle class. In far too many schools today, the educational system appears to be conducting an active campaign to convince children to think in a politically correct fashion. Middle-class parents have become alarmed at the thought of classroom education being extended to instruction regarding alternate sexual lifestyles. Many middle-class parents see the Federal government as the agency that barred public expression of religion in public school but now endorses perverted lifestyles as normal, even though the majority of the middle class reject such views.

The human cost of forced busing to the children, parents, and communities is beyond calculation and comprehension. Yet, another cost of busing is within the scope of comprehension. The devaluation of real estate values in middle-class neighborhoods that are zoned by a Federal judge into the "wrong" school district has placed many families into economic "hot water." Across the South numerous middle-class homeowners have lost a large part of their home equity by the simple act of a Federal judge drawing a school busing district. One of the first questions a prospective purchaser will ask a home seller is, "What school district are you in?" If the home has been zoned into a district that buses its children across town to a predominantly black area with high crime, then the seller will find it extremely difficult to realize the full equity price for his home. In other words, the arbitrary and unconstitutional actions of a Federal judge have cost the seller thousands of dollars! The liberal establishment does not care about the individual's loss; all it cares about is the furtherance of its ill-conceived, left-wing social experiments.

In Baton Rouge, Louisiana, a black civil rights leader was asked why he was pushing the busing agenda when it appeared to harm local education. His reply was to the effect that he did not care about education, all he cared about was integration. This was in a city in which the Federal judge met with local civil rights groups, such as the NAACP, to discuss busing issues but refused to meet with local parents, even though the local parents represented a far larger number of citizens and paid the bulk of school taxes! The Federal courts were not interested in justice, only in imposing new decrees for the unrepresented middle class to follow.

The high cost of forced busing cannot be fully understood until it is recognized that tax dollars that could have been spent for real education were spent to maintain and operate an expensive bus system solely to move children from place to place. In Kansas City, Missouri, the Federal court went so far as to order the implementation of a 25% income tax and a doubling of local property taxes to pay for its forced integration plan![70] Do you recall what happened during the colonial period when the British Parliament attempted to tax the colonies without their consent? The people rebelled against the government crying, "No taxation without representation!" The cost of the Kansas City integration plan was in excess of $1.2 billion. Yet, according to a study done by the liberal Harvard Project on School Desegregation, the plan has not been successful in integrating local schools![71] The liberal social experiment of busing is a billion-dollar failure, financed by the unrepresented middle-class taxpayer and endured by those thousands of middle-class students. Added to this is the expense of private education that many middle-class parents found necessary to impose upon themselves. The liberal establishment has undemocratically forced the middle class to bear the economic burden of numerous unconstitutional social experiments.

The Federal Supreme Court, in 1990, ruled that the district Federal judge could not directly tax the local citizens to pay for his school desegregation plan. What appeared to be a victory for local self-government quickly evaporated when the Federal Supreme Court allowed the same district Federal judge to order the local school board to implement his plan and they (the local school board) would have to figure out how to pay for the plan.[72] If the local

70 Ibid

71 *The Wall Street Journal*, April 26, 1994, editorial page.

72 *The Wall Street Journal*, December 21, 1994, A19.

school board refused to fund the Federal judge's plan, then the Federal judge would hold them in contempt and order the school board to Federal prison.

The school district of Rockford, Illinois, has labored under a Federal desegregation court order since 1989. By 1994, the local taxpayers had footed the $54 million cost of implementing the Federal judge's orders. Local authorities estimate that the Federal desegregation plan will cost $100 million by 1996. What did the local community get for their expenditures in Federalized "education"? They were forced to hire an "Associate Superintendent of Equity" by the name of Stephen J. Wesley. This individual was not hired by the local school board, though the local school board paid the salary, but he was hired by a Federal court-appointed "master of desegregation." Thirteen months after the Federally appointed "master" hired Wesley, it was discovered that he had been convicted of embezzling while employed by a Colorado school district, he falsified his credentials with counterfeit degrees, and he lied about being trained as a Jesuit priest.[73]

The system of forced busing is supported by the Democratic party. In response, the middle class has looked vainly to the Republican party to champion its right of freedom of choice in education. Unfortunately, the GOP has been negligent in its duty to the middle class. In 1968, Governor George C. Wallace stood up for the middle class and denounced Federally mandated busing. As is common, the media attempted to fix the label of racist upon those people campaigning against busing. The Republican party tried to ignore busing as an issue, but the threat of Governor Wallace's campaign forced Richard Nixon to assume much of Wallace's anti-busing rhetoric. Nixon used the middle-class's anti-busing anger as a tool to capture their votes. As soon as Nixon was elected, the issue was dropped. Nixon's and the GOP's attitude toward the middle class is best explained by reading what Nixon's attorney general told a group of black civil rights activists shortly after Nixon's election: "Look at what we do, not what we say!"[74] What the national Republicans were saying is, "We lied to the middle class just to get their votes; now what can we

---

73 Ibid

74 Richard Nixon's Attorney General-Designate John Mitchell, addressing a group of Southern civil rights leaders in 1968, after Nixon's election, as quoted in William J. Quirk and R. Randall Bridwell, *Abandoned: The Betrayal of the American Middle Class Since World War II* (Lanham, MD: Madison Books, 1992) 201.

do to further the anti- middle class civil rights agenda?" As we have already explained in Chapter 4, the reason the GOP did this was to capture the "last vote." They knew that the middle class would never vote for the extreme liberal Democratic candidate, therefore the GOP was confident that it could "cut a deal" with the "protected minorities"—after all, the middle class had nowhere to go.

The education of our children is too important to be controlled by faceless Federal bureaucrats or callous Federal judges. Control of our children's educational institutions must be reclaimed by the middle class, and that control must be maintained at the local level. Those opposing this idea include the Federal government, the liberal media who attempt to paint all who oppose them with the tar brush of racism, and the liberal education establishment. All of these liberal establishments have a vested interest in preventing the middle class from regaining control, not over our schools, but over our children! The only way we can prevent the current or future Federal government from controlling local schools is to have a strong sovereign state that will interpose its sovereign authority between an aggressive Federal government and local schools. In order to maintain a society that is based upon the Jeffersonian principle of equality of opportunity, "We the people" of the sovereign state must ensure a color-blind society. As history has demonstrated, we cannot rely upon the Federal government to do this for us. As we demonstrate in Chapters 1 and 25, "We the people" of the sovereign state have the right to protect our liberties from an aggressive Federal government. Instead of Federally imposed forced busing—Why Not Freedom!

SUMMARY
Questions and Answers

Q. If forced busing is such a problem in the South, why don't we hear more about Southerners complaining about it?

A. In cities and rural areas all across the South, Federal interference with local education has become a common fact of life. Most young people in the South have grown up not knowing what it is like to go to a school that is administered according to the wishes of the local community. At one time in the South, the local school was the center of all community activity and a source of community pride. But, with the advent of forced busing, the community has lost its traditional source of pride. Even in the black community, voices have been raised in protest over the loss of community spirit and pride because of the loss of control over the local school. This loss has proven to be detrimental to society at large. Parents who no longer feel close to teachers, administrators, and schools do not reinforce values taught by the community, which deprives society of one of its main pillars of support. Yes, forced busing has been and continues to be a problem in the South and in certain areas of the North. But in the South, with its history of total military defeat at the hands of the Federal government, people are more acutely aware of the results of too great a resistance to Federal tyranny. With the liberal voting block in the South constituting up to 40% of the voters, it is very difficult to elect statesmen who will stand up to the Federal government. But, there is hope. As time goes on, more and more Southerners are realizing that they must take a stand against Federal tyranny.

CHAPTER 9

Instead of Crime in Our Streets—
Why Not Freedom!

In the United States of America violent crime has reached epidemic proportions. In the nine years from 1960 to 1969 it increased by more than 200%![75] Look at what happened in our country in 1994:

Every 21 minutes—an American died due to violent crime
Every 5 minutes—an American woman was raped
Every 40 seconds—an American was robbed
Every 5 seconds—an American home was burglarized.[76]

After spending nearly five trillion dollars on social welfare programs, providing special rights for criminals, installing air-conditioned gyms and other prison accommodations, and tying the hands of the police, the liberal establishment has given Americans a society verging upon unbridled chaos. Nowhere is the disastrous result of liberalism's attack upon traditional American values more evident than in the alarming increase in violent crime.

In the late 1960s, George Wallace made "law and order" a key plank in his bid for the presidency of the United States. At the time of Governor Wallace's presidential campaign, the liberal media attacked Wallace's emphasis on law and order. They even claimed that he had stolen this theme from a plank in the Nazi party platform! The liberal establishment assured Americans that they had nothing to fear from crime. Liberals assured Americans that there was no real increase in violent crime and that, even if there were an increase, their liberal social programs would solve the underlying causes of crime. The causes of crime in Wallace's time and in our

75 Wayne LaPierre, *Guns, Crime, and Freedom* (Washington, DC: Regnery Publishing, Inc., 1994) 117.

76 Ibid, 113.

time, according to liberals, are racism, poverty, discrimination, hunger, and the unwillingness on the part of many Americans to "do their part" to overcome past abuses suffered by the disadvantaged. Twenty-five years of experience have demonstrated to the middle class that Governor Wallace's prediction about crime in America was closer to reality than anything offered by the liberal establishment.

The New York subway has provided us with numerous examples of violent criminal activity. It has also provided us with an excellent example of how the liberal-controlled government has abandoned the safety of Americans and now favors the special rights of criminals. In 1984, Jerome Sandusky, a retired seventy-one-year- old worker, was waiting for the scheduled arrival of a train in a Manhattan subway station. Suddenly he was set upon by a group of thugs. One of the thugs, twenty-three-year-old Bernard McCummings, a career criminal, grabbed Sandusky in a choke-hold and, according to Sandusky, attempted to kill him. A couple of transit police officers heard Sandusky's screams for help and rushed to his assistance. According to one of the officers, McCummings attempted to attack the police after receiving a warning signal from a juvenile member of the group. The juvenile's warning consisted of shouting out "yo" at the approach of the officers. According to police reports, McCummings lunged at one of the officers, who shot the thug. The transit officer, a fourteen-year veteran of the force, was cleared of wrongdoing by an internal investigation. McCummings' wound caused a spinal cord injury and eventual confinement in a wheelchair.

McCummings, the thug who had attempted to rob and murder a law-abiding citizen, then filed suit against the Transit Authority for excessive use of force. The court system of New York awarded him $4.3 million dollars. The New York Supreme Court upheld the award, and the United States Supreme Court (a court that never found it difficult to interfere in the business of Southern states) refused to hear the case—that is, the United States Supreme Court allowed the award to stand! In liberal America "crime pays." But it seems that the liberal establishment has forgotten about the victim. Sandusky did attempt to go through New York's "crime victims compensation" process. He received nothing because McCummings was officially listed as an indigent at the time.[77]

77 Eric Breindel, "Who Says Crime Doesn't Pay?" *The Wall Street Journal*, December 15, 1993, A17.

Let us not forget who has to ante-up the $4.3 million dollars—that's right, the taxpayers! Not only are we the victims of criminals in the streets, but we are also the victims of an insane and criminal liberal "justice" system.

The devastating effect that a sharp rise in violent crime can have upon a free society was described by Herrnstein and Murray in *The Bell Curve*.[78] They warned that as crime increases it will eventually destroy a free society. This is because a free country depends upon the voluntary acceptance of its citizens of a general code of conduct. Free people expect everyone to follow the "rules of conduct" generally accepted by society. When crime becomes a problem and a large segment of the population no longer respects the property rights and security rights of the rest of the population, then society must substitute governmental coercion for the cooperation once obtained by the voluntary conduct of civilized citizens. Any time government uses its police power to enforce conduct, the first victim is the freedom of the law-abiding segment of society. For example, in order to enforce the law regarding not driving while under the influence of alcohol, the entire driving population must now be subject to arbitrary, roadside breath-a-lizer exams. In addition, the very ease by which we once moved about our cities and neighborhoods, and even the security we once felt in our own homes, is taken away. Crime robs society not only of property, but freedom and security. Bars on windows, double locks on doors, and high-priced electrical security systems are no substitute for the safe society we enjoyed before crime seized our society.

Herrnstein and Murray were describing the problems faced by numerous middle-class Americans, who, at the time of their retirement, suddenly realize that their American dream, a home that they have worked all their life to pay for, is located in a "transitional" neighborhood. Suddenly, through no fault of their own, they find themselves prisoners in their own home, afraid to go out at night. The security and comfort of their retirement years are taken away by forces beyond their control, the force of Big Government with liberals at the controls. The figures for violent crime, the type of crime that makes people feel insecure in their homes at night or on the streets during the day, has constantly increased since the mid-1960s. From 1964 to 1971 the trend line for crime jumped sharply

78 Richard J. Herrnstein and Charles Murray, *The Bell Curve: Intelligence and Class Structure in American Life* (New York, NY: The Free Press, 1994) 236-37.

and continued into the 1980s at which time it increased even more rapidly.[79]

The crime rate data demonstrate a sharp increase around the time that liberalism gained virtually complete control of American society. In the mid-1960s, the Federal government greatly increased its powers with the passage of the 1964 "Civil Rights" Act and again in 1965 with the passage of the "Voting Rights" Act. From that point forward, the liberal establishment has been able to marshall its welfare and quasi-welfare block vote to defeat "conservative" candidates who oppose the enlargement of Federal powers. Such activities as forced busing, racial quotas, race norming, and gun control (just to name a few) have all been used by the liberal establishment to increase the ability of the Federal government to interfere in the lives of American citizens. It should come as no surprise that the trend line demonstrating the sharp increase in violent crime remained flat until the mid-1960s. After liberalism "dethroned" traditional middle-class values, such as rewarding merit and insisting upon fast and effective punishment for criminals, the criminal element seized control of our streets. As long as criminologists and social scientists viewed crime and criminals basically the same as the middle class viewed them, i.e., crime was wrong; the criminal was responsible for his conduct; punishment should fit the crime, be swift, and sure: as long as this view was held in common with the middle class, then crime was more or less under control. After the mid-1960s the social scientists began to advocate the theory that it was not the criminal's fault but that society was at fault and contributed to the criminal's acts of violence. Liberal social scientists and criminologists began to theorize that the criminal was only getting even with a society that had mistreated and abused him. In short, liberal social scientists began to advocate the theory that society had victimized the criminal.[80]

When confronted with the reality of criminal activity, the liberal establishment tends to blame society rather than the criminal. To the liberal, the criminal is not at fault, it is society that is to blame. Modern liberalism advances the theory that criminal activity is caused by a society that discriminates against the perpetrator of crime, thereby forcing him into a life of crime. Or, perhaps, his anti-social lifestyle

79 Ibid.

80 Ibid, 237.

is the result of numerous unnamed ancestors being taken from their idyllic homeland and forced into a life of slavery. Liberalism of the 1950s began to teach generations of Americans not to spank their children and not to punish criminals. Middle-class solutions to real problems are out of the question for liberals. Unlike the middle class, liberals will engage the errant child throwing a temper tantrum in "meaningful" dialogue; they will attempt to rehabilitate criminals and punish police officers for using "undue" force. The result of the acceptance of untested liberal sociology is evidenced every day in the headlines of America's daily newspapers! The United States is faced with the breakdown of law and order—just as predicted by Governor Wallace in 1968. Liberal policies have created a vast underclass that does not understand the basic principle of civilization. Meanwhile, liberal policies in education are slowly "dumbing down" future generations of middle-class citizens—not a bright picture for the future of American civilization. Too many people have never learned the basic principle that a free civilization depends upon a high degree of self-control and individual responsibility. Our welfare society, as well as a large segment of America's average citizens, do not realize that in order to remain free they must fulfill their duty to obey rules of "civilized conduct." Voluntary self-control is not required of subjects of an oppressive dictatorship. They are forced to comply with governmental rules by the police power of the state. This is not the type of society that our Founding Fathers had in mind. They envisioned a civilized society in which the people voluntarily complied with general social norms of conduct. They knew that a people who were a part of a civilized culture would not require the force of the police state in order to maintain their society. Civilized people can be trusted with freedom. As crime becomes a larger part of our social fabric, we lose an important part of our civilized society and our freedom.[81]

The threat of crime in the streets is more than just the suffering of individual victims—though this, in and of itself, is tragic. The breakdown in law and order that Americans currently contend with is the result of programs and policies forced upon an unwilling middle class. Very few of the social programs instituted by America's liberal elite would have ever lasted if the middle class had been in control of their community. These liberal policies are said to have

81 Ibid, 254.

been "forced" upon the middle class because none of these policies would have been possible if (1) the liberal propaganda ministry of the media had given equal and fair treatment to traditional middle-class American values, and (2) the sovereign states had not been unconstitutionally denied the right to defend their citizens from these abusive, liberal, Federal policies. For example, the police department for the city of Denver, Colorado, decided to crack down on violent crime. In an effort to reduce gang-related violence in the metropolitan area, they established a crime data base on gang members. Yet, the response of the liberal establishment sheds much light on how the left-of-center mindset in this country deals with the threat of middle-class America defending its rights. The Denver area American Civil Liberties Union attacked the program because more members of minority groups were listed than other groups. It made no difference to the liberal ACLU that more minority members were part of gangs than whites. Nor did it matter that the police had established a system whereby an individual who had no contact with the criminal justice system for a specific period of time was dropped from the list.[82]

Notice why the liberal ACLU attacked this effective crime-fighting technique—not because it was ineffective or because it violated a specific provision of the Constitution, but because the numbers were not "right." Again and again, middle-class rights have been sacrificed to the liberal idea that, in matters of race, "the numbers must be equal." One would suspect that liberals would blame the middle class because there are not enough white Colorado gang members!

Liberals insist that, in society, race is never responsible for variation in data relative to human behavior. Therefore, if more blacks are on death row, then it must be, according to liberal thinking, the result of discrimination, oppression, or racism. But data collected from the FBI's *Uniform Crime Reports* suggest a different conclusion. If the crimes committed by blacks in America are removed, the result is a crime rate similar to that of Europe. Yet, the liberal establishment is quick to demand gun-control laws because Americans have easier access to guns than Europeans, and this, according to liberals, is the reason for our higher crime rate.

---

82 Amitai Etzioni, "How Our Towns Fight Crime," *The Wall Street Journal,* December 31, 1993, editorial page.

If you break down the U.S. crime statistics by race (white and black), what you get is the following: In 1992, American whites committed 5.1 murders per 100,000, while American blacks committed more than eight times as many—43.4 per 100,000. American whites committed 126 robberies per 100,000 in 1992, while American blacks (per 100,000) committed more than 10 times as many—1,343. The white American murder rate (5.1) is thus even less than the average murder rate of the four European nations (5.5). . . . White Americans, who have easy access to guns, are less likely to kill each other than are the British, who are almost completely disarmed.[83]

The relationship of race and criminal activity was also noted in a study that compared Seattle to Vancouver.

[G]un ownership in Seattle is four times that of Vancouver, so if guns are responsible for crime, as the anti-gun crowd would have you believe, surely the homicide rate in Seattle should be 400 percent higher than that of Vancouver rather than a mere 60 percent. Dr. Brandon Centerwall reported in the *American Journal of Epidemiology,* December 1, 1991, that the homicide rates among non-Hispanic whites in Seattle and Vancouver were almost identical at just over six per 100,000, and that blacks and Hispanics could not be meaningfully compared because so few live in Vancouver. . . . The minorities in Seattle had astronomical homicide rates–36.6 per 100,000 for blacks and 26.9 for Hispanics. . . . [E]xcepting blacks and Hispanics, Seattle's homicide rate was actually lower than Vancouver's.[84]

The liberal establishment insists that it can cure crime with its social programs. Liberals will demand that middle-class Americans turn over more and more of their wage property to the government so liberals can finance their social programs. The liberal will attempt to make middle-class Americans feel guilty because more blacks are in prison than whites—the inference being that most of the blacks are incarcerated because of the failure of society and, therefore, it is the fault of the middle-class Americans that prisons are populated by a larger number of blacks. Yet, a 1991 study of adult burglary and robbery defendants demonstrated that race or ethnic background had very little effect on the likelihood of conviction or the imposition

83 Samuel Francis, "The Truth About Guns and Race," *Southern Partisan,* 2nd Quarter, 1994, 48.

84 LaPierre, 172-73.

of a subsequent penalty. According to this study, race or group identity bore little if any relationship to the outcome.[85]

The liberal's solution to crime is to disarm law-abiding citizens, tax
the middle class, and use those funds, not to build more prisons or to
enable stricter law enforcement, but to enact new social programs
to address the inequality and discrimination that liberal ideology
claims is responsible for crime. Clinton's "Crime Bill" is an excellent example of liberal ideology in action. With the stroke of a pen,
liberals were able to turn millions of law-abiding gun owners into
Federal criminals and, at the same time, establish new social programs for liberalism's "protected minorities"—programs such as midnight basketball! The false promise made by the liberal crime
bill—that crime can be solved by spending more Federal money—
is, in many people's mind, worthy of an indictment.[86] But liberalism
marches on, using the police power of Big Government to remove
middle-class property forcefully, in the form of taxes, and spending
tax money on social programs the liberal claim will cure the very
problem that earlier liberal programs and policies created.

The deleterious effects of liberal social programs can be seen in
such programs as the affirmative action or racial quota acts. These
types of liberal programs work together to create a social environment that tends to increase criminal activity in society. The use of
quotas in the selection of police officers offers an excellent example
of such evil. Many Northern urban and most Southern police departments either are under a court-ordered affirmative action hiring
plan or have adopted a "voluntary" quota hiring plan. Of course,
these "voluntary" plans are not, in fact, voluntary but are the attempt
of the local police department to avoid costly Federal suits. The liberal establishment has used its political power and its control of the
media to force police departments across the country to use quotas
to make sure they reflect the right racial mix. In order to achieve
the right racial mix, many police departments abandoned the merit
system and began to hire by the numbers depending upon the race
of the applicant. It did not matter if a better qualified white candidate was passed over. After all, to the liberal mind, numbers and
race are all that matter. Discrimination does not matter just so long

85 John J. DiTulio, Jr., "The Black Crime Gap," *The Wall Street Journal,* July 11, 1994, editorial
page.

86 "Crime Bill Illusion," *The Wall Street Journal,* September 7, 1994, A12.

as it is a white male who is suffering. But of course it is not just the white male who suffers. His whole family suffers, but since liberals do not hold a high regard for the traditional family, then their suffering should not matter much either. As police departments rushed to meet their quota of new minority employees, a disproportionate number of officers were hired who did not have the background required for police work. The result is that in New York a larger number of indicted policemen have come from the ranks of those hired during the quota-hiring frenzy. A very similar result has also been reported in cities such as Washington, D.C., and Miami.

The quota-hiring frenzy has led many police departments to lower their testing standards and relax their background checks. In a number of the cities where police officers have been indicted it has been discovered subsequently that these same officers had the very lowest test scores. This is what happens to a society that practices social "dumbing down" in order to reach equality by the numbers. Some of the minority officers even had felony backgrounds that the police departments ignored.[87] Our entire society and civilization has been put at risk just to achieve the right mix of minorities.

The failed policies of liberalism, more than any other single factor, have given rise to the current wave of crime in the streets of America. Beginning in the early 1930s, liberalism slowly seized control of American society. By the mid-1960s, the liberal establishment had gained enough power that it could, at last, force middle-class America to accept radical changes in the manner that our society treats social maladies. Under liberalism, the criminal became the victim, prisons became air-conditioned hotels, the police became the enemy of civil liberties, and the middle class became the tax "cash-cow" to pay for an unending string of untested liberal social schemes.

After nearly $5 trillion dollars spent on welfare and social programs, after an unprecedented rise in violent crime, after the spilling of vast quantities of innocent blood, instead of crime in the streets—Why Not Freedom!

---

87 William McGowan, "The Corrupt Influence of Police Diversity Hiring," *The Wall Street Journal,* June 6, 1994, editorial page.

SUMMARY
Questions and Answers

Q. You often make references to former Governor George Wallace of Alabama. How can we look to such a person for ideas and inspiration in making a new free society; after all, wasn't he a racist?

A. One of the favorite tools the liberal establishment uses against anyone fighting for limited government, as opposed to Big Brother Government, is the tar brush of racism to distort what is being said and to paint as evil anyone standing up for middle-class values. If anyone will review Governor Wallace's complete life, rather than just focusing upon one area, he will see a man who consistently fought against the growth of unlimited Federal power. Over that same time period, Governor Wallace evolved from a die-hard segregationist to one who embraced the idea of equal rights for all; yet, he never let up on his demand for local control of our lives, as opposed to the centrally planned society of modern liberalism. During that same time frame, the South, in general, moved, from a society which embraced state-sponsored discrimination to a society which embraced faith in equality before the law. What has continued to trouble the liberal establishment is that the South has not embraced the central tenant of liberalism, which is, abject human equality. Southerners, and no doubt most Americans, have no problem accepting the idea that all people should be treated equally before the law. Where Southerners' attitudes have not changed is in regard to the idea or the notion of complete human equality. Southerners, and many other Americans, view this as nothing less than a Marxist myth, and, for this reason, liberals continue their attack upon everything truly Southern, including the life and legacy of Governor George Wallace.

Still, the results of Governor Wallace's presidential bid have had a tremendous effect upon American politics. Wallace was the man who forced many middle-class issues onto the political agenda, issues that the American voters believed in but the liberal establishment had refused to acknowledge. He was one of the first nationally known politicians to warn the rest of the country that the Federal government had grown out of control. Although we may disagree with some of his early statements, his overall contribution to the fight against Big Government should not be overlooked.

Q. How can reducing the size of the Federal government make my hometown a safer place to live?

A. After billions on top of billions of dollars have been spent by the Federal government "fighting" crime, we should understand by now that the Federal government cannot correct the problem of criminal activity in our hometowns. Who can solve hometown America's problems with crime? No one is better suited for that job than Mr. and Mrs. Hometown America. Although the Federal government's inability to make our hometowns safe is obvious to anyone, that has not deterred the Feds from preventing Mr. and Mrs. Hometown America from instituting proven solutions to their crime problems. By putting control of the Federal government back where it belongs, with "We the people" of the sovereign states, we can at least control the adverse action of the Feds and get them off our backs long enough for us to institute proper crime-fighting methods. As every hometown is different, there will be different methods of crime control being tried. What works well in an industrialized urban area may be ridiculous for a rural area. Nevertheless, we must be free to solve problems that are facing each community. It is at the level of the states that such activity has been traditionally found. If you want a safe hometown, you must have the right to institute the solutions that your state deems necessary.

CHAPTER 10

Instead of Intrusive Federal Regulations—Why Not Freedom!

A fourteen-year-old boy was lost for two days in the New Mexican wilderness. After a massive search, the boy was located by one of the search helicopters. The search team requested permission to land and rescue the boy. The U.S. Forest Service denied permission for the helicopter to land! Why? Because a government regulation prohibited mechanical vehicles from entering the "wilderness" area. The boy was forced to spend a third night in the government "preserve."[88] What has happened in America when a regulation enacted by some unknown, faceless bureaucrat is more important than the rescue of a lost child? The problem is that we now live under a Federal government that no longer recognizes any limit to the exercise of governmental power. "We the people" no longer have a sovereign state to stand between us and an abusive Federal government. If you and I do not belong to one of the Federal government's "protected minorities" or other special- interest groups, then we will be the victims of Federal power, not the beneficiaries of constitutional protection of our civil liberties. The explosion of new and powerful Federal regulations since the mid-1960s has created new and more efficient ways for the liberal establishment to push its left-wing political agenda.

The interesting thing about Federal regulators is that they can always give a logical and socially sound excuse for their existence. For example, who would be opposed to assuring that people confined to wheelchairs have access to public buildings? No one would oppose such a "noble" cause. But the liberal establishment has used Americans' basic compassion to enact laws that can then be interpreted very loosely. The end result is that "We the people" are deprived of our property rights, in violation of the "taking" clause of the Fifth

88 Woody West, Associate Editor, "Federal Behemoth Should Make Americans Wonder If Secessionists Were Right," *Insight*, August 22, 1994, 40.

Amendment and without "due process," a violation of the infamous Fourteenth Amendment.[89]

The Americans With Disabilities Act (ADA) was just such a law. Its laudable purpose was to assure that the disabled were not discriminated against solely because of their disability. By appealing to Americans' basic sense of fair play, the liberal establishment, assisted by the Republican administration, was able to enact a law that gave the Federal government far more power than was ever intended by the original Constitution. In political science, as in physical science, every action has a reaction. There is no such thing as a neutral action by government. This is important because the power assumed by the Federal government had to come from somewhere. Where did this "extra" power the Federal government now exercises come from? The Federal government cannot create power. It must come from some preexisting power source. How, then, does the Federal government accrue more power? It simply takes power from the reserved rights of the sovereign states, the repository of our common civil rights as a free people.

When the Federal government assumed the right to be the sole judge of how much power it would exercise, "We the people" of the sovereign states lost the right to control the exercise of governmental power. As long as State's Rights existed, the Federal government was controlled by "We the people" at the local level. With the loss of local (state) control of the Federal government, all we can now do is hope that those who possess such enormous power over us will exercise it prudently. But, as James Madison warned us, "Where there is power and an interest to use it, wrong will be done," or as John C. Calhoun stated, "Government has within it a tendency to abuse its powers."

A sixty-six-year-old Certified Public Accountant (CPA) residing in the state of California, Newton Becker, found out just how easy it is to fall prey to government regulators. Becker established a CPA review course for accountants studying for the CPA exam. Becker was asked to provide sign language interpreters for a student with hearing disabilities. Unfortunately for Becker, the cost of his providing interpreters would be more than the cost for the course. In other words, the Federal government was telling a private businessman that he had to provide a service to "protected minorities" even though he

---

89 For a discussion of the unconstitutional enactment of the Fourteenth Amendment, see James R. Kennedy and Walter D. Kennedy, *The South Was Right!* (Gretna, LA: Pelican Publishing Company, 1994) 167-76, 369-79.

would be losing money in the process. And, by the way, Becker was specifically prohibited from adding the cost of the interpreters to the tuition of the disabled student. Every private businessman in America is under this same requirement! Becker took on the Federal government—he had rights too, or so he thought! The fight cost the sixty-six-year-old man hundreds of thousands of dollars in legal expenses. This demonstrates why "We the people," the individual citizens, need the protection of the sovereign state. Becker was fighting an adversary with an unlimited checkbook—the Federal government. With no one to help him, this private citizen surrendered to the Federal government. He was forced to provide the interpreters even though the cost exceeded the money he received from the course tuition![90]

Yes, each of you Newton Beckers of America, there is a cruel lesson here for the middle class to learn. Even if we do have rights (which we doubt, under the current governmental arrangement), we do not have the resources to fight the Federal government. That is why under the original constitutional system, "We the people" maintained all of our rights under the protection of our sovereign state. Our wise Forefathers knew that a central government that is far removed from the people cannot be trusted. The sovereign state was supposed to be the mechanism by which "We the people" could effectively erect barricades against unwarranted Federal encroachments of our reserved rights.[91]

The Occupational Safety and Health Administration (OSHA) is another example of good intentions being used by the liberal establishment to ensure the enactment of laws that can be used to further its liberal (socialist) agenda. OSHA came to us as a gift from the Republican administration of Richard Nixon. Yes, that's right, Nixon's Republican administration gave America OSHA, affirmative action, and forced busing. Despite this fact, there are some Americans who believe that all is right with the United States as long as the Republicans are in control. How long will it take for Americans to once again understand that, until "We the people" of the sovereign states are in control of "our" Federal government, our "dearest interests" will never be secure?

90 "Disabilities Dissenter Crushed," *The Wall Street Journal*, May 18, 1994, editorial page.

91 Alexander Hamilton, *The Federalist Nos. 31,32*, quoted in George W. Carey and James McClellan, *The Federalist: Student Edition* (Dubuque, IA: Kendall/Hunt Publishing Company, 1990) 152-58.

Under OSHA's general duty clause, an employer is required to provide a safe work environment. Good idea, but how is "a safe work environment" measured? Small and large business have been assessed huge fines by OSHA inspectors for failure to keep records and other such nebulous charges. American businessmen spend millions of dollars annually in an attempt to "get ready" for an OSHA inspection that may never happen. If these funds were spent on pure work place safety, it would at least be arguable that some good is coming from the exercise, but the truth is that most of it is a paper exercise, done in anticipation of an inspection.

The arbitrary and capricious nature of the OSHA bureaucracy is typified by a change in the way OSHA assesses fines and penalties. Under the Clinton administration, the department began assessing mega-fines. This change was made by bureaucrats in OSHA. Overnight, non-elected Federal officials decided to subject American businessmen to exorbitant penalties. Clinton's response to this and other substantive changes in the enforcement of the law was to ask OSHA's head to go to Congress and ask Congress to change the law to make it conform with the regulations! Our Forefathers fought a war because of taxation without representation—what would they have said about Federal government subjecting American businessmen to regulation without representation?

Nowhere is the arrogance of Federal bureaucratic power more pronounced than in the department of Housing and Urban Development (HUD). In Chapter 20 we will detail the results of HUD's attack on freedom of speech. Even though HUD has "promised" not to go to the same extreme again, "We the people" have little reason to feel secure. After all, HUD's admission was forced; it did not suddenly suffer pangs of guilt because of its violation of the First Amendment. In the Berkeley Three case, which we will examine later, HUD was more like the criminal who is sorry that he got caught, but not sorry he committed the crime!

This case raises questions about the legitimacy of government agencies that have assumed police powers and are now using those powers against private citizens. Think about the numerous HUD fair housing attorneys who troll local newspapers hoping to find "social misfits" such as the lady in Wisconsin who violated our national conscious by placing an ad in the local paper for a "Christian handyman"; the ever-present EPA vigilantes who eagerly strike out at environmental criminals who destroy national treasures such as backyard "wet lands"; or the man in New Jersey who was hit by two summonses for killing a rat! Is there a legitimate place in our so-called free country for people who have such power, who use this governmental power to further their personal, left-wing, political agenda? These people now have the police power and full resources of the Federal government to assist them in forcing middle-class Americans to conform to their politically correct social theories.[92]

"The road to hell is paved with good intentions" is an admonition given to us and to most other Southerners by our mothers. This could be the epithet for our lost freedoms. Take visionary legislation and add to it questionable constitutionality and the denial of the once-sovereign state to protect "We the people," and the end result is the destruction of liberty—all done under the guise of "good intentions."

We all want a clean environment. So why not enact legislation to clean up all toxic dumps? Good intentions, good cause, bad results. The Superfund legislation was enacted by the Federal Congress with the same fuzzy, warm-all-over "good feelings" common to every liberal boondoggle. The purpose was to use taxpayers' money to clean up abandoned toxic waste sites. Since 1980 the EPA has consumed approximately $20 billion and has managed to clean up less than 20% of the twelve hundred toxic waste sites. Where did all of our tax money go? According to a Rand study, approximately 33% of the Superfund clean-up money was paid for what the EPA calls "transaction cost"—attorneys and such![93]

The moral of the Superfund story is the same as it is with all such schemes, that is, Big Government is basically inefficient. The taxpayer never receives fair value for his money. Even without a liberal establishment using the Federal government to further its political agenda, the Federal government is still intrinsically inefficient. The farther government moves away from the source of power and revenues, the less efficient and more despotic it becomes. Big, centralized Federal government is not only dangerous and unconstitutional, it is also ineffective—"We the people" of the sovereign state don't need a master up in the "big house" to look after us!

---

92 "HUD's Thought Police," *The Wall Street Journal*, August 23, 1994, editorial page.

93 "Not So Super," *The Wall Street Journal*, October 4, 1994, editorial page.

Thanks, but we can do it better ourselves, and, if we don't do it better, we will have no one to blame but ourselves. Big Government—who needs it? Who needs Big Governments? Try out these names: Hitler, Stalin, Mussolini, and Tojo, just to name a few. You see, Big Governments do have their supporters, but a free people should never be in that number.

What the Federal government says when it is pushing through some "good" legislation and what it actually does once it has grabbed a little more of Americans' personal liberty are two different things. Take, for example the 1964 Civil Rights Act. Senator Hubert Humphrey, a liberal supporter of the act, declared that it would not punish employers for accidental discrimination (whatever that is), nor would it require the use of quotas. In short, he claimed that the only way an employer could be penalized under the Civil Rights Act was for the employer to have intentionally discriminated against a "protected minority." The verbiage of the 1964 Civil Rights Act specifically prohibited racial quotas and busing. Yet, despite the promises made by the liberals in Congress, the president, and the entire liberal establishment, America has suffered decades of quotas and busing. Middle-class Americans have learned by sad experience that they cannot trust the Federal government.

The 1964 Civil Right Act established a new arm of intrusive and oppressive Federal power, the Equal Employment Opportunity Commission (EEOC). The bureaucrats in the EEOC chose to ignore the intent of Congress and moved toward a quota system of employment in which American businessmen are presumed to be in violation of the act if their work force does not represent the general population. The businessman is presumed to be guilty, and the Justice Department through the Office of Civil Rights can, in effect, indict, try, judge, and sentence the businessman. Of course, the businessman can resist, but who has enough money to fight the Federal government? The mere threat of an EEOC claim has forced the majority of employers to assume an official or unofficial affirmative action hiring plan—quotas.

The history of the EEOC reveals the typical arrogance of Federal bureaucrats who hold unlimited power over the lives of middle-class citizens. By enacting confusing and convoluted regulations they set themselves up as the sole source of information regarding these regulations and as the sole judge as to whether or not middle-class citizens are complying with these confusing regulations. In 1978 the EEOC published its notoriously confusing *Uniform Guidelines* for employment practices. The Federal government's own General Accounting Office (GAO) stated that the guidelines were written on a reading difficulty level of grade 23—post-graduate level! Federal bureaucrats in the EEOC admitted that they created the guidelines to be used by lawyers and psychologists. The guidelines were supposed to assist managers in complying with Federal "fair hiring" laws. Yet, these very same guidelines were purposely designed to be too difficult for the average citizen to read and comprehend! If the average businessman violated any of the numerous and incomprehensible regulations, he would be subject to thousands of dollars in legal fees, back pay, and Federal fines. The EEOC is just one of many Federal agencies that now rule our lives with virtually dictatorial powers. It exemplifies the arrogance of power exercised by the Federal government every day in this once-free land.

The non-elected and unconstitutional Federal equality police have forced their liberal agenda upon middle-class Americans. In the process of pushing their left-wing agenda, they have subjected Americans to decades of quasi-judicial terrorism.

The Office of Federal Contracts Compliance Programs (OFCCP) was created by Executive Order Number 11246 issued by President Lyndon Johnson. Johnson, a Democrat, used this executive order to pressure contractors doing business with the Federal government to hire "protected minorities." Not to be outdone by the Democrats, a Republican president, Richard Nixon, imposed MANDATORY racial goals upon Federal contractors. The Republicans were searching for the "last vote" and knew that by adopting and furthering the Democratic social agenda they could capture some of the Democrats' minority votes.[94] The OFCCP has been very active in the promotion of equality of results through quotas. It denies the use of quotas, but by way of heavy fines and penalties it is able to intimidate businessmen and force them to hire by the numbers in order to prevent their businesses from running afoul of America's equality police. The OFCCP forced an Illinois bank to pay $14 million to settle a claim of discrimination. In Louisiana a bank was compelled to pay $1.9 million to settle an allegation that it had violated Federal anti-discrimination regulations. What private businessman can

94 See the discussion of the "last vote" theory in Chapter 4.

afford to risk the wrath of such a powerful and intrusive Federal government? The safe bet for the business community is to hire by the numbers. Quotas by any other name is still just as repulsive.

It should be remembered that these companies, and scores of other companies, were forced to settle these claims not because they were actually guilty of "intentional" discrimination, but because their numbers were not right—according to the judgment of some unknown bureaucrat! The Federal equality police do not need evidence of intent to discriminate; all they need is to count the number of red, yellow, black, and white faces—if the numbers are not right, according to the Federal bureaucrat, then the individual or company is guilty! Such was the fate of an Illinois small businessman who was convicted and fined more than $100,000 by the EEOC because his establishment did not employ at least 8.45 blacks.

The more discretionary authority government acquires, the fewer freedoms the individual citizen enjoys. Our current Federal government has seized unlimited discretionary power. The powers exercised by the Federal government were delegated from the sovereign state. If "We the people" ever hope to protect our "dearest interests," our property rights, and our civil liberties, we must force the Federal government to return to limited Federalism, State Sovereignty, and State's Rights. Instead of intrusive Federal regulations— Why Not Freedom!

SUMMARY
Questions and Answers

Q. You continue to talk about how "We the people" of the sovereign states must reclaim our right to control the Federal government. Does not history prove that the states are no match for the power of the Federal government? Is it not just a pipe dream to speak of restoring State's Rights?

A. Thomas Jefferson is reported to have once stated that "Eternal vigilance is the price of liberty." If "We the people" had maintained that vigilance spoken of by our Forefathers, we would not be living in a society in which the central government acts in such unrestricted manner. It is left up to "We the people" of each state to begin the process of re-establishing the means whereby the rights and freedoms of the people are protected. The road back to the Republic of

Republics of our Forefathers will be difficult and probably a long one. Our history as Americans proves beyond a doubt that "We the people" do have the means and tradition to be the world's foremost freedom fighters. We the authors have no misgivings about the ability of Americans to regain their lost rights.

CHAPTER 11

Instead of Trillions of Dollars of Federal Debt—Why Not Freedom!

The government of the United States is drowning in red ink, yet the policy of borrow-and-spend continues in Washington, D.C. But, the good sense of the American people has been displayed by the Committee of Fifty States which was organized early in the 1990s by a group of citizens from the American Northwest. This organization, though founded by Westerners, declared that it may be necessary to dissolve the Federal Union! Why would anyone, especially a group of non-Southerners, take such a radical stand? The problem of the national debt so concerned these citizens that they were willing to stand up and tell America that, if the Federal government does not abide by the Constitution, the Federal Union will be dissolved. The Committee of Fifty States advocates the use of "The Ultimatum Resolution" in its attempt to control the runaway national debt. Its objective is to have thirty-eight states pass the resolution declaring that, if the Federal debt reaches six trillion dollars, then the Federal Union will be dissolved. Let the president, Congress, the Supreme Court, and thirty-one million Federal employees file for unemployment. The logic of the Committee of Fifty States is that the states created the Federal government, and the states can dissolve and reorganize the Federal government, and should do so when it no longer performs its proper duties.

This may sound extreme when you first hear about it, but the fact remains that the unprecedented growth of the Federal debt poses a serious challenge to free government. Someone must take control, and, since the Federal government has refused to control itself, perhaps it is time for the states to assert their sovereign right to discipline their agent.

Debt is anti-democratic; it is the ultimate form of "taxation without representation" because it requires future generations to pay for spending done by the present generation. It presents a pernicious

117

danger to the sovereignty of the country internationally, and it destroys the liberty of citizens of generations yet to be conceived. Thomas Jefferson believed that

> No generation can contract debts greater than may be paid during the course of its own existence. . . . The conclusion then, is that neither the representatives of a nation, nor the whole nation itself assembled, can validly engage debts beyond what they may pay in their own time.[95]

James Madison warned Americans of three great dangers to their civil liberties: war, armies, and debt. The fact that Madison listed debt as one of the three major dangers threatening civil liberties should give contemporary Americans additional reason to be concerned.

> War is the parent of armies; from these proceed debts and taxes; and armies, and debts, and taxes are the known instruments for bringing the many under the domination of the few.[96]

James Madison was not the only early American patriot to sound a warning about the national debt. Thomas Jefferson, writing to a friend concerning the Federal debt, declared

> I wish it were possible to obtain a single amendment to our Constitution. I would be willing to depend on that alone for the reduction of the administration of our government of the genuine principles of its Constitution: I mean an additional article, taking from the federal government the power of borrowing.[97]

The placing of an undue burden of accumulating debt upon the backs of unrepresented generations was viewed by Jefferson as a violation of the principle of the "consent of the governed" and, therefore, as a violation of the civil liberties of unborn generations of Americans. Jefferson championed a principle that middle-class Americans have held for years; that is, we do not have the right to mortgage the future of generations of Americans yet to be born. Jefferson knew that the only way a democratic republic could maintain its moral right to govern was by raising the funds for government on a pay-as-you-go basis. Borrowing, though perhaps necessary during

95 William J. Quirk and R. Randall Bridwell, *Abandoned: The Betrayal of the American Middle Class Since World War II* (Lanham, MD: Madison Books, 1992) 12.

96 Ibid, 13.

97 Ibid, 15-16.

an emergency, is not a democratic method of financing a free government.

How a government finances its operations will go a long way in determining if it is or will remain a free society. In a healthy democratic republic, the people, acting through their elected representatives, must agree upon what they want their government to do and how they intend to pay for government programs. The safest and most democratic method is a pay-as-you-go method in which taxes are set to ensure that the government collects enough revenues to pay for its programs. The chief executive (president or governor) proposes a budget and the taxes necessary to pay for government programs, and the legislative branch of government must approve, modify, or reject the proposed budget. Both the chief executive and the legislators know they will answer to the electorate. If they tend to be too extravagant with the people's property (remember, taxes are a taking of personal property), then the people will remove their elected servants at the next election. This serves as a check against the tendency of politicians who would otherwise vote for pork-barrel programs. Pay-as-you-go financing forces politicians to face the people and explain why they increased their taxes. It is pro-democratic because it requires representatives to justify their actions. They must give good reason for spending other peoples' money. This system forces politicians to remember the taxpayer every time they decide to raise taxes.

Debt (or borrowing which creates the debt), on the other hand, is anti-democratic. Because it requires no immediate increase in taxes to fund government programs, government officials can initiate new programs without worrying the taxpayer! By borrowing, there is no need to report to the people or to justify an increase in taxes in order to pay for new government programs. Debt allows politicians to avoid the embarrassment of public debate regarding new taxes necessary to finance pork-barrel programs. Governmental debt removes the incentives for politicians to be frugal with other people's money. Politicians hate to raise taxes, but they love to enact pork-barrel programs to "help" their constituents—constituents who, by the way, will be asked to vote for these same politicians at the next election. Debt allows politicians to enact pork-barrel programs without having to bother the voters with new taxes. What a plan! The chief executive proposes such and such a program to alleviate a great

social ill, and legislators, now uninhibited by the necessity of increasing taxes, rush forward to claim their share of the credit for providing the "goodies." They can then go back home and brag to the local
Rotary and Civitan clubs that they are good for their districts because
they know how to bring their share of the pie home to the people.
No one ever thinks to ask, "How are we going to pay for all of these
special, and in many cases good, programs?" The whole scheme is
one giant merry-go-round, borrow and borrow, spend and spend,
and the people are too dumb to know any better—or so it is thought.

The cost of these new programs is easily shifted to unrepresented
future generations. Political accountability is destroyed, there is an
increased temptation to use government programs to buy votes at
the next election, and slowly the public's confidence in their government is undermined. With a pay-as-you-go system it was difficult
for political leaders to entangle the country in unpopular, no-win,
wars. Political leaders could not find enough popular support to pass
the necessary tax increase to finance foreign intrigue. But now with
the assistance of debt and borrowing, the unpleasant talk of taxes is
avoided, at least for the time being. Today and the next election are
the primary concern to politicians. No wonder Thomas Jefferson and
James Madison were opposed to government debt.[98]

From the very early beginning of the United States, popular government programs were financed on a pay-as-you-go basis. As the
nation moved into the era of militant, anti-middle class liberalism,
unpopular government programs began being financed by borrowing. For a government that needs to finance unpopular government
programs, borrowing has the great advantage of allowing the promotion of these unpopular programs without the necessity of getting
people's approval. In other words, borrowing allows the government
to hide its true intentions. Financing unpopular government programs by borrowing removes the necessity of holding public debate
regarding the need to increase middle-class taxes. Since unpopular
government programs would go down in defeat if the general public knew it had to pay for them, borrowing became the liberal establishment's method of circumventing middle-class resistance to its
programs. Left-wing social engineering could continue full pace
without fear of the middle class finding out what was being done to
them by "their" Federal government. Under this system, the middle-

98 Ibid, 14.

class sheep will never find out what the main course will be at the feast planned by their liberal shepherd.

For the past fifty years our country has had to bear an ever-increasing load of debt. In 1960 taxpayers were footing the bill on a $291 billion debt by paying $9 billion annually in interest. Note, interest, not payment on the principal. In 1991 taxpayers were handed a bill for the interest alone on the national debt to the tune of $283.1 billion! But don't be concerned, the liberals have assured us it's all right because "we owe it to ourselves." Today only forty cents of every tax dollar goes to fund the operations of government. The balance is used to pay the interest on the national debt. The interest continues to roll along at a rate of $32 million an hour. Sooner or later the chickens will come home to roost. Sooner or later someone will have to pay the huge debt our undemocratic, liberal establishment has incurred. Sooner or later, you can bet "We the people" of the middle class who were not responsible for the debt will be told to "pay the bill." After all, who paid the bill for the Savings and Loan bail out? The middle class, America's tax "cash-cow"— that's who![99]

Liberals in Washington, D.C., have consistently assured Americans that debt is not bad; after all, "we owe it to ourselves" they have repeatedly told us. Yet, with this country's debt at three to four trillion dollars, the interest alone will eventually consume the total of current income tax collections. When one bankrupt individual is owed money by another bankrupt individual, neither has improved his financial condition! But even worse, in the 1980s, it became apparent that we do not owe it to our fellow Americans. More and more U.S. government bonds were being bought by foreigners— especially Japanese. When foreigners hold a financial lien on a country's future, there are serious questions regarding the sovereignty of the debtor nation. Our debt increased as it became politically profitable to enact pork-barrel programs to ensure re-election for incumbent politicians. The pro-democratic restriction of pay-as-you-go government was replaced with the anti-democratic principle of governmental debt. "We the people" were bypassed, and suddenly there was no way to control the growth of government, or so we were told. Of course, those who were telling us that they could not control government growth were exactly the same ones who had a vested interest in the growth of government—politicians of both parties! Those

99 Ibid, 4.

who controlled the Federal government wanted to spend money on things that middle-class Americans would not approve, or, in the case of reverse discrimination and quotas, to which the middle class were vehemently opposed. This opposition no longer presented a barrier to borrow-and-spend politicians. They merely bypassed the middle class and borrowed against the future of generations of middle-class citizens yet unborn and completely unrepresented. Thomas Jefferson's nightmare of governmental debt has become a reality in politically correct America. Unpopular wars, foreign intrigues, destructive social legislation, and much more has been forced upon America's middle class, and all the while it has been done without upsetting citizens with debate on new taxes.[100]

The liberal establishment gained control of the Federal government and was determined to use the force of government to re-engineer society according to its left-wing ideology. The average American would not allow his taxes to be raised to pursue such unworthy goals. The liberal establishment's answer was the wholesale adoption of undemocratic methods to finance the Federal government's social spending agenda. By taxing unborn generations through government borrowing, the liberal establishment has managed to finance its social schemes. Unfortunately, the load of debt has become unbearable for us and nearly unpayable for future generations of Americans. A sad day is coming in the future of America, the day when we of this generation will have to explain to those being born today that they must pay their tax burden as well as ours. How will we, as older Americans, have the courage to explain to a younger generation that we spent their money? The ever-increasing national debt also puts our country's sovereignty at risk; it hinders domestic economic development, and it threatens the financial security of middle-class families.

How do we control the Federal appetite for "easy" money? How can "We the people" of the sovereign state limit the spending enthusiasm of a faraway Federal government? Instead of trillions of dollars of debt—Why Not Freedom!

---

100 Ibid, 52-53.

SUMMARY
Questions and Answers

Q. I hear people talking about the national debt all the time, but it is hard for me to understand just how much money is one trillion dollars. It doesn't seem real; I can't comprehend it; is it real?

A. Most middle-class Americans have little or no idea what our political leaders mean when they refer to such huge quantities of money. This has served to the advantage of the tax-and-spend crowd and to the disadvantage of the middle class. The late Senator Everett Dirksen, noting the ease with which the Federal government talks about and spends money, once stated, "A billion [dollars] here, a billion there, the first thing you know you are talking about *real money!*" Real money indeed; it's our tax money, or, more to the point, it's our property that is being spent. It is very hard to understand the scope of the national debt because we do not routinely deal with such numbers.

Here is an example of what spending a trillion dollars would be like. *First step.* If you were given a box with a thousand one thousand dollar bills in it and told to spend one thousand dollars ($1,000) every day, how long would it take you to spend one million dollars ($1,000,000)? In one year, at one thousand dollars per day, you would have spent $365,000. At that rate, it would take you almost three years to spend a million dollars. *Second step.* It takes a thousand one million dollar bills ($1,000,000) to make one billion dollars ($1,000,000,000). If you continued to spend one thousand dollars ($1,000) each day of the year, how long would it take you to spend one billion dollars ($1,000,000,000)? Just a little less than three thousand years. *Third step.* Knowing that there are a thousand one billion dollar bills ($1,000,000,000) in one trillion dollars ($1,000,000,000,000), how long would it take you to spend a trillion dollars? Just under three million years.

Now, remember that the Federal government is somewhere between (at this time) three and four trillion dollars in debt, and you will begin to understand the scope of America's problem with an uncontrolled Federal government. How much more proof do we need before we understand that we cannot trust Big Government, regardless of liberal or conservative leadership, to control its own lust for spending money and its abuse of delegated powers?

No one, other than "We the people" of the sovereign states, can solve this problem.

CHAPTER 12

Instead of Tax-and-Spend Federalism— Why Not Freedom!

Nothing about the Federal government affects the life of middle-class families more than its tax policies. According to an article in *The Wall Street Journal,* due to the personal exemption allowed a family of four in 1948, almost 80% of their family income was shielded from the Federal tax collector. To give the same family similar protection today, the Federal government would have increase its personal exemption from the current $2,300 to $8,200![101] From this example we can see that tax-and-spend Federalism has been steadily leaching the economic life blood from the American family. The Federal Supreme Court in 1803, in *Madison v. Marbury,* acknowledged that the power to tax invokes the power to destroy. Current Federal tax schemes have taken a dead aim on America's middle class with disastrous results for individuals, but, most tragically, it has crippled the American family.

The 1911 Federal Income Tax law was designed to "raise revenue for the government." The 1911 Federal Income Tax law consisted of fifteen pages of easy-to-understand regulations that taxed the first $20,000 of income at 1%, income between $20,001 and $50,000 at 2%, and topped out with a 6% tax on income over $500,000. Theodore Roosevelt needed the money to pay for his Great White Fleet. The old method of raising Federal revenues by tariffs would not pay for such trappings of an empire. Not only did the income tax provide the government with a seemingly endless source of revenues, but it also provided government with a tool to re-engineer society by "taking from the rich and giving to the poor." Federal officials could now play Robin Hood. Redistributing income became the leading goal of liberalism, which soon had complete control of the Federal government.

Internal Revenue Service codes that were originally fifteen pages

101 Wade F. Horn, "Putting Parents First," *The Wall Street Journal,* May 28, 1993, editorial page.

long have grown to more than four thousand pages of bureaucratic waffle words. Special-interest groups have used their political influence in Congress to carve out special tax code exemptions for themselves. Because the middle class has no special-interest lobby, we have the honor of making up the loss in tax revenues due to tax breaks given to the special interests. In addition to these tax breaks, the Federal government has been using IRS codes to redistribute middle-class wealth and to implement other liberal social engineering programs. The IRS takes from the middle class and funnels our property to the Federal government where liberal politicians and Big Money lobbyists eagerly distribute it in the form of innumerable social programs and tax breaks. Of course, these "good" social programs just happen to benefit the liberal politicians who will run for reelection by reminding their clientele of how effective they have been in supplying them with their share of Federal funds. But you and I know whose money it is that is being "redistributed."[102]

The tax code is used to determine who will become wealthy and who will remain in the middle and lower classes. The wealthy do not pay taxes, while the middle and even the lower classes pay a disproportionate percentage of taxes. The Democratic-controlled Congress enacted, and a "conservative" Republican president, Ronald Reagan, signed, the 1986 Reform Act. This act provided for transitional rules that allowed certain "Princes of Wealth" to avoid paying their share of taxes.

> These transitional rules were the core of the Reagan tax policy in practice. These rules created 174 special exceptions for corporations including Unocal, Phillips Petroleum, Texaco, Pennzoil, General Motors, Chrysler, Goldman Sachs, Manville, General Mills, Walt Disney, Pan Am, Northwest Airlines, Delta, Control Data, Multimedia, Metromedia, . . . Mitsubishi and Toyota.[103]

The effect of these tax policies has been to shift the burden of an ever-increasing tax-and-spend Federal government onto the hard-working middle class.

> The code's capriciousness is matched by its disparate impact on taxpayers. Certain industries, for example, are effectively exempted from taxation by Congress. The House-Senate Joint

102 William J. Quirk and R. Randall Bridwell, *Abandoned: The Betrayal of the American Middle Class Since World War II* (New York, NY: Madison Books, 1992) 112.
103 Ibid, 127.

Tax Committee reported in 1983 that the chemical industry had an effective tax rate of *minus* 1 percent meaning that they ended up with a credit towards future tax years. The construction industry at the time paid 0.7 percent tax on its earnings. As of 1985, General Electric had not paid a dollar in federal corporate income tax for three years, despite earnings of 5 billion dollars during that period.[104]

The preceding offers a very important lesson for "conservatives." We should note that both liberal Democrats and conservative Republicans worked hand in hand to place the heavy yoke of Federal taxation upon the middle class. The liberal Democrats wanted more middle-class money to spend on social welfare programs, and the "conservative" Republicans wanted to defend the special interests of Big Money by shielding them from the Federal tax collector. Of course, the revenue short-fall caused by the shielding of the big corporations was made up by imposing a heaver tax burden upon the middle-class taxpayer.

> Congress, since World War II, has directed the tax system more and more against the middle class. Under traditional income tax theory, an individual is not supposed to be taxed at all until he has earned enough money to provide for the essentials of life—food—shelter, etc. A family of four making the median income is not able to, and should not pay, any income tax. This is known as a "tax threshold." This was the idea behind the personal exemption which was $1000.00 in 1939. . . . Today, just to adjust for inflation, the personal exemption should be $6,000-$8,000, not the $2,050 it is. . . . [I]n 1948, the median income for a family of four was $3,468. However, because of the personal exemption and standard deduction, only $801—or 23 percent of income—was subject to any tax. Today the same family had an income of $29,184 of which $20,421—or 70 percent—is subject to tax.[105]

By increasing the amount of the middle-class family's income that is subject to taxation, the Federal government effectively reduced the standard of living and the quality of family life for the vast majority of Americans. Three years after the end of World War II the average middle-class family of four had only 2% of its income taken for

104 Ibid, 113
105 Ibid, 114.

Federal income tax. That has grown to its 1990's rate of 24% to the Federal government and up to an additional 10% going to state and local governments. This sharp increase in the taking of private property from the middle-class family's income by the government has caused parents to work longer (usually by requiring the wife to take or remain in a job even though many working mothers would prefer to stay at home with the more important job of raising children). Federal tax-and-spend policy has forced middle-class parents to spend more time at work, away from their families—just to stay even and "make ends meet."[106]

The marriage penalty is another example of how the Federal tax code is undermining middle-class values and families. A married couple filing a joint return, whose joint earnings in 1993 were $58,000, would owe the Federal tax collector $8,398. If they were not married but living together and filed separate tax returns, they would owe the Federal tax collector $7,136.[107]

Middle-class consumers pay a hidden tax caused by the cost incurred by businesses attempting to comply with Federal income tax regulations. Accounting cost is computed as part of business overhead and, as with all costs, is passed along to the consumer in the form of higher prices for goods and services. The estimated total cost for the Fortune 500 companies to comply with the Federal income tax code in 1992 was $1.055 billion.[108] It has been estimated that the accounting cost to comply with the income tax code for corporations with less than $1 million in assets was more than 390% greater than what these corporations paid in actual taxes. In plain English and simple math, for every one dollar ($1.00) these businesses paid in taxes, they paid an additional three dollars and ninety cents ($3.90) in accounting cost.[109]

The wasting of middle-class tax monies only compounds the sense of outrage felt by the over-taxed, over-regulated, and abused taxpayer. In 1993, in excess of 250,000 people collected Federal disability payments valued at $1.4 billion.[110] The reason these 250,000

---

106 Horn, *The Wall Street Journal*, May 28, 1993.

107 *The* (New Orleans, LA) *Times Picayune*, March 18, 1994, C1.

108 Arthur P. Hall, "Accounting Cost, Another Tax," *The Wall Street Journal*, December 9, 1993, editorial page.

109 Ibid.

110 "Tax-Subsidized Addicts," *The Wall Street Journal*, February 8, 1994, A16.

people were collecting the money belonging to middle-class families was that they were addicted to drugs or alcohol. Many were not even checked to make sure they were in a treatment program. Yes, that's right—the middle-class taxpayer was paying for the addict's drugs and alcohol! A recent General Accounting Office report stated that 172,000 substance abusers who were currently drawing disability were not being monitored for continuing substance abuse. In other words, the Federal government gave these people our tax money but made little if any effort to assure that the recipients were not using our hard-earned money to subsidize their substance abuse. The Federal government's own guidelines state that "a substance addiction in and of itself" could qualify an individual for disability payments. These checks average over $5,000 per year tax free. A Federal court recently handed down a decision declaring that a heroin addict who sold illegal drugs cannot be barred from receiving his disability payments![111]

The "tax exempt" foundation is another scheme by which the Federal government shields special-interest groups from paying their fair share of the tax burden and thereby shifts a larger portion to the middle-class taxpayer. Even though conservative or moderate trustees outnumber liberal trustees on exempt foundation boards, the conservatives and moderates tend to avoid politically sensitive areas. They appear reluctant to tread in the politically correct mine field, whereas the liberals are very aggressive in pushing their left-wing political agenda. When we look at the money given by these foundations to individuals and groups working in the social policy arena, we find that tax exempt foundations that promote liberal causes are three times more numerous than those that promote conservative causes.[112] These "tax exempt" foundations are using money that would have been paid into the government as taxes to further their primarily left-wing, anti-middle class social agenda. Of course, the revenue short-fall created by the tax exempt status of these liberal foundations will be shifted to the middle-class taxpayer.

Of all the laws enacted by the Federal government, none has been more disastrous to the middle class than the 1986 Tax Reform Act. This act was touted as an attempt to make the tax code fairer for the

111 Ibid.

112 Stanley Rothman, "The Philanthropists' Agenda," *The Wall Street Journal,* March 2, 1994, editorial page.

middle class. The liberals in Congress boasted about the benefits accruing to the common man as a result of the "reforms" initiated by Congress. The news media gave us daily conditioning treatments on every national news program about the tax relief pending for the average American. Even our beloved "conservative" president, Ronald Reagan, bragged after the passage of the bill through the Senate, "Taxpayers 1, Special Interest 0." Yet, when *The New York Times/CBS* poll was conducted, the media, the Federal establishment, and the liberal establishment were shocked to find out that not a single demographic group in America believed that the bill would produce a fairer tax system, and only 11% thought that they would pay less tax as a result of the passage of the bill.[113] The middle class have learned that, any time the government talks about tax reform, what the politicians are really doing is trying to figure out a better way to put their sticky fingers into our wallets.

> The 1986 act took dead aim on the middle class. The promised across-the-board tax reduction was in fact a tax increase for them. Consider a family of four with $30,000 in wage income, $200 in interest income, and $500 in dividends. They formerly took deductions of $2,250 for an Individual Retirement Account, $6,000 in mortgage interest, $3,000 in interest on a car loan, $1,700 in state and local income and property taxes and $300 in sales tax, and paid tax of $1,843. Their tax bill jumped to $2,200 under the 1986 law, a startling 21 percent tax increase. . . . Under the 1986 act, basic middle-class deductions—including interest on car loans, credit cards and education loans—were abolished or weakened. A wealthy person could deduct all the interest on two $500,000 homes, but a middle-class person could not deduct the interest on a loan to put his children through college.[114]

The average working man and woman in America were shocked to find out that their Federal government considered them as belonging to the "high income" group of citizens. What the Federal government was calling "high income" for tax purposes was actually bedrock middle-class America. The 1986 act benefitted the richest segments of our country (Republicans can be counted on to look out for their Big Money special interests), and it also provided more

113 Quirk and Bridwell, 118.
114 Ibid, 125.

money for social programs (the liberal democrats got something for their social welfare, special-interest group), and the middle-class—we all know what we got. Among other things, we got the bill! The super rich at the top, the social welfare and quasi-welfare at the bottom, and, in between, being squeezed out of existence—none other than the middle-class taxpayer.

The Reagan administration not only presided over the tripling of the national debt, but also watched the mammoth increase in the number of pages in the Internal Revenue Code. *Money* magazine, beginning in 1988, asked fifty tax experts to complete the tax forms for an average family. In 1988, *Money* received fifty different answers regarding the amount the family owed in Federal taxes ranging from $7,202 to $11,881! Over the next three years, the answers became more divergent. In 1991, only one "expert" got the correct answer! That same year, the IRS reported that compliance with Federal tax codes by small businesses had sharply decreased since the 1980s. The reason given was the complexity of the tax codes. Why do the politicians allow such confusing and costly tax codes to hamper the productivity of competitiveness of America's business? One of the reasons is that the confusing tax codes allow the politicians to hide handouts and special privileges to special-interest groups, and it provides a way for the "Princes of Privileges" to shield their wealth from the tax collector.

The time has come for the long-suffering, middle-class taxpayer to demand less government and the liberty to use his own money, not for the support of government projects, but for the support of his own family. Instead of a tax-and-spend Federal government—Why Not Freedom!

SUMMARY
Questions and Answers

Q. You make the point about the tax penalty for married couples. According to the figures given, the so-called penalty amounts to less than $1,200 for a couple earning $58,000. Do you really think that a man and woman will refuse to get married because of a $1,200 tax penalty?

A. The point being made about the marriage penalty in the Federal income tax code has more to do with how the Federal government treats the most important institution in our society, the family, than it does with the issue of whether this amount of money will prevent people from getting married. It is likely that there are some couples who do not get married because of the tax penalty, although the number is probably very small. The tax penalty is only one of many abuses the family has had to suffer because of Federal tax policies. What is needed is a government that understands, or is forced to recognize, the intrinsic value of stable families in a free society. Without stable families, our society cannot survive, yet the Federal government has consistently attacked many of the core beliefs of the traditional family unit. The question that must be answered is, "How can the family be protected from an abusive Federal government?" The history of these United States gives us the answer to that question. Each Sovereign Community, that is, each sovereign state, is composed of citizens nurtured by the family unit. The legitimate source of all political power comes from the people at the local level as they form their states, which then act together to form the Federal government. It is here with "We the people" of the sovereign states that our ultimate protection of our right as a free people will be maintained.

CHAPTER 13

Instead of Unfunded Federal Mandates—Why Not Freedom!

Nothing demonstrates the uncontrolled excesses of the liberal tax-and-spend Federal government more than unfunded Federal mandates. Over the past several years, the Federal Congress has enacted laws that command the states to raise the appropriate funds to fulfill the demands of laws the Congress has passed. In doing so, the Federal government has been treating the states as nothing more than a dependent or subservient agent of the Federal government. King George III did not even have such power over the colonies. The liberal political establishment in Washington, D.C., has used the revenues collected from the middle class to repay special-interest groups for voting it into office. Numerous social programs have been enacted for the benefit of liberalism's welfare clientele, its "protected minorities." Not only have these privileged groups benefitted from middle-class tax monies, but also an entire bureaucracy has grown up around these social programs. Untold thousands of "pointed head bureaucrats" are paid handsome salaries to provide benefits and services for welfare and other protected classes. In fact, these bureaucrats have also become an indispensable part of liberalism's clientele. Most of these programs grew out of Lyndon Johnson's Great Society legislation enacted in the mid-1960s. Today, after spending 4.5 trillion dollars on welfare,[115] America's social problems are worse than when the liberals began their spending spree (spending money of the middle class, of course). The failure of liberalism's tax-and-spend solutions has had no detrimental effect on its propensity to tax the middle class and to spend money belonging to the middle class. During the 1980s, Federal spending grew so far out of control that even the liberal Congress could not raise taxes fast enough to keep up with its enormous appetite for middle-class money. A normal person

115 Wayne LaPierre, *Guns, Crime, and Freedom* (Washington, DC: Regnery Publishing, Inc., 1994) 117.

would conclude that, since the Federal government could no longer acquire the money it needed for new social programs either by direct taxation or by borrowing,[116] then it would stop enacting new programs. Wrong!

During the years from the early 1960s to the early 1990s, the Federal government "discovered" a very convenient way to continue providing pork-barrel programs to its clientele. The Federal Congress simply passed laws requiring states and local governments to pay for Federally mandated programs! What a clever trick! Federal mandates are a pork-barrel politician's dream come true. With the new system of unfunded Federal mandates, the pork-barrel politician can go back home and brag to his constituency that he has voted them thus-and-such program and that he has done so without even having to increase their Federal taxes. Of course, the lying politician conveniently forgets to tell the voters that he has shifted the responsibility for paying for such programs to the people of the (now not-so sovereign) state. Guess who has to pay for these Federally mandated programs? That's right—you and I.

Nowhere in the Constitution is there authority for the Federal government to enact unfunded mandates. Yet, as we have seen so many times before, lack of constitutional authority or even explicit language forbidding such Federal action has been no hinderance for an out-of-control Federal government. What has been the effect of these unfunded Federal mandates? The Congressional Budget Office estimated that Federal mandates imposed on local governments from 1983 to 1990 cost the taxpayers approximately $12.7 billion![117] Of course, the liberal media, liberal politicians, and their clientele will assure us that these new regulations were needed for some all-important social good. Lofty liberal verbiage is used with the intent of making middle-class taxpayers feel guilty or selfish if they oppose any such grand "social advancement." The questions that were never asked were why, if these programs were so important, did we need a Federal law to force us to pay for these programs, and did the Federal government have the constitutional authority to force us to accept these programs?

---

116 Borrowing is really a technique by which politicians tax unborn generations to pay for social programs to be spent on a contemporary clientele. According to Thomas Jefferson, it is an unethical act because, as far as the future generation is concerned, borrowing represents taxation without representation.

117 *The Wall Street Journal,* May 18, 1994, A14.

In Hollywood, Florida, Federally mandated regulations required the city to spend $250,000 to prove that its slightly salty run-off would not harm the highly salty Atlantic Ocean. Mayor Richard Daley of Chicago stated that his city was forced to spend a minimum of $160 million in 1991 for unfunded Federal mandates. He noted that this money, taken from local taxpayers, could have been used to pay for 3,200 new police officers.[118] But, the citizens at the local level had no choice. They were faced with orders from their master in Washington, D.C. Fire protection, police protection, street repair, or education all take a back set to Federal mandates! You and I have no choice, just as we have no choice about where we send our children to school—the Federal government is master, and we are its subjects!

All across America, people at the local and state levels are demanding that the Federal government relent in its use of unfunded mandates. For the first time in more than forty years, the Federal government is being challenged by the states. The impressive thing for Southerners is that, thus far, it has been non-Southern states that have led the fight against the Federal government's unwarranted exercise of power. Governor George V. Voinovich of Ohio declared that the Federal government's unfunded mandates were putting great pressure on taxpayers throughout the country. He warned that the Federal government's actions threatened to cripple states by forcing them to use local tax revenues to pay for Federal mandates. He noted that Washington had begun to shift its budget deficits from the Federal government to the states.[119] The state of Ohio estimated that Federal mandates would cost Ohio taxpayers $356 million in 1994 and a total of over $1.7 billion in 1992-95. One Federal mandate alone will cost the taxpayers of Ohio $50 million per year! The governor pointed out that, if the people had a choice of where to spend their tax monies, they could pave nearly 700 miles of rural roads or rebuild 137 bridges.[120] Yet, the Federal government will not allow "We the people" of the sovereign states to make these decisions. Whatever happened to the Ninth and Tenth Amendments? Oh yes, we do recall that Federal Supreme Court Judge Salmon P. Chase in 1866, declared that State Sovereignty (i.e., State's Rights) died at

118 Ibid

119 *The Wall Street Journal,* January 31, 1994, editorial page.

120 Ibid.

Appomattox.[121] The consequences of the "death" of State's Rights are now being felt by all Americans, not just the descendants of Robert E. Lee's Confederate Army. It must be pointed out here that the right of a people of a sovereign state to rule themselves is a grand American concept. State's Rights, just like any other right, may be suppressed but can never be destroyed. It is one of those "unalienable" rights spoken of by our Forefathers in the Declaration of Independence.

The state of Colorado became so alarmed over the abuses of Federal powers and the continuing burden of unfunded mandates that it passed a Tenth Amendment Resolution. Representative Charlie Duke of Colorado introduced the resolution that made the point that states, under the constitutional provisions of the Tenth Amendment, have the right to reject unfunded Federal mandates. Across the country, citizens at the local level are beginning to view the Federal government as an oppressive and out-of-control bureaucratic monster.

The outcry from the people of the states has compelled certain Congressmen to offer to limit the use of unfunded Federal mandates. Some have even offered to renounce their use. On the surface this appears to be a step in the right direction. But, "We the people" of the sovereign states must always remember that a government that promises to no longer oppress its citizens can be forced to honor its promise only by an authority greater than the one making the promise. If, after making such a promise, a later Congress decides to renew the use of unfunded mandates, what can "We the people" of the sovereign states do to prevent it?

There is an underlying problem here that has not been admitted to by the Federal government. The problem is not in the size of the unfunded Federal mandate; it is in the fact that the Federal government has overstepped its constitutional authority in this matter. It, the Federal government, NEVER, NEVER had a constitutional right to issue the first mandate to the sovereign states. Relinquishing the act of issuing unfunded mandates is one thing; admitting that Congress does not have the right to issue such mandates is, indeed, a horse of a different color. The Federal government has, as yet, never admitted that its actions were illegal. Our current problem is that

121 Judge Salmon P. Chase, quoted in James R. Kennedy and Walter D. Kennedy, *The South Was Right!* (Gretna, LA: Pelican Publishing Company, 1994) 219.

"We the people" of the sovereign states have no mechanism to defend our rights when those rights are infringed upon by an abusive Federal government. Experience has already demonstrated that the Federal government cannot be trusted to respect the limitations imposed upon it by the Constitution. Something more effective must be established in order to control the Federal government.

Instead of unfunded Federal mandates—Why Not Freedom!

SUMMARY

Questions and Answers

Q. How can State's Rights be of any benefit to Americans today if it is true that "State Sovereignty died at Appomattox?"

A. The statement that "State Sovereignty [i.e., State's Rights] died at Appomattox" was made by Federal Supreme Court Justice Salmon P. Chase one year after General Lee had surrendered. Although the loss of the War for Southern Independence did give the radicals in the Federal Congress an opportunity to change the nature of this constitutional Republic of Republics, that change holds no validity because it was done without the "consent of the governed." Surely, any superior military force can trample upon the rights of a people, but those rights are just as valid even if the people are not allowed to exercise them. The thing for us to remember is that "We the people" may at this time have many of our rights suppressed, but by determination and willpower we can once again put our house back in order and re-establish a constitutional Republic of Republics in which "We the people" will once again be the true masters.

CHAPTER 14

Instead of Liberal Attacks Against Western Civilization and History— Why Not Freedom!

Since the early days of Soviet Communism, the American liberal establishment has viewed Western civilization as "imperialist," "oppressive," and an "exploiter" of the downtrodden peoples of the world (and, because America is a part of European or Western civilization, the liberal's hatred for Western civilization is imputed to America). Modern-day liberals are guilty of vicarious chauvinism. Liberals maintain an attitude that the culture of groups other than their own is superior to that of Western civilization. They hate their own civilization, not because it has harmed them, but because, in their opinion, Western civilization has "victimized" the undeveloped people of the world. Instead of promoting and supporting Western traditions and civilization, they have become its greatest critics.

To the liberal's way of thinking, the success of Western civilization was purchased at the price of colonialism in Asia and Latin America or the slave trade in Africa. Liberalism, with its anti-Western attitude, overlooks the conquest and imperial expansion of Asian nations, disregards internal strife and repression caused by Latin American dictators, and, of course, completely ignores the aspect of black-on-black slavery within Africa. In other words, even though Western civilization has produced great advances in art, science, and political thought, none of this makes up for the "sins" attributed to that civilization by liberal ideology. The liberal happily enjoys the miracles of modern Western medicine and technology, but he harbors hatred for the culture and political system that made such advances possible. Even though Western civilization has produced the greatest expansion of technology and civil liberties in world history, the liberal still loathes the idea of honoring this civilization. In a word, the liberal is compelled to feel guilty constantly about Western civilization, the very civilization that made it possible for him to be so critical. In order to mitigate his self-imposed and illogical feelings

of guilt, the liberal has assumed the position of implacable critic of
Western and specifically American civilization.

The contempt with which the liberal establishment views American society demonstrates itself often during the discussion of American military ventures. Modern liberals have often condemned the
Colonial Patriots because they were, according to liberal rhetoric,
fighting to protect the rights of only the rich merchants and planters
of America. According to these liberals, the Mexican-American War
was a war of aggression fabricated by warmongers in the United
States against the peace-loving people of Mexico. Never mind that
the Mexican leader, Santa Anna, was a dictator who was threatening
the peace of Texas. The Spanish-American War, according to liberal
mythology, was an imperialistic war to gain Cuba for the United
States. Of course, everyone knows how liberals feel about the war in
Vietnam. But one of the most outrageous attacks upon American culture has been the recent assault by the liberal elite upon America's
World War II war effort.

During the Second World War, American fighting men and
women were engaged in combat against an aggressive enemy. The
Japanese had launched an unprovoked attack upon the United
States at Pearl Harbor. After several years of struggle, the United
States faced the dangerous task of invading the Japanese homeland.
American military leaders were predicting U.S. casualties numbering
in the hundreds of thousands. They were given the chance of avoid-
ing these American casualties by dropping newly developed atomic
bombs on Japan. To the patriotic American military leaders, there
was no choice. They elected to drop the bombs hoping to force
Japan to surrender without having to put hundreds of thousands of
Americans in harm's way. Their choice proved to be the correct one.
Yet, in spite of all of this, contemporary politically correct liberals
have taken it upon themselves to insult the courage of American
veterans by labeling the atomic bombing of Japan an act of genocide.

The Smithsonian Institution's exhibit on the atomic bombing of
Japan is an example of such politically correct interpretation of history. The graphics at the Smithsonian's display revealing the estimated casualties the United States would have suffered had it been
forced to invade Japan were first set at 229,000. National Air and
Space Museum director Martin Harurit decreased the estimated U.S.
casualties to 63,000. The American Legion was outraged. It

demanded that the exhibit be canceled because it portrayed the United States as the aggressor.[122]

This callous insult of America's veterans should come as no surprise to those who understand the liberal's overwhelming and consuming sense of guilt.

> Guilt is integral to liberalism, and the feeling of guilt is an integral element in the liberal motivation. . . . The harassed liberal is relentlessly driven by his Eumenidean guilt.[123]

The liberal's consuming guilt drives him to try to do something about every social problem that strikes his conscience. If the ozone layer is being depleted, then the liberal wants to use the police power of government to try to restore it; if the kangaroo rat is in danger of extinction, then the liberal would use the iron fist of government bureaucrats to confiscate private property and use it as a rat preserve! The destruction of middle-class values, property, or freedom is never the focus of the liberal's moral outrage, nor is it even given any serious consideration. The American middle class represents to the liberal all that is wrong with Western civilization. When the middle class ask liberals why middle-class tax money should be spent on "protected minorities," the usual answer is, "Because we owe it to these people," or, as George McGovern inferred of busing, it was necessary for white Americans to endure busing "in order to pay for our sins of racism."[124]

> Within the United States, as in other advanced Western nations, the same moral asymmetry is present. The liberal community not only flagellates itself with the abusive writings of a disoriented Negro homosexual, but awards him money, fame and public honors. The spokesmen of the Black Muslims can openly preach racial hatred, violence and insurrection to their heart's content, with never a challenge from police, courts or the self-appointed guardians of civil liberties. The guilt of the liberal is insatiable. He *deserves*, by his own judgement, to be kicked, slapped and spat on for his infinite crimes. The shooting of a Negro in Mississippi, purportedly the act of a crazed and isolated white man, reverberates from liberal sounding boards into weeks

122 *The USA Today,* January 20, 1995, 1A.

123 James Burnham, *Suicide of the West* (New York, NY: John Day Company, 1964) 195.

124 Robert W. Whitaker, *A Plague on Both Your Houses* (Washington—NY: Robert B. Luce, Inc., 1976) 206.

of world headlines; the shooting of white men in Maryland by rioting Negro gangs slides back into an obscure and unread paragraph. The truncheons of hard-pressed police struggling to preserve the minimum elements of public order against unloosed chaos become Satanic pitchforks; the rocks and broken bottles of the mob, angelic swords.[125]

One of the clearest examples of the anti-Western bias of liberalism is the history standards produced by President Clinton's Goals 2000 Act. The National Education Standards and Improvement Council produced a guideline for the teaching of American history. This guideline or standard produced by representatives of the liberal education establishment makes only fleeting references to George Washington and never describes him as our first president. These liberal educators found it noteworthy to emphasize the founding of the extreme left-wing National Organization of Women (NOW) and the founding of the Sierra Club, but not the first gathering of the United States Congress.[126]

The liberal education establishment had intended to use these standards as an attack upon Western civilization. They recommended that students consider that the Constitution sidetracked the developing movement to abolish slavery and to think about the achievements and grandeur of Mansa Musa's court and wealth of Mali.[127] That well-known black female Harriet Tubman was listed six times, yet contemporary white males such as the little-known Gen. Robert E. Lee were not mentioned, and Gen. Ulysses S. Grant was mentioned but once. General Lee is in good company because Alexander Graham Bell, Thomas Edison, Albert Einstein, Jonas Salk, and the Wright Brothers were also ignored.[128]

While Paul Revere, J. P. Morgan, and Thomas Edison received no mention, the liberal education establishment did think it necessary to portray America in as bad a light as possible by giving McCarthyism and Senator Joseph McCarthy a total of nineteen references. The Ku Klux Klan came in with seventeen references. The liberal education establishment, true to form, managed to quote at least one

---

125 Burnham, 200.

126 Lynne V. Cheney, "The End of History," *The Wall Street Journal,* October 20, 1994, editorial page.

127 Ibid

128 Ibid

congressional leader. It quoted Speaker of the House Tip O'Neill as claiming that President Ronald Reagan was "a cheerleader for self-ishness."[129] No doubt, this is the America that liberals see when they look at our history.

The liberal establishment has declared war upon American culture by attacking our common history. Down South, black extremists supported by their fellow travelers in the liberal media have been engaged in a vicious campaign of cultural genocide against everything Southern.[130] The liberal media have attempted to portray the struggle for Southern Self-Determination in 1861-65 as a conspiracy of treason by a racist society. Their favorite technique has been to accuse the South of fighting to maintain and extend the system of African slavery. Southerners have traditionally maintained that the Cause of the South in 1861 was the same as the Cause of our Colonial Forefathers in 1776—a struggle to maintain inalienable rights and to withdraw from conflict with an abusive government. The South, in 1861, was following the tradition established by the Declaration of Independence; that is, to establish a new government more conducive to the maintenance of its liberty.[131] Southerners find it difficult to understand why their Cause should not be given a fair and equal treatment with that of their Colonial Forefathers. Liberals have denied the South an equal and impartial hearing for the Southern view of the War for Southern Independence because of the existence of the system of slavery. Yet, Southerners have often stated that this very same system of slavery existed in all thirteen colonies in 1776, when the American colonies seceded from the British Union. In addition, the New England colonies were actively engaging in the nefarious African slave trade at the time of America's secession from the British Empire. If self-determination was right for the American colonies in 1776, then why would it not have been right for the South in 1861? Surely, no one could logically use the argument that the existence of slavery in the South was reason enough to deny self-determination to the South in 1861, while ignoring that same system of slavery which existed in all thirteen American colonies in 1776

---

129 Ibid

130 James R. Kennedy and Walter D. Kennedy, *The South Was Right!* (Gretna, LA: Pelican Publishing Company, 1994) 271-303.

131 See Confederate President Jefferson Davis' inaugural address, quoted in Kennedy and Kennedy, 321-26.

and the existence of the African slave trade during the era of the Revolutionary War.

Liberals refuse to accept this logical explanation offered by Southerners who desire to display the flags and symbols of their Southern Heritage proudly. Black extremists and their lackeys in education, politics, and the media have demanded the removal of all symbols of Confederate heritage. Why? Because, they claim, it represents, "slavery," "treason," or "racism." Liberals feel guilty about these "sins" of America and attempt to allay their self-imposed guilt by denying Southerners the right to display the symbols of their heritage. Black extremists will demand the removal of a Confederate flag or monument because they find it "offensive." Yet, according to a Louis Harris poll, such flags are not viewed as offensive by the overwhelming majority of black Southerners. Sixty-eight percent of blacks (a majority of better than two to one) responded that they do not find the Confederate flag offensive. Americans in general have stated that the use of the Confederate flag as part of a state's flag is not offensive and that these states should not be forced to remove it. (From Dixie, we would like to say—Thank you, America!) As expected, the poll demonstrated even greater support from Southerners. Down South, the support for keeping the Confederate flag as part of a state flag is 71%.[132]

As we have demonstrated, this ongoing assault upon the history and, therefore, the culture of American civilization is nothing less than an attempt to erode respect for the values of the Founding Fathers and succeeding generations of America. At the time of the writing of this book, the most severe attacks are being launched against the honor and history of the veterans of World War II and the Confederate veterans. One point must be made here; no matter where we are born in America and regardless of which war or historical period our individual ancestors were involved in, when the culture and history of any American is attacked by the liberal establishment, everyone should come to his defense. Truth knows no boundaries. When New England's Founding Fathers are attacked as "witch burners" or "holier than thou" religious extremists, Southerners should come to their defense. When the liberal establishment demands the removal of a Confederate monument or flag down in

132 *The Washington Times,* July 4, 1994.

Dixie, Yankees should set up a howl of protest. Our common heritage as Americans is under attack. The enemy is, at present, using the old method of divide and conquer. It is time for Americans to stand up with pride and defend their common heritage.

Liberals have been using their control of education, the media, and politics as an opportunity to attack our heritage as Americans. Whether it is an attack upon World War II veterans, an attack upon Western civilization in general, or an attack upon the heritage of one section of this country, the liberal establishment has been actively engaged in an attempt to rewrite history to support its left-wing political agenda.

Instead of rewriting our history to support a politically correct, liberal agenda—Why Not Freedom!

SUMMARY
Questions and Answers

Q. As a Southerner, I have been fighting to defend Southern history and culture. Most of the time I have experienced little help and many times a lot of harm from Yankees; why should I trouble myself with defending their history when they are doing so much to destroy mine? Further, I find much about their history shocking and deplorable; why would I want to defend that?

A. General Robert E. Lee used to make the point that we don't always do the right thing because we like the ones it will help, but because a gentleman will always do the "right thing." I am sure that there are many Northerners who misunderstand Southern history, just as there are many Southerners who do not understand Northern history. As Americans, the important thing to remember is that each section of our country and every ethnic group within it should be allowed free access to the market place of ideas. According to the Jeffersonian idea of equality of opportunity, each segment should be allowed to give its views, openly and freely, and then each of the remainder can decide for itself what views are appropriate. Always remember that the liberal, politically correct crowd will use every method at their disposal to trash or otherwise downgrade our common heritage as Americans. When you, as a Southerner, help your Northern neighbors defend their heritage and history from attacks by the politically correct intellectual gestapo, you are assisting them in defeating the same enemies who are attacking your Southern Heritage. As far as finding portions of their history "shocking and deplorable," may I suggest that you try to be a little more open-minded about Northern history; after all, this is the same thing you are asking Northerners to do about portions of Southern history that they find "shocking and deplorable."

Q. What are the benefits to the liberal establishment for attacking American history?

A. The liberal establishment owes its existence to its electorial clientele. These are the people who continue to block-vote for the left-of-center candidates. By attacking the values and heroes of the American majority, the liberal establishment is repaying the minority block-voters for their support. This approach also gives the minority an excuse to demand more middle-class tax dollars. After all, if the majority of Americans are descendants of those who waged illegal wars, traded in slaves, or owned slaves, then, of course, "we (middle-class Americans) owe it to them (minorities)." For this reason the people of America cannot allow the liberal elite to keep them cowed "upon stools of everlasting repentance."

CHAPTER 15

Instead of HUD Projects in Middle-Class Neighborhoods—Why Not Freedom!

The Federal government has recently stepped up its attack against the middle class with an assault on suburbia. Housing and Urban Development (HUD) is doing to housing what Federal court-ordered forced busing did to education. HUD claims that inner-city crime, drug addiction, and poverty can be cured by forcefully trans-planting the "projects" into middle-class subdivisions. The Clinton administration asked for millions of taxpayers' dollars to be used to remove the poor from poverty centers and integrate them into America's middle-class neighborhoods. The Washington bureaucrats describe this as economic integration. HUD has a $25 billion budget it plans to use to "economically integrate" middle-class neighborhoods. The Federal government is providing millions of dollars worth of rental vouchers to people currently living in public housing projects.[133] These vouchers will be used to move Federally approved "poor" people into middle- and upper-income neighborhoods. Your Federal tax dollars are hard at work destroying the equity of middle-class homeowners! In 1990, while a Republican was president, a group of black welfare recipients sued to end, what they claimed to be, segregation of poor blacks in public housing. The Clinton administration is actively attempting to relocate these black welfare recipients into middle-class, predominantly white neighborhoods. It should be noted that these middle-class neighborhoods are not restricted to white-only residents, but are open to anyone who can qualify for home ownership. This issue, like so many other issues, is not about race, but about the rights of taxpayers as opposed to the demands of tax consumers.

What happens when people are relocated into a subdivision without having earned the right to be there? More specifically, what

133 Howard Husock, "Voucher Plan for Housing: A Trojan Horse," *The Wall Street Journal*, December 21, 1994, editorial page.

147

happens to private property values of middle-class Americans when a group of people who formerly lived in a high-crime district take up residence among them? What happens to property values when people move into an area who have no vested interest in maintaining the high quality of the community in which they now find themselves? An Illinois official complained that the sudden influx of HUD-subsidized families caused a neighborhood to turn into a slum. Another city's mayor warned of the economic disaster that occurs when people are artificially introduced into a formerly tax-paying neighborhood. Thanks to HUD, an entire neighborhood is changed from taxpayers into tax consumers. Suddenly the city must supply more municipal services for new citizens who do not contribute to the tax rolls. The *Chicago Sun-Times* noted that people naturally resent it when the government gives someone property the rest of society has to work to obtain. Americans resent the government's use of their tax monies to make tax consumers the economic equivalent of the tax-paying segment of society. Even the mayor of Boston complained of the welfare tenants that HUD had moved across the street from his residence (who says there is no justice left in the world?). He complained that the welfare tenants were disturbing the natural peace and quiet of his neigborhood, using drugs, and generally threatening the security of the neighborhood. But what was worse was that there was nothing that the local citizens could do to prevent the deterioration of their neighborhood. Due to lenient Federal rules, it was practically impossible to remove individuals from the HUD program. The *St. Louis Post Dispatch* reported a rising crime wave following HUD arrivals and noted that the increasing numbers of HUD-subsidized homeowners were undermining the city's neighborhoods.

The mentality of the liberal advocates of "economic integration" is frightening. They are moving unqualified residents into middle-class subdivisions with the same callous and arrogant attitudes that they used to bus middle-class children out of those same neighborhoods. Liberals believe that, if the environment is changed, then bad people will automatically become good (by this we do not mean to imply that everyone who lives in government projects is bad). They assume that a criminal who is taken away from a government project and placed, via Federal vouchers, into a middle-class neighborhood will be less likely to commit crimes because he is in the midst of relative affluence. This is the kind of thinking that currently controls the liberal establishments of education, media, and government—no wonder we are in such a sad situation!

HUD's own "Crime in Public Housing" report declared that "crime rates in public housing complexes are in some cases . . . ten times higher than the national average." By the way, Mr. or Mrs. Middle Class, the people who want to move outsiders next door to you are the same ones who also want to take away your right to keep and bear arms! The economic damage done by high crime-rate public housing is not confined to the "projects" alone. The high crime rate of public housing areas drives down private property values in the adjacent neighborhoods. Just think about it; you work hard all your life, you pay your taxes, you obey the laws, you serve your country if called upon, you save, and finally you have a home to call your own. To you, just like to the average middle-class American, your home represents the largest asset acquired during your lifetime. It is your plan to live quietly and safely during your retirement in your mortgage-free home. And then, along comes the Federal government, HUD vouchers in hand and welfare recipients in tow. Your safe, secure neighborhood is invaded by people who don't know the meaning of working, saving, and sacrificing, all of which you had to endure to acquire your home. They are given a home next to you— paid for with your tax money—you might say that you paid for your home and your new neighbor's home as well! Now, call your real estate agent and see what your home is worth. Overnight the Federal government has destroyed your life's work, your savings, your sacrifice, your dreams of a pleasant and safe retirement. What is worse, under the current system of Federal government, there is nothing that you can do about it. You must keep quiet and suffer in silence—otherwise, you may be prosecuted for housing discrimination, as described in Chapter 18.

The loss to the private citizen is a real, tangible, monetary loss that he will realize when he decides to sell or borrow against his home. A member of the Detroit Board of Assessors stated that HUD's activities had cost every homeowner one-fifth of the value of his home. The *Chicago Tribune* characterized the Federal activities as worse than any recorded natural disaster. Within forty-eight months the Federal government's activities changed a clean, safe neighborhood into a slum. The Federal government is using its police powers to steal the private property of middle-class citizens. The Constitution clearly forbids such "taking" by the Federal government. The Fifth Amendment declares: "No person shall . . . be deprived of life, liberty, or property, without due process of law; nor shall private property be taken for public use without just compensation." But, as we already know only too well, the Constitution is no protection for the middle class when they are faced with a Federal agent intent on implementing a politically correct Federal court order, Federal program, or Federal law.

Don't you think it's time for a change? Isn't it about time that the middle-class citizen had a mechanism to protect his rights and his liberties when confronted by an abusive Federal government? We have learned from more than forty years of sad experience that the Federal government can be used to infringe on our rights. We also know that, even if "conservatives" should gain control of the Federal Congress, the Supreme Court, and the president's office, that alone would not assure the future security of our "dearest interests" and liberties. What happens if in the next election the "conservatives" lose control of the Federal Congress or fail to elect a "conservative" president? Must our liberties be at risk at every election? We must have a balance of power between the Federal government and "We the people" of the sovereign state. That "balance of power" was originally designed to be exercised by the people at the local level through their agent, the state.[134]

Instead of the tyranny of Federal HUD agents—Why Not Freedom!

SUMMARY
Questions and Answers

Q. How does HUD's voucher system for "poor" people work?

A. The "under-privileged" homeowner voucher system of the Federal government works much like the school voucher plan that the liberals and the Federal government have worked so hard to defeat. A "poor" person will apply to the appropriate department of the Federal government for a voucher that can be used to obtain housing in middle- and upper-class neighborhoods. Unlike the voucher system

134 James Madison, *The Federalist No. 46,* quoted in George W. Carey and James McClellan, *The Federalist: Student Edition* (Dubuque, IA: Kendall/Hunt Publishing Company, 1990) 240-45.

for schools, in which most of those who apply for said vouchers are taxpayers, those applying for homeowner vouchers are, for the most part, non-taxpayers. In reality, the hard-working homeowners of the subdivision invaded by the so-called underprivileged will be the ones paying for the new non-working and, therefore, non-taxpaying, residents. The middle-class citizen who has sacrificed so much time and effort to buy and maintain his home and his home equity will see it disappear in a matter of days. Most of these middle-class people will never be able to recover the loss because their investment represents a lifetime of work.

Q. Your resistance to "poor" people moving into your neighborhood sounds like a code word or phrase for black people. Isn't it true that you are just trying to keep black people out of white neighborhoods?

A. We don't use code words. If we feel a particular way about a subject, we just tell it like it is. The truth is, middle-class neighbors have a common desire to protect their hard work and investment. This is true of all people and not a trait peculiar to whites. Black people, who by their own efforts become members of the middle class, have a similar value system as that of white people in the middle class. We have known many black middle-class people who respond just as any white person responds, when confronted with the loss of their home equity or retirement security. Liberals are just going have to get used to the idea of black middle-class conservatives. Black middle-class conservatives have more in common with the white middle class than they do with the so-called poor people, black or white. Middle-class values transcend color.

CHAPTER 16

Instead of Socialized Medicine—
Why Not Freedom!

Late in 1993, President Bill Clinton delighted the liberal establishment by announcing his (and his wife Hilary's) long-awaited health care reform. The president's health care reform plan proved to be the boldest Federal power grab since the War for Southern Independence. The Clintons' nationalized health plan would have enabled the Federal government to bring under its control more than one-seventh of the economy of the United States! Liberals, socialists, and other politically correct centralists were ecstatic! It appeared that, at last, their dreams of a socialist America were to be realized. All at the expense of Americans' individual liberty!

The liberal establishments in the media and politics avoided any substantive discussion of the two most important questions regarding the proposed health care reform. First, did the United States Constitution grant the Federal government authority to regulate the individual citizen's choice regarding health care, and, second, would the American people accept the limitations imposed by the Federal government relative to their choices of health care insurance coverage (or not to have such coverage) and their choice of personal physicians and hospitals?

The mindset of the average socialist is one of absolute abhorrence of societal inequality. To the socialist, all conditions of people's lives should be equal. Abject or total human equality is the central theme of the "religion" of socialism. Nowhere is this theme of socialism more obvious than in the realm of economics. Anyone who has studied socialism knows that its primary aim is the redistribution of wealth in a manner that faceless social planners have determined to be "fair." Clinton's health care reform was just such a plan. It would have required the very young and healthy to subsidize the older and sicker population. It would have required those who lead a healthy lifestyle to subsidize those who engage in risky lifestyles that tend to produce more accidents or diseases. In order for such a plan to work, the government must have the authority to *force* everyone to participate. In addition, the government must pay for such a program by direct taxation on the person being covered or indirectly by forcing someone other than the person being covered to pay the cost, such as the person's employer. In the case of indirect taxation, the additional cost of health care would be added to the cost of doing business, and, as with all cost, would be passed along to the consumer in the form of higher prices. As we all should know by now, there is no such thing as a free lunch—eventually, the consumer, primarily the middle-class consumer, pays for all such government mandates on employers. In addition to higher prices, the additional cost to businesses decreases the amount of revenues available for salary increases for employees. In effect, in such a plan the Federal government requires the employer to be an unpaid tax collector; the consumer pays the indirect tax twice, once in higher prices and twice by decreased wages!

Where did the Federal government obtain such imperialist power over the health and well-being of its "subjects"? Where does the Constitution grant to the Federal government the authority to require private citizens to participate in a government-sponsored health care system? As we have demonstrated, the original Constitution was a compact between sovereign states whereby they agreed to create the Federal government. This newly created government was to be one of specific and limited powers.[135] Even the most ardent Federalist, Centralist, or Monarchist of 1787 would have never suggested that the Federal government should have the power to enforce a program like Clinton's health care reform. But, as we have already seen, contemporary political correctness does not recognize the limitations of a written constitution. Therefore, the liberty, freedoms, and rights of Americans are enjoyed only as long as they do not hinder the social progress envisioned by the liberal establishments of government, education, or the media.

According to modern liberalism, the Federal government obtains its authority to regulate Americans' choice of health care from the

---

135 "[The] States Governments would clearly retain all the rights of sovereignty which they before had and which were not by that act *exclusively* delegated to the United States." Alexander Hamilton, *The Federalist No. 32,* quoted in George W. Carey and James McClellan, *The Federalist: Student Edition* (Dubuque, IA: Kendall/Hunt Publishing Company, 1990) 156.

commerce clause of the Constitution. Remember the "glancing geese" theory discussed in Chapter 5. The same commerce clause that can be used by the EPA to claim authority over your use of a pool of water in your back yard is also used as the excuse for the Federal government to regulate your health care decisions. The commerce clause gives the Federal government power to "regulate commerce with foreign Nations and among the several States." The purpose of the commerce clause was to provide a free trade zone among the states of the Union. This limited interpretation of the commerce clause was upheld until the 1930s and 1940s. During Franklin D. Roosevelt's terms as president, he successfully packed the Supreme Court with men who would support his Big Government social programs. It was during this period that the Federal Supreme Court for the first time began to use the commerce clause as an excuse for granting new and intrusive Federal powers over the states and the people thereof. In 1942, the United States Supreme Court, using the commerce clause of the Federal Constitution, even ruled that a farmer could not grow wheat for his own consumption.[136]

The liberal establishment showed its true colors with the dangerous precedent set by the Clinton health care reform plan. The liberal establishment declared that the Federal government had a right to regulate citizens because they were living within the domain of the Federal government. Very few people even challenged the logic of this giant Federal power grab. In other words, the philosophy behind socialized medicine is that you and I are not free to choose for ourselves; our lives do not belong to us, but we are in effect property of the Federal government which will exercise its authority to decide how to take care of its property! This socializing philosophy does not recognize the limitations of the Constitution, rather, it replaces the Constitution with the new concept of an America in which Big Brother Federal government owns the right to "take care of its citizens" without consulting those very citizens—the Federal government knows best! This gives Big Government a blank check on the liberties of all Americans. With this power, there is nothing that the Federal government cannot order us to do. The commerce clause can now be cited to justify banning fatty foods or foods high in salt, or to establish mandatory exercise classes for citizens![137]

136 *Wickard v. Filburn,* 317 U.S. 111 (1942).

137 *The Wall Street Journal,* September 29, 1993, editorial page.

Just think about what this loss of freedom really means. If Congress can regulate our choice of health care just because we breath air that crosses state boundaries (and, therefore, is in interstate commerce) or some other absurd reason, then Congress could mandate that all its subjects (formerly referred to as citizens) who are too fat will be put on a diet. Or, if certain Americans are not in good physical condition, Congress could legislate daily exercise programs. Or, if some citizens eat too many fatty foods, Congress could outlaw hamburgers, hot dogs, french fries, pizza, etc.! An article in *The Wall Street Journal* questioned the wisdom of justifying social legislation by using the commerce clause. Using such logic, bureaucrats or ambitious politicians could attack any limitation of their Federal authority. Even the Bill of Rights would be vulnerable. Strange as it may appear, while the whole world is discovering that Big Government and centralized planning do not work, here in America our liberal establishment is still attempting to force it upon free citizens.[138] "We the people" of the sovereign states must make the decision of whether or not we are individuals responsible for our own actions and personal well-being or whether we are subjects of an all-powerful central government to which we have surrendered all our liberty in exchange for the promise of social well-being—a well-being defined by the politically correct liberal establishment.

Another problem with the liberal proposal of socialized medicine is that it will deny freedom of choice in health care matters. This is necessary as a form of rationing health care. But, of course, the liberals would never admit that they are rationing health care. What they say is that they are controlling cost. In another article, "Removing Our Freedom," a study was done to measure the restraint of individual freedom inherent in various health care bills. A study performed by The National Taxpayers Union Foundation examined the influence on American freedom of the Clinton health care reform plan. This was done by counting words in the law that tended to restrict choice. Words such as "ban," "fine," "penalty," "prison," "require," and "sanction" were counted. Clinton's plan topped the list with nearly fifteen hundred such words.[139] Also interesting was the fact that Clinton's plan included verbiage requiring limits (quotas) for health care professionals along racial and ethnic lines. It

138 Ibid

139 *The Wall Street Journal,* June 27, 1994, editorial page.

would require medical students to be chosen, not on merit, but, in part, on the basis of their race. The Clinton plan would create a national council that would decide, among other things, when and if a particular medical specialty (brain surgeons for example) had the appropriate number of minorities. But why stop here? Using the same logic, the Federal government could establish quotas for medical care. Whites might not be treated until an appropriate number of minorities were also treated. After all, as we revealed in Chapter 6, the Federal government has determined that the key to fighting discrimination is to play by the numbers. So, why not apply the magic of liberal social science to the actual administration of health care? The logic is the same—in the long run the results will be the same—an embittered and resentful middle class being forced to watch as liberal politicians destroy not only their rights but also their very lives! No, instead of an unlimited Federal government that forces socialized medicine upon hapless subjects—Why Not Freedom!

SUMMARY

Questions and Answers

Q. You refer to socialism as a "religion." How can such an idea be considered as a religion?

A. Socialism is not a new innovation, but, rather, it has been around for a long time. The Pilgrim Fathers of New England even tried a form of socialism when they first came to the New World. It was a total failure, and they were saved from starvation by the implementation of a free market economy. Our Forefathers had enough good sense to recognize the failure of a planned, collectivist economy. Modern-day liberals and other socialists cling to the myth of socialism even though it has proven to be the twentieth century's most economically and morally bankrupt system. This century has seen the rise of Fascism, Nazism, and Communism, all of which believed in a system of government in which the few, at the top of government, ruled the many at the bottom. All these systems were anti-private property and anti-civil rights. Big Government has been in its heyday during this century, but it has also proven itself to be a system that cannot produce a free or prosperous society. Yet, America's liberal elite still maintain a child-like faith in a planned economy. America's liberal elite still demand the right to rule from Washington because they, as they understand it, know better than the common people how to make the world a "better" place. This faith in socialism is not based in reality but in a religious type of blind faith that goes beyond rational thinking. Thus, we say that socialism is a religion; not that it has a moral system or believes in a higher being, it does not. Socialism is humanism to the core; it believes in the idea that mankind and mankind alone holds the answers to its problems. Thus, the god of socialism appears to be man himself. A sick man, who is his own doctor, is indeed to be pitied.

Q. You state that you do not want the Federal government to dictate health care policy. What if the states desire to institute socialized medicine? How would you feel about health care run from the state level?

A. From the point of freedom and good economics, state-run health care is still a poor choice for people who desire to be free. Granted, the Federal government has no constitutional authority to pursue such a policy. In our federal system of government, the people of a sovereign state have the right to institute such a policy, but we would oppose such a system for the reasons just mentioned. Many states, such as Louisiana, have a good system of indigent care hospitals. This system negates the demand of the bleeding heart socialist for socialized medical care because care is offered to everyone regardless of income. These hospitals were established by the people of the sovereign state of Louisiana for the care of its people. As long as the people freely chose to do this and are not under the compulsion of a "higher" authority, we applaud their willingness to assist others. But nowhere is there to be found a "right" of the indigent to force the people of the sovereign state to provide this care. A cardinal rule in dealing with these matters should be "minimize force and maximize freedom."

CHAPTER 17

Instead of an Anti-Middle Class Liberal Media—Why Not Freedom!

As we have already demonstrated in Chapter 3, the left-of-center liberal media are not an independent group dedicated to fairly presenting the news. They have become the unofficial propaganda ministry of the politically correct, liberal establishment. The liberal media have vigorously maintained their monopoly in the market place of ideas. They have, to a large degree, been successful in preventing conservative leaders from presenting their ideas and views on national and local issues. As good propagandists, they have used current events in an attempt to mold the thinking of the masses. While working diligently for those with whom they agree, they have, on the other hand, been arrogant and condescending in their dealings with anyone who would dare oppose their opinions.

The liberal media have assumed the position that the First Amendment applies only to the official media. Therefore, only the chosen few of the liberal establishment have the right of free expression—by this we mean that only "their" position is allowed favored, or even equal, status. The average middle-class citizen is free to stand on the street corner and shout to the top of his lungs about issues such as gun control, racial quotas, busing, and high taxes, but such issues will never be given a fair presentation on the evening news or on the editorial page of a major national newspaper or magazine. Yes, the middle class still has its First Amendment right to free speech, but, in our modern technological society, the liberal media have isolated him and his views from the American public. Yes, in modern America, the press is free but only for those who control access to it. The liberal, politically correct media have effectively barred candid discussions of the excesses of unlimited Federalism or conservative alternatives to Big Government. The unofficial liberal ministry of propaganda has become the key element in maintaining a left-of-center, intellectual dictatorship in America's market place of ideas.

159

Without the support of their liberal propaganda machinery, the liberal establishments of education and government would collapse.

The liberal media will insist that they are an unbiased news outlet. They will maintain that they never allow their personal views to cloud or influence their conduct as "journalists."[140] Yet, recent polling has demonstrated that the American people do not trust "journalists." How have journalists managed to lose the respect of a majority of Americans? An establishment that has had the ear of virtually all Americans for the last fifty years now finds itself held in contempt—why? According to the "talking heads" of the liberal media, the blame for all their trouble with middle America rests upon talk radio. But, is there something else going on? Is it possible that the liberal media have been less concerned about a fair and impartial presentation of the news and more concerned about advancing their pet liberal political agenda? Perhaps middle-class Americans have grown weary of being cast as bigots, racists, and ignorant bumpkins just because they refuse to follow the liberal party line presented on nightly news shows.

When contemplating America's media, many Americans have the perception of a media establishment that would rather smear a conservative than debate him on the issues. An example of this smear effort was displayed in the attempt of the liberal media and politicians to remove the Confederate battle flag from the Georgia state flag. The liberal media, both national and state, declared that the flag of Generals Robert E. Lee and "Stonewall" Jackson was racist and evil. The *Atlanta Journal Constitution* even likened the Confederate flag to the Nazi Swastika! Their plan was making great headway until the scalawag governor of Georgia accepted an invitation to debate a representative of the Sons of Confederate Veterans[141] on "Larry King Live." The scalawag governor was publicly humiliated on national television and the proud people of Georgia saved their flag and the honor and dignity of their gallant ancestors. When given both sides of a story, such as the truth about the Confederate battle flag and not liberal bias, the American middle class usually makes the choice on the side of conservative ideas. This is the real reason the liberal establishment feel liberals cannot withstand the truth; that is why they try

140 Gerald F. Seib, "Confidence Gap: Press Trapped in Own Cynicism," *The Wall Street Journal,* August 31, 1994, A14.

141 Charles Lunsford, "Larry King Live," CNN, February 19, 1993.

with all their power to maintain a monopoly in the market place of ideas. Whether dealing with Southern heritage issues or issues of limited government, the liberal establishment use their near monopoly in the market place of information transmission to advance those issues toward the liberal point of view.

> In the Left's ongoing war against conservatives and conservative ideas, slander and libel have become routine. A contemporary liberal would much rather damn conservatives with a toxic label—"racist," "homophobe," "fascist"—than actually debate their ideas on the merits.[142]

When Georgia Senator Newt Gingrich stated that the Clinton White House was dominated by "counterculture McGoverniks," the liberal press sent up a howl such as has rarely been heard in Washington, D.C. Yet, little note was made, and certainly no complaints were heard, when Vice President Al Gore described Republicans as desiring ". . . to create as much . . . discord and hatefulness as they possibly can and follow a scorched-earth political strategy: burn down the house in hopes that you'll inherit the ashes."[143] The average American, after viewing such double standards for years, has begun to suspect that a left-of-center, double standard is being applied to the reporting of the news. This double standard can be demonstrated by looking at the invectives used to describe Senator Jessie Helm's joke about President Clinton needing a bodyguard in Helm's state. In his report of the incident, NBC reporter Jim Miklaszewski used such terms as "Prince of Darkness," "rabid attack dog," "bigot," "sexist," and "homophobe."[144] Did anyone condemn this liberal reporter? Of course not!

Another liberal "journalist," Sunniu Khalid of National Public Radio described Newt Gingrich as a man looking for "a more scientific, a more civil way of lynching people."[145] Did the fair and non-biased media send up a howl of protest? Of course not, because they are not fair and unbiased! The politically correct, liberal media constantly protect their own, and, by way of modern technological

---

142 Jeff Jacoby, "Liberals spent the year smearing their opponents," *The Boston Globe*, as published in *The* (New Orleans, LA) *Times Picayune*, January 3, 1995, B5.

143 Ibid

144 Ibid

145 Ibid

communication, they attempt to assassinate the character of anyone so foolish as to oppose their liberal agenda.

Race baiting has been an efficient tool for the liberal media. By waving the "bloody shirt" of racism, liberals can scare off those who would normally tend to oppose them. By using the bloody shirt of racism, liberals can also destroy the credibility of those so foolish as to stand up to the liberal establishment. As always, the race card is a popular weapon to use against the defenders of middle-class values. Charles Rangel, Harlem's left-wing Democratic Congressman, blasted Republicans' tax-cut pledge of 1995 not by calling it bad economics, but by calling it—racism.

> "It's not 'spic' or 'nigger' anymore," he commented poisonously. "They say, 'Let's cut taxes.' " The same slander was hurled at Gingrich personally. In a cataract of abuse titled, "Newt Gingrich, Authoritarian," the *New York Times* indicted his "race-based" politics. "A proxy for race-baiting," chimed in *New York Magazine*'s Jacob Weisberg, adding: "George Wallace was big in rural Georgia too." And Sam Donaldson of ABC accused Gingrich of bigotry to his face: "A lot of people are afraid of you. . . . Worse, you're an intolerant bigot."[146]

In another example of liberal bias against conservatives, a columnist for *The USA Today,* one of America's most liberal propaganda papers, blasted Supreme Court Justice Clarence Thomas:

> I hope his wife feeds him lots of eggs and butter and he dies early like many black men do of heart disease. . . . He's an absolutely reprehensible person.[147]

Did the media send up a howl of protest? Of course not! Did middle-class America expect them to do so? Of course not. Why? Because they have learned to expect their propaganda tricks—the propagandists of the liberal media have been found out; the middle class does not trust them because liberals have demonstrated that they do not deserve trust. The self-righteous and arrogant liberal media moguls assume that middle-class Americans are fools who will never catch on to their propaganda tricks—but they are wrong. America's middle class has seen the handiwork of the media elite too often to be fooled forever.

146 Ibid

147 Ibid

The liberal establishment in the media has a long record of smearing as racist any Southern conservative candidate who opposes racial quotas or busing. It has become one of its main political ploys to maintain control of the "Democratic" South.[148] It has been so successful with this propaganda technique down South that, in 1994, the liberals attempted a national variation on this theme. Their plan was to smear the religious right as being "intolerant," "ignorant," and "dangerous." They hoped to create a new "religious" bloody shirt that they could use to frighten off potential voters.

The Democratic Congressional Campaign Committee, directed by Vic Fazio, instructed fellow Democrats to attack the religious right. He urged Democrats to portray conservative Protestants, traditional Catholics, and Orthodox Jews as radicals. Democrat Michael Woo of Los Angeles used TV ads to attack Reverend Pat Robertson and to allege that his Republican opponent was an integral part of the religious right. Woo was defeated by his "religious right" opponent by a whopping 54%. In Arkansas, Mike Huckabee, a candidate for lieutenant governor and a Baptist minister, was described by his Democratic opponent as being too extreme and strident ever to be trusted in elective office. In spite of such illogical and strident attacks, the former minister won the election in Bill Clinton's home state. In both Oklahoma and Kentucky, liberal Democrats attacked conservatives on religious grounds. The conservatives won in both states, with a vote of 55% in Kentucky, and a vote of 54% in Oklahoma.[149]

While the liberal Democrats were attacking religion from their political base, the liberal media were performing their role of anti-religion propagandists. One terrorist expert on the "Larry King Live" show, in an effort to impugn the character of all Bible-believing Christians, stated that the so-called cult at Waco represented "Christian fundamentalism."[150]

The liberal media's attack against traditional religious values stands in sharp contrast to their support of "homosexual" causes. Accuracy In Media, Inc. reviewed the coverage given "gay" causes in an issue of *The New York Times:*

148 James R. Kennedy and Walter D. Kennedy, *The South Was Right!* (Gretna, LA: Pelican Publishing Company, 1994) 245,252.

149 Grover Norquist, "Bashing the Religious Right Is a Losing Strategy," *The Wall Street Journal,* October 23, 1994, editorial page.

150 Reed Irvine, *The News Manipulators: Why You Can't Trust the News* (Smithtown, NY: Book Distributors, Inc., 1993) 31.

> Picking up a recent Sunday edition of the *Times,* we counted four major articles that served their [homosexuals] agenda. If someone didn't know better, they would have sworn the *Times* was an organ of the gay rights movement . . . in its Style section. Two-thirds of one page was taken up by a photograph of a sweet-looking 17 year old girl who believes she is a lesbian. The story told how she goes into high schools teaching kids that homosexuality is a legitimate alternative lifestyle. Except for a few critical words from an official of the Catholic Church, the tone of the article was positive about the role of what were called "gay youngsters." . . . [T]he front page of the Metro section [gave] a favorable profile of Nicholas Rango, who coordinates AIDS policy for New York State. . . . [T]he business section featured a major article about employees of major corporations who are coming out of the closet and admitting they are gay. . . . [F]our major articles promoting gays in just one issue. . . . [151]

The liberal media both promote and protect those who agree with their politically correct agenda. For example, most will recall the ABC miniseries "Roots" based upon a book of the same name written by Alex Haley. The book and ABC's miniseries were portrayed as being an accurate history of the experiences of the author's ancestors. The author claimed that he had traced his ancestry back to Africa. Many Southerners who are active in genealogy research were more than a little skeptical regarding this claim. How could someone write such a detailed history based upon oral history supposedly passed down generation to generation since the time his family was taken from their "idyllic" African home?

> The answer is found partly in a lawsuit that was filed against him [Alex Haley] in 1978 by Harold Courlander, an author who charged that substantial parts of Haley's family history were actually taken from a book he had written called *The African.* . . . Alex Haley settled with Harold Courlander out of court, agreeing to pay him $650,000 and acknowledging his debt to Courlander's creativity. Normally, this would be a stain on an author's reputation that the media would not let anyone forget, but our media so loved Alex Haley and his *Roots* that they have neglected to mention that it was a work of fiction that was in large measure copied from another novel. [152]

151 Ibid, 9-10.

152 Ibid, 151-2.

While the liberal media have been quick to promote and protect those books and authors who support the liberal agenda, they have been equally quick in denouncing those who dare to disagree with liberal doctrines. During the time when *Roots* was the rage of "sensitive" book reviewers and critics, another book that analyzed the system of slavery in America suffered the denunciation of liberalism. The book was *Time on the Cross*. The authors, both professionals in economics, applied scientific research techniques and data gathering to amass the details necessary to complete their study. Of the many shocking conclusions reached, subsequent to detailed research and analysis, was that the average slave in the American South was treated better than his contemporary, white wage slave in the industrial sweat shops of the North.[153] Such "un-American" conclusions were treated as heresy by the liberal establishments of media and academia. The authors were severely criticized and their work summarily dismissed. Unfortunately for the liberal media and liberal academia, the Nobel Peace Prize Committee was not informed that the work of these two scholars had been "disproved" by liberal theoreticians. In 1994, these scholars were awarded the Nobel Prize in economics for their work which culminated in their book, *Time on the Cross*.[154]

There is no greater area of media bias demonstrated than in the area of "gun control." When it comes to the discussion of guns in the hands of law-abiding citizens, the liberal media have primarily one answer, "Get rid of all guns." Michael Gartner, president of NBC News, declared that no one in the country should be allowed to purchase, own, possess or use a handgun. He stated that only the military and the police should be allowed to have handguns and that the only way to achieve this goal was to change the Constitution.[155]

---

153 According to the data, as reported in *Time on the Cross*, the life expectations of American slaves were much longer than the life expectations of free urban industrial workers of either the United States or Europe. In a survey, done in the early 1890s on housing of workers in New York city, as reported in *Time on the Cross*, it was disclosed that the median number of square feet of sleeping space per person of household was thirty-five feet. Therefore, the "typical" Southern slave cabin of the late antebellum period likely contained more sleeping space per person than most of New York city's workers had available to them fifty years later. See Robert W. Fogel and Stanley L. Engerman, *Time on the Cross* (Boston, MA: Little, Brown and Company, 1974) 116,126.

154 "Nobel Economists: On Institutions and Slavery," *The Wall Street Journal*, October 13, 1993, A20.

155 Michael Gartner, quoted in Wayne LaPierre, *Guns, Crime, and Freedom* (Washington, DC: Regnery Publishing Inc., 1994) 201.

Organizations such as the National Rifle Association (NRA) have been demonized by the media. Not only have the media been unfair in reporting incidents of violence in America but, at times, they have even refused to accept paid advertisements sponsored by the NRA.[156] This is an excellent example of how the media maintain their monopoly in the market place of ideas.

Media Research Center (MRC) looked at 107 network news stories aired during the debate over the Brady Bill. In their research, they determined that there was a distinct pattern whereby the liberal media would concentrate on reporting activities and research conducted by gun control advocates. For example, 62% of the stories gave pro-gun control advocates more time than anti-gun control spokesmen, the so-called experts who supported gun control outnumbered their gun rights counterpart by a ratio of two to one, and when discussing the Brady Bill the liberal media's anti-gun bias was demonstrated by a three to one ratio of pro-Brady Bill news stories.[157]

MRC researched seventy-eight stories that were not related to the Brady Bill and found that only 4% were devoted to the rights of gun owners.[158] MRC noted that, during the debate over the Brady Bill, NBC permitted air time for only six opponents of the Brady Bill while allowing thirty-four supporters access to the airways. Gun control advocates were given a 4 to 1 majority on CNN; CBS tilted in favor of gun control speakers 13 to 6; and ABC 12 to 8.[159] Is it possible that there is a trend developing here? Perhaps the liberal media are not as even-handed and professional as they would have the American people believe. Tony Mauro of *The USA Today* admitted the radical difference between the media and the American people:

> In the news room of USA Today for example, which prides itself on drawing its staff from a cross-section of the nation, it was hard to find editors and reporters who had ever owned a gun. In other workplaces, it would be difficult to find anyone who hadn't.[160]

156 Ibid, 204-5.

157 Ibid, 207.

158 Ibid

159 Ibid, 208.

160 Ibid, 209.

The left-wing tilt of the news has turned it into an effective propaganda organ for the liberal establishment—all done under the protection of the First Amendment. Yet, who protects the middle class's First Amendment right to free speech, to free expression, to a free press when the press controls access to the medium and vigorously maintains a monopoly in America's market place of ideas?

Instead of a politically correct, liberal propaganda ministry masquerading as a news media—Why Not Freedom!

SUMMARY
Questions and Answers

Q. How can a return to the original constitutional republic have any influence on the so-called liberal media? After all, they are independent of political control, aren't they?

A. In answer to the second part of your question, yes, the media are independent of political control, and should be so. Yet, there is a close relationship between the liberal media and the liberal establishment which now controls Washington, D.C. By returning power to "We the people" of the sovereign states, the power base for the liberal alliance in Washington, D.C., will be broken. Although we may feel that our local media are somewhat liberal, when compared to the media in Washington, D.C., they, more often than not, reflect the views of the local population. With the return of local control of our government and lives, the local media will have an upper hand in the "news" business, whereas, at present, all power is in Washington, D.C. Therefore, the liberal media that reflect the official "Big Government" line have the advantage. This is just one more reason for "We the people" to reassert our right to govern ourselves at the local level.

CHAPTER 18

Instead of Attacks Upon Family Values— Why Not Freedom!

Family values and family issues have at long last caught the imagination of mainstream political America. With both political parties and even the establishment media vying to jump on the "family values" bandwagon, it would be wise to look at what is at issue here as far as middle-class America is concerned.

Can there be a viable society, other than in the depraved mind of some Hollywood movie producer, that can last any length of time without some form of moral and ethical standard? Hearth and kin, mom's apple pie, the old homestead, regardless of what image it may call to mind, home, the seat of the family, has a strong attraction and influence for most people. Yet, this most necessary element of a strong society has undergone a relentless attack at the hands of America's liberal elite.

It is from the collective instruction of the family that a society derives its general opinions on moral and ethical values. If a society is described as a building, then families are the bricks that make up the structure. As long as its building blocks are strong, a society can weather many storms. It is families that connect one generation of a society to a new and developing generation and, by doing so, maintain the society as a living entity. A society's history and heritage is the material that bonds the present generation to the past and enables it to judge correctly from the fountain of experience how to prepare the way for future generations.

The collective knowledge of man, both secular and biblical, teaches us that every society has attempted in some manner to collect and hand down to its young people the knowledge gleaned from its past experience. The act of passing down to future generations the "wisdom of the ages" is an act of self-preservation for any society. Many years ago, man first learned that a rattlesnake bite could kill. Armed with this knowledge, man passed on to future generations this valuable information, thereby freeing his society from having to continue suffering the disastrous results of rattlesnake bites. A society that scorns the wisdom of its past will eventually die.

Now, what do snake bites and life in modern society have in common? What is obvious to any rational person as far as snake bites are concerned is somehow lost on modern liberals when society begins to talk about the middle-class value system. A system is nothing more than the accumulated knowledge of past generations. The established system of morality and ethics has made it possible to provide stability and permanence to American society. Without stability, no one would feel safe enough to raise a family (we call this the inalienable right to life) and, without permanence, no one would feel safe to engage in economic activity (here we see the inalienable right to liberty and property). Without these elements, a society becomes nothing more than a nomadic tribe of marauders (without conscience and without roots). With stability and permanence, a society develops a system of law, and, from that point forward, civilization grows.

It should be noted that the most fundamental aspect in the development and maintenance of a lawful society is the family unit. It is from this unit that law is developed, and, from the family unit of succeeding generations, respect for that law is taught and passed on to new generations. The family unit is essential for a healthy society. Yet, in America today, liberalism has put on a full-court press in its assault on the middle-class value system. Liberalism has no compunction about attacking the most traditional notion of right and wrong held by the middle class. Middle-class Americans have no problems in punishing violent criminals, but liberals, with tears of pity flowing down their cheeks, will say that criminal activity is the fault of an unjust society—meaning, of course, middle-class society. Victims of crime get little or no pity from modern liberals who insist that criminals be taken care of in the most extravagant manner. The criminal must have his rights read to him, must have a lawyer provided, must have every amenity possible afforded him—all, of course, at the expense of the taxpayers—but what about the victim?

The system of moral and ethical values in middle-class American society today is the product of the accumulated wisdom of many prior generations. The knowledge that our Forefathers brought with them and which they have handed down to us through time should not be lightly discarded. No society has ever outlived the rejection of its historic moral value system. The society may not die overnight, but, once it no longer recognizes the value of the accumulated wisdom of its Forefathers, it will surely perish.

As Americans, we have a long and virtuous history in the development of our value system. The American value system is based on a biblical world view. Simply put, that means that those who came to this continent did so with a set of beliefs that were based upon the concept that man is the product of divine creation and is not to be trusted with his own well-being. Man, according to the biblical world view, is to live as God ordained him to live. This attitude established a stable and permanent society, even in the wilds of a "new world." Those liberals who advocate the abandonment of the world view of the Founders of this nation are as irresponsible to our society as those in earlier societies who would advocate forgetting the wisdom established by their Forefathers as it relates to rattlesnakes.

From the very beginning of this country, the reality of God and God's law was recognized. For example, the very charter that was granted to Rhode Island by King Charles II proclaims "That they [the colonists of Rhode Island], pursuing with peace and loyal minds their sober, serious, and religious intentions, of Godly edifying themselves and one another in the holy Christian faith and worship. . . ."[161] Most early documents dealing with the establishment of colonies in America make such reference to the promotion of the Christian religion. After the various colonies proclaimed their independence, many wrote new state constitutions. Within these documents, modern Americans can read and learn about the genesis of America's value system. In its new constitution, written in 1780, Massachusetts informs us how it felt about God's nature and man's responsibility to God. In Part I, Article II, of the Massachusetts Declaration of Rights, we read, "It is the right, as well as the duty, of all men in society, publicly, and at stated seasons, to worship the Supreme Being, the Great Creator and Preserver of the universe."[162] The people of Massachusetts recognized at this early time not only man's right to worship God, but also man's duty to worship God. We feel compelled once again to point out that this duty was not given to man by *any*

---

161 Charter of Rhode Island, as cited in *The American's Guide to the Constitutions of the United States of America* (Trenton, NJ: Moore and Lake, 1813) 101.

162 Constitution of Massachusetts, as cited in *The American's Guide to the Constitutions of the United States of America*, 69.

government nor can *any* government legitimately deny to man the right to worship; this is an inalienable right, a right that predates any government. The constitution of the state of Maryland states "That as it is the duty of every man to worship God in such manner as he thinks most acceptable to him, all persons professing the Christian religion, are equally entitled to protection in their religious liberty. . . ."[163] In Article VIII of the constitution of the state of South Carolina we find the following: "The free exercise and enjoyment of religious profession and worship without discrimination or preference, shall, for ever hereafter, be allowed within this state to all mankind. . . ."[164] In 1796 the state of Tennessee petitioned Congress to be admitted into the Union. The first constitution of Tennessee demonstrates the type of value system the people believed in at that time. To qualify to hold office in their state, the people of Tennessee required that "No person who denies *the being of God or a future state of rewards and punishments,* shall hold any office in the civil department of this state."[165] Not only did the people of Tennessee want their elected officials to believe in God, but, most of all, they desired that their elected officials have a belief in a hereafter, where a just God would judge and punish all men. Here we see why it is so important for American society to maintain its core value system. This system will produce the type of people who will adjust the desires of their life to live in accord with biblical concepts. A society that teaches its members of a time to come where they will have to answer for all that they have done here upon earth ("a future state of rewards and punishments") will yield a more stable and safe community. Most people would rather do business with or interact with someone who has been raised to believe that, even if he is smart enough to "rip them off," sometime in the future he will have to answer to an all-powerful God for his actions.

The most fundamental document of United States history is the Declaration of Independence. It is in this document that the sovereign communities announced to the world their independence. The Declaration of Independence boldly states that all men are *created*

163 Constitution of Maryland, as cited in *The American's Guide to the Constitutions of the United States of America,* 190.

164 Constitution of South Carolina, as cited in *The American's Guide to the Constitutions of the United States of America,* 242.

165 Constitution of Tennessee, as cited in *The American's Guide to the Constitutions of the United States of America,* 342.

by God and that God had granted to man certain "*unalienable*" rights. The Founding Fathers indeed had a strong faith in God, which served as the source of their value system.

The biblical world view served America well during the first three hundred years of its existence. Although the biblical world view has been the view held by the majority of America's middle class, early in the nineteenth century the secular view of man and his world began to be accepted by a small but vocal minority as the view upon which America's value system should be based. Under the banner of "progress," the self-appointed guardians of America's soul began a slow but continuous attack upon traditional values held by the rest of Americans.

Today, the protracted war waged against the traditional values of middle-class America by the liberal establishment is having disastrous consequences. With the loss of our traditional biblical world view, we have lost more than just a few moss-covered Bible-thumpers. Every aspect of our society is feeling the pain of the loss of our moral and ethical compass. Today, in public high schools approximately 25% of all seniors will discover that they have a sexually transmitted disease.[166] In American society, we find that 22% of all white children and 70% of all black children are born out of wedlock,[167] or about 30% of all children born in America are born out of wedlock. In the modern, progressive America of today, 40% of the nation's children do not live with both parents.[168] While the moral and ethical values of our Forefathers have been relegated to the trash heap of history, Aid to Families with Dependent Children (AFDC) has escalated from an insignificant (by Washington's standards) $556 million in 1950 to a profound $24.9 billion (that's billion with a "b") in 1992,[169] and at the same time, the heavy hand of Big Government has been dipping deeper and deeper into the pockets of middle-class families. In 1948, the average family paid only 4% of its income to the Federal government, but by 1993 the average family was paying more than 35% of its income to the Federal government. This has had a most injurious consequence in the lives of middle-class Americans.

166 Kenneth Mulligan, "The New Counterculture," *NET Policy Insights* 616, September, 1994, 1.

167 Table No. 101, *Statistical Abstract of the United States*, 1993.

168 Tables 78, 80, *Statistical Abstract of the United States*, 1994.

169 Table 577, *Statistical Abstract of the United States*, 1994; Table 449, *Statistical Abstract of the United States*, 1970.

Most middle-class Americans, even if they do not attend church, have an intuitive or "gut" feeling about what is right and what is wrong. This sense of right or wrong has been developed by families over many generations and, therefore, tends to be very conservative in nature; that is, it is stable and resistant to radical change. To the fire-eating liberal extremists who believe they know more and care more than anyone else in society, this cannot be tolerated. In past years, the liberal elite have mounted an unprecedented attack upon those who have and promote the traditional biblical world view, the view espoused by the Founding Fathers of this country. A few examples of liberal extremism are in order.

In September of 1993, Attorney General Janet Reno reinterpreted the definition of what is or is not child pornography, thereby allowing more latitude for the promoters of child pornography. This was done even though the vast majority of America's middle class were horrified at the thought of making child pornography easier to obtain. In October 1993, the Federal bureaucrats in the so-called Equal Employment Opportunity Commission proposed a rule via the infamous *Federal Register* that had the possibility of making it a crime for the owner of a private company to have Bible study on his own property. This rule could have been interpreted by Federal judges in such a manner as to make it a crime to talk to anyone on the job about his religion. If such rules are approved by the Federal government in the future, who will protect "We the people" at the state and local level? Does it not now become clear why Patrick Henry warned Americans not to trust their "dearest interests" to anyone but "We the people" of the sovereign states?

No action by any recent American president has so shocked the good sense of the middle class as the appointment by President Bill Clinton of Dr. Joycelyn Elders as America's Surgeon General. Elders quickly became known as America's condom queen. She came on the American scene at a time when all of liberaldom appeared to have fallen in love with condoms or at least had some type of condom fetish. "A condom in every pocket and two in every purse" seemed to be the motto of the liberal establishment. Every excuse was used as a reason to promote the use of condoms. Making condoms freely available in order to control sexually transmitted diseases and unwanted pregnancies including, of course, teenage pregnancy became a fad with the liberal politically correct movement.

When the middle class tried to reassert its moral values by advocating abstinence for their children, they were ridiculed by the liberal establishment. "Old fashioned," "puritanical," and "out of touch" were common slurs cast at those who desired to teach good morals rather than good sex to their children. Never would liberals allow Americans to think that such archaic ideas as abstinence and chastity could work in post-Christian America.

In 1994, the Southern Baptist Convention began its "True Love Waits" campaign. This campaign consisted of counseling young people about the duty of love and marriage, and the danger of an immoral lifestyle. Once the young people accepted the concept that "True Love Waits," they signed pledge cards to remain abstinent until marriage. More than 200,000 pledge cards were signed and carried to Washington, D.C., to be displayed on the Capitol Mall. A news conference was called; President Bill Clinton, Dr. Joycelyn Elders, Donna Shalala (Director of the Department of Health and Human Services) were all invited to attend and make comments on this inspiring sight. NONE attended! You see, Big Government is not interested in middle-class values, middle-class solutions, or middle-class children. Tom Strode, Communications Director of the Southern Baptist Convention, noted, "It's clear that the administration is not comfortable with abstinence as an appropriate response to teen sexual activity. What these kids are doing and pledging violates one of the cardinal tenets of the liberal faith: It's OK for unmarried kids—for unmarried adults, as well—to be sexually active. They just need to be educated about how to do it. That's the 'safe-sex' myth. And people die from it."[170]

As radical and ridiculous as some of the antics of Dr. Elders have been, it must be remembered that she was confirmed by the United States Senate, with the backing of so-called conservative Democrats and at least twelve Republicans. Again, it must be pointed out that the middle class cannot expect the politicians in Washington to be the sole guardians of their "dearest interests." No one can be trusted with the job of guardian of our life, liberty, and happiness other than we ourselves. Remember the old Greek warning, "Who shall guard the guards?" If we allow the central government in Washington to be the guardian of our "dearest interests." how will we know if it ceases to be our agent and becomes our master?

---

170 Roy Maynard, "Staking Their Lives On It," *World*, August 13, 1994.

The Federal courts have led the way in the liberal attack upon the biblical world view of America's middle class. In 1994, a Federal appeals court ordered a picture of Jesus to be removed from display in a high school hallway. The court ruled that the presence of the picture "entangles" government and religion. The "offending" picture had been hanging in the hallway of that school for no less than thirty years. No doubt, many of the parents of the children attending that school had themselves passed the same picture as they attended "their" school. Most middle-class parents cannot understand why the Federal government desires to involve itself with such purely local matters. Indeed, it is beyond the comprehension of most parents why such a display should cause so many problems; it just does not make good sense to them, and their natural good sense is right.

One of the most offensive attacks upon the Faith of our Fathers and their biblical world view was played out in San Jose, California, whose city fathers spent more than $500,000 of taxpayer money to erect an icon (of course, they called it a statue) to Quetzalcoatl. Quetzalcoatl? Yes, Quetzalcoatl, the pagan Aztec god. You may remember the Aztecs; they had a rather unique idea about religious worship. It involved such uplifting values as human sacrifices, in which hearts were cut out of the chests of screaming victims, and altars covered with the cascading blood of slave sacrifices. The injury to the biblical world view occasioned by the erecting of this icon not being sufficient, the city parks board demanded the removal of a nativity scene from the same park during the Christmas season (you know, separation of church and state!). Thus, the liberal establishment continued its attack up the traditional biblical world view of the middle class. The liberal philosophy seems to be, "Bloody, pagan, Aztec god, yes; Baby Jesus, no!"

The good judgment of the middle class is based upon their common experience. It tells them that the traditional values that they were taught are the same set of values they desire for their children. The hand of history and experience is a strong teacher; the middle class, with their natural desire for stability and permanence, is the natural enemy of the radical, liberal social engineers.

Edmund Burke, the renowned British conservative philosopher, noted that "It is ordained in the eternal constitution of things, that men of intemperate minds cannot be free. Their passions forge their fetters." A common problem faced by every society in its developmental stage is how to control the wild or unrestrained nature of man in his relationships with his fellows. Because of our traditional biblical world view, inherited from our Founding Fathers, America has a mechanism in place to prevent its passions from forging its fetters. Our common history and heritage are the tools needed for the work of controlling "intemperate" minds, but it is in the family where these tools are put to use. This is the one reason the liberal establishment has done all within its power to destroy the one thing that holds society together, America's biblical world view.

Liberals know that the innate conservatism of America's middle-class is a reflection of its cultural inheritance. Because it has a social memory that extends, at least, back to the Founding Fathers of America, the middle class has a tendency to judge the acts of the radical elements of liberalism as the acts of an incendiary at the temple door. To America's middle class, their heritage and history are a deep well of their collective experience as a people. They intuitively know that those who refuse to draw and drink from this well are condemned to die of thirst. The collective experience of Americans teaches each generation that they are the recipients of the labor and sacrifice of others. Armed with this knowledge, they will seek to advance the well-being of their children in the same manner and, in so doing, make a better country for all the children of this land. But, modern liberalism seeks to remove from the middle class their faith in and knowledge of their cultural roots. Without the proper understanding of their heritage, middle-class families cannot defend their place in America.

If there is any doubt as to why we need a strong moral compass, such as our biblical world view, notice the words of one of America's eminent patriots, John Adams: "Our Constitution was made for a moral and religious people. It is wholly inadequate for the governance of any other." James Madison stated that the free government of America was not in the hands of the government but depended upon the ability of the people to govern themselves and to ". . . control ourselves, to sustain ourselves, according to the Ten Commandments of God." But Mr. Madison, haven't you heard about the separation of church and state? Every liberal will defend his role as an antagonist of true religion in America based upon the myth of the "wall of separation between church and state." Yet, as we have demonstrated, no such wall was ever put into place by the

Constitution. If it had, men such as Madison would have never made the preceding statement.

John Adams, James Madison, and a whole generation of American patriots knew that the secret to self-government at the state or Federal level is grounded in our ability as individuals to govern ourselves first. The proven, time-honored, and traditional value system of America demonstrated its ability to produce self-sufficient individuals. Strong individuals, will, in turn, be equipped to play an active role in a free society, which, in turn, will produce a strong free government. Such people do not need government agents or bureaucrats. A self-sufficient society is the death knell to liberalism. Perhaps, this is one reason the liberal establishment is so insistent on the destruction of the core values of the middle class.

More and more Americans are becoming irate when faced with the alterations in our society which are being forced upon all by an arrogant liberal elite. The American middle class is becoming tired of innumerable social engineering projects from a cadre of faceless Federal agents. Attacks upon middle-class religious faith, advertisements for condoms and safe sex rather than abstinence for youth, the normalization of every aberrant sexual behavior known to mankind, the imposition of taxes that make normal family life impossible, and the arrogance of a self-serving Big Brother government that is totally out of control are just a few of the items on the middle class's list of grievances against the Federal government.

As in the other sections of this book, we again ask the question, the most pertinent question for anyone who loves freedom and desires to see true freedom passed on to future generations: "How can America's middle class regain the rights and freedoms already taken from us, and how can we be secure in our freedom once we regain it?" As always, we return to the words of Patrick Henry who warned Americans to be skeptical of those who have the power to infringe upon our "dearest interests." As Henry pointed out, an individual's liberty is secure only when that individual can be the guardian of his own liberty. Instead of attacks upon family values—Why Not Freedom!

SUMMARY
Questions and Answers

Q. If family values are as important as you say, what role would you have the Federal government play in keeping the family strong?

A. None! Nowhere in the Constitution is authority delegated to the Federal government to intercede for or act on behalf of the family unit. All that should be demanded of the Federal government is that it not create an environment that is harmful to the development of strong family units. There are many things the Federal government can, and does, do that will harm the family, but it has little real ability to make families stronger. The Federal government's meager ability to influence the family constructively has driven the liberal establishment mad. Liberals still cling to the false idea that government can solve any and all problems. This socialist idea of government has been proven wrong many times this century, but America's liberal establishment will persist in its efforts to mold and shape families with its state-devised, state-imposed rules and regulations. Thus, "We the people" must reassert our right to govern ourselves and to allow families to develop as the healthy matrix of our society.

CHAPTER 19

Instead of Mob Rule at the Voting Booth—Why Not Freedom!

In a democracy, by definition, the people rule. Their rule is given voice by way of the franchise. The right of free men to vote on their leaders is an integral part of a democracy. Yet, though it may astonish many Americans, this country was not established as a pure democracy. The Founding Fathers made a distinction between the American republic and a democracy. They were concerned about the pernicious effect of "mobocracy" which sooner or later will develop in an unrestricted democracy.

> [A] pure democracy. . . . A common passion or interest will, in almost every case, be felt by a majority of the whole. . . . [Such governments] have ever been found incompatible with personal security or the rights of property. . . . [T]his species of government, have erroneously supposed that by reducing mankind to a perfect equality in their political rights, they would, at the same time be perfectly equalized and assimilated in their possessions, their opinions, and their passions.[171]

John Stuart Mill, the great English civil libertarian, was also concerned about the possibility of mob rule in a democracy.

> The Demos, too, being in America the one source of power, all the selfish ambition of the country gravitates towards it, as it does in despotic countries towards the monarch. The natural tendency of representative government, as of modern civilization, is towards collective mediocrity: and this tendency increased by all reductions and extensions of the franchise, their effect being to place the principal power in the hands of classes more and more below the highest level of instruction in the community.[172]

---

171 James Madison, *The Federalist No. 10,* quoted in George W. Carey and James McClellan, *The Federalist: Student Edition* (Dubuque, IA: Kendall/Hunt Publishing Company, 1990) 46.

172 John S. Mill, *Representative Government,* quoted in *Great Books of the Western World,* Maynard Hutchins, Ed. (Chicago, IL: Encyclopedia Britannica, Inc., 1952) XLIII; 375, 381.

The liberal establishment prefers the concept of "universal franchise," or as the Federal court defined it, "one man, one vote." Liberals favor schemes such as "motor voter bills" in which an individual can register to vote when he gets a driver's license (of course, he has to pass a test and prove that he has the ability to drive a car, no such accounting is required for the act of voting) OR when he applies for welfare. The fact that under this plan thousands of illegal aliens are allowed to vote is of no concern to the liberal. Illegal aliens, according to liberal logic, are human beings (which is not the point of contention for conservatives) who now live in America, they pay taxes when they buy goods, and, therefore, they deserve the right to vote. The concept that voting is a "right" that automatically belongs to everyone, instead of a "privilege" to be obtained after demonstrating certain, non-arbitrary qualifications, is the primary dividing line between a "mobocracy" and the "democratic" republic established by the Founding Fathers.

The liberal establishment has used the "one man, one vote" universal franchise scheme to ensure the electorial victory of its candidates. Once a society starts down the road to unlimited franchise, it opens itself up to massive election frauds. Liberals are experts in manipulating the present franchise system to ensure victory for their candidates. Judge Clarence Newcomer stated that, during the November 1993 elections in Philadelphia, the liberal campaign engaged in a "massive scheme" that included ballot fraud, forgery, intimidation, and voter harassment.[173] Election officials, who were a part of the liberal ruling establishment, were permitted to take absentee ballots around to black and hispanic neighbors "helping" with "a new way to vote."[174] The liberal Justice Department had reacted quickly in a case involving conservative Ed Rollins and allegations that he paid black ministers to support conservative candidates. Yet this same Justice Department was slow to investigate the documented cases of illegal voter fraud across the river in Philadelphia.[175] A United States district judge ruled that the liberal Democrats participated in a "civil conspiracy"[176] in an attempt to throw the election by defrauding the electorate.

173 "A New Way to Vote," *The Wall Street Journal,* February 25, 1994, editorial page.

174 Ibid

175 Ibid

176 "Aside," *The Wall Street Journal,* May 4, 1994, editorial page.

Liberals want a loose and easy scheme for voter registration because it makes it easier for them to mass their welfare and quasi-welfare voting block. It also makes it easier to conduct voter fraud as they did in Philadelphia during the November 1993 election.

We are confronted with a dilemma when we discuss voter qualifications. On one extreme, we can have a society that has no qualifications—just show up and vote—and on the other extreme we can have such restrictive qualifications that only a very small percentage of the population can vote—such as in the former Soviet Union where only Communist party members could vote in party elections.

When conservatives begin to discuss the topic of legitimate voting qualifications, the liberal establishment reacts as if an unpardonable sin has been committed. Is universal suffrage one of those sacred dogmas of democracy? Is it a form of democratic heresy even to discuss the topic other than to praise it? The liberal establishment will attempt to discredit anyone who dares to examine universal suffrage or who doubts its efficacy. The term "universal suffrage" conceals a gross fallacy. The authors are not aware of any elected liberal who supports the concept of "universal" suffrage. Even liberals believe that some qualifications should be established prior to allowing an individual to exercise the privilege of voting. The question is not if there should be qualifications, but whether those qualifications should be loose and easy or restrictive. To our knowledge, there are no elected conservatives who support the concept of establishing arbitrary qualification standards that would permanently preclude a given group or individuals from enjoying the privilege of voting. The concept of "universal" suffrage, by definition, is not advocated by liberals, because even liberals restrict voting to those eighteen and older. On the other hand, conservatives do not advocate a restrictive franchise such as occurred in early America when women, non-whites, and non-property holders were denied the privilege of voting. Some people may honestly question why conservatives should advocate non-arbitrary qualifications to qualify for the franchise.

Let us suppose that we live in a democracy with a population of four million people whose government supports the concept of "one man, one vote," that is, universal suffrage. In this hypothetical democracy, let us assume that there are one million citizens who are less than eighteen years old and therefore are not allowed to vote; let us further assume that there are another one million citizens who have been convicted of and are in prison for committing violent crimes and, therefore, not allowed to vote; and, just to make it interesting, let us assume that there are one million citizens who suffer from extreme psychological impairment and are permanently committed to mental health facilities and thus not allowed to vote. The result is that, even in our "one man, one vote" democracy that practices universal suffrage, only 25% of the citizens are actually allowed to exercise the right to vote. In other words, 75% of the population of this democracy is denied the right to vote, therefore, the 25% numerical minority deny the numerical majority their right of suffrage. How can one-fourth of the population justify denying three-fourths of the population their "right" to vote in a democracy? The numerical minority does this by appealing to the principle of *incapacity*—that is, some people are not *qualified* to vote.

> Universal suffrage means, then, universal suffrage for those who are capable. . . . Who are capable? Are minors, . . . insane persons, and persons who have committed certain major crimes the only ones to be determined incapable? A closer examination of the subject shows us the motive which causes the right of suffrage to be based upon the supposition of incapacity. The motive is that the elector or voter does not exercise this right for himself alone, but for everybody. The most extended elective system and the most restricted elective system are alike in this respect. They differ only in respect to what constitutes incapacity. It is not a difference of principle, but merely a difference of degree.
>
> If . . . the right of suffrage arrives with one's birth, it would be an injustice for adults to prevent . . . children from voting. Why are they [children] prevented? Because they are presumed to be incapable. And why is incapacity a motive for exclusion? Because it is not the voter alone who suffers the consequences of his vote; because each vote touches and affects everyone in the entire community; because the people in the community have a right to demand some safe guards concerning the acts upon which their welfare and existence depend. . . .
>
> . . . [T]his controversy over universal suffrage . . . would lose nearly all of its importance if the law had always been what it ought to be. . . . In fact, if law were restricted to protecting all persons, all liberties, and all properties; if law were nothing more than the organized combination of the individual's right to self

defense; if law were the obstacle, the check, the punisher of all oppression and plunder—is it likely that we citizens would then argue much about the extent of the franchise?

. . . Is it likely that the excluded classes would refuse to peaceably await the coming of their right to vote?. . . . If the law were confined to its proper functions, everyone's interest in the law would be the same. Is it not clear that, under these circumstances, those who voted could not inconvenience those who did not vote? But on the other hand, imagine that this fatal principle has been introduced: Under the pretense of organization, regulation, protection, or encouragement, the law takes property from one person and gives it to another; the law takes the wealth of all and gives it to a few—whether farmers, manufacturers, ship owners, artists, or comedians. Under these circumstances, then certainly every class will aspire to grasp the law, and logically so.

The excluded classes will furiously demand their right to vote—and will overthrow society rather than not to obtain it. Even beggars and vagabonds will then prove to you that they also have an incontestable title to vote. They will say to you: "We cannot buy wine, tobacco, or salt without paying the tax. And a part of the tax that we pay is given by law—in privileges and subsidies—to men who are richer than we are. Others use the law to raise the prices of bread, meat, iron, or cloth. Thus, since everyone else uses the law for his own profit, we also would like to use the law for our own profit. We demand from the law *the right to relief,* which is the poor man's plunder. To obtain their right, we also should be voters and legislators in order that we may organize Beggary on a grand scale. . . .

As long as it is admitted that the law may be diverted from its true purpose—then everyone will want to participate in making the law, either to protect himself against plunder or to use it for plunder.[177]

The preceding words are all the more dramatic when we realize that they were not written by a contemporary, conservative American political analyst but by Frederic Bastiat, an 1850 French political observer! He made three important points: (1) the law can be used as a legal excuse to plunder the property of private citizens, (2) the

---

177 Frederic Bastiat, *The Law* (1850, Irvington-On-Hudson, NY: The Foundation For Economic Education, Inc., 1979) 14-18.

right of suffrage is not a purely individual right, but a right that affects society at large—this is due to the ability of government to engage in "legal" plunder of the property of individual citizens, and (3) some individuals are incapable of exercising the right to vote in a manner that would be consistent with the maintenance of a free society. For these reasons, conservatives must insist upon reasonable, non-arbitrary voting qualifications being met before an individual is allowed to exercise his right to vote. Our purpose is to ensure that the tax-consuming portion of our society is not given a blank check upon the property rights of the tax-paying portion of society.

The liberal establishment has constructed an efficient political machine that has organized the welfare and quasi-welfare voters into an efficient voting block to ensure the election of liberal, social welfare candidates who, after being elected, will enact social programs that have the effect of transferring the property of the middle-class taxpayers to the tax-consuming, liberal voting class. Liberals will resist any conservative plan to strengthen voting qualifications. Why? Because they know that any effort to prevent tax consumers from plundering the property of the taxpayers will cause a decrease in their liberal welfare and quasi-welfare voting block. In short, liberals will lose the voting strength they depend upon to win elections.

Most Americans assume that the right to vote is the primary means that they have to protect their liberty. While the right of suffrage is important, its importance is maintained only when used within the framework of limited Federalism, State's Rights, and State Sovereignty. Voting alone is not sufficient to protect the liberties and property of the average citizen when that citizen is confronted with an abusive and oppressive Federal government. John C. Calhoun noted that the right of suffrage is

> [T]he indispensable and primary principle in the foundation
> of a constitutional government. When this right is properly
> guarded, and the people sufficiently enlightened to understand
> their own rights and the interests of the community. . . .[178]

Calhoun warns that, even though a large number of people think that suffrage alone is sufficient to form a constitutional government, they are dangerously wrong. Calhoun, writing in the late 1840s, agrees with Bastiat that government has within itself a tendency to

---

178 John C. Calhoun, *The Works of John C. Calhoun* (New York, NY: D. Appleton and Company, 1844) 12-13.

abuse its powers. This tendency toward plundering other people's property cannot be counteracted by the right to vote.

> The right of suffrage, of itself, can do no more than give complete control to those who elect, over the conduct of those they have elected. . . . The sum total, then, of its effects, when most successful, is, to make those elected the true and faithful representatives of those who elected them. . . .[179]

Calhoun is warning us of the danger of relying on universal suffrage to protect the interests of the entire country. In a democracy, the majority rules—but does majority rule authorize the legalized plundering of the numerical minority?

> [Suffrage] only changes the seat of authority, without counteracting, in the least, the tendency of the government to oppression and abuse of its powers.[180]

As Bastiat noted, if the purpose of the law were limited to protecting only the liberty and property of all citizens, then there would be no struggle to control government. But, because the control of government may be used to plunder the property of some for the benefit of others, then various interests strive to gain control of government either to prevent the seizure of private property or to plunder the private property of those who have no effective means to protect their property from the government tax collector. The liberal establishment would not dare use the term "plunder" to describe their activities. They would garnish it with such verbiage as "equitable income redistribution," "soaking the rich," or some other bombastic verbal smoke screen to disguise their plundering of middle-class private property.

Some may ask why the democratic principle of majority rule would present such a risk to a free society; after all, majority rule is the foundation of free government. Yes, it is the foundation, but it is not the entire structure! Calhoun explains why the unbridled rule of the numerical majority can be so dangerous to the liberty and property of the numerical minority:

> If the whole community had the same interests so that the interests of each and every portion would be so affected by the action of the government, that the laws which oppressed or impoverished

179 Ibid, 13-14.

180 Ibid

one portion, would necessarily oppress and impoverish all others, or the reverse, then the right of suffrage, of itself, would be all-sufficient to counteract the tendency of the government to oppression and abuse of its powers. . . .[181]

Patrick Henry had warned Southerners about the conflicting interests that existed between the commercial interests of the Northeast and the agricultural interests of the South. He predicted that the day would come when the "dearest interests" of the South would be legislated away by a Northern-controlled Congress intent on protecting the commercial interests of their section.[182] The Tariff of Abomination in 1828 and South Carolina's nullification brought about a constitutional crisis that was still burning in Calhoun's memory. Calhoun and Southerners in general had first-hand knowledge of the dangers inherent in the democratic rule of the numerical majority.

[N]othing [is] more easy than to pervert its powers into instruments to aggrandize and enrich one or more interests by oppressing and impoverishing the others; and this too, under the operation of laws, couched in general terms; and which, on their face, appear fair and equal. Nor is this the case in some particular communities only. It is so in all. . . .[183]

John C. Calhoun clearly demonstrated the danger of relying upon suffrage as the only mechanism to control the tendency of government to abuse its power, oppress its citizens, and plunder their property.

John Stuart Mill (1806-1873), an English defender of civil liberties, established the basic qualifications for a citizen to meet in order to earn the privilege of exercising the right to vote. The basic principle of the franchise is that citizens would not be disqualified except through their own fault, and no arbitrary barriers should be established by which any person is permanently excluded from voting. The privilege must be open to all who are willing to earn it.

The first qualification recommended by Mill was that anyone who desired to exercise the right to vote must first learn how to read and write as well as gain basic knowledge in history, geography, and mathematics.

181 Ibid

182 Patrick Henry, quoted in William Wirt Henry, Ed., *Patrick Henry: Life, Correspondence, and Speeches* (1891, Harrisonburg, VA: Sprinkle Publications, 1993) III; 520.

183 Calhoun, 15.

[I]t is wholly inadmissible that any person should participate in the suffrage without being able to read, write, and I will add, perform the common operations of arithmetic . . . people would no more think of giving the suffrage to a man who could not read, than of giving it to a child who could not speak; and it would not be society that would exclude him, but his own laziness. When society has not performed its duty, by rendering this amount of instruction accessible to all, there is some hardship in the case, but this is a hardship that ought to be borne. . . . No one but those in whom an a priori theory has silenced common sense will maintain that power over others, over the whole community, should be imparted to people who have not acquired the commonest and most essential requisites for taking care of themselves. . . . It would be eminently desirable that other things besides reading, writing and arithmetic could be made necessary to the suffrage; that some knowledge of the conformation of the earth, its natural and political divisions, the elements of general history and of the history and institutions of their own country, could be required from all electors. . . . [A]fter a few years it would exclude none but those who cared so little for the privilege, that their vote, if given, would not in general be an indication of any real political opinion.[184]

Mill agrees with Bastiat that those who cannot read and write do not possess the capacity to govern their fellow citizens. Their incapacity is not necessarily a permanent disqualification. They have within themselves the capacity to remove their incapacity. Liberals will ask why conservatives believe in punishing the illiterate. We conservatives should reply with our own question to the liberal, "Why would you punish the entire community by making ignorance equal to knowledge?"

It is not useful, but hurtful, that the constitution of the country should declare ignorance to be entitled to as much political power as knowledge. . . .[185]

The second requirement is that being a taxpayer should be a prerequisite to voting.

Mill stressed the point that those who are required to pay the taxes will make a more intelligent and thoughtful decision as to whom they

---

184 John S. Mill, *Representative Government*, quoted in *Great Books of the Western World*, Maynard Hutchins, Ed. (Chicago, IL: Encyclopedia Britannica, Inc., 1952), XLIII; 382-83.

185 Ibid, 387-88.

put in charge of the tax collecting authority. Mill also emphasized that he did not consider an indirect or easy tax to be sufficient to fulfill this requirement. In other words, a sales tax or payroll tax that is paid in what amounts to easy installments will not affect the average citizen enough to make him conscious of the fact that his government is depriving him of his property.

> It is also important, that the assembly which votes the taxes, either general or local, should be elected exclusively by those who pay something towards the taxes imposed. Those who pay no taxes, disposing by their votes of other people's money, have every motive to be lavish and none to economize. As far as money matters are concerned, any power of voting possessed by them is a violation of the fundamental principle of free government. . . . It amounts to allowing them to put their hands into other people's pockets for any purpose which they think fit to call a public one . . . the indirect taxes. . . . But this mode of defraying a share of the public expenses is hardly felt: the payer, unless a person of education and reflection, does not identify his interest with a low scale of public expenditure as closely as when money for its support is demanded directly from himself. . . . It would be better that a direct tax, in the simple form of a capitation, should be levied on every grown person in the community; or that every such person should be admitted an elector on allowing himself to be rated extra ordiem to the assessed taxes; or that a small annual payment, rising and falling with the gross expenditure of the country, should be required from every registered elector; that so everyone might feel that the money which he assisted in voting was partly his own, and that he was interested in keeping down its amount.[186]

The ability of politicians to pass "easy" taxes has been a key element in the growth of Big Government at both the state and Federal levels. By linking the right to vote to the obligation of paying for more government, we could change the ease with which politicians use the taxpayer's money to pay off their political debts.

The third requirement of voting is that those who supply their existence with public relief (welfare, public housing, etc.) should not be allowed to exercise the privilege of voting.

I regard it as required by first principles, that the receipt of

186 Ibid, 383.

parish relief should be a peremptory disqualification for the franchise. He who cannot by his labor suffice for his own support has no claim to the privilege of helping himself to the money of others. By becoming dependent on the remaining members of the community for actual subsistence, he abdicates his claim to equal rights with them in other respects. Those to whom he is indebted for the continuance of his very existence may justly claim the exclusive management of those common concerns to which he now brings nothing, or less than he takes away. As a condition of the franchise, a term should be fixed, say five years previous to the registry, during which the applicant's name has not been on the parish books as a recipient of relief.[187]

The fourth qualification for voting established by Mill is similar to the third. It would deny the privilege of voting to those who take advantage of bankruptcy and thereby shift their personal burden upon society who must, through higher prices, insurance rates, lending rates, and, as in the Savings and Loan bail outs, higher taxes, finance another's failure.

To be certified bankrupt, or to have taken the benefit of the Insolvent Act should disqualify for the franchise until the person has paid his debts or at least proved that he is not now, and has not for some long period been, dependent on eleemosynary support.[188]

The authors would add a fifth qualification, one that unfortunately is necessary in our day, but the need for such an exclusion was unthinkable in Mill's day. Any person who has been convicted of a felony should not be allowed to exercise the right of voting for some specific time after he has completed his prison sentence. In other words, as far as suffrage is concerned he is on probation for say five years after he has completed his time in prison. If he keeps a "clean" record and meets the other qualifications, then he will have earned the right to exercise the right to vote. A criminal who has "paid his debt to society" by remaining behind bars for the duration of his prison term has offered society no evidence of his rehabilitation. Before he is allowed to help govern society, he must first demonstrate that he has reformed his life.

187 Ibid
188 Ibid

A restrictive franchise that is administered fairly and equally will help to maintain our democratic republic and prevent it from being turned into a pure democracy or, as we have termed it, a "mobocracy." It should be restated that no qualification should be allowed that would permanently deny an individual the right to earn the privilege of voting. A restrictive franchise will help prevent the government from being used as an instrument of plunder. The ability of government to plunder middle-class[189] property by way of taxation must be controlled by those who pay for that government and not those who enjoy the monies taken by government from the hard-working people of the country. There must be a barrier between the property of the taxpayers and the insatiable appetite of the tax consumers. This barrier must be established by "We the people" of the sovereign state. The legislature of the sovereign state of New Jersey clearly declared and defended the state's right to enact such legislation. New Jersey denounced an act of the Federal Congress that would

> ... transfer to Congress the whole control of the right of suffrage in the State, and to deprive the State of a free representation by destroying the power of regulating suffrage within its own limits, a power which they have never been willing to surrender to the general government, and which was reserved to the States as the fundamental principle on which the Constitution itself was constructed—principles of self-government.[190]

The people of New Jersey, through their representatives in their state legislature, acknowledged the fact that regulation of the franchise belongs to the state as a reserved right under the original Constitution. This reserved right of the sovereign state is a right that is inseparable from the principle of free government.

Instead of mob rule at the voting booth—Why Not Freedom!

---

189 We emphasize protecting middle class property because the larger share of income is paid by the middle class as taxes, but the same principle is true for all people regardless of what economic class they belong to.

190 James R. Kennedy and Walter D. Kennedy, *The South Was Right!* (Gretna, LA: Pelican Publishing Company, 1994) 373.

SUMMARY
Questions and Answers

Q. What chance would people in the minority have in obtaining a fair and equal opportunity to vote if there were not a strong Federal government to protect their right to vote?

A. Your comment about a strong Federal government providing for the right to vote reminds us of the cliche that declares, "Any government strong enough to give you anything is also strong enough to take anything you have away." Let's look at American history and see if, indeed, the Federal government must play a role in making it easier for a group of non-voters to receive the franchise. Early in American history, many states required relatively large property ownership as a qualification to vote. Yet, before the Federal government became a "voter qualification" activist, people who owned little or no property received the right to vote. In the 1840s, the state of Rhode Island had such a stiff voter requirement that less than one-half of the adult male population could exercise the right to vote. Yet, this inequity was solved by the people of the sovereign state of Rhode Island without Federal intervention.

The right of women to vote was extended to many women in various states before it became the law of the land by the passage of the Nineteenth Amendment. It should be noted that this took place by constitutional methods, and not by Federal edict. Thus, the sovereign states acted as was prescribed in the Constitution.

CHAPTER 20

Instead of the Federal Government's Assault on Free Speech— Why Not Freedom!

"Congress shall make no law . . . abridging the freedom of speech"; these precious words are found in the First Amendment of the United States Constitution, a part of what we fondly refer to as the Bill of Rights. The language cannot be clearer. The Bill of Rights was intended as a clear and concise limitation on the power and, therefore, the ability of the Federal government to infringe upon the right of free speech. Our Founding Fathers had every intention of making sure that Americans would never have to live in fear of punishment by the Federal government simply because they spoke their minds. As we have noted throughout this book, clear limitations written into the Constitution are no guarantee that the Federal government will respect the rights and liberties of "We the people" of the sovereign states. The case of the Berkeley Three is an excellent example of just how far America has traveled down the slippery slope of Federal tyranny.

Three private citizens and homeowners in Berkeley, California, became concerned about the possible loss of their property value because of the announced plan of Housing and Urban Development (HUD) to establish a housing project for the homeless in their neighborhood. The American dream of home ownership is one of the hallmarks of the hard-working American middle class. The middle class's home equity is usually the greater part of their financial resources. It should be no surprise that the middle class would respond negatively when a Federal agency announces a policy that would have the effect of driving down the value of homes in the affected area. As explained in Chapter 15, the use of Federal tax resources to implement programs that cause middle-class homeowners to lose property value is a direct violation of the "taking" section of the Fifth Amendment. As we shall now see, the Federal government has no more respect for the constitutional provisions

protecting freedom of speech than it has for the constitutional prohibition against unjust taking of private property!

The Berkeley Three labored under the false notion that, in America, a citizen is free to speak his mind on public policy issues. Wrong!
Today, you and I are free from possible persecution only if we freely
parrot left-wing, politically correct ideas—something middle-class
Americans tend to refrain from doing. When news of their public
opposition reached the HUD thought police, a Federally sponsored
investigation of the three was initiated. What law had they broken?
According to HUD officials, opposition to HUD housing proposals
constitutes harassment of disabled minorities, and, therefore, such
speech is not protected by the First Amendment! For speaking up for
their property rights, the Berkeley Three faced up $100,000 in fines
and a year in jail! One can only imagine the chilling effect this had
on free speech. Who would dare voice opposition to the government
program and subject himself to Federal investigations, fines, and jail?
No, most people would opt to "go along just to get along." But, can
you really blame people who find themselves in such a situation?
Who can afford to match the spending power of the Federal government in court? The cost of a legal defense for a private citizen,
even if he should win, would be in the hundreds of thousands of
dollars. The average law-abiding, taxpaying citizen just can't afford to
take on the Federal government.

Luckily for the Three, *The Wall Street Journal* and talk radio
reported their case.[191] The exposure of HUD's outrageous attack
upon constitutionally protected free speech by these sources caused
HUD to relent in its attack on the Berkeley Three. Yet, we must
remember here that the Federal tyrant did not relent with its attack
on free speech because of the Federal government's respect for the
right of free speech, but because its crime had been exposed! Others
are not so lucky. Strange, but middle-class Americans who oppose
certain Federal agencies are now in a situation similar to the Rus-
sian dissidents in the former Soviet Union. The only way the Rus-
sian dissidents could gain protection was to be lucky enough to have
their names and stories printed in a Western newspaper. According
to *The Wall Street Journal*, HUD has established new guidelines to prevent gross violations of the First Amendment. Unfortunately for us
all, these new Federal guidelines, established to protect our right to

191 "HUD's Thought Police," *The Wall Street Journal*, August 23, 1994, editorial page.

free speech, are shot through with loopholes and bureaucratic waffle words.[192] From experience we can expect that these loopholes and waffle words will eventually be used by zealot liberals to enforce their politically correct agenda upon an unwilling middle class.

The Assistant Secretary for Fair Housing and Equal Employment published an article in which she warned Americans that we "can expect more cases" similar to the Berkeley case. Even though the Federal agency published new rules that were assumed to guard against infringement of free speech, the agency has dropped only eleven of the thirty-four pending investigations. Expecting the Federal government to police itself is tantamount to asking a hungry fox to guard the hen house! If the chickens expect to survive, they had better find a way to slam the door on the fox as soon as he tries to stick his nose into the hen house.

The left-wing liberal media will rush in and defend the Federal government by claiming that the Berkeley Three case was an isolated incident. As always, never trust the liberal media. While the Berkeley Three case was being prosecuted, the Federal government was also prosecuting (or is it persecuting?) a similar case in Manhattan's Gramercy Park. It seems that a group of citizens there joined together and attempted to outbid a developer because they wanted to purchase the site in question to prevent the development of a proposed shelter for the homeless. The Federal government decided that it would not tolerate such free-market competition. In America these days, it is easier for the Federal government to drag private citizens through its courts on charges of housing discrimination than it is to take criminals off the streets or defend America's borders from an invasion of illegal aliens.

The Federal government has agents who scan the classified ads of local newspapers in an attempt to bring discrimination criminals to Federal justice. In Wisconsin, a fifty-year-old divorced woman ran a simple ad in an attempt to rent a room in her home. The criminal language of the ad read: "Apartment for rent, 1 bedroom, electric included, mature Christian handyman." This ad cost the lady $8,000 in legal fees and fines.[193] You see, she was guilty of religious and sexual discrimination. In 1988, Congress changed the Federal Fair

192 Heather MacDonald, "HUD Continues Its Assault on Free Speech," *The Wall Street Journal*, September 14, 1994, A23.

193 "HUD's Thought Police," *The Wall Street Journal*, August 23, 1994, editorial page.

Housing Act to make it illegal for a private individual to place an ad that may appear to discriminate. This Federal law is so onerous that it was used by the politically correct crowd to bankrupt a chain of California newspapers. The papers ran an ad that used the words "adults preferred." There goes freedom of the press along with freedom of speech! The interesting thing about the 1988 revised Federal law is the name of the president who signed it. Or, perhaps more specifically, the political party to which belonged. The signature is that of President George Bush, Republican, conservative, or so we thought. The point is made again; we cannot trust either the Republican or the Democratic party to protect the rights and liberties of "We the people." As exhibited here, party politics are more important to the Republican leadership than the struggle to preserve and protect the rights and freedoms of America's middle class. We must devise or, more aptly, re-invent, a better system than mere party politicking if we intend to protect our constitutional liberties.

The Federal government's assault on freedom of speech has even invaded the Federal Bureau of Investigation. The FBI, in an October 1993 letter, admitted that other Federal agencies were using the FBI to investigate individuals who were applying for jobs in those agencies. The purpose of the FBI's investigation was to make sure that the applicants were "free of biases against any class of citizens." The FBI is being used to make sure applicants not only are free from personal discriminatory acts but also are free from discriminatory thoughts. The applicant's neighbors are asked by the FBI if they have ever heard the applicant tell a racist joke or say anything that would indicate he is prejudiced.[194] It has been reported that recent presidents told racial jokes or used racial slurs. Would they have passed FBI thought police muster? Do we need a Federal thought police? Who defines what is and what is not acceptable, government-approved speech. Are redneck jokes racist? If a black comedian uses the "n" word (which happens on modern TV) is he a racist? What if the comedian is white—is there a different standard for white people?

The use of Federal power to investigate private speech is beyond the scope and purpose of any constitutional provision regarding legitimate Federal powers. Who can protect the individual citizen when he finds himself confronted and harassed by the virtually

194 Jeremy J. Stone, "PC Invades the FBI," *The Wall Street Journal,* November 2, 1993, editorial page.

unlimited power and resources of the Federal government? If we love our liberty, we must find the answer to this essential question. But, be of good cheer! The answer has already been found and effectively used by two of America's greatest statesmen, Thomas Jefferson and James Madison!

Congress, in 1798, violated the Bill of Rights when it passed the Alien and Sedition Acts. The purpose of these acts was to stifle political opposition to President John Adams. Essentially, these acts made it a Federal crime "to oppose any measure or measures of the government of the United States . . . if any person shall write, print, utter, or publish [that opposition]. . . ." Sounds strangely familiar to certain contemporary anti-discrimination laws passed by the Federal government! What can a citizen do when his rights are infringed upon by the Federal government? Neo-conservatives and liberals alike will tell us that we can always take our case to the United States Supreme Court. Of course, that presumes we have the financial resources to fight the government in its own courts. In 1798, as is the case most of the time today, the United States Supreme Court sided with the Federal government (surprise, surprise). The supposed guardians of our dearest rights and liberties actually championed the cause of oppression!

Look at how well the United States Supreme Court defended the civil liberties of American citizens. Supreme Court Justice Samuel Chase used the Alien and Sedition Acts as an excuse to indict the editor of the *Richmond Examiner* for sedition.[195] The editor was tried and found guilty. A Vermont Congressman published an article critical of President John Adams. He was indicted for sedition, tried before Supreme Court Justice William Patterson, found guilty, and sentenced to four months in jail. Another American refused to divulge the names of his friends who shared his anti-Federalist views. Federal Justice Chase was so enraged that he fined the man $450 and sentenced him to jail for eighteen months. All of these things were happening, here in America, a mere decade after the ratification of the Bill of Rights. (Do you still feel that the Federal courts are the true protectors of your civil liberties?) What was the popular reaction to this unconstitutional attack on individual rights by the Federal government? The response was quick and decisive.

195 James R. Kennedy and Walter D. Kennedy, *The South Was Right!* (Gretna, LA: Pelican Publishing Company, 1994) 231.

No two men did more to establish the principle of individual liberty in America that Thomas Jefferson and James Madison, both Southerners from Virginia. When, in 1798, the Federal government unconstitutionally extended its authority over the private citizen and when its own Federal court system endorsed the unconstitutional acts, the people looked to the one remaining check against undue Federal intrusion—they looked to their sovereign state to protect their liberties. The states of Virginia and Kentucky declared the Alien and Sedition Acts to be unconstitutional and, therefore, unenforceable within the sovereign states of Virginia and Kentucky. The famous Virginia and Kentucky Resolutions[196] were written by James Madison (also known as the father of our Constitution) and Thomas Jefferson (author of the Declaration of Independence). Here we see the grand function of local self-government as the state interposed its protective sovereign authority between its defenseless citizens and a belligerent and oppressive Federal government. The words of the Virginia Resolution resound down to this day with the promise of protection for the little man when faced with the unlimited resources of an aggressive Federal government: "Resolved, that the several States composing the United States of America are not united on the principle of unlimited submission to their general government . . . whensoever the general government assumes un-delegated powers, its acts are unauthoritative, void, and of no force . . . this government, created by this compact [the Constitution] was not made the exclusive or final judge to the extent of the powers delegated to itself. . . . [E]ach party [each state] has equal right to judge for itself." These resolutions demonstrate the central premise of the original American government, the right of local self-government, the duty of the state to stand between an aggressive Federal government, and the civil liberties of the people of the state. The authority of the sovereign state has been used by states such as Massachusetts and Wisconsin to nullify sections of the Constitution, acts of Congress, and Supreme Court decisions that the people of those states felt were in violation of their moral obligations to humanity. The Constitution provided for the return of fugitive slaves in Article IV, Section 2. Because of the change in sentiment of many Northern states, this constitutional provision was held to be in violation of

196 Ibid, 165.

their moral values regarding slavery.[197] Yet, the Constitution plainly required them to return runaway slaves. They had agreed to those conditions when they accepted the proposed Constitution, so what were they to do? Simply, within the bounds of their sovereign state, all such laws were declared null and void. The states, as declared in the Virginia and Kentucky Resolutions, were the final judge. In his farewell address to the U.S. Senate, Jefferson Davis acknowledged the validity of nullification as practiced by the Northern states.[198] Yes, our Constitutional Forefathers provided us with a remedy for acts of the Federal government that are unconstitutional. But, what happened to this grand American defense for civil liberty?

The key to protecting the private citizen from an oppressive Federal government is the strength of the sovereign state in which the citizen resides. According to Supreme Court Justice Salmon P. Chase (1864-1873), "State Sovereignty died at Appomattox." Strange that a judge would use trial by combat to justify a radical change in constitutional government. Ever since the defeat of the South in the War for Southern Independence, the Federal government has assumed the right to be the exclusive judge of the extent of its power. What would have happened if the people of Virginia and Kentucky had been forced to rely upon the Federal government to protect their liberties in 1798? The answer is clear. We cannot trust the thief to be the arbitrator of whether his conduct is right or wrong. We cannot trust a hungry fox to guard the hen house. Today, "We the people" of the sovereign states are left to fend for ourselves when our rights and liberties are oppressed by the Federal government. Who will guard the guards? We must trust our dearest rights and liberties to no one other than ourselves. Instead of a Federal government that denies its citizens free speech—Why Not Freedom!

SUMMARY
Questions and Answers

Q. How does the Federal government's attempt to promote better living conditions for the poor constitute an attack upon free speech, and, even if it did, how does this noble effort cause a problem as far as our political rights?

197 Ibid, 214-15.
198 Ibid, 316.

A. Any time government attempts to stifle the free expression of ideas, a precious element of our free society is diminished. If government can repress speech because it is deemed by the government to be critical of a government policy, then any opposition to government policy is destroyed. In a free society, the government must stand in the public eye and abide by the criticism of the members of that society. Without such criticism, no free government will remain free. William Rawle of Philadelphia, Pennsylvania, made the following statement about free speech in his 1825 textbook on the United States Constitution: "The foundation of a free government begins to be undermined when freedom of speech on political subjects is restrained; it is destroyed when freedom of speech is wholly denied." When considering our rights as citizens of this country, we should realize that all freedoms are interconnected. If we lose one freedom, such as freedom of speech, then all others are equally in peril of being taken away from us. When it comes to political matters, as a free society we must be careful to allow free speech its fullest latitude—even in those areas in which we may not fully agree with the opinions being expressed.

CHAPTER 21

Instead of Federal Attacks Upon Private Property Rights—Why Not Freedom!

The right to the peaceful and secure use and enjoyment of private property is a key element in the creation of a free society. As John C. Calhoun noted, man needs government to enforce rules that prevent a stronger person from abusing the property of the weaker person. Government was established to prevent the chaos that results when the law of the jungle becomes the order of the day. Domestic tranquility (law and order) provides an environment in which legitimate commerce can take place leading to the growth and development of higher societies and civilizations.

The property rights of a serf are dependent upon the will of the Lord of the Manor. A free man's use of his private property is encumbered only by those restraints his society places upon the use of inherently dangerous property. For example, a citizen who owns a gunpowder manufacturing plant would not be allowed to place the plant next to a school even though he owns the property adjacent to the school building. There are a few restrictions, but, by and large, a free man is unencumbered as to the use or disposition of his private property.

The importance of property rights was recognized by our Colonial Forefathers. The Virginia Declaration of Independence, penned by Thomas Jefferson, states that there are certain inalienable rights, three of which are the right to "life, liberty, and property." Sound familiar? In the joint Declaration of Independence of July 4, 1776, the term "pursuit of happiness" was substituted for "property." Jefferson and the Founding Fathers recognized the relationship between property rights and the "pursuit of happiness."

Amendment V of the United States Constitution states, "No person shall . . . be deprived of life, liberty, or property, without due process of law; nor shall private property be taken for public use, without just compensation." The "taking" clause and the "due process" clause of the Fifth Amendment plainly establish, as an American principle, respect for private property rights. Arthur Lee of Virginia in 1775 declared, "The right of property is the guardian of every other right, and to deprive the people of this, is in fact to deprive them of their liberty."[199] The "taking" clause was placed in the Constitution by the Founding Fathers to protect our inalienable property rights.

In 1938, Franklin D. Roosevelt's Supreme Court made a frontal attack against private property rights. In *U.S. v. Carolene Products Co.*, the United States Supreme Court ruled that government actions (such as regulations) affecting economic rights will be less closely scrutinized than those affecting fundamental rights such as speech and voting, or the rights of minorities. With this decision, the Federal Supreme Court declared that middle-class property rights were secondary to any right that could be asserted by the Federal government's "protected minorities." This began an era in which the liberal-controlled Federal government looked upon two classes of rights protected by the Constitution. Those rights are described as "civil rights" and all other rights enumerated in the Bill of Rights. For instance, the Second Amendment protection of the right to keep and bear arms was (according to the liberal interpretation) of less importance than, say, the right of a "protected minority" to receive a welfare check. The rights reserved to the sovereign state by "We the people" in the Tenth Amendment were less important and would receive less protection from the Federal tribunals than, say, the right of a criminal to have an air-conditioned cell and access to gym equipment. Of course, it was merely chance that the greater percentage of those criminals just happen to belong to the Federal government's "protected minorities." Read the Constitution as closely as you may, and you will never find even a hint that the Founding Fathers intended to treat some rights as more important than others. Nowhere will you find even an implied intention to place property rights second to any other civil right. Yet, the Federal Supreme Court has assumed the right to re-write the Constitution to the detriment of America's middle class.

Bill Ellen's case is typical of the numerous Federal abuses of private citizens and their right to use their private property. Ellen is a

---

199 Arthur Lee, quoted in James Ely, *The Guardian of Every Other Right: A Constitutional History of Property Rights* (NY: Oxford University Press, 1992) 14.

Vietnam veteran who was sent to prison by the same government that he had so faithfully served. His crime was that he had built duck ponds on his private property as a personal effort to help conserve wildlife. He carefully obtained at least thirty-eight permits from various government agencies. He consulted the Army Corps of Engineers who informed him that the land he wanted to use was not listed as wet lands. After Ellen began construction of his duck ponds, the Army Corps of Engineers changed their opinion, issued a new definition of wet lands, and ordered him to cease and desist. Within two days of receiving the Federal order, he halted construction. Yet, the Federal government has insisted on charging Ellen with being an environmental criminal. A Federal prosecutor is determined to send this public criminal to prison.[200]

The Federal Ninth Circuit Court ruled in 1987 that, to invoke the "taking" clause of the Constitution, a private citizen must ". . . demonstrate that all or substantially all economically viable use of the property has been denied."[201] Rhode Island's Senator John Chaffee announced that a private citizen should have no right to "just compensation" as provided by the Fifth Amendment to the U.S. Constitution unless the citizen could prove that "all" viable economic use has been denied him as the property owner.[202] When the Federal government is the exclusive judge of the extent of its powers, we can rest assured that those powers will be abused, all the time maintaining the fantasy that the government's action is for the good of the public.

Environmental extremists have used the Endangered Species Act to deprive private property owners forcibly of their right to use their own property. In Texas, Marj and Roger Krueger purchased a home for $53,000 with plans to improve it. Before they could begin expanding and remodeling their home, the Federal government stepped in. It seems that an endangered species, the golden-checked warbler, was spotted in "the canyons adjacent" to the Krueger's home site. The U.S. Fish and Wildlife Service has burdened property owners with countless edicts prohibiting such everyday activities as clearing brush or removing trees. According to our

200 "Bill Reilly's Family Values," *Washington Times*, September 28, 1992, editorial page.

201 David L. Callis, "Property Rights: Are There Any Left?" *Urban Lawyer*, Vol. 20, summer 1988, 597.

202 *Congressional Record*, June 12, 1991, S7556.

all-knowing Federal officials, these activities might modify nearby habitats.[203]

The Endangered Species Act is responsible for a substantial portion of the estimated one billion dollar property loss suffered by the citizens of California because of the wild fires of 1993. Prior to the fire season, the local county fire department recommended that the citizens "abate the flammable vegetation" around their homes. Down South we call this simple fire safety technique "cutting a fire break." It is usually done by plowing or discing a strip around your property or building that you desire protecting; but that was before the age of an all-encompassing, all-powerful Federal government. When the U.S. Fish and Wildlife Service found out about the recommendation, they informed the county and citizens in a letter that discing fire-breaks would harm an endangered species living in the area—the K rat (yes, a rat). The U.S. government warned the people of the area that "It should be noted that the Act provides for both criminal and civil penalties" for cutting a fire break, on their own property! The desire of Federal bureaucrats to turn private property into a rat preserve had more authority than the desire of homeowners to save their homes from dangerous fires![204] In passing, we would like to note that, since the K rat was listed as an endangered species, approximately 100 million taxpayer dollars have been spent on saving the little creature.

Patrick Henry foresaw the day when a strong, centralized Federal government would oppress our "dearest interests." When he was invited to attend the Constitutional Convention, he refused, stating, "I smell a rat"! Perhaps it was a K rat that Patrick Henry smelled. Surely, if Patrick Henry were alive today, he would tell us, "It's time for an old-fashion rat killing."

The Clean Water Act, passed with good intentions to help preserve the environment, has become a tool of despotism in the hands of Federal officials who have no respect for the private property rights of American citizens. In Port Bolivar, Texas, Federal officials have attempted to put a seventy-three-year-old man in jail because he violated the Clean Water Act. Marinus Van Leuzen had owned a parcel of land with an ocean view for twenty years. He decided to build a

203 "Enraging Species Act," *The Wall Street Journal*, April 19, 1994, editorial page.

204 Ike C. Sugg, "California Fires—Losing Houses, Saving Rats," *The Wall Street Journal*, November 10, 1993, editorial page.

retirement home on his land. To Leuzen's dismay, the Army Corp of Engineers and the Environmental Protection Agency cited him for violating the Wet Lands provisions of the Clean Water Act. It might be of interest to know that the term "wet lands" does not even appear in the Clean Water Act, so, even if Leuzen had read the act, it most likely would not have done him any good! The Federal court had some interesting punishment for this "environmental criminal." He was required to construct a billboard ten feet high and twenty feet across that carried a public announcement of illegal wet land destruction, what was being done to restore the land, and that he was the responsible party. The Federal government forced this private citizen to publicly admit to being, in the government's eyes, an environmental criminal. Such cruel, public confessions would be more appropriate for the former Soviet Union or Red China during its Cultural Revolution, than for the United States of America. In addition to his court-ordered public humiliation, Leuzen is required to pay $350 a month into a special government account for the next eight years. Poor man, the Federal government is in effect forcing him to pay it rent on his own home. The money will be used by the government to remove the offending structure (his home). He must also use a large part of his life savings to restore the land to its former state. This vast tract of wet land that this "environmental criminal" contaminated is less than half an acre in size.[205]

This "taking" of private property by the Federal government was authorized by the U.S. District Court for the Southern District of Texas. But this is not the only example of such Federal abuses. All across the country, private citizens are barred from using their own property. In California an immigrant farmer has been threatened with a year in prison and $300,000 in fines for slaying five rats while tilling land on his farm. In Texas thousands of marchers demonstrated against the U.S. Wildlife Service's plans to label 800,000 acres in thirty-three Texas counties as "critical habitat" for a migratory songbird.[206]

The Federal Congress, in 1986, designated the Columbia River Gorge to be a wild and scenic river. This designation allowed the Federal government to restrict the use of land owned by private citizens

205 Jonathan Tolman, "A Sign of the Times," *The Wall Street Journal,* September 20, 1994, editorial page.

206 "Endangered Property Rights," *The Wall Street Journal,* September 12, 1994, editorial page.

along the river. Overnight, land owners were informed by Federal bureaucrats that they could not construct a home on their land unless they owned a minimum of forty acres. The citizens of Skamania County, Washington, voted ten to one to fight the scenic river restrictions. But popular votes carry little authority with the agents of Big Government. The Federal government won, and now it even dictates to the people in the area what color they can paint their own homes!

Liberals will insist that property rights should be secondary to civil rights and public environmental rights. Yet, as we have seen, when a government no longer recognizes the critical importance of property rights, the civil liberties of all citizens are at risk. Our civil liberties are in reverse proportion to the size of the Federal government—the larger the government, the smaller our liberties. When it comes to property rights, we must remember that a government that is controlling property is actually controlling the property owner.

How do "We the people" of the sovereign state provide for adequate protection for our property rights? It is evident that the current "safeguards" have not worked. What, then, shall we do? It is time that "We the people" quit relying upon power-seekers or office-holders in faraway Washington, D.C. It is time we assumed the responsibility to guard our own liberty. Instead of the Federal government's assault on private property rights—Why Not Freedom!

SUMMARY
Questions and Answers

Q. Doesn't all this talk about property prove the greediness and selfishness of conservatives? Why don't you think about other people who are in need?

A. No, the talk about property rights has nothing to do with being greedy or selfish, it has everything to do with being free. Private property and the right of being secure in the ownership of property has a biblical foundation which is reflected in the writings of the early colonialists. One of the Ten Commandments instructs us, "Thou shall not steal." A government that does not recognize its citizens' right to be secure in the ownership of property is nothing less than a tyranny. No citizen of a Fascist, Nazi, or Communist government is secure in his property. Our Forefathers knew how important this right is to a free people; thus, they provided us with the safeguard of the Fifth Amendment to the Constitution. The most needy person in the world is that person who is not allowed to be free because he is held in bondage by a tyrannical government. Indeed, we do wish to help all such needy people.

CHAPTER 22

Instead of an Activist Supreme Court—
Why Not Freedom!

Today, in America, nearly twelve hundred local public school districts are under some form of Federal court-ordered desegregation decree. Forty years after *Brown v. Topeka Board of Education*, we are still no closer to realizing "desegregation" of our public schools. Why? Initially the Federal excuse for the slow rate of school integration was that the Southern states were resisting lawful Federal authority. Southerners, according to the Federal government and the liberal establishment, were resisting court-ordered desegregation by fabricating absurd predictions that their children would not be safe in desegregated public schools, offering unsubstantiated complaints that educational standards would be lowered, and expressing prejudicial fears that desegregated public schools would promote the cultural and social values of "protected minorities" to the detriment of the cultural values of the larger but unprotected middle class. After forty years of Federal control of a purely local matter, the education of middle-class children has yet to produce the Federally assured promised land of human equality, brotherhood, love, and justice. For more than four decades, the Federal government has effectively seized control of education, removing it from parents at the local level and delivering it to faraway, left-wing social scientists, the NAACP, and Federal bureaucrats. Americans of all races have been assured by the Federal courts that these experts know how to create a better society than the one being produced by "We the people" and that they know how to solve all of the nation's social problems. The Federal courts, and their apologists in the media and the education establishment, have maintained that they have stripped the middle class of their inherent right to control the education of their children for the good of the middle class. The Federal courts have turned middle-class children over to self-proclaimed experts who are engaged in left-wing social experiments, all the while assuring the

American people that they know what is best for us and our society.

One of the problems associated with desegregating public schools is how to determine when a school is, in fact, desegregated. This is not a problem for normal, average, middle-class citizens. A school is desegregated, just like a lunch counter, when anyone, regardless of his race, can go there with no distinction made between him and anyone else. Simple? No, not if you are a Federal judge. Freedom of choice is not the criterion used by the Federal courts when judging whether a school is desegregated. The Federal courts have adopted a different criterion. They have renounced a color-blind public school in favor of a color-conscious public school. They have assumed the right to use the police power of the Federal government to force "correct" black-to-white (or any other color of the human rainbow) pupil ratio. The workings of the Federal courts are strange to the extreme. In 1895, the United States Supreme Court ruled that *race could* be used to assign position in society. In 1954, the United States Supreme Court ruled that *race could not* be used to assign position in society. In the mid 1960s, the same United States Supreme Court ruled that *race could* again be used to assign position within society, in this case, in school attendance.

Vacillating on important issues is a dangerous characteristic for a judicial system, but there are even more dangerous actions of the Federal court, actions that can and do attack the very foundation of a free society. Federal Judge Russell Clark ordered a local school district in Missouri to increase the local tax levee to pay off $1.2 billion to aid in the desegregation of public schools. This tax burden on the local middle-class population was in addition to the taxes the citizens had voted on themselves to support their local schools.[207]

Where did the Federal courts acquire the power to control local education, to use children in social experiments, and to *tax* citizens without benefit of the consent of the taxed? The Federal courts have assumed similar arbitrary powers in other areas of our lives. For example, in the area of criminal justice, the Federal courts have been actively encouraging greater respect for the rights of criminals at the expense of the victims (and potential victims). The Federal courts have hampered the ability of law enforcement officials to

---

207 Michael Warder, "Keep Tax-Happy Judges Away From School Boards," *The Wall Street Journal*, December 21, 1994, A19.

protect society from the criminal element that preys upon the law-abiding citizenry. Many police officers have begun to question why they should put their lives on the line, only to have some judge release the criminal on a mere technicality. This activist Federal judicial system has had a chilling effect upon law enforcement. This chilling effect is costing the law-abiding citizenry not only in loss of property and higher insurance rates, but also in the incalculable loss of personal security that affects most of us today. The case of Kenneth McDuff offers a good example of the consequences of the actions of the Federal courts in this matter.

McDuff was convicted of a series of burglaries committed in 1964. During his crime spree, he raped a woman, slashed her throat, and left her to die. The trial court sentenced him to fifty-two years in prison. He served less than a year and was paroled! Two years later, in 1966, he killed a pair of teenagers, a seventeen-year-old boy and the boy's sixteen-year-old girlfriend. He executed them by shooting them in the head and face. McDuff was tried, convicted, and sentenced to death by a Texas trial court. But, thanks to the intervention of the United States Supreme Court, his death sentence was changed to life in prison (at taxpayers' expense, nonetheless). It seems that the Federal court thought that a death penalty under these circumstances would be "cruel and unusual" punishment, thereby violating McDuff's constitutional rights. The activist United States Supreme Court gave the criminal more consideration than was given to the safety of society. This is only one of numerous examples of how our Federal courts have undermined the ability of our local law enforcement officials to safeguard our society from predatory criminals.

Why the concern for the rights of criminals? There is a rational explanation. An accused person is just that, an accused person who has the presumption of innocence. Therefore, we must make sure that the civil liberties that make and keep us free are carefully protected. An accused person should not be subjected to the torture rack merely because the police suspect that he has committed a crime. In a 1936 case, the Supreme Court overturned a conviction based upon the confession of an accused person who had been physically tortured by police. In a 1946 case, an accused person had been interrogated by the police, using the stereotypical "hot lights" in the eyes for over thirty-six hours straight! None of us can be sure that one day we may not be the one who is falsely accused of a criminal offense. It is in our best interest to ensure that due respect for the rights of the accused is afforded. But, "bad cases make for bad laws." The activist Supreme Court has taken a good issue, protecting the accused from police state tactics, and carried it to its logical extreme; then using the police power of the Federal government, it has forced its extremist and activist decisions upon law-abiding citizens.

Citing the *Miranda* case, the United States Supreme Court overturned Robert Minnick's murder conviction. Minnick was arrested and held in California in 1986 on a murder charge for which he had been arrested in Mississippi. He was read his Miranda rights (right to remain silent, right to have an attorney, etc.). After his arrest, he was permitted several visits with his attorney. When the sheriff from Mississippi arrived and asked to speak with the suspect, the suspect consented. Information obtained from the interview was used as evidence against Minnick during a subsequent trial in Mississippi. Minnick was found guilty of murder, and his conviction was upheld by the Supreme Court of Mississippi. Minnick's conviction was thereafter overturned by the Federal Supreme Court!

In a sharply worded dissenting opinion, Chief Justice William Rehnquist and Justice Antonin Scalia noted

> The Court today establishes an irrebuttable presumption that a criminal suspect, after invoking his *Miranda* right to counsel, can *never* validly waive that right during any police-initiated encounter, even after the suspect has been provided multiple Miranda warnings and has actually consulted his attorney. . . . [T]he Constitution's proscription of compelled testimony does not remotely authorize this incursion upon state practices. . . .[208]

Activist judges on the United States Supreme Court have followed the traditional liberal tactic of taking a morally good cause and using it as an excuse to promote their leftist agenda. For example, the natural desire of Americans to help the downtrodden has been used as the pretext for the creation of a multi-billion-dollar welfare establishment, financed by middle-class tax monies. The same can be said about the Federal Supreme Court. The good cause of allowing parents the freedom to choose which public school they want to send their children to, regardless of race, has been turned into the Federal court's right to remove authority for local schools and local taxes

---

208 *Minnick v. Mississippi,* 498 U.S. 146 (1990).

from "We the people" and to give that right to left-wing social activists. The eminently good cause of protecting civil liberties has been turned into an excuse to coddle criminals and encourage social spending to rehabilitate law-breakers and to correct the underlying cause of crime—and, of course, liberals are quick to tell us what those causes of crime are: poverty, discrimination, racism, and an unwillingness of the middle class to share its wealth with the disadvantaged "protected minorities." How did the United States Supreme Court acquire such power over the lives of "We the people"?

The possibility of the Federal Supreme Court subverting the local authority of the state was one of the reasons that anti-Federalists opposed the adoption of the United States Constitution. In 1787, William Grayson of Virginia, who had an uncanny knack of predicting the future role of the Federal court, stated

> This court [the Federal Supreme Court] has more power than any court under heaven. . . . What has it in view, unless to subvert the State governments?[209]

Another Virginian, George Mason, had an equally skeptical view of the proposed Federal court system:

> When we consider the nature of these courts, we must conclude that their effect and operation will be utterly to destroy the State governments; for they will be the judges how far their laws will operate. . . . The principle itself goes to the destruction of the legislation of the States, whether or not it was intended. . . . I think it will destroy the State governments. . . .[210]

A Massachusetts case offers an example of how this activist Federal Supreme Court has destroyed the legislation of a sovereign state and prevented the state from protecting its most vulnerable citizens. In the case *Globe Newspaper Company v. Superior Court for the County of Norfolk* (Massachusetts), the United States Supreme Court overturned a state law passed to protect the identity of minors who were victims of sexual assaults and who were testifying in court. The Federal Supreme Court declared the state law unconstitutional! In a stinging dissent, Chief Justice Warren Burger lashed out against the activist members of the court who voted to overturn the state law.

---

209 William Grayson, quoted in James R. Kennedy and Walter D. Kennedy, *The South Was Right!* (Gretna, LA: Pelican Publishing Company, 1994) 230.

210 Ibid, 230.

[T]oday the Court holds unconstitutional a state statute designed to protect not the *accused,* but the minor *victims* of sex crimes. . . . Although states are permitted, for example, to mandate the closure of all proceedings in order to protect a 17-year-old charged with rape, they are not permitted to require the closing of part of criminal proceedings in order to protect an innocent child who has been raped. . . . [T]he court today denies the victims the kind of protection routinely given to juveniles who commit crimes. Many will find it difficult to reconcile the concern so often expressed for the rights of the accused with the callous indifference exhibited today for children who, having suffered the trauma of rape or other sexual abuse, are denied the modest protection the Massachusetts Legislature provided.[211]

Robert Yates, an early anti-Federalist from New York, declared,

This power in the judicial will enable them to mould the government, into almost any shape they please.[212]

For the last sixty years, an activist Supreme Court in conjunction with the liberal establishment in Washington, D.C., the media, and the education establishment has been busy "molding" the Federal government according to its left-wing agenda.

The proponents of a strong, centralized, national government have championed the concept that *only* the Federal Supreme Court can decide if an act of government, state or Federal, is constitutional. In addition, this decision is to be final. This scheme has been enforced by the police power of the Federal government and has become an accepted article of faith in our modern-day liberal democracy. This has not always been a universally held opinion. Our first president, George Washington, felt that the president should be the one to interpret the Constitution.[213] The Jeffersonian-Republicans did not object to the concept of judicial review (the theory that the Supreme Court could determine if an act of government was constitutional), but they did object to the assertion that *only* the

---

211 *Globe Newspaper Company v. Superior Court for the County of Norfolk* (Massachusetts), 457 U.S. 596 (1982).

212 Robert Yates, quoted in David M. O'Brien, *Constitutional Law and Politics* (New York, NY: W. W. Norton & Company, 1982) II; 26.

213 Forrest McDonald, *A Constitutional History of the United States* (Malabar, FL: Robert E. Krieger Publishing Company, 1982) 42.

Federal Supreme Court had such authority. The Jeffersonian-Republicans knew that, in order to protect the liberties of the people, the people would need some means to erect a barrier between the arbitrary and abusive use of Federal power and the individual citizen. That means would be the sovereign state. The Jeffersonian-Republicans insisted that "We the people" of the sovereign state, acting through our state, had the right to judge whether or not an act of the Federal government was "pursuant" to the Constitution.[214]

The anti-Federalists, as well as the Jeffersonian-Republicans, were fearful that the Federal Supreme Court would become embroiled in politics. They knew that judges, being human, would tend to support those who held views and interests similar to their own. This is exactly what happened in 1798 with the passage of the Alien and Sedition Acts. The Federal Congress, president, and Supreme Court attempted to infringe upon the First Amendment rights of free speech and free press. It should be no surprise to learn that, of the ten people who were indicted, tried, convicted, and sentenced by the Federal courts for violating the Sedition Act, all were Jeffersonian-Republicans![215] The sovereign states of Virginia and Kentucky, in effect, nullified these unconstitutional acts. The states' brave efforts to defend their citizens from an abusive Federal government led to the election of Jeffersonian-Republicans who eventually removed these unconstitutional acts. The important point for us to remember is that there is no magic in making men and women Supreme Court justices. They are given lifetime appointments, but this does not prevent them from acting to support particular political interests even though those acts may be in violation of constitutional authority. Only in a monarchy is a human being given the lifetime right to judge the acts of citizens, officials, and governments. Yet, in America, we have adopted the worst aspect of monarchy, life tenure (when was the last time a Supreme Court justice was impeached?) without any means to assure that the "justice" dispensed is "pursuant" to the Constitution. If the Supreme Court rules in favor of and in conjunction with an establishment, special-interest group (protected minorities, for example), then there is no effective avenue to redress the injustice forced upon society. Thus, the Supreme Court can order local school districts to ignore the concept of a color-blind society and

214 Ibid, 60.
215 Ibid, 54.

make pupil and teacher assignments according to skin color. And, where can the law-abiding, tax-paying, middle-class citizen seek redress for the loss of local control of his children's schools? He can't look to his state because, according to accepted theory, the state is subservient to the Federal government. He can't look to his Federal senator or representative because, if they are a part of the liberal Democratic party, they will not want to do anything to upset the liberal's "protected minority" clientele, or, if they are "conservative" Republicans, they will be too timid to confront the national media and the possibility of being branded as "racists."

There are those who think the lifetime tenure of Supreme Court justices will prevent them from becoming involved in contemporary politics. This has not been the case from the very beginning. Robert Yates, a New York anti-Federalist, noted the dangers inherent in a Supreme Court appointed for life:

> There is no authority that can remove them, and they cannot be controlled by the laws of the legislature. In short, they are independent of the people, of the legislature, and of every power under heaven. Men placed in this situation will generally soon feel themselves independent of heaven itself. . . .[216]

The Federal Supreme Court has a legitimate function in our Republic of Republics. But, it is not the *exclusive* judge of the constitutionality of acts of the various governments in our Republic of Republics. Its decisions should ordinarily be followed, but, if a question arises as to the constitutionality of an act of government, and if that decision has the potential to infringe upon the liberties of citizens of the sovereign state, then the sovereign state has the duty to decide for itself if said act is "pursuant"[217] to the Constitution. In such a case, the decision of the Federal Supreme Court would have persuasive but not mandatory authority. The final arbitrator of our liberties must always be "We the people" of the sovereign state. This is both the letter and the spirit of the Virginia and Kentucky Resolutions of 1798. It is also the constitutional principle upon which our

---

216 Robert Yates, quoted in O'Brien, II; 26.

217 "[It] will not follow . . . that acts of the larger society [Federal government] which are *not pursuant* to its constitutional powers but which are invasion of the residuary authorities of the smaller societies [states], will become the supreme law of the land. These will be merely acts of usurpation, and will deserve to be treated as such." Alexander Hamilton, *The Federalist No. 33*, quoted in George W. Carey and James McClellan, *The Federalist: Student Edition* (Dubuque, IA: Kendall/Hunt Publishing Company, 1990) 161.

American Republic of Republics is founded. It is the very essence of our inalienable right to live under a government based upon the "consent of the governed." Instead of an activist Federal Supreme Court—Why Not Freedom!

SUMMARY
Questions and Answers

Q. You have made several glowing references to William Rawle, the author of an 1825 textbook on the United States Constitution, yet when I read Rawle's textbook, he seems to have a high regard for the Federal court system. Why don't you feel the same way about our Federal courts?

A. You are correct; Rawle, a lawyer and judge, had a high regard for the Federal court system. Yet, he had a great fear of what such a system could do if left unchecked. Rawle said, "[I]t is said that there is generally a propensity in public functionaries to extend their power beyond its proper limits, and this may at some future time be the case with the courts of the United States." Rawle, in this statement, was anticipating the travesty which occurs when the Supreme Court becomes a legislative activist, thereby substituting its will for objective interpretation of the Constitution or the laws of the several states. The reason we feel so much distrust of the current Federal court system is because it has done that which Rawle warned Americans to be on guard against. How can "We the people" of the sovereign states protect ourselves from such an abusive Federal court system that Rawle warned us about? The only safety for our "dearest interests" is within ourselves, by the actions of "We the people" of the sovereign states. A reading of Rawle's textbook on the United States Constitution points out that it is within the purview of the people of the sovereign states to protect their rights. Never accept the liberal myth that the United States Supreme Court is the sole protector of our constitutional rights. It, just like the IRS, cannot be trusted to protect our rights.

CHAPTER 23

Instead of Political Correctness— Why Not Freedom!

During the late 1980s, the liberal academic establishment introduced an era of thought control that has eviscerated all pretenses of academic freedom. The liberal establishment has forced upon America our first modern experience with "thought control." Not since the time of the Alien and Sedition Acts of 1798 have Americans been so afraid to speak their minds freely. Political correctness (PC) has become academia's primary tool to assure liberalism's monopoly in the market place of ideas. Political correctness has grown beyond the universities and is now invading the various branches of government and spilling over into private agencies and groups. We can now look forward to the day when the police power of government will be used to enforce political correctness.

Reeling under the attacks of the middle class because of their politically correct ideology, liberal idealogues and academics have denounced the middle-class revolt against liberalism's political correctness. The liberal establishment has even attempted to deny the existence of political correctness; yet, proof of political correctness can be found in any state. In California, for example, all colleges and universities, if they want to receive government money from loans and to certify that they are legitimate colleges or universities and not "diploma mills," must be accredited by the Western Association of Schools and Colleges (WASC). WASC issued guidelines requiring that all schools desiring accreditation must meet its new "diversity" standard. According to WASC, "diversity" is essential for a proper education, and any school that did not meet its standard would not be accredited. In short, what WASC said to the schools in California was, "If you want to stay in business, then you had better be politically correct." The PC diversity police were enforcing America's new standard of favoring protected minorities, feminists, and those with non-traditional sexual preferences.[218]

218"The Diversity Standard," *The Wall Street Journal*, December 29, 1993, editorial page.

This is an example of how the PC Gestapo can use its power to force its left-wing political agenda on institutions supported by middle-class taxpayers. Left-wing, quasi-governmental agencies such as WASC can intrude into any American urban or rural school and force it to accept standards and curricula that would be repulsive to the average middle-class citizen.

Westminster Theological Seminary, a small Presbyterian school, was put on probation by WASC when the diversity inspectors discovered that the seminary did not have the right quota of females on its governing board. The diversity Gestapo in New York refused to reaccredit Baruch College because investigation revealed that the college had not been sufficiently concerned about multicultural goals. Our colleges and universities are now encouraging an atmosphere in which students, parents, and the middle class in general must live with the threat of censorship, speech codes, hiring quotas, and admission quotas. All of this is part of the left-wing, liberal attempt to force its view of political correctness on American society. Modern campus radicals are not students, but PC administrators and professors. Together they are attempting to condition middle-class children about what to think instead of teaching them how to think.

Another example of political correctness on campus is the rise of student judicial boards. These boards are run by students and politically correct faculty members. These boards rule on questions of fact, similar to the way a jury decides questions of guilt or innocence. The major difference is that few, if any, of the constitutional rights of the accused are honored. Our constitutional tradition of due process and fair hearing are abandoned as these judicial boards rule on the mundane, a dispute between students as to potentially criminal charges, such as accusations of date rape or violation of hate speech codes. The politically correct crowd has seized these boards in order to use them to fight the student and public backlash against the attempt to enforce PC liberal agendas on America's college and university campuses. These boards, under the direction of doctrinaire liberals, have become modern-day censors on campus. What student will raise his voice in opposition to speech codes and thereby risk the possibility of character assassination at the hands of liberal zealots? The campus hate speech police have had a chilling effect in the one-time bastion of free speech.[219]

219 "A Mockery of Justice on Campus," *The Wall Street Journal*, September 27, 1993, editorial page.

At the University of California-Riverside, a fraternity incurred the wrath of the university's thought police when it issued a T-shirt advertising a party with a theme of "South of the Border." It seems that a group of Chicano activists were offended by the T-shirt. Just as the thought police were preparing to administer a public "intellectual" caning to the fraternity, a small group called the Individual Rights Foundation stepped in and prevailed. Not only was the university administration forced to relent in its harassment of the fraternity, but also two of the administrators had to agree to attend seminars on the meaning of free speech.[220]

The crusade for political correctness has now moved from the academic arena into our everyday life. It should not be surprising to discover that those who receive a politically correct education will attempt to impose their PC values on their peers when they enter a profession. In 1994, the American Bar Association's (ABA) Standing Committee on Ethics and Professional Responsibility proposed a new rule governing professional conduct for attorneys. The proposed PC rule would dramatically restrict an attorney's right to free speech. It would classify as unethical behavior for a lawyer to "knowingly manifest by words or conduct, in the course of representing a client, bias or prejudice based upon race, sex, religion, national origin, disability, age, sexual orientation or socioeconomic status."[221] If an attorney knowingly committed an enumerated politically incorrect act, he could be sanctioned or even disbarred.

Professor Richard F. Duncan, University of Nebraska College of Law, asked the counsel for the ABA for a ruling. His question was: "If an attorney is engaged in personal conversation and is asked his opinion about a proposed law regarding 'gay rights' and the attorney states that he is opposed to the legislation 'because homosexuality is immoral and unnatural,' would the attorney be in violation of the ABA's proposed ethics rule?" The ABA counsel admitted that the attorney "might be in violation" and that the "reach of the rule is practically limitless."[222] The same interpretation could be made if an attorney complained that welfare was wrong because it encourages dependency and illegitimacy. This would imply a bias against the poor or "protected minorities" who represent a disproportionate

---

220 "Aside," *The Wall Street Journal,* December 7, 1993, editorial page.

221 "A Speech Code for Lawyers," *The Wall Street Journal,* February 3, 1994, editorial page.

222 Ibid

share of welfare recipients. According to the proposed ABA rule, this could represent a bias against an identifiable "socioeconomic" group. If a conservative professional in any field speaks his mind, he stands in danger of being assaulted by the left-wing, politically correct, thought police. This is the first time in modern America that citizens can be harassed and punished for speaking their minds. The PC movement has had an enormously chilling effect on middle-class free speech. But, of course, it was intended to do just that! Freedom of speech is not a consideration; thought control is the goal of the liberal establishment. The intention is to maintain a monopoly in the market place of ideas. Liberals do not intend to allow equal time for any idea contrary to the officially sanctioned PC view.

The PC movement has even attacked freedom of the press. In 1988, the revised Fair Housing Act was pushed through Congress and signed into law by the most "conservative" Republican president in history, Ronald Reagan. This law made it a crime for an individual to place an advertisement or for a newspaper to allow an advertisement to run that "may appear to discriminate."[223] Private PC groups now routinely troll newspaper classified ads looking for an unsuspecting individual who may have inadvertently—yet nonetheless—violated the Federal law. This law and many other similar laws now allow private liberal groups to enforce their PC ideology in the name of enforcing the Federal law. Using such laws, the PC police in California forced a chain of twenty newspapers into bankruptcy! When the law becomes the enemy of the law-abiding people of the country, it no longer deserves the name or the respect of law!

The PC police have even enlisted the Federal Bureau of Investigation to help ferret out hate speech and thought crimes. In an October 18, 1993, letter the FBI disclosed that anyone who had ever uttered a statement they considered to be "insensitive" to any minority group could be disqualified from holding a government job. Federal agencies have asked the FBI to investigate private comments made by applicants to determine if an applicant is free of biases. The FBI is not merely inquiring into overt acts but is building a file on applicant's comments made in private.[224] Shades of *1984*, Big Brother is watching and listening to you!

---

223 "Politically Correct Classified," *The Wall Street Journal*, December 13, 1993, editorial page.

224 Jeremy J. Stone, "PC Invades the FBI," *The Wall Street Journal*, November 2, 1993, editorial page.

The mere knowledge that the FBI is checking up on potential job applicants will have an enormously chilling effect on free speech. The fact that "our" Federal government thinks that it has a right to invade the private thoughts and conversations of American citizens should give us all reason to fear the powers of a government that is arrogantly drunk on its power and that holds the privacy and civil liberties of the "We the people" in total contempt.

Will "We the people" allow those in power to continue to abuse the power of the Federal government in order to further their PC, liberal social and political agendas? If we do, then this country will become another Soviet Union, in which the people are afraid to speak frankly to their friends and neighbors. Do "We the people" want America to become a society in which everyone is afraid of the ever-watchful and all-powerful Big Government?

Remember George Washington's warning that "Government is not reason, it is not eloquence, it is like fire; a dangerous servant but a fearful master." All across the South, thanks to the unfair South-only Voting Rights Act, the Federal government has redrawn voting districts, gerrymandering them to ensure that the Federal government's "protected minorities" will have majority districts. When opposition to racial gerrymandering mounts as a result of the virtual disenfranchising of the white minority in the district, the PC police in the media launch a vicious and slanderous character assassination against those in opposition to the liberal gerrymandering. A white candidate who attempts to run against a black candidate in a racially gerrymandered district will be subjected to great pressure from the politically correct crowd. According to Professor Carol Swain, Princeton's Woodrow Wilson School, contemporary, politically correct doctrine has declared it incorrect for a white candidate to run for office in a minority dominated district.[225] The PC thought police are slowly turning the Federal government into our fearful master.

In a review of a book about political correctness, the reviewer for *The Wall Street Journal* noted that a vast multicultural bureaucracy now dominates most of America's institutions. The PC crowd at a Philadelphia newspaper demanded the removal of an editor who recommended the use of Norplant for unwed mothers and branded the editor as a racist. Some universities have forced resident dorm

---

225 "Black Majority Districts, a Rotten Litmus Test," *The Wall Street Journal*, December 27, 1993, editorial page.

advisers to watch hard-core homosexual pornography and have had sensitivity trainers roaming the room with cameras to catch expressions of disapproval on the face of dorm advisers. Of course, such expressions would be evidence of bias against homosexuals. Grade schoolers in Brookline, Massachusetts, have been reported to ask, "Why do they teach us that white people suck?"[226] Yes, we all would like to know—some of us already know—thank God it was a child from Massachusetts who asked such a piercing question and not a child from Mississippi!

The liberal education establishment is using its control of education as a means of presenting its left-wing propaganda to middle-class children. Parents who object to this abuse of their children can open themselves up to public criticism and ridicule from the education "experts." In some cases, these politically correct educators have attempted to make it a crime for parents to criticize politically correct education. Debra Saunders, a syndicated columnist, detailed the attempt of school administrators to make such criticism a criminal activity. "This story reflects the treatment meted out to many parents across the country who protest the educrats' unfailing efforts to impose their values on America's children."[227]

An example of the PC madness is seen in a program fostered by Petaluma Public School. It seems that the Petaluma school administrators decided to set up a PC program called Human Interaction (HI). In this class, the teachers would ask the students who their parents voted for in the 1980 election, if any member of their family were alcoholics, and if the children were "happy" most of the time. Some of the parents objected to such personal inquiries and attempted to pull their children out of the class. The educators proposed to deal with the parental protest by requiring the parents to submit in writing the reasons they did not want their children to attend HI and also to declare that the parents would provide "appropriate alternative educational experiences." This signed statement would, according to the administrators' proposed rule, subject the parents to the "penalty of perjury," which happens to be up to four years in prison!

Who gave the Petaluma schools the right to require parents to

226 William McGowan, "A Politically Incorrect Study of PC," *The Wall Street Journal*, January 4, 1995, A10 [book review, *Dictatorship of Virtue: Multiculturalism and the Battle for America's Future*, by Richard Bernstein, Knopf].

227 Debra Saunders, "Parents: Don't cross educrats," as carried by *The* (New Orleans, LA) *Times Picayune*, October 10, 1994, B5.

discuss social, religious or political issues with their kids? Who made Petaluma schools the Parents Police Department? . . . [T]he threat of hard time would come across as intimidation, a warning to any parent who would criticize their pet class that she or he could be subject to intense personal scrutiny. . . . The message: Parents, don't cross us.[228]

Thanks to the help of a religious freedom advocacy group, the Rutherford Institute, the school administrators removed the threat of criminal penalty. But the tyrannical control of educators over the children continued. Students who do not take the HI class are not allowed to substitute another class. One parent stated that her son was not allowed to take another class and was assigned to a work detail in the office during the vacant period. The education "experts" are experts in administering punishment to those who refuse to follow their liberal, politically correct party line.

The availability of education for the children of middle- and lower-income families has been cited as a major element in the American dream. But, for the last thirty years, the value received by the taxpayer has been in reverse relationship to the taxes paid—the more money pumped into the education system, the lower the "intellectual" outflow.[229] The spending per student in elementary and high schools has increased by 180% since 1960, even after being adjusted for inflation. There has been no substantial increase in enrollment, nor have teacher salaries increased after adjusting for inflation. No, we are not paying our real teachers too much—the cost is in the increase of personnel. The ratio of non-teacher to student has almost doubled since 1960. Schools have convinced the public that it is their function to do the work that was done so well by parents for so many years.[230] Efforts by middle-class parents to reintroduce basic education curricula has too often met with entrenched opposition from the education establishment. The middle class have a vested interest in assuring that good teachers are paid a salary sufficient for the profession and also an interest in making sure their tax monies are used for education and not left-wing propaganda.

The pervasive intrusion of Federal court orders, Federal

228 Ibid

229 Bruno V. Manno, "Deliver Us From Clinton's School Bill," *The Wall Street Journal,* June 22, 1993, editorial page.

230 Lindley H. Clark, Jr., "The High Cost of High (and Lower) Schools," *The Wall Street Journal,* October 4, 1994, editorial page.

guidelines, Federal edicts, and Federal subsidies into every aspect of our daily lives has created an environment that allows the liberal establishment to use both private and public groups to enforce political correctness. The use of the force of government to police the thoughts and speech of Americans must be brought under control. "We the people" of the sovereign state cannot rely upon the Federal government to control itself. We must have a better guarantee for our "dearest interests." That something else is the sovereign state, the final bulwark between an abusive, politically correct Federal government and "We the people" of the sovereign state. Instead of political correctness—Why Not Freedom!

SUMMARY
Questions and Answers

Q. One good point about the drive for political correctness that you did not talk about is the attempt to punish criminals for hate crimes. Don't you think this is a good example of a positive benefit of, as you call it, the liberal establishment?

A. To answer your question in its simplest form—no. We do not see the drive to institute what liberals call "hate crimes" into the legal system of America as a positive drive. Here is the problem with the so-called "hate crimes" mythology. Who will define what is and is not hateful, and who will decide what punishment is appropriate for this heretofore unknown crime? As victims of criminal activity, we do not believe the crime was committed against our property by a criminal with love in his heart; is this, then, a hate crime? Is a man shot and killed by a person with "love in his heart" any less dead than one killed by a murderer with "hate in his heart"? Liberals desire to use the so-called "hate crime" mythology in order to reward certain groups of its liberal constituency with punishment aimed at the middle class. For example, it has already been stated by the NAACP that black people cannot be racist because, to be a racist, one must have power over a victim. According to this liberal group, black Americans do not have power over white Americans; therefore any crime committed against a white person by a black cannot be based on race, and therefore is not racist (therefore it is not a "hate crime"). Using such convoluted logic, the liberal establishment can condemn most crimes committed against a minority individual by a member of the majority as a "hate crime." The "hate crime" movement has the potential of destroying every freedom the American middle class has left. We believe America would be better served if all criminal activity, regardless of the criminal's skin color, was punished quickly and severely.

Q. I find it very offensive when someone uses racial or ethnic slurs. What is wrong with government enforcing some form of civility among its citizens?

A. You are not alone in your revulsion at hearing coarse and harmful remarks made about individuals or groups of individuals. The authors, as very young children growing up in Mississippi, were taught by our parents not to use words such as "nigger" or otherwise be disrespectful of black people. This may not fit the liberal-enforced stereotypical view of Mississippi during the 1950s, but we can assure you from personal experience that such training by parents in the South at that time was common. It did not take the power of government to enforce such a sense of respect for our fellow man. This sense of respect for our fellow man did require a deep-seated faith in and adherence to the traditional biblical world view. "Do unto others as you would have them do unto you" is not amenable to government control. When the liberal establishment attacks and destroys the traditional biblical world view that enabled parents in Mississippi and around the nation to teach their children a system of respect for others, liberals had to introduce a system that would attempt to restore that respect. They have failed. Respect, like love, must be given by free choice of the individual; it cannot be coerced into existence. As for the second part of your question, you ask, "Why can't government enforce some form of civility among *its* citizens?" Here we see one clear difference between the neo-socialist (that is, liberal) view of government and the traditional (paleo-conservative) view of government. Government does not own "its" citizens; rather, "We the people" own our government. In a free society, such as the original constitutional Republic of Republics, "We the people" told the government what to do, not the other way around. Much has changed during the past two hundred years, and it is time to revisit the old Republic of Republics in order to reestablish the lost liberty and freedoms of "We the people."

CHAPTER 24

Instead of the Arrogance of Power—
Why Not Freedom!

Because they believe in individual responsibility, America's middle class have one primary expectation of government, that is, that it leave them alone. America's middle class have never felt that they need a watchful master up in the "big house" providing for them and making sure they are being "taken care of." The liberal establishment does not share such provincial middle-class views of government. To the liberal, government is a tool to be used to reshape and perfect society; of course, "liberal" perfection has very few followers in the middle class. Nowhere in this liberal plan is there a place for "input" from the common man. Liberals are possessed of an attitude of moral superiority. They would have us believe that they are the only ones who truly care about society, peace, the sick, the elderly, the downtrodden, etc. Liberals believe that their sense of caring gives them the moral right to reshape American society in their pre-conceived image.

Liberals are wed to their belief of moral superiority to which they hold with a determination equal to any religious fanatic or cult member. They are worse than cult priests. At least cult priests claim that the priesthood receives its authority from a higher source than themselves; but, not so with liberalism. Liberals are so egotistical that they do not need a god to commission them to "go ye therefore and forcefully reshape society." Their authority comes from within themselves—because they "care" more; they are more "compassionate" and more concerned about "sensitive" issues. Therefore, according to their politically correct logic, they deserve the right to use the police powers of government to force the "brutish cattle" (the middle class) into accepting liberalism's social policy. Liberals have become society's self-appointed priests of the new politically correct social order. The power they control through the education establishment, the media, and the government has given them the

231

persona of petty, tyrannical gods. An arrogance of power typifies modern liberalism. Of course, all gods need an evil force to contend with; middle-class issues, values, and leaders are therefore demonized by modern liberalism in order to provide the petty gods of liberalism with an appropriate enemy with which to contend.

Any time liberals need to prove that they are the only ones who care about crime, the media will trot out a "special report" about the crude, evil, and dangerous National Rifle Association; or, to prove that they are the only ones who care about race relations, they will present a "documentary" about how "racists" use "code words" to prevent the adoption of more affirmative action plans; or, any time they need to prove that racism is a controlling element down in Dixie, they will do an "expose" on Confederate flags and racism. All these are done with the intention of (1) making liberals feel good about themselves—one can almost hear them congratulating themselves because, like the self-righteous Pharisee, they are "not as other men are"[231] and (2) discouraging (perhaps "conditioning" would be a more appropriate word) the general public from questioning the edicts of the gods of liberalism.

Liberals have been America's ruling elite for the past fifty years. With the willing assistance of the unofficial ministers of propaganda in the media, liberals successfully use the force of government to enact their undemocratic social programs. Over the past half-century, they have developed an unprecedented assumption of moral superiority, political arrogance, and self-delusion that they have a right to rule the American people. To America's ruling elite, the middle class are the sheep, and liberals are the shepherds.

A New York newspaper columnist portrayed former Governor Mario Cuomo of New York as the archetypical, arrogant, elitist liberal. Shortly after Cuomo was removed from office by the people of New York, he was asked to assess "what went wrong"; why did he lose the election? Addressing the National Press Club a month after the lost election, Cuomo gave a frightening account of a liberal's estimation of the worth of self-government by the common people, that is, the middle class. Using the metaphor of shepherd and sheep, Cuomo complained that the sheep were actually now attempting to lead the shepherds! Prior to the advent of an arrogant, liberal, ruling elite, would any politician in America have dared to compare the

---

231 Luke 18:11, *The Holy Bible.*

American people to sheep? Until the advent of liberalism's ruling elite and their willing lackeys in the media and education, no politician who valued his political life and who had no yearning for a layer of feathers fastened to his hide with warm tar would have had the gall to insult America's hard-working and long-suffering taxpayers publicly. Prior to this speech, this liberal governor had made another speech in which he urged people to read the Sermon on the Mount, and then he questioned, "Can a conservative really be a Christian?"[232] The governor also used the "loving" concept of "family":

> "Family" is a fine word to suggest compassion, which Gov. Cuomo often wants to suggest. But it is not good as a model of democratically organized societies for the simple reason that a democracy has as its fundamental principle that of citizen equality. [Equality before the law.]
>
> "Family" implies an unequal relationship, like that of father and son, state and ward, shepherd and sheep. The shepherd and sheep metaphor was actually used by the governor in the Press Club speech.
>
> Mario Cuomo and his fellow Democrats found politics to be unobjectionable, of course, as long as they were the shepherds. But, as he complained at the Press Club, today the "sheep are leading the shepherds."
>
> He believes elected officials are meant to lead, to refashion society, to engineer social improvements and to recreate government if necessary—not at the direction of ordinary citizens but as the "shepherds'" own more highly tuned moral sensibilities dictate. The people are seen largely as an unthinking body of greedy, mean-spirited "haves" who, as Gov. Cuomo hinted, may very well be on the verge of instructing their new leaders to ignore the sick and poor while turning their attention to young children only long enough to victimize them. . . .
>
> The people who rebelled on Election Day [November 8, 1994] were not voting against the downtrodden but against a government they believe does not trust them to run their own lives and imputes evil motives to them when they attempt to do so.[233]

Thus, we see an example of the arrogance of power. But, this is only one of many examples that could be cited. Note the arrogance

232 Dan Davidson, *Albany* (NY) *Times Union,* as carried in *The* (New Orleans, LA) *Times Picayune,* January 1, 1995, B7.

233 Ibid

of elected members of the Federal Congress who are elected from conservative districts, but, when they get to Washington, D.C., vote liberal. When asked how they keep getting re-elected, their response was, "Press release conservative, vote liberal."[234] Another example of the arrogance of power is found in the listing of thirty-one members of Congress who promised to cut Federal spending but actually delivered more spending, as reported in *The Wall Street Journal*. They did this by sponsoring bills to cut Federal spending, but, all along they knew that these bills did not have a chance of passage. Yet, the bills were the topics for hot news releases back home. The folks back home got useless rhetoric, while the liberal special interest got more and more of the middle class's property in the form of tax revenues. Of the thirty-one big spenders, six were Republican and sixteen, both Republican and Democrat, were from the South, supposedly the conservative South.[235] The arrogance of political power breeds a condescending contempt for the common man.

Another example of political arrogance is the way our elected Federal officials of the 103rd Congress handled the A to Z Spending Cuts Bill. The A to Z Spending Cuts Bill required an open debate with an up-or-down vote on specific budget outlays. No hiding in secret committees, no empty rhetoric and useless posturing for home consumption, just a simple on-the-record vote, for or against less government spending. To introduce the A to Z Bill on the floor for a vote, the conservatives in Congress needed a "discharge" petition in order to get the bill out of a liberal-controlled committee. Even though thirty-three House members had gone on record as supporting the bill (that is, they had issued hot news releases for home consumption), they refused to sign the discharge petition, and the bill died in committee. Once again, of the thirty-three House members claiming to be for the A to Z Spending Cuts Bill, fifteen were from the South.[236] The arrogance of power allows elected Federal officials to treat middle-class Americans as if they were a bunch of dumb sheep. Arrogant Federal officials know that they can lie to the middle class, and pretend to be conservative, while doing the bidding of their liberal masters in Washington, D.C.

Because of their self-assumed attitude of moral superiority, liberals

---

234 *The Wall Street Journal*, September 30, 1993, editorial page.

235 Paul S. Hewitt, "The Hypocrisy Index," *The Wall Street Journal*, October 12, 1994, A18.

236 "Beltway Production Off," *The Wall Street Journal*, October 12, 1994, A18.

are perfectly comfortable controlling the reins of power. They believe everything they do is good for society, and, therefore any complaint from the middle class can be legitimately ignored—after all, the liberal is convinced that he is the moral guardian of society, commissioned by some unknown power to perfect our imperfect world by whatever means is necessary.

Liberals are not the only ones who have become intoxicated with the arrogance of power. The arrogance of power is intoxicating to every political association that is exposed to it; that is why "We the people" must have in our hands the means of checking such unrestrained actions of Big Government. This arrogance produced the Savings and Loan failures and subsequent bail outs, paid for, of course, by (guess who) middle-class taxpayers. This is just one example of how the arrogance of the Big Money establishment is evidenced by our recent history. In the early 1950s, the Federal government exercised its assumed right to treat unsuspecting American citizens like laboratory rats. The Federal government conducted numerous radiation experiments, such as giving pregnant women radiative pills, detonating radiation bombs near private homes, and exposing the genitals of prisoners to x-rays—all done by "our" Federal government secretly during the Cold War. The Federal government from 1948 to 1952 intentionally released radiation into the atmosphere to see how far it would travel. The release sites were all populated: Los Alamos, New Mexico; Dugway, Utah; and Oak Ridge, Tennessee. Some of the radiation traveled as far away as seventy miles. In Nashville, Tennessee, 751 pregnant women were secretly exposed to radiation thirty times greater than natural radiation. Follow-up records have been "destroyed," but it is known that a five-year-old child of one of the victims died of lymphatic leukemia, which is associated with radiation exposure.[237]

Now, please remember that this was not being done to Americans by Nazi or Communist tyrants, but by "our" own Federal government, a government that recognizes the authority of no one other than itself. Under the original Constitution, the Federal government could be brought under control, but that relief from Federal tyranny has been taken away from Americans since 1865. Hopefully, Americans can begin to understand why we must restore the natural equilibrium in power between the state and Federal government. Here

237 *The USA Today,* December 21, 1993, 1A-2A.

we see examples of how dangerous government can be. We see how easily normally "good" people can convince themselves that they are better equipped to rule society than "We the people" of the sovereign state. We see how this self-delusion can lead to a ruling elite who view themselves as wise and anointed shepherds of "their" dumb sheep. We see how even the Federal government of these United States can sink to the low level of secretly conducting lethal experiments on unsuspecting citizens. We see the arrogance of power in action. This is why the Founding Fathers feared a strong central government. This is why they were determined to create a limited Federal government and why they reserved all non-delegated powers to the states. The Founding Fathers hoped that the sovereign state would be capable of erecting "barriers against the encroachments of the national authority"[238] to protect the people from an abusive or oppressive Federal government.

Another example of extreme arrogance of power occurred on August 21, 1992—while Republican President George Bush was in office. The Federal government's agents murdered a fourteen-year-old boy and his mother and seriously wounded the father, Randy Weaver (see "Bury Our Freedom on Ruby Ridge" in the Addenda section). Janet Reno's Justice Department issued a confidential Justice Department report admitting that the Federal government's action "contravened the Constitution of the United States." The Federal government's unconstitutional actions resulted in the death of Vicki Weaver and her fourteen-year-old son. One senior Federal official involved in the case was quoted as saying, ". . . [Weaver] was not going to last long . . . [the Federal agents knew that he would be] taken down hard and fast."[239]

> Later, federal prosecutors obtained an indictment charging Weaver in the killing of the deputy marshal. Both were acquitted as the case collapsed in the welter of accusations that the government had mishandled the entire episode.[240]

How many Ruby Ridges or other secret abuses of Federal power

238 Alexander Hamilton, *The Federalist No. 85*, quoted in George W. Carey and James McClellan, *The Federalist: Student Edition* (Dubuque, IA: Kendall/Hunt Publishing Company, 1990) 453.

239 David Johnston, *The New York Times*, as reported in *The* (New Orleans, LA) *Times Picayune*, December 14, 1994, A4.

240 Ibid

have occurred in these United States is unknown. One thing is certain; if we allow a large central government to be the exclusive judge as to the limits of its powers, then it is certain that eventually those powers will be abused. That is why our Founding Fathers were determined to leave "We the people" of the sovereign state a means whereby we would be able to defend our "dearest interests" against an intrusive Federal government.

America's arrogant, liberal, ruling elite share numerous common characteristics:

1. They are always eager to rule. They have no confidence in the ability of the average man to govern his society. No detail of the average man's life, society, or culture is too insignificant to be left alone. The ruling elite can intellectually justify any intrusion into people's lives, regardless of how grandiose or petty.

2. They are eager to experiment with the lives of the people over whom they rule.

3. They always rule poorly—they invariably do a poor job, at least as far as those of the middle class who have to endure their rule and pay the taxes to support their social schemes are concerned.

4. They tend to favor large social programs covering as many people or groups of people as possible, such as socialized medicine, equal housing, and affirmative action. This gives them a better opportunity to reshape society, to transform it to meet their predetermined, left-wing social agenda.

5. They hate popular discontent and organizations attempting to channel such discontent into popular political action. For example, the ruling elite of education will spend millions of dollars to defeat school choice or voucher plans; the elite of government will marshall all resources necessary to defeat a ballot initiative relative to illegal immigration, or they will slander and smear as a racist anyone leading a crusade against forced busing. Indeed, this may represent a form of envy. The ruling elite have increasingly detested the way in which the collective action of the common man tends to achieve great things so naturally, and without direction or assistance from liberals. Why, the mere thought that THEY may not be needed is pure heresy!

6. They always treat people subject to their jurisdiction as children and constantly stress their children's waywardness and dependence on the guidance of liberal judges. The citizen cannot decide

to have local limitations on taxation but must yield to judicial taxation, even though it defeats the citizens' financial and personal planning and residential preference. The limits and boundaries of local
taxing authorities may be freely expanded and remodeled to catch
the wandering taxpayer who desires to escape the judicial tax levy.
In short, every aspect of the individual's personal preference is regulated. He may not move about or associate freely.[241]

The election of November 8, 1994, was a rude awakening for many
arrogant politicians. Regardless of how impressive a given conservative election victory may be, it must be remembered that election
results can be overruled in a few, short years. We need something
more permanent than "good" conservative Federal officials to protect our liberties and property.

George Washington warned Americans that "Government is not
eloquence, it is not reason, it is like fire; a dangerous servant but a
fearful master." For the last fifty years, under the control of a liberal
establishment, the Federal government has insidiously grown from
a dangerous servant and is now becoming our fearful master. It is
now up to us, "We the people," the source of a legitimate government, to rein in the excesses of Big Government by establishing a system by which "We the people" of the sovereign state may erect
proper barriers to safeguard our "dearest interests" from a ruling
elite, intoxicated on the arrogance of governmental power. Instead
of the arrogance of power—Why Not Freedom?

SUMMARY OF SECTION II

Questions and Answers

*Q. You keep talking about the abuse of Federal power, but what about the
abuse of state power such as segregation?*

A. First of all, you must understand that in our Republic of
Republics, Federal authority is not original. Federal authority is
derived from the states through the Constitution. State authority is
original because our sovereign states derive their authority from "We
the people," the only legitimate source of governmental authority.

241 William J. Quirk and R. Randall Bridwell, *Abandoned: The Betrayal of the American Middle
Class* (Lanham, MD: Madison Books, 1992) 337-39.

It is the responsibility of the sovereign state to police the actions of its agent, the Federal government, and to erect appropriate barriers against said agent to assure that the liberty and property of citizens are not infringed upon by an abusive Federal government.

In the event that a state abuses its power, then the people of said state have the responsibility of correcting and if necessary punishing those who abuse their powers. Suppose one state passes a law that causes harm to certain segments of its citizens. As bad as the results may be, it is at least limited to that state alone. Now, suppose the Federal government passes the same law. Instantly, the evil result is imposed upon the entire country. What is even worse is that it is much more difficult to correct Federal error than it is to correct state error. "We the people" will receive much better response when we visit our state capitol and ask our local representatives for assistance than we will if we make a similar pilgrimage to Washington, D.C.

As for segregation, there is more segregation in Northern cities today than there is in the South. Segregation was yesterday, this is today—our cause is the cause of individual civil liberty. The use of governmental force to impose any social scheme, segregation or busing for example, is wrong because it violates the right of individuals to choose freely. Big Governments make for small citizens.

Q. Aren't local and state politicians just as likely to abuse their power as national politicians?

A. No, they are not as likely to abuse their power. The reason why state and local officials are not as likely to abuse their power is that they are too close to the electorate. For instance, a local sheriff who abuses his office will be faced with complaints from the population everywhere he goes. He cannot hide in faraway Washington, D.C. He does not have a huge, faceless, cold, bureaucracy to shield him from the public. He cannot count on a judiciary that enjoys lifetime appointments to rule in his favor. He knows that his fellow citizens will make the relatively short trip to the county courthouse or the state capitol to complain about his abuse of power. Local and state officials by necessity are more responsive to "We the people." That is why the Founding Fathers purposely reserved the vast majority of powers to the states. A democratic republic works best close to home. This does not mean that abuses will not occur, but it does mean that when they do occur their effects will be limited to that state and that "We the people" of that sovereign state have a better opportunity to correct the abuses.

SECTION III

THE PRESCRIPTION FOR THE CURE

INTRODUCTORY COMMENTS

In Section I, we identified the parties in the struggle to gain control of the Federal government. We demonstrated how the various groups all attempt to gain control of the Federal government in order to use the government's police power to protect their special interests. Of course, this means that, regardless of who is in control of the Federal government, the middle class still pays the bill. In Section II, we gave examples of present-day abuses of Federal powers. We demonstrated how liberal special-interest groups have used the Federal government to give advantages to their clientele ("protected minorities") and to enact radical regulations that allow government agents to confiscate private property, and how the activist Federal courts have assumed the right to govern local communities.

In this section, we will outline the technique by which "We the people" of the sovereign states can organize for the struggle to restore our constitutional government, a government of limited Federalism, State's Rights, and State Sovereignty. Once organized, "We the people" will be prepared to take on the monster of Big Government—this historic battle will occur, not in Washington, D.C., but at the local level. The key to dethroning Big Government is to return to "We the people" the right to use the sovereign state to serve as a barrier between us and an abusive Federal government. That power will be returned to the people of the states with the passage of the Sovereign Authority Amendment. At last, "We the people" will have the means to halt effectually Federal intrusion upon our reserved rights; at last, "We the people" will have the constitutional weapon necessary to enforce the Tenth Amendment! At last, our original constitutional Republic of Republics will, once again, be controlled by "We the people" of the sovereign states!

241

CHAPTER 25

A Philosophy of Freedom

In Section II, we discussed contemporary political issues that affect middle-class Americans. These are issues that the politically correct liberal establishments continue to ignore. Issues such as reverse discrimination, tax-and-spend liberalism, and gun control receive little attention from the liberal establishments, except in an attempt to dismiss their importance or to brand conservative opponents of such liberal schemes as racist, uncaring, or just another group of "dumb Bubbas."

There exists a tremendous gulf between the thinking of middle-class Americans and that of the liberal establishments of media, education, and government. The liberal establishment has used the force of the Federal government, the propaganda force of the left-wing media, and a politically correct education establishment to force its values upon the majority of middle-class Americans. Most Americans do not support the concept of discriminating against a white male just because of the color of his skin. Yet, the liberal establishment has forced the middle class to endure decades of Federally enforced affirmative action plans, quotas, and numerous other plots to allow liberal clientele (also known as "protected minorities") special rights. The majority of Americans reject the notion that their children should be assigned to schools according to the color of their skin. Yet, the Federal courts and their liberal aides-de-camp, such as the NAACP, have forced the middle class to endure decades of forced busing. The majority of Americans do not believe that gun control laws are the best way to fight crime. Yet, the liberal Congress aided by liberal propagandists in the media have forced the middle class to endure the violation of its Second Amendment right to keep and bear arms. The majority of Americans reject the notion that homosexuality and other sexual perversions are acceptable alternative lifestyles. Yet, in 1993, the liberal Federal government forced

243

young people, most of whom were from middle-class families, to accept homosexuals in the military. Throughout this list two issues are constant. One, the will and consent of the middle class stands in opposition to the political and social agenda of the liberal establishment. Two, the liberal establishment has assumed the right to use governmental force to impose unpopular social experiments, ideas, and legislation upon middle-class citizens. Free and unfettered consent and the application of governmental force, in this case as in all such cases, are the dividing line between a free republic and tyranny.

Because most middle-class Americans believe in individual responsibility, they do not look to Big Brother government as their provider. Individual responsibility is an indispensable element in the formation of a democratic republic. As already noted, a people who cannot or will not provide for themselves will never be free. A people who cannot or will not provide for themselves have never instituted a free, democratic republic. If such a people by some stroke of extreme fortune, were to inherit a free republic, they would, over the course of a few short decades, consume that free government and plunge their society into an impoverished and dismal socialist commune—Haiti being a prime example.

Unlike the average middle-class American, the liberal establishment does not believe in individual responsibility. Listen to the excuses given by liberals to rationalize the actions of individuals. "Poverty, crime, disease, slums, drug rings, AIDs are all the fault, not of individuals, but of society." "*Society* is at fault, not the criminal." "It is society's fault that so many unwed mothers are on welfare." "It's not the criminal's fault; it is society's fault for not rehabilitating the poor victim of discrimination." Liberals and their clientele look to government to provide opportunity, training, health care, housing, food, and—let us not forget—midnight basketball!

Many Southerners and other Americans have asked why there are so many tax-and-spend liberals elected in the South. This is contrary to the traditional conservatism and individualism that is so often associated with the South. Many liberals have taken great pleasure in attacking the South because of its traditional anti-Big Government views, yet they say, the South pays less tax into the United States Treasury and receives more tax dollars in return. It is true that the South pays less tax than any other section of the United States, not because it desires to do so, but because of its post-War poverty. Before 1861, the South's per capita income was in the middle range of American income; since Appomattox the South has been on the bottom of America's income range. Yet, liberals condemn the South because it does not pay as much tax into the National Treasury as Northern states pay. Liberals condemn the South because it receives so many tax dollars from military retirement funds and military installations. Here liberals condemn Southerners for being patriotic and serving in the military. Because of the region's high poverty level, many people seek a career in the military and therefore receive retirement benefits; is this a reason to condemn the South? The South has always provided more than its share of men in the defense of America; why should it be condemned because of this act of patriotism?[242] But the real reason that so many tax dollars are funneled into the South is simple; it is payment from the liberal elected officials to its faithful welfare clientele (not something the average Southern middle-class voter desired).

The reason liberal politicians are elected in the South is because, in the South, there is a disproportionate number of people who acquire their living from government programs. Since 1865, the South has been an economic second-class citizen of the American Union. This poverty in the South has proven itself to be a political gold mine for tax-and-spend liberals. Liberals use the welfare and quasi-welfare block vote to assure political victory to candidates who will vote for more left-wing social programs. These social programs serve as a repayment to the liberal block voters—the largest percentage of this liberal block vote is made up of black Southerners. But who do you think is paying the taxes for these liberal, tax-and-spend social programs? That's right, the middle class—primarily the white middle class! A Southern candidate who desires to protect the middle class from the "legalized" pillage of the liberal welfare block vote must overcome this 30-40% solid block vote in order to win an election. In other words, in a state in which the welfare and quasi-welfare block vote represents 40% of the total potential vote, the Southern conservative candidate must win 80-90% of the remaining 60% potential votes to win. This is no easy task to accomplish. All the liberal (usually Democrat) candidate has to do is to promise more goodies (midnight basketball, etc.) to the block vote and trick

242 James R. Kennedy and Walter D. Kennedy, *The South Was Right!* (Gretna, LA: Pelican Publishing Company, 1994) 257.

enough middle-class voters into voting for him, and he wins. This is the reason why the South sends so many liberal tax-and-spend Democratic politicians to the Senate, the House of Representatives, governor's mansions, etc. The liberal candidate will "talk" conservative, but, once elected, he votes liberal.[243] Elected Federal officeholders from all sections of our country have been secretly doing this for years. For example, the first day Rep. Jim Inhofe was in office he questioned his fellow Oklahoma Congressman about how he managed to stay in office so long, coming from a conservative state, with such a liberal voting record. The reply was both shocking and enlightening. The Congressman told Rep. Inhofe that it was easy, "All you have to do is vote with the liberal leadership, and then make conservative press releases for your constituents to read."[244] This is exactly what our politicians have been doing for the last fifty years—claiming to represent middle-class values but following the directions of an anti-middle class, liberal leadership.

Representative Charles Stenholm provides us with another example of how our political leaders act once conservatives send them to Washington. In 1993 he was the head of the Conservative Democratic Forum. According to an editorial in *The Wall Street Journal*, even though he was elected as a conservative, his whole career has been a show whereby he takes a public stand against the liberal leadership but at the last moment surrenders to the demands of the liberal leadership![245] As with other politicians, Rep. Stenholm and his cadre of "moderates" make hot speeches and press releases for home consumption. All this amounts to is a deception of "We the people." It is nothing more than a fake stand against the liberal leadership. The liberal leadership allow these so-called moderates to make their speeches because they know that when it comes time to vote, these so-called moderates can be brought back into line by sharp party discipline.[246] This has been happening across America for decades. It has been especially pernicious in the South because we have so many "marginal" districts—districts with large welfare and quasi-welfare votes.

It is very unfortunate that there are not more black Southerners in

243 *The Wall Street Journal,* September 30, 1993, editorial page.

244 Ibid

245 *The Wall Street Journal,* June 1, 1993, editorial page.

246 Ibid

the Southern middle class. As we have already pointed out, the only way black Southerners can be made to feel the necessity of voting a conservative line is by encouraging an economic climate that will allow more black Southerners to move into the economic middle class. The chief physical characteristic of the middle class is ownership of property. Property sets the middle class apart from the economic lower class. With the ownership of property comes the desire to maintain and protect one's hard-earned possessions. Thus, the middle class is antagonistic to the plunder of their property either by criminals or by the more omnipresent variety of plunderers known as tax collectors. Color is of little importance when you are being forced to spend your hard-earned money for social welfare programs that will only serve to increase your tax burden. Black Southerners will vote "middle-class" values only when they by their own efforts become a viable part of the economic middle class. The movement of black people into the middle class is an on-going reality, but it must be accelerated. Liberals have a vested interest in preventing this from happening, whereas the middle class have a vested interest in assuring the movement of more black Southerners into the middle class. This movement must be made possible by having a free society with free markets open to all citizens. The movement of minorities into the middle class, and thus incorporating middle-class virtues, will never be possible by artificial means such as quotas or reverse discrimination. As is discussed in Chapter 6, such Big Government projects will only increase racial conflict.

One reason for the slow movement of black Americans into the mainstream middle class is their view of the role of government in the lives of Americans as opposed to the traditional middle-class view of the role of government. The philosophical difference between the majority of white and black Americans was documented in a September 1994 poll conducted by *The Wall Street Journal* and NBC News. When asked which institution was more responsible for creating jobs, 67% of blacks answered "government." Only 41% of whites answered "government." Greater emphasis on government spending was advocated by 68% of blacks, but by only 36% of whites. A majority of whites thought a better option for solving social and individual problems was to emphasize "private initiative and personal responsibility."[247] To point out these differences is to leave oneself open to

247 *The Wall Street Journal,* September 29, 1994, A12.

hate-filled and slanderous attacks from the liberal media. The liberal establishment does not want such "secrets" discussed. Anyone "foolish" enough to bring to light these points will be branded with the label of "racist," "bigot," and "ignorant redneck" by the left-wing liberal media. But it is important, not only for Southern middle-class voters but also for all Americans as well, to understand the differing philosophies that guide the thinking of these two divergent and, too often, antagonistic groups. In a nutshell, the best way to describe the differences is to say that the tax consumers (represented by the liberal block vote—the larger percentage of that vote in the South being black) prefer a strong government that redistributes other people's wealth via social programs designed for their constituents. The taxpayers (middle class, primarily white) on the other hand, desire a limited government, limited taxation, and an insistence that individuals assume responsible for their own well-being. The tax consumers (the liberal block vote) are using the force of the government tax collector to take property away from the middle-class taxpayers and redistribute middle-class property to those who vote for liberal candidates.

Remember that, before government "gives" something to someone, it must first take that something away from someone else! Government has no wealth or property of its own; nor can it create wealth. It acquires its money the same way the highwayman or robber acquires his money—by the use of force and against the will of the victim! Anyone who does not believe this is challenged to refuse to pay his income tax. What will happen? The government will send its agents, armed with court orders and, if necessary, physical force, to remove the property to satisfy the government's demand to "stand and deliver." What is the difference between a highwayman and the tax collector? The highwayman hides from the law to acquire his ill-gotten goods, while the tax collector uses the force of law to gain his goods. Taxation is nothing less than "legalized" theft.[248] Taxation is the taking of an individual's private property by organized society. The taking is none the less onerous because a mass of people attach a "social" rationale to the taking. If the taking were done by anyone other than government, it would be treated as criminal activity. Where does government acquire the right to take a person's

---

248 Frederic Bastiat, *The Law* (1850, Irvington-On-Hudson, NY: The Foundation for Economic Education, Inc., 1979) 11.

private property? That great American from South Carolina, John C. Calhoun, stated that God ordained that man should live in a social order. Man, as a fallen creature, was prone to do evil. Man tended to be more concerned about what affected himself than about what affected others or society at large. In a manner of speaking, man tended to be selfish. If man, as an individual, were strong enough, he would take from his fellows their property to use as his own. Man as a fallen creature needed spiritual salvation and redemption in order to gain heaven after death, and he needed government to ensure that he did not oppress his fellows while living an imperfect existence here on earth.

The primary function of government is to prevent domestic strife, that is, to maintain law and order and to protect its borders from the international strife of invasion. (Headlines from daily papers prove that the current Federal government has failed both of these requirements.) "We the people" allow government to exercise a degree of control over us in exchange for government's role of defending our borders and assuring domestic tranquility (law and order). Government cannot perform these functions without financial resources. Therefore, the necessity of taxation. Taxes are a necessary evil. The collection of taxes even by an honest and efficient government in payment for essential functions is still the involuntary taking of an individual's earnings. As governments become bigger and more impersonal, the taxpayer will often feel that his property (his tax money) is being used for purposes that he would not have voluntarily given his money to support. As George Washington said, government is force! Washington stated that "Government is not reason, it is not eloquence, it is like fire; a dangerous servant but a fearful master." That is why our Colonial Forefathers placed strict limitations on the powers granted to the Federal government under the original Constitution. The people of the sovereign states knew that the new government they were creating, the Federal government, had within it the potential to abuse its powers. They feared the tyranny of a centralized Federal government. That is why states such as Virginia and New York specifically reserved the right to withdraw any power they had delegated to the Federal government (an act of secession) if those powers granted to the Federal government were ever used against the people of the states.[249]

249 Kennedy and Kennedy, 162.

Modern liberals, on the other hand, have decided that it is government's role to create a society in which everyone has equal wealth, equal housing, equal health care. Absolute equality has become the liberals' political fetish. This equality fetish of modern liberalism extends even to the mental process of thinking. Liberalism's drive for equality of thought has produced political correctness in which all politically incorrect speech and conduct are proscribed and punished by the government. Liberalism must rely upon the force of government and intimidation from the liberal media to enforce compliance with its detrimental policies. Who would voluntarily give one-third to one-half of his earnings to a government that wasted his money? How many middle-class Americans would voluntarily bus their children for the sake of some bizarre, unproven, and cruel liberal social theory? How many white Americans would voluntarily refuse a much-needed job offer, thereby sacrificing their family's future, in order to give a less-qualified "minority" the job? The answer is, very few if any would. The liberal is faced with the dilemma of how to bring about his dreams of a politically correct America when the middle class refuse to cooperate. But the liberal will not be dismayed. He will simply use the force of government, aided by the intimidation factor of the left-wing propaganda media, to compel the middle class to do what they would not otherwise freely consent to do.

Liberalism's power is based upon force. Free government is based upon the principle of consent. Between these two there can be no compromise. To accept a political system that allows the government to deprive its citizens of their hard-earned wages for any purpose declared to be "social welfare" would be to give government the right to destroy the property rights of its citizens. Deprive a man of the right to his property, and you transform him into a slave. Thus, the need for a limited government, low taxation, and individual responsibility if you desire to live in a country that is free. Government, even good government, is the enemy of free men. Taxation is the tool by which liberals legally plunder the hard-earned property of taxpayers and reward liberalism's tax-consuming clientele. We must return to a Federal government described by Thomas Jefferson as "a frugal government that does not take from the laborer the bread he has earned."

The Declaration of Independence, though it has no constitutional authority, is one of history's finest statements regarding the right and duty of a people to defend and, if necessary, establish a free government. In that document, Thomas Jefferson, who penned the Declaration, declared that all mankind have certain "unalienable rights." What he meant was that no matter what a king, or parliament, or any other government, past, present, or future, may do, it can never legally deprive a people of these God-given rights. This concept is very important to the present-day middle class as we struggle to restore our original rights under the Constitution. The liberals will declare that the original Constitution is now outdated and, therefore, modern Supreme Court judges are duty bound to ignore the "archaic" limitations the Founding Fathers placed upon the Federal government. This liberal constitutional theory allows the Supreme Court to declare any right reserved by the sovereign state to be unconstitutional. If a Federal judge decides that a state should provide air-conditioned weight rooms for violent criminals held in state prisons, then the Federal judge, under this liberal constitutional theory, merely issues the Federal court order to the state. In such a system, the state is no longer sovereign but is merely an administrative subdivision of the national government.

What, you may ask, does this have to do with our "unalienable rights?" One of the most important "unalienable" rights a free man has is the right to live under a government ordered upon the principle of the consent of the governed.[250] The Declaration of Independence declares this right to be so important that, if a government violates consent, then the people have not only a right but also a duty to remove that government and replace it with a new government ". . . organizing its powers in such form, as to them shall seem most likely to effect their Safety and Happiness." The right of the people to consent to government was not denied to the states in the Constitution. According to the Tenth Amendment, all rights not specifically denied to the states remain with the states and the people thereof. When the people of the South, in 1861, withdrew their consent and established a new government according to the "unalienable" rights enunciated in the Declaration of Independence, the numerical majority who controlled the Federal government in Washington, D.C., responded by using military force to deny this most important "unalienable" right. This set a precedent that has been and will

250 See "Consent of the Governed—Key to Liberty" in the Addenda section.

continue to be used as an excuse by the liberal establishment to deny all Americans our right to reform the present Federal government. Their logic will be that "you give your consent every time you vote." While this may be nominally true, it is not inclusive of the entire concept of consent. Those who oppose the restoration of the original Constitution will attempt to brand this effort as illegal. They will do this by declaring our efforts to be in violation of the existing Constitution. They will declare that we have consented to the current Federal government as demonstrated by numerous votes cast during national elections. Therefore, according to our opposition, we are in rebellion against legitimate Federal authority, and they will threaten to send in their troops to enforce the civil authority of the national government. With this facade established, they are then free to use the moral suasion of bloody bayonets to deny the "unalienable" right of a people to consent to their government. All of this is based upon the assertion that by casting a ballot "We the people" have given our consent to the current abusive and unconstitutional Federal government.

If we accept the liberal's proposition that voting is all that is necessary to prove consent, then, by demonstrating prior voting in Federal elections, the liberals are free to use force to prevent a change in the government controlled by the liberal establishment. If voting is all that is necessary to prove consent, then the Irish, who voted in elections for representation in the British Parliament, gave their consent to English rule in Ireland and, therefore, their call for Irish Liberty was illegal. Of course, we know that this concept is entirely wrong. The same can be said for the people of Quebec who voted in Canadian elections, or the people of Lithuania who voted in Soviet elections. There is more to consent than casting a ballot. The liberal establishment and the interests of Big Money have never offered the middle class a candidate who was primarily interested in representing middle-class interests. They have, at various times, given the middle class candidates who "talked" conservative or who engaged in popular middle-class rhetoric, but they have never sacrificed their primary interest groups to help the middle class. The left-of-center media (the unofficial propaganda ministry for the liberal establishment) have never given equal time to the issues and leaders of the middle class. The left-of-center education establishment has exercised a monopoly in the academic arena and has viciously harassed and ostracized middle-class spokesmen and blocked the open and fair discussion of middle-class issues. For consent to be legitimate, it must be given freely by individuals who have been adequately informed regarding all aspects of their decision. The Federal government, controlled at one time by the interests of industrial wealth and at another time by the forces of the liberal establishment, has consistently denied to the middle class the opportunity to vote for a viable candidate who would represent their "dearest interests."

The propaganda ministry of the liberal establishment (the media) has vilified and slandered middle-class leaders and issues. The politically correct education establishment has exercised a tyrannical monopoly in the academic market place of ideas by denying middle-class leaders an opportunity to an equal hearing and by refusing to allow an unbiased presentation of middle-class issues. The liberal establishment, in conjunction with the Federal government, is therefore guilty of denying the middle class the "unalienable" right to consent to the government under which they live.

The only way we can guarantee that the current or a future Federal government will not abuse its powers is to require the state to fulfill its original function as the ultimate defender of American civil liberties. The state must once again assert its authority to interpose its sovereign power between an abusive Federal government (the Congress, the Supreme Court, the president, or any agent or department thereof) and "We the people" of the sovereign states. This is what Thomas Jefferson and James Madison did in their famous Kentucky and Virginia Resolutions of 1798. This is what Federalists such as Alexander Hamilton predicted the states would do if they were faced with an unconstitutional act by the Federal government: ". . . the State governments will, in all possible contingencies, afford complete security against invasions of the public liberty by the national authority."[251] The ability of the sovereign state to protect its citizens from an abusive Federal government has been denied ever since the loss of the War for Southern Independence. The time has come for all Americans to recognize and reclaim the vital constitutional mechanism of State Sovereignty. Our Founding Fathers

---

251 Alexander Hamilton, *The Federalist No. 28*, in George W. Carey and James McClellan, *The Federalist: Student Edition* (Dubuque, IA: Kendall/Hunt Publishing Company, 1990) 141.

recognized it as the ultimate remedy for the unconstitutional violation of our most precious liberties. Instead of an anti-middle class,
collectivist government—Why Not Freedom!

SUMMARY
Questions and Answers

*Q. You state that you desire to see more black Americans move into the
middle class because they will then take on middle-class values and vote
accordingly. If this is true, then why don't you support the concept of helping
minorities move into the middle class by supporting racial quotas and minority set-asides?*

A. The principle of free people in a free society, thus free markets, will not abide the idea of governmental intrusion into the lives
of a free people. Thus, the very idea of having some paternalistic government supervising and otherwise usurping the rights of a free people will not allow us to condone reverse discrimination. In a free
society, people will move into and out of markets by their will and
intellect. No one in a free society has any grounds for complaint if he
is frustrated in honest competition for advancement in the market
place. The cardinal rule is that all men are allowed free access to
the market to offer their skills. The choice is to be made upon ability and not skin color. If a group is given favor because of their ethnic
background rather than their ability, they will only increase a state
of bitterness between themselves and those who make up the majority. This does not advance relations between these groups. As for
those who are artificially placed in the middle class because of governmental discrimination, they are beholden not to their own
efforts, but to the government which is in a state of war with the
majority of the members of society. These "artificial" middle-class
people will not take on standard middle-class values because they see
Big Government, just as the welfare clientele see it, as their benefac-
tor. Thus, the liberal establishment by the use of its hold on governmental power can produce quasi-middle class voters for themselves.
Real damage is done to the many honest and capable minority workers who are judged according to the standard workmanship of those
who hold such positions not by merit, but by the force of governmental edicts. Those who are capable should be encouraged to

compete for their place in the market and thereby establish the precedent of hard work and skill as the mode of advancement. Once this is done and the market is secured from governmental interference, minorities will become active participants in middle-class America with the attendant values and voting patterns. This concept is the one great reason why the liberal establishment does not want its welfare clientele to move, by its own merit, into the middle class.

Q. You often mention "unalienable" rights. What are these "unalienable" rights, and where do we get them—from the Constitution?

A. The Founding Fathers of this nation held a common view of the world often referred to as a "biblical world view." This simply means that they viewed the world and man as the product of a divine Creator. Thus, you will note that the Declaration of Independence states that mankind is "endowed by their creator with certain unalienable rights." Your right to life, liberty, the pursuit of happiness, and the right to live under a government founded upon the "consent of the governed" is not a grant from any government or any man; it is a grant from the divine Creator. Since this right is given to man by God, it cannot be taken from man by a man or by any group of men. Thus, these rights are said to be "unalienable." Yes, "unalienable" rights are often trampled upon by tyrants, but this in and of itself does not destroy an "unalienable" right; it only denies to the individual the exercise of his God-given right. From this view of God, man, and government comes the early American view of a Federal Constitution that was established to protect the God-given rights of Americans. Nowhere, in the Constitution, is there found the notion that the Federal government is "creating" or "giving" rights to its subjects. God created rights, therefore, they are "unalienable." The duty of government is to protect those God-given rights.

CHAPTER 26

A Strategy for Freedom

This chapter is addressed generally to all middle-class Americans and specifically to Southerners. The theme of this book is the necessity of re-establishing the original constitutional government of limited Federalism, local control, State Sovereignty, and State's Rights. These are principles that have traditionally been associated with the conservative South. Southerners such as Patrick Henry, Thomas Jefferson, John C. Calhoun, and Jefferson Davis were early defenders of these principles. The post-War Radical Republicans and the current liberal establishment have used the War for Southern Independence, slavery, and racism as a propaganda tool to cause some Southerners to feel guilty about their gallant heritage. This has resulted in a reluctance by some Southerners to take the lead in championing the virtues of State Sovereignty, State's Rights, and limited Federalism. Since the early 1990s, many non-Southern leaders have taken a bold stand in the defense of these principles. Colorado has passed a Tenth Amendment Resolution; former Governor Bracken Lee of Utah has endorsed "The Ultimatum Resolution" which declares that, if the Federal debt reaches six trillion dollars, then the Federal Union will be dissolved; and Ohio's Governor, George V. Voinovich, has blasted such Federal intrusion in his state as unfunded Federal mandates. To date, the South, instead of leading, is lagging far behind. This chapter is addressed to Southerners as a challenge to join our brave Northern kinsmen and renew our battle to uphold the principles of the original Constitution.

According to polling data and the results of the November 8, 1994, elections, the vast majority of Americans have lost confidence in the Federal Congress.[252] It appears that Americans have decided that the Federal government is incompetent, ineffective, and injurious to

252 John H. Fund, "The Revolution of 1994," *The Wall Street Journal,* October 19, 1994, editorial page.

the average person's liberties. The threat of an unconstitutional and abusive Federal government has now become a reality in the everyday life of American citizens. Southerners have a long history of warning our fellow citizens about the threat to liberty posed by an unbridled Federal government. The Southern League[253] is an organization that offers Southerners and all Americans the solution to the problem of an abusive Federal government. This solution is found in the traditional constitutional principles of State Sovereignty, State's Rights, limited Federal powers, and the right of sovereign states to interpose their sovereign authority between their citizens and an abusive Federal government or to secede from the abusive government if no other method of protecting our liberties will provide a remedy. Under our original Constitution, the sovereign state was the final bulwark between individual liberty and an oppressive Federal government.[254] It is this bulwark that must be re-established if the average citizen is to have any protection for his civil liberties. Where can the average citizen go for protection from an abusive Federal government if that right is taken from the sovereign state? This bulwark of protection for the average citizen from a Federal government that will not recognize the limits of its power must be restored if "We the people" are to be secure in our freedom. Unfortunately, since Appomattox, the Federal government has recognized no limits to the exercise of its power.[255] This situation must be reversed.

The Founding Fathers' original intentions to establish a Federal republic with limited and specific powers and their almost universal apprehension of a strong, centralized national government have been thoroughly documented.[256] Even so, there are those who deny the right of "We the people" of the sovereign state(s) to nullify unconstitutional Federal intrusions or to secede from an oppressive and unresponsive Federal government. When average Southerners are told that the only way they can protect their society from unwarranted Federal intrusion is to reestablish the constitutional principles of State

253 For more information, see "Organizing for Freedom" in the Addenda section.

254 See the Virginia and Kentucky Resolutions of 1798, quoted in James R. Kennedy and Walter D. Kennedy, *The South Was Right!* (Gretna, LA: Pelican Publishing Company, 1994) 164-65.

255 "State Sovereignty died at Appomattox" according to U.S. Supreme Court Justice Salmon P. Chase, quoted in Kennedy and Kennedy, 219.

256 William Rawle, *A View of the Constitution of the United States: Secession as Taught at West Point*, Walter D. Kennedy and James R. Kennedy, Eds. (1825, Simsboro, LA: Old South Books, 1993) 41-42.

Sovereignty, including the right of the state to nullify unwarranted Federal actions and, if necessary, the right to secede, they are shocked to the point of total disbelief! As soon as they manage to regain their composure, the following reply gushes forth: "That won't work; we have already tried it!" Let us examine the proposition that, since the South has already tried nullification and secession, these constitutional remedies are not available to protect our ancient liberties. We will then examine a possible strategy that an organized South could use to gain the power necessary to force the Federal government to relent in its unconstitutional oppression of our ancient rights.

Richard Weaver in *The Southern Tradition at Bay* noted that one of the greatest mistakes that the South made was that it took the decision of Appomattox too literally.[257] As a result, Southerners have tended to retreat before the onslaught of liberal ideas and interests. Even when an attempt is made to protect Southern ideas and values, the leadership of the South usually think only in defensive terms. Today, when faced with a Federal government that is actively disarming law-abiding citizens, taking over a third of our wage property under the guise of taxes to support social programs, and callously infringing upon the right of free speech as in the case of the Berkeley Three (who were prosecuted for voicing their concerns over HUD's plans to locate a federally funded housing project in their middle-class neighborhood)—even in light of these and numerous other blatantly unconstitutional actions of the Federal government—Southerners still find it difficult to admit that states, both North and South, had a right to secede in 1861 and that the same right exists today!

If the American colonies were right to speak of withdrawing from their union with Great Britain[258] in 1776, then that same right to withdraw from an existing union that no longer honors its ancient charters and rights exists for us today. If the colonies were right to

257 Richard Weaver, *The Southern Tradition at Bay* (New Rochelle, NY: Arlington House, 1968) 390.

258 The attitude of the American colonists is demonstrated by the language of the state constitutions written after each colony had withdrawn from the British Union. Note the words of North Carolina: "Whereas allegiance and protection are, in the nature reciprocal, and the one should of right be refused, when the other is withdrawn. . . . [Therefore] the said colonies now are, and for ever shall be free and independent states." The constitution of North Carolina, quoted in *The American's Guide to the Constitutions of the United States of America* (Trenton, NJ: Moore and Lake, 1813) 224.

declare to the world that their current government no longer
governed with the consent of the governed and that the colonies
would therefore assert their right and duty to remove themselves
from said government, then that same right exists for us today. If
the right to interpose the sovereign powers of the state between
unconstitutional Federal actions existed in 1798 when James Madison and Thomas Jefferson penned the Virginia and Kentucky Resolutions declaring that the states ". . . are not united on the principle
of unlimited submission to their general government; . . . whensoever the general government assumes undelegated powers, its acts
are unauthoritative, void, and of no force; . . . this government, created by compact, was not made the exclusive or final judge to the
extent of the powers delegated to itself; . . . each party has equal right
to judge for itself,"[259] then that same right exists for Southerners and
all Americans today. If the right of secession as taught in *A View of
the Constitution,* used by the Federal government's own military academy at West Point, was correct in 1825, then it is still correct today.[260]
The passage of time cannot destroy the veracity of high principles
nor can longevity bestow virtue upon crime. The passage of time
cannot justify the crime of denying a people their inalienable right of
self-determination. As strange as it may seem to some, that is what
happened at Appomattox. Although the South was militarily
defeated, it was the American principle of self-government and self-
determination that actually suffered defeat at Appomattox. In the
American experience, secession is valid because the principles of self-
determination and consent of the governed are valid. That which was
right in 1776 was right in 1861 and is still right today! The success
or failure of a military struggle to maintain a government based upon
these principles does not reflect upon the principle of freedom. The
legitimacy of a government is not decided by some medieval trial by
combat but by the test of free and unfettered consent. To deny the
right of secession is to deny the right of the United States to exist outside the British Empire. The question should be settled as far as
Americans who believe in the principles of the Declaration of Independence are concerned—secession is an inherent and inalienable
right that cannot be negated by the moral suasion of bloody bayonets!

259 See the discussion of the Virginia and Kentucky Resolutions of 1798, quoted in Kennedy
and Kennedy, 164-65.

260 Rawle, 234-44.

The existence of a right does not mean that the right will be or should be exercised. Therefore, a more germane question should be asked, "Can secession or the threat of secession be used in our current political environment as a method of reclaiming our lost rights?" This question advances us from the discussion of political theory to one of practical politics—will it work? Could secession (or the threat thereof) be an effective tool to force an abusive and unconstitutional Federal government to recognize and respect the rights of "We the people" of the sovereign states?

As we have already noted, the answer to this question is often mistakenly given in a knee-jerk reaction—"No, secession won't work; we've tried that before." The reply is usually uttered with a most solemn and remorseful demeanor, almost as if the individual replying is experiencing the emotion of grief as a result of the answer he feels forced to offer. As Richard Weaver noted, Southerners have taken the decision at Appomattox too literally. General Lee surrendered an army, not an inalienable right—the right to live under a government founded upon the principle of the consent of the governed. He surrendered an army, not the Tenth Amendment! Let us then look to history for evidence of the successful use of secession.

To be successful, a secession movement should be supported by a population that has a sense of community. The people must be united by a common culture that holds individuals together: a memory of a common heritage, ties of kinship, and a degree of spiritual unity. A successful secession movement is not based on economics or philosophy, though these may play an important role; it is based upon a common cultural identity, an identity that is threatened by an alien power. Texas seceded from Mexico. Cultural differences were at the root of the antagonism and became the underlying strength of the resistance movement.

The mere threat of secession has been used in modern times to gain important concessions from a more powerful force. The Scottish National Party used the threat of secession to force the British Parliament to allocate larger shares of North Sea oil royalties for the Scottish people. In Quebec, the Canadian Federal government was forced to grant specific cultural advantages to the French-speaking province. These advantages remain in place even though the French separatists lost the plebiscite on secession twenty years ago. Currently, the Canadian Federal government has tacitly acknowledged the right of Quebec to secede from the Federal Union. British Columbia, another Canadian province, is now discussing the possibility of seceding.

The story of Lithuania's secession from the Soviet Union is well known. The Lithuanian people were forced to live for almost fifty years under the most cruel empire in history, an empire that actively practiced cultural genocide, and yet the people of Lithuania were able to force the empire to grant them their liberty. In India, an humble spokesman for the independence of India from the British Empire was able to use the moral persuasion of non-violence to force the British to "quit India." Mahatma Gandhi proved to the world that it takes more than cold steel to defeat a people who are determined to exercise their inalienable right to self-determination. In these examples, it should be noted that most of the secession movements did not rely upon military force to gain their goals.

Charles Stewart Parnell's political revolt against British tyranny could serve as an example for future Southern and other conservative state secession movements. (Remember, the remedy of secession is not an exclusive tool for Southern use only. Secession is an American, not a Southern, right.) The separation of Ireland from the British Empire was an occasion of numerous insurrections. Yet, Parnell led a political revolt against the British that almost won Irish freedom without relying upon military force.

Parnell was born at Avondale, Ireland, of English and American descent, a country gentleman who had been educated at the best English schools and who inherited from his mother a hatred of England and a fierce, implacable dedication to the Irish national cause. He once told a friend, "These English despise us because we are Irish; but we must stand up to them. That's the way to treat an Englishman—stand up to him!"

Parnell was elected as an Irish representative to the British Parliament after several unsuccessful attempts. He entered Parliament as a virtual rebel. He knew that physical force was of no avail against the might of the Empire, so he chose the tactic of political exasperation.

The old, traditional Irish party politicians had achieved nothing for Ireland but contempt from the English and complete control of all Irish affairs from London. The Irish party members went half-heartedly through the motions of free debate, observed all the rules of the British Constitution, and politely obeyed their English masters. They did not even have enough power and determination to force the English to relieve the Irish famines of the 1840s. During these famines, over a million Irish men, women, and children starved to death!

Faced by a government under the control of the English, Parnell initiated a policy of organized obstruction in Parliament. He would have no alliance with either English party. He would support each, in turn, with sole regard to the balance of power in Parliament. Every question became an Irish question. Every debate was interrupted with arguments about the Irish issue. The grievances of Ireland and the plight of her people were dinned into English ears day after day, night after night. Within ten years, Parnell built up his faction from a mere handful to eighty-six members of Parliament. After the election of 1885, he became the unofficial broker of political power between the two rival English political parties.

At the very height of power and with Irish freedom within sight, disaster struck. Parnell became involved in a scandalous divorce in which he was named as correspondent. The repercussions shortened his life. If he had lived, he would have undoubtedly brought about Irish Home Rule before the turn of the century and without the necessity of armed revolt.

Could a similar political movement supporting secession win a political struggle with the American liberal establishment? What would happen if there arose in the South an organization that used various media to advocate secession as the only way to force the Federal government to adhere to the limits of the original Constitution? Such an organization would inform Americans that only by an appeal to the right of secession could Southerners and those Northerners who live in urban areas, ever hope to end forced busing, or that the only way to force the evil power brokers in liberal Washington, D.C., to relent in their campaigns of reverse discrimination, open borders immigration policies, violation of the right to keep and bear arms, infringement upon private citizens' property rights, anti-Southern cultural genocide, and denial of freedom of speech would be an appeal to secession. Such an organization could demonstrate that the only sure way to protect Americans from an abusive Federal government would be an appeal to secession. Secession would be the tool whereby "We the people" could notify the arrogant elite in

Washington, D.C., that we are the ones who command and possess the source of authority in America—to put it bluntly, it could be the means by which we tell the Washington elite that "We the people," not the elite, are "the boss"! Suppose this and other organizations would raise the Southern public's conscious identification with their Southern culture by defending Confederate flags and symbols. More importantly, these organizations would keep the political questions of State's Rights, State Sovereignty, and limited Federalism (questions such as busing, reverse discrimination, high taxes, and gun control) before the American public.

After the initial shock at the introduction of the concept of secession, the public would understand that secession (or the threat thereof) is an act of self-determination by which our original constitutional Republic of Republics would be restored. Once secession was viewed in its constitutional context, as an act of self-determination, the American public would embrace the idea. The inalienable right of self-determination is the only way to permanently resolve political issues such as reverse discrimination, gun control, and unfunded Federal mandates. Southerners, as well as other conservative Americans, would soon understand that issues such as quotas, busing, high taxes, and crime are issues that traditional, business-as-usual politicians have purposefully refused to address but that now "We the people" of the sovereign state have the means to correct these problems. The principle of self-determination would have the effect of removing the Big Government, Federal politician from the governmental power equation. By this means "We the people" would do an end run around the Federal political establishment in Washington, D.C.

At some point, the organization supporting the principle of self-determination would begin sponsoring political candidates who would offer secession (or the threat of secession) as the primary means of restoring the balance of power between the states and the Federal government. At last, the middle class would have found the means and political leaders to reclaim their lost rights. The ineffective and dismal voting records of Democratic and Republican politicians relative to issues such as busing, affirmative action, and taxes would be continually presented to the public. Candidates elected from this "State's Rights" cadre would promote and build this organization at the grass-roots level and make every issue brought before them a question of the restoration of the original constitutional government, limited Federalism, State Sovereignty, and State's Rights.

The organization would train members to convert the population into supporters of State's Rights. Aside from direct political action, the population would be directed into specific social actions such as selective buying campaigns, recall elections aimed at liberal politicians who betray middle-class values (referred to in the South as scalawags), mass protests, and other social actions that would support the political goal of the restoration of middle-class freedom. For example, physician members of the organization would send letters to all other physicians in their respective states describing how Federal efforts to socialize medicine could be completely blocked by supporting the principle of secession and those candidates who advocate it. Small business owners in every American city and town would receive information reminding them how much EEOC, ADA, OSHA, and other Federal compliance programs are costing them and how this will cease only when the sovereign state reclaims its legitimate authority to protect them from an abusive Federal government. Each year during the week of April 15, the organization could purchase radio spot ads reminding the taxpayer that the liberal establishment that controls the Federal government is using middle-class tax revenues to "pay off" liberalism's tax-consuming, liberal-voting, welfare clientele.

Recent polling data support the conclusion that Southerners still think of themselves as residents of a special region or even as a people who share a common past. A recent Louis Harris poll noted that 71% of the Southern people support the use of the Confederate battle flag on state flags.[261] Another poll conducted by *The Atlanta Journal Constitution* revealed that 20% of Southerners think that the South would be better off as an independent nation![262] This 20% of Southerners who currently believe in independence is truly an amazing number of people when we consider that they hold this opinion without the benefit of an organized, pro-independence public information effort and in the face of liberal media that are virulently anti-South. The American people, North, South, East, and West are willing to give freedom a chance!

The preceding hypotheses and recent polling data demonstrate

261 "Survey Finds Tolerance for Confederate Flag," *The Washington Times,* July 4, 1994.

262 Lewis Grizzard, *Hattiesburg* (MS) *American,* July 11, 1993, 11A.

that the possibility for a successful Southern mass movement against the current unconstitutional, liberal, Federal power structure is possible. The examples of Texas, Scottish Nationalists, Quebec, Lithuania, Gandhi, and Parnell all support the possibility of a successful secession movement. The South (and other states seeking to reclaim their sovereign authority) would, for the first time, have a convincing claim to the moral high ground. We could present our Cause to the Court of World Opinion—a court that already has a less than enthusiastic opinion regarding big, centralized empires. The Southern people, proud of their heritage and determined to reassert their inalienable right to live under a government ordered upon the principle of the free and unfettered consent of the governed could be the catalyst for the development of an American social force capable of breaching the strongest barricades of tyranny and overrunning an entrenched, politically correct, and dictatorial ruling elite.

This chapter has been addressed in a general manner to all Americans, regardless of which section they may live in, but more specifically it has been addressed to Southerners. At one time in the history of the United States, the South was in the vanguard of those defending State's Rights and limited Federalism. As we have shown, that is no longer the case. The once-forceful South has become the timid South, the reluctant South, the frightened and intimidated South. If Americans are ever to regain their lost rights, they must see a renewal in the fighting spirit of the South. Conservatives from other areas of the country need the support of Southern conservatives in order to defeat the leviathan of Big Government. It is hoped that an invigorated South will once again take its stand for constitutional government and thereby encourage our fellow Americans in other parts of the country to join with us in the struggle to restore limited Federalism, State's Rights, and our original Republic of Republics. Thus, this chapter is offered in the hope of explaining to those outside the South some of the problems the middle class people of the South are contending with and also as an effort to infuse back into the hearts and mind of Southerners the courage and determination that once was the South's and that once inspired the world.

Deo Vindice!

SUMMARY
Questions and Answers

Q. You talk about secession as an answer to the problems Americans now face from the Federal government. Don't you think that by promoting secession you are undoing the work of history and over 600,000 Americans who died to keep America one nation?

A. No one can go back into history and change it. What we have said is that the problems confronting Americans are a direct result of the inability of "We the people" at the local level to check the abuse of our rights by the Federal government. This usurpation of our rights by an abusive Federal government is a fact of life regardless of what section of the country we live in. Whatever the Federal government determines to do with you or me or with one of our rights, it can do, and no one at this point in American history can prevent it from acting in such an unconstitutional manner. At one time in the history of this Republic of Republics, "We the people" did possess the tools for the defense of our "dearest interests." Since Appomattox, the power of the sovereign states has been removed from "We the people" and its powers concentrated in the hands of those in control of the Federal government. If all men were good and honest, there would be little problem with this arrangement. Under those conditions, the letter and spirit of the Constitution would be upheld and our "dearest interests" would be secure. But, as we know from secular as well as biblical history, given man's basic nature and his ability to abuse his fellow creatures, abuse will eventually occur. Because of the nature of mankind and mankind's government, a system of checks and balances must be placed upon all instruments of governmental power to prevent misuse. State's Rights or, if you prefer, State Sovereignty, is the natural check upon a Federal government's ability to overstep its legitimate authority. The act of secession is the ultimate, not the first, response of a people attempting to defend their threatened rights. As John Locke stated, ". . . a people are never truly free if there be no means to escape tyranny."

Your question about maintaining America as "one nation" cannot be answered without first knowing what type of nation you are attempting to maintain. In a free society or nation, there are some things that simply cannot be done, because to do those things would

negate the very idea of freedom itself, thereby making the maintenance of a free society impossible. Thus, for instance, if we desire to
maintain America as a free nation in which religious freedom is recognized, the Federal government cannot enforce a state religion. If
it attempted to enforce a state religion and some state of the American Union responded by seceding, would the Federal government of
"free" America be justified in waging a war against that state in order
to "keep America one nation"? You see, in this hypothesis, America
ceases to be "free" when it no longer recognizes freedom of religion, and, certainly, when it wages war upon a particular section of
the country in order to enforce one section's views upon another.
When this happens, the nation is no longer "free", i.e., the nation is
no longer governed with the consent of the governed. Now, if what
you desire is purely maintaining the geographical integrity of the
borders of America without any reference to the nature of its government, whether it be a free government or a dictatorship, then you
may choose war and aggression to achieve your goals. But you cannot
rationally say that what you are doing is promoting freedom, because
your very action is destroying the foundation upon which all free
societies are built. By forcing your desire to maintain the geographical borders of America, you are destroying the principle of government based upon the consent of the governed.

The notion of states having an obligation to their citizens to be the
guardian of their rights, and the people acting through their states
having the right to secede from an abusive Federal government may
seem rather hard to understand at first. The act of secession is an
act of "tough love" by those who created the Federal government.
Oftentimes this principle of tough love is exercised by parents who
find no other way to control unruly children. It is done not because
the parents desire harm or even punishment for their children, but
because tough love is the only solution for a given problem. When
the Federal government acts like a spoiled child and refuses to
respond to the wishes of "We the people" of the sovereign state, the
very ones responsible for the life of the Federal government, tough
love is in order. This is the reason that Alexander Hamilton stated
that he hoped that the equilibrium between the state and Federal
government would be maintained. Hamilton even noted that the
legislatures of the states would have sufficient means at their disposal

to protect this equilibrium. Like a sick child needing a strong dose of unpleasant-tasting medicine, the Federal government needs some "tough love" from "We the people" of the sovereign states.

CHAPTER 27

The Cure for the Disease of Big Government

Our purpose in writing this book is more than merely to demonstrate that the Founding Fathers intended to establish a government of limited Federalism, reserving the residual powers to "We the people" within our respective sovereign states. We also intend to do more than just give vivid examples of contemporary abuse of Federal power and the modern-day destruction of civil liberties of American citizens by an uncontrollable Federal government. This has been done by other authors many times before. What is unique about this book is that in it we offer a political solution to the abuse of Federal power. We offer a cure for the disease of an unresponsive, tax-and-spend Big Government. We offer the only means by which "We the people" of the sovereign state can assure that an abusive Federal government will never again violate any American citizen's inalienable rights. We offer nothing new. We offer a return to the system of constitutional government that our Founding Fathers intended when they ratified the original Constitution and Bill of Rights.

It should be obvious to all that the middle class cannot rely upon the national political parties to bring about this radical restoration of constitutional government. These parties have both, at one time or another, abandoned the middle class. While so easily abandoning middle-class issues, they have been most reluctant to sacrifice any issue that is dear to their special-interest groups. While it is important for conservative middle-class citizens to participate in and attempt to control the party most nearly advocating middle-class values, this alone will never suffice for the restoration of limited Federalism, State's Rights, and State Sovereignty. Both national parties have as their primary goal the control of the Federal government and the use of that government to advance their party and its leaders. Anything that tends to reduce Federal power will tend to reduce the perks of power available for the national party to be divided among the party faithful. Regardless of how "conservative" any national political party is, it will always find it difficult and contrary to man's political nature[263] to reduce its power. This is not to imply that we feel it unwise to work within national political parties. While working within a national party, we must always keep in mind that the party alone will not provide the solution for the abandonment of the middle class. A political party, under the control or direction of true conservatives, can be a tool that is carefully used to help achieve our goal. A political party is a tool to achieve the ultimate goal of restoration of the original constitutional Republic of Republics and must not be confused with the goal itself. Under conservative control, a political party can be a means to the end, but it is not the solution needed to protect the "dearest interests" of America's middle class.

In the late 1960s, conservative Southern Democrats were ejected from the national Democratic party. They were replaced with the likes of the predominantly black Freedom Democratic party which brought to the party its anti-middle class values. Since then, many Southern conservatives have maintained a split political personality. Southerners have voted Democratic in state and local elections and Republican in national elections. This has worked to the great disadvantage of the conservative movement nationwide. It has allowed the Democratic party to maintain its hold on a large share of Southern state legislatures and governors' mansions. The national Democrats avoided any punishment for ejecting conservative Southerners and seating liberal radicals who did not represent the interests of middle-class Southerners. The national Republican party, on the other hand, reaped a windfall. The Republican party virtually inherited, without having to bargain for it, the majority of the Southern middle-class vote during national elections. These votes were "gratis"; they cost the Republicans nothing, because Southern conservatives gave their votes away without extracting anything of value from the national Republican party in return, except rhetoric. As we have demonstrated in Chapters 5 through 24 the Republican party has given conservatives rhetoric, reserving the real action for the "protected minorities" who represent the "last vote." While the national Democratic party engaged in an open frontal assault against

---

263 John C. Calhoun, *Disquisition on Government*, quoted in *The Works of John C. Calhoun* (New York, NY: D. Appleton and Company, 1844) I; 3.

America's middle-class, the national Republican party secretly betrayed the middle class (especially the Southern middle class).

Thomas Jefferson was the leader of the original Republican party.[264] These early Jeffersonian Republicans used the power of their party to overturn many of the unconstitutional acts of the Federalist party which had preceded them in office. The original Republicans used their national party to support their views. Still, it should be remembered that eventually all parties lose power. If we depend solely upon party power as a defense for our liberties, then we put our "dearest interests" at risk during each election. To protect our "dearest interests," something more permanent than party politics must be established.

Many conservatives place all their hopes for protecting constitutional government in the simple technique of electing enough "good conservatives" to national office. This, they reason, will allow us to control the Federal government. According to these conservatives, it really does not matter which party the "conservative" belongs to, just as long as he is a "conservative." Their logic is that, if conservatives can control both Houses of Congress, elect conservative presidents, and pack the Supreme Court with conservative judges, then the "dearest interests" of the middle class will be safe. There are two main problems with this logic. First, *the Federal government is a special interest within itself.* Therefore, merely electing "conservative" Federal officials will not remove those officials from the distorting influence of the special interests of the Federal government. As we have already noted, it is difficult for an elected official to vote for measures that have the effect of reducing his importance—a vote to eliminate Federal distribution of welfare monies, for example would reduce the elected official's importance to the people whom he will ask to vote for him in the next election. Elected conservatives also have their own special-interest groups who seek special favors from them. These efforts, just as the efforts of the liberal's clientele, will at some point in time have an impact upon the rights and liberties of "We the people" at the local level. How can "We the people" protect ourselves from "our" conservative elected officials who may become part of the "Federal scene?" There is also a natural and intended antagonism between the special interests of the Federal government and the

264 Forrest McDonald, *A Constitutional History of the United States* (Malabar, FL: Robert E. Krieger Publishing Company, 1986) 46.

interests of state and local governments—not to mention the interests of the middle-class taxpayer. "We the people" of the sovereign state cannot trust our "dearest interests" to the governance of benevolent Federal officials *even when they claim to be and indeed are conservative.* It will always be to their political advantage to have a large central government that can "give" special favors to those who elect Federal officials and therefore assure their re-election, patronage, or well-being. John C. Calhoun described this tendency when he noted that government "has itself a strong tendency to disorder and abuse of its powers, as all experience and almost every page of history testify." He also observed that government "must be administered by men in whom, like others, will, if left unguarded, be by them converted into instruments to oppress the rest of the community."[265]

As far as the Supreme Court is concerned, it should be noted that, under our current system, after a "conservative" is approved for the Supreme Court, "We the people" of the sovereign state have no control over his actions. He may be nominated and approved as a "conservative," but once approved he may be influenced to change and become antagonistic toward his former friends. President Dwight D. Eisenhower nominated Earl Warren, believing that he would be a moderate jurist. After he was seated, Warren led the charge to the left as one of the court's most liberal, activist chief justices in modern history. A similar event occurred with President James Madison's appointee. Madison, author of the Virginia Resolution of 1798, wanted a Supreme Court justice who would support the original intent of the Constitution. He appointed Joseph Story who became one of America's strongest advocates of centralized Federal power and an enemy of state sovereignty.[266] No, "We the people" cannot rely upon "good conservatives" elected or appointed to Federal offices for the ultimate protection of our "dearest interests."

The second danger in relying upon the Federal government to protect our "dearest interests" is that national political party discipline, applied by fellow elected officials in Washington, D.C., is stronger and more influential than an individually elected Federal official's commitment to the unorganized mass of voters "way back" home. The elected official faces the voters every other year at most, but he faces the party whip every day. If the party whip tells him to

265 Calhoun, I; 7.
266 McDonald, 54.

vote for the Panama Canal Treaty, gun control, or a quota civil rights bill, even though he knows his unorganized constituents oppose such legislation, he will follow the party whip's directions regardless of how many letters he receives from the folks back home. Sometimes, in order to help the poor beleaguered fellow out, the party leadership will allow legislators from conservative districts to take turns voting against unpopular liberal legislation. This allows an elected official to send the word back home about how he voted against "bad" liberal legislation. What he does not tell his constituency is that the party whip had already counted the votes and thus knew that the few negative votes allowed for home consumption would not hurt the passage of the unpopular liberal legislation. At other times, the party will arrange for two different votes on unpopular liberal legislation. One is made in public, but it is then reversed in the privacy of a committee. This is the way Federal elected officials are used by the party to advance the special interests of "protected minorities" and other special-interest groups. The elected "conservative" talks conservatively but votes with the party leadership.[267] The party system that controls the Federal government works just as well for Big Money as it does for "protected minorities"; in either case "We the people" of the middle class are left out of the equation, our responsibility being only to serve as the Federal government's tax "cash-cow." Neither reliance on national parties nor on "conservative" control of the Federal government will provide the middle class with the means to protect our "dearest interests."

What mechanism, then, can the middle class rely upon to protect our rights and liberties? Some would say that we must rely upon a written constitution. Yet, a written constitution only gives the directions for government to follow. A written constitution is only as good as the "good faith" of the men and women who implement the plan outlined by that constitution. The actual implementation of those directions can provide ample opportunity for special-interest groups to enrich themselves at the expense of society at large. If a group of people gain control of the various branches of the Federal government, they may choose to ignore the written limitations imposed by the constitution.[268] In such a case, what recourse would "We the

267 *The Wall Street Journal*, Sept. 30, 1993, editorial page [to put it frankly—our elected federal officials have made a lucrative career out of lying to the American people].

268 James R. Kennedy and Walter D. Kennedy, *The South Was Right!* (Gretna, LA: Pelican lishing Company, 1994) 156-58.

people" have? Suppose the Federal Congress passed laws oppressing the civil liberties of Americans, and the Federal president
enforced those unconstitutional laws while the Federal Supreme
Court refused to declare said laws unconstitutional; what protection
would be afforded "We the people" by the written constitution? This
is the situation that will eventually arise in any solitary, centralized
republic. Eventually, the numerical majority will gain complete control of the national government and use it to the advantage of the
numerical majority and to the disadvantage of the numerical minority.[269] Thus, the need exists for some mechanism outside of the Federal government to control the abuse of Federal powers and to act
as a counterbalance to the tendency of any Federal government to
abuse its powers.

Conservatives believe in the principle of individual responsibility.
Therefore, we must look first to ourselves to protect our rights and
liberties. We know that no one can protect our "dearest interests"
better than we can. "We the people" at the local level are the first to
feel and respond to the oppressive acts of government. We are better
qualified to initiate a reaction to unconstitutional infringement of
our liberties, not Big Government, not an impersonal Supreme
Court, not national politicians intoxicated with the arrogance of
power and residing in faraway Washington, D.C. The constitutional
protection of individual liberty is best accomplished by the people
who have the most to lose if constitutional government is not maintained. This is the great benefit of State Sovereignty and State's
Rights. "We the people" of the sovereign states are empowered
through the corporate body of our state to judge whether an action
of the Federal government is unconstitutional. Under the system of
co-ordinate Federal/state governments,[270] we are not required to
appeal to the Federal government to judge whether it (the Federal
government) is abusing its powers. This, after all, would make the
one accused of the crime the same one to judge his own guilt or
innocence. The original intention of our Founding Fathers was to
create (and, in fact, they did create) a Republic of Republics. Prior to
the loss of the War for Southern Independence, our country was
referred to in the plural, i.e. "The United States *are* a great

---

269 Calhoun, I; 303-4.

270 Ibid, I; 265-67, 299.

country."[271] This reflected the generally accepted opinion that our country is composed of a federation of sovereign republics governed by a compact[272] styled in the Constitution for the United States of America. Unfortunately, too many Americans have been deluded by post-Appomattox nationalist propaganda. By following this "manifest destiny" propaganda line, "We the people" have been led away from the foundation and strength of our liberty—the sovereign state—and into the entangling embrace of an overgrown, tax-and-spend, out-of-control Federal government that no longer recognizes any limit to the exercise of its powers.

As a result of the conservative victory in the November 8, 1994, election, many people began to discuss the possibility of the Federal government "allowing" the states to take over a larger part of the responsibility for certain Federal programs. The truth is that the Federal government never had any business taking over these state functions to begin with. The idea that the Federal government may "allow" the states more participation in these programs is based upon a fallacy. The Federal government receives its authority from the states; it therefore cannot grant to the states new rights. If the Federal government is exercising any rights not granted in the original Constitution (as legally amended), then its acts are not "pursuant" to the Constitution and are therefore void.[273] The Federal government is not the original source of sovereign power—"We the people" of the sovereign states are the source of original power, and we still possess our inalienable right to limit or withdraw our authority at the pleasure of the Sovereign Community.

The struggle to restore the original Constitution is not a business-as-usual political exercise. It is a revolution akin to America's original struggle with the British Empire. "We the people" must determine to rein in the tentacles of an abusive Federal government. "We the people" must determine to establish a mechanism that will control the innumerable agents of Leviathan, that is, the agents of the

271 William Rawle, *A View of the Constitution of the United States,* Walter D. Kennedy and James R. Kennedy, Eds. (1825, Simsboro, LA: Old South Books, 1993) 37, 78, 234.

272 "When the Constitution was framed, its framers, and the people who adopted it, came to a clear, express, unquestionable stipulation and compact." Daniel Webster (1851), quoted in Albert Taylor Bledsoe, *Is Davis a Traitor?* 2nd. ed. (St. Louis, MO: The Advocate House, 1879) 99.

273 Alexander Hamilton, *The Federalist No. 33,* quoted in George W. Carey and James McClellan, *Federalist Papers: Student Edition* (Dubuque, IA: Kendall/Hunt Publishing Co., 1990) 161.

Federal government, who have become intoxicated with the arrogance of power. "We the people" must be dedicated to establishing a system by which the "dearest interests" of the common man, at the local level, will be secure from the greed and calloused indifference of faraway political bosses. "We the people" not only have the right but also the duty to protect our civil liberties and the civil liberties of generations yet to come. "We the people" must make our claim to the authority to change, alter, abolish, or replace the current Federal government, not from the Constitution, either past or present, but from the inalienable right of a people to establish the government that rules over them.[274] This is a right that was acknowledged by our Declaration of Independence:

> . . . Governments are instituted among Men, deriving their just powers from the consent of the governed,—That whenever any Form of Government becomes destructive of these ends, it is the Right of the People to alter or to abolish it, and to institute new Government. . . .[275]

The right and duty of "We the people" to alter or abolish any government that does not serve the happiness and safety of the people existed before the Constitution and the Declaration of Independence. "We the people" have the supreme authority to establish a government that governs by the authority of the free and unfettered consent of the people.

In our American system, "We the people" express our sovereign will through our state government. John C. Calhoun described the state as the Sovereign Community. People as individuals are not sovereign, but together as a community they exercise their sovereign authority to create state constitutions authorizing specific functions for government at the local and state level. Serving as the agent of the people of a Sovereign Community, the state, in conjunction with other states, each acting as an independent entity, created the Federal government. This government was created by independent

274 Although the principle of "government by the consent of the governed" is very American, it has many noble antecedents. See Junius Brutus, *Vindiciae Contra Tyrannos: A Defence of Liberty Against Tyrants* (1689, Edmonton, AB, Canada: Still Waters Revival Books, 1989) 59-60, and Samuel Rutherford, *Lex Rex* (1644, Harrisonburg, VA: Sprinkle Publications, 1982) 126.

275 See The Unanimous Declaration of the Thirteen United States of America, In Congress, July 4, 1776.

communities for their own betterment. The states did not intend to create an agent to serve as their lord and master. The Federal government is the agent of the states. The state is the agent of the Sovereign Community. "We the people" are individual members of the Sovereign Community, and through its elected representatives to its state legislature or state constitutional convention, we ratified the creation of the Federal government and any subsequent constitutional power granted to either government (state or Federal).

The concept of State Sovereignty is indispensable to the operation of our original constitutional system.[276] The principle of the states as independent and sovereign political entities predates the existence of the Federal government. The state of Virginia declared her independence from Great Britain in May of 1776, a full month before the joint declaration issued by the thirteen American colonies on July 4, 1776. After the conclusion of the American Revolution, the British recognized the freedom and independence of each of the thirteen former British colonies. When the British signed the Treaty of Paris, the former colonies became thirteen free and independent states. In 1781, these states organized a Federal government under the Articles of Confederation. Article II of the Articles of Confederation left no question regarding the status of each state in this self-styled "perpetual" union (this "perpetual" union lasted only seven years, at which time each of the states seceded from it and later acceded to the new union under the Constitution of 1787. The Founding Fathers did not use the term "perpetual" again). In plain language, Article II of the Articles of Confederation states

> Each state retains its sovereignty, freedom, and independence, and every Power, Jurisdiction and right, which is not by this confederation expressly delegated to the United States, in Congress assembled.

From the plain language of Article II of the Articles of Confederation, it can be seen that the sovereign states were intent upon (1) establishing the fact that each state was a free, independent, and sovereign entity, and (2) declaring clearly that their union together was not an implied reenunciation of their sovereign authority. The right of "We the people" of the sovereign state to alter or abolish an

276 Kennedy and Kennedy, 219-35.

abusive central government has been demonstrated as an inalienable right, a sovereign right of our respective state as evidenced by the language of the Treaty of Paris and the Articles of Confederation. Some may ask, "But what about the Constitution?" Though not essential to the existence of our right to change or abolish an abusive Federal government, it is enlightening to consider the attitude of our Founding Fathers regarding the questions of State Sovereignty and the right of the state to challenge unconstitutional acts of the Federal government.

The Federalist, Number 39, declared that the new Constitution would be ratified by the people of America,

> . . . not as individuals composing one entire nation, but as composing the distinct and independent States to which they [the people] belong. It is to be the assent and ratification of the several States, derived from the supreme authority in each State, the authority of the people themselves. The act, therefore, establishing the Constitution, will not be a *national,* but a *federal* act.
> . . . Each State in ratifying the Constitution, is considered as a sovereign body, independent of all others, and only to be bound by its own voluntary act. In this relation, then, the new Constitution will, if established, be a *federal,* and not a *national,* constitution.[277]

The Federalists (those who supported the adoption of the Constitution) were attempting to calm the fears of many of the citizens of the states who were afraid that the new Federal government proposed under the Constitution would become national in character. As a national government, so reasoned men such as Patrick Henry, the Federal government would assume the right to treat states as inferior governmental districts. The people of America had recently seceded from a union with the British Empire[278] and did not relish the thought of creating another centralized, national government that could abuse the dearest rights of "We the people" of the sovereign state. The Federalists, again and again, assured the people of the states that anti-Federalists such as Patrick Henry were overreacting.

277 James Madison, *The Federalist No. 39,* quoted in Carey and McClellan, 196-97.

278 "*Resolved,* That the union that has hitherto subsisted between Great Britain and the American colonies is thereby totally dissolved, and that the inhabitants of this colony are discharged from any allegiance to the crown of Great Britain." Virginia Convention—Independence, quoted in William Wirt Henry, Ed., *Patrick Henry: Life, Correspondence, and Speeches* (1891, Harrisonburg, VA: Sprinkle Publications, 1993) I; 396.

Unfortunately, history has proven that Patrick Henry's warnings were more prophetic than the assurances of the Federalists.

During the debate on ratification of the Constitution, there was little if any doubt as to the sovereign status of the states. Even such an ardent advocate of a strong national government as Alexander Hamilton admitted, "The State governments, by their original constitutions, are invested with complete sovereignty."[279] Not only did such Federalists recognize the sovereignty of the states, but James Madison, a Federalist at this point in his life, also noted the dependency of the Federal government upon the state for the Federal government's very existence. On the other hand, he noted that the states did not require the Federal government in order to exist as states. "The State governments may be regarded as constituent and essential parts of the federal government; whilst the latter [the Federal government] is no wise essential to the operation or organization of the former [the states]."[280] He also noted the importance of the states as a primary defender of the "lives, liberties, and properties" of the citizens of each state.

> The powers delegated by the proposed Constitution to the federal government are few and defined. Those which are to remain in the State governments are numerous and indefinite. The former [Federal powers] will be exercised principally on external objects, as war, peace, negotiation, and foreign commerce; with which last the power of taxation will, for the most part, be connected. The powers reserved to the several States will extend to all the objects which, in the ordinary course of affairs, concern the lives, liberties, and properties of the people, and the internal order, improvement, and prosperity of the State.[281]

Alexander Hamilton noted that the powers reserved to the states are necessary for the day-to-day functioning of the state and that these activities are best controlled by the people at the local level. Hamilton made specific mention of those things our Founding Fathers referred to in the Declaration of Independence as certain "unalienable" rights: life, liberty, property, and internal order. These attributes are fundamental to people in a free society; without them we cannot be free. Hamilton, though an avid nationalist and

279 Alexander Hamilton, *The Federalist No. 31*, quoted in Carey and McClellan, 154.

280 James Madison, *The Federalist No. 45*, quoted in Carey and McClellan, 237.

281 Ibid, 238.

supporter of a strong centralized Federal government, knew that the people of the sovereign states would not accept an American Federal government that claimed the right to control local and state affairs. When it came to convincing the early Americans to form a new central government, Hamilton made sure that everyone knew that the type of government he was advocating was one of a limited Federal nature.

While it is important to understand the Founding Fathers' acceptance of the principle of state sovereignty, another more important point to understand is that they believed it was necessary for the sovereign state to have the power to defend its citizens from an abusive and oppressive Federal government. Hamilton knew that "we the people" of the sovereign state ". . . will always take care to preserve the constitutional equilibrium between the general and the State governments."[282] The Federalists were quick to assert that the people had nothing to fear from the proposed Federal government. Their confidence was supposedly based upon the conviction that the sovereign state would always be available to defend citizens whose civil liberties or property rights were threatened by an unwarranted act of the Federal government. Hamilton was convinced that the state governments could and would offer the people of the states the protection they needed from an abusive Federal government. In *The Federalist Papers,* Hamilton states

> It may safely be received as an axiom in our political system, that the State governments will, in all possible contingencies, afford complete security against invasions of the public liberty by the national authority.[283]

During the debates contemplating the ratification of the Constitution, anti-Federalists such as Patrick Henry of Virginia and John Lansing of New York warned Americans about the potential for abuse of the powers that the states were delegating to the Federal government under the proposed Constitution. Again and again, the Federalists would counter with promises and assurances of the safety provided the people by the state because the state would always be the ultimate barrier between the liberty of "We the people" and an abusive Federal government. The Federalists implied that the

---

282 Alexander Hamilton, *The Federalist No. 31,* quoted in Carey and McClellan, 155.

283 Alexander Hamilton, *The Federalist No. 28,* quoted in Carey and McClellan, 141.

anti-Federalists were overreacting, were misguided extremists, or were simply lacking in a proper understanding of the proposed Constitution. The Federalists seemed to be perplexed as to why the anti-Federalists were so concerned about the possible abuse of Federal powers:

> I am unable to conceive that the State legislatures, which must feel so many motives to watch, and which possess so many means of counteracting, the federal legislature, would fail either to detect or to defeat a conspiracy of the latter [the Federal government] against the liberties of their common constituents.[284]

Even though the Federalist assurances were to be proven incorrect, it still demonstrates the fact that our Founding Fathers' original intention was to establish a co-ordinate Federal/state system in which the state could protect the people from an abusive Federal government. In the closing paragraphs of the last *Federalist Paper*, Hamilton once again assured the citizens of the sovereign states that they would always have the right and power to protect their "dearest interests" from an oppressive Federal government:

> We may safely rely on the disposition of the State legislatures to erect barriers against the encroachments of the national authority.[285]

From these examples of the promises made to the American people by those who were advocating the adoption of the Constitution, ample proof is offered that the generally accepted proposition of state sovereignty was a political reality in early America. We can also see that the Founding Fathers who proposed the Constitution and the sovereign states who ultimately ratified it all believed that the state legislature or the people of their state in convention would always have a means to erect a barrier between their rights and liberties and an abusive Federal government.

The Founding Fathers and the people of the ratifying states did not contemplate a Federal system in which the Federal government or a branch thereof would be the final judge as to the constitutionality of Federal actions. This is an important point that has been lost

---

284 James Madison, *The Federalist No. 55*, quoted in Carey and McClellan, 288.

285 Alexander Hamilton, *The Federalist No. 85*, quoted in Carey and McClellan, 453.

to most contemporary Americans. Under the original Constitution, the sovereign state had many means to prevent unconstitutional acts by the Federal government from infringing upon the liberty of its citizens. When faced with an unwarranted Federal action, the state could appeal to the Federal Congress. But, suppose the Federal Congress was the offending party? In such a case, the state could appeal to the Federal executive, the president, to veto the unconstitutional act of Congress. But what if the president supported the abusive legislation? The state could appeal to the Federal Supreme Court to overturn the act on constitutional grounds. But suppose the Federal court had been packed with avid Federalists who supported a strong national government—what recourse would be left to "We the people" of the sovereign state? According to today's prevailing political orthodoxy, the state would be bound to accept and enforce the unconstitutional infringement of its citizens' civil liberties. Under the current political system, the state is merely an administrative district or a political subdivision of the central government. According to contemporary, politically correct, constitutional theory, once the Federal government has procedurally reviewed its own actions and declared them to be constitutional, then no recourse is left to the state and people thereof but to accept the onerous Federal edict. Yet, as we have seen from the writings of the Federalists, this was not their concept of the state/Federal relationship nor their intention for the Federal government. Each branch of the Federal government has a responsibility to assure that its actions and, to the extent possible, the actions of the other branches of the Federal government, are "pursuant to the Constitution." But the Federal government was not granted an exclusive right to judge the constitutionality of its actions. This right remained with those who created the Federal government—the states.

The anti-Federalists were successful in forcing the adoption of a Bill of Rights that they hoped would prevent the Federal government from oppressing the civil liberties of the people of their states. Here again, we are faced with the sad state of contemporary knowledge regarding the rights and liberties of citizens of sovereign states in this republic. Most Americans think that the Bill of Rights is an enumeration of the rights and liberties of American citizens. Americans are amazed when presented with evidence of how liberal education and left-wing media have misinformed them.[286] The average person is shocked to find out that the Bill of Rights applies to the Federal government but not to the states.[287]

The first ten amendments to the Constitution, commonly referred to as the Bill of Rights, were passed at the insistence of the states during their ratification debate. The anti-Federalists wanted stronger language to assure that future politicians would not attempt to use the delegated Federal powers to infringe upon the rights and liberties of the people of their states. They specifically noted that "Congress" could not make laws abridging the freedom of speech, the freedom of the press, the freedom of religion, and the freedom to assemble. It was no accident that the Second Amendment declared that the right to keep and bear arms was a necessary component of forming a militia and that the militia was necessary to maintain a free *state*. A careful rereading of the Second Amendment will demonstrate that the maintenance of a free nation or free Federal government was not mentioned. Why? Because the Federal government had a standing army to enforce its powers, whereas the Founding Fathers left the states the power of its armed citizens to protect the state. The states had voluntarily agreed not to maintain regular troops (as opposed to a militia) during times of peace in Article 1, Section 10, of the Constitution. Yet, in Amendment III, the states ratified an amendment prohibiting soldiers from being quartered in any house without consent during a time of peace. Why did they pass this amendment if not to limit their newly created Federal government? The Federal government, in our Federal/state co-ordinate governmental system, was the only government that was constitutionally authorized to maintain "troops." It is plain that the states intended the limitation to apply to the Federal government. Amendment Nine is of particular significance. In essence, it declares that just because "We the people" of the sovereign states did not list a specific right in the Constitution (such as the right of a sovereign state to judge an act of its agent to be unconstitutional, to nullify said act, or, if necessary, to recall our delegated rights by the act of secession) merely because these rights were not listed, that does not mean

286 [National education will have the effect of] "extinguishing Catholic or religious education and to form one homogeneous American people after the New England evangelical type." Kennedy and Kennedy, 275.

287 In *Barrow v. Baltimore*, 77 Peters 243 (1833), the United States Supreme Court ruled that the limitations imposed by the Bill of Rights "contain no expression indicating an intention to apply them to the state governments."

that they do not exist! The Ninth Amendment is based upon the principle that "We the people" of the sovereign state are the source of all sovereign authority, that we reserve all that we have not specifically delegated, and that we maintain our right to exercise those rights when we think it to be most appropriate.

The Tenth Amendment repeats the same principle of the Ninth Amendment but adds emphasis by explaining that the Federal government is composed of powers delegated from the states and that all powers not specifically delegated to the Federal government are retained by the states individually. What the thirteen original states were saying was, "All rights and liberties not specifically listed are hereby made a part of this agreement. Those of you who are agents of the Federal government, you bureaucrats, you professional politicians, or future tyrants, take warning! We the people of the sovereign state will take whatever action is necessary to protect our 'dearest interests.'"

The actions of "We the people" of the sovereign states of Virginia and Kentucky in 1798 are an excellent example of how our system of co-ordinate Federal/state government should work. The civil liberties of the common man were defended by his state when the state interposed its sovereign authority to defeat the Federal government's effort to infringe upon the freedom of speech and of the press. The Jeffersonians (original Republicans) did not object to judicial review as such; they merely insisted that each branch of the Federal government and each of the state governments had an equal right and duty to determine constitutionality for itself.[288] The right of the sovereign state to judge for itself the constitutionality of a Federal action is based upon the principle that, being sovereign, a state cannot be commanded or compelled to act against its will. The states pointed to the facts that their sovereign nature was recognized by the Treaty of Paris, that as sovereign states they had acceded to the "perpetual" union under the Articles of Confederation, that as sovereign states they had seceded from the old union under the Articles of Confederation, and as sovereign states they had acceded to the new union under the Constitution thereby creating the Federal government as their agent. At all times, they were especially careful to protect and maintain their sovereign character, and, according to the first text-

288 McDonald, 60.

book used to teach the Constitution at the Federal Military Academy at West Point, ". . . the state sovereignties are, in all respects not voluntarily ceded to the United States, as vigorous as ever."[289]

"We the people" of the sovereign state must reassert our state's sovereign authority to judge whether Federal actions are an unconstitutional infringement of our dearest rights. This is an act that cannot be done by an individual or a group of individuals acting outside of their state government.[290] This is the unique characteristic of the American constitutional government; this is what makes us, or should make us, a Republic of Republics. In our system of government, "We the people" acting through our sovereign state are co-equal with the Federal government. "We the people" of the sovereign state have the right to declare acts of the Federal government that are not "pursuant to the Constitution"[291] as unconstitutional, and, for that particular state, those unconstitutional acts are null and void. If the rest of the Union wishes to endure an unconstitutional abuse of their rights and liberties, then that is their business—but for the nullifying state, the abusive Federal acts must cease. This is the legitimate function of our co-ordinate state/Federal system. The authors of *The Federalist Papers* felt that this co-ordinate characteristic was so necessary to the type of Federal government they were striving to establish that they referred to this system of government as a compound republic:

> In a single republic, all the power surrendered by the people, is submitted to the administration of a single government; and the usurpations are guarded against by a division of the government into distinct and separate departments. In the compound republic of America, the power surrendered by the people, is first divided between two distinct governments [Federal/state], and then the portion allotted to each, subdivided among distinct

---

289 Rawle, 197.

290 Judge Abel Upshur explains the nature of our free government thusly: "[S]overeignty does not reside in any government whatever, neither State nor federal. Government is regarded merely as the agent of those who create it, and subject in all respects to their will. . . . The true sovereignty of the United States, therefore, is in the States, and not in the people of the United States, nor in the Federal Government." Abel Upshur, *The Federal Government: Its True Nature and Character* (1840, Houston, TX: St Thomas Press, 1977) 184-85.

291 ". . . it will not follow . . . that acts of the larger society [the Federal government] which are not pursuant to its constitutional powers, but which are invasion of the residuary authorities of the smaller societies [the states], will become the supreme law of the land. These will be merely acts of usurpation, and will deserve to be treated as such." Alexander Hamilton, *The Federalist No. 33*, quoted in Carey and McClellan, 161.

and separate departments. Hence a double security arises to the rights of the people. The different governments will control each other; at the same time that each will be controlled by itself.[292]

The authors of *The Federalist Papers* accepted and promoted the concept of a co-ordinate Federal/state system because they knew the American people would not allow a single, centralized government to rule over their erstwhile free and sovereign states. To counteract and discredit the predictions of the anti-Federalists that the Federal government would destroy the reserved rights of the sovereign states, the Federalists promised the American people that they would always have their state legislatures to appeal to if the Federal government abused its powers.

> . . . [I]t has on another occasion, been shown that the federal legislature will not only be restrained by its dependence on the people, as other legislative bodies are, but that it will be, moreover, watched and controlled by the several collateral legislatures, which other legislative bodies are not.[293]

From the historical record as reviewed, it can be seen that the Founding Fathers did not create an all-powerful, centralized, national government; it can be shown that the thirteen sovereign states did not surrender their sovereign power in favor of the newly created Federal government; even the Federalists, who desired a strong Federal government (relative to the government under the Articles of Confederation), accepted and promoted the concept of the sovereign state as a co-equal government in our Republic of Republics—a government that would serve as the final defender of the dearest rights and liberties of "We the people" if those rights and liberties are threatened by an abusive Federal government. Yet, as we have repeatedly demonstrated, "State Sovereignty died at Appomattox." It now remains for us to explain how "We the people" of the sovereign state may reclaim our state's sovereign authority and once again allow our sovereign state to perform its constitutional function of protecting our "dearest interests."

---

292 James Madison, *The Federalist No. 51*, quoted in Carey and McClellan, 268.

293 James Madison, *The Federalist No. 52*, quoted in Carey and McClellan, 276.

THE STATE SOVEREIGNTY AMENDMENT

Because conservatives have spent the last fifty years as the numerical minority in American politics, they have a mindset that tends to view with skepticism any plan to improve their political standing. For the past half-century, conservatives have been fighting a rearguard action against the assaults of liberalism. The time has now arrived for conservatives to take the initiative and let the liberals fight a rearguard action. This will require conservatives to accept the concept that they can and must set the political agenda. It is their responsibility to frame the issues and to offer their solutions to the incorrigible problems that have faced the middle class for five decades.

In the South, conservatives have the problem not only of overcoming the disastrous defeats dealt conservative ideas over the past fifty years but also of overcoming the psychologically disastrous consequences of the defeat of the South in the War for Southern Independence. Non-Southerners may find this hard to understand. It is something that only a people who share the memory of invasion, conquest, and occupation can easily understand. As Richard Weaver declared, the South took the decision of Appomattox too literally. It cast a pall upon all future action. Instead of entering the twentieth century as the fighting South, vigorously defending its tradition of conservatism, State's Rights, and limited Federalism, it became the timid South, cautiously compromising with the powers that be in Washington, D.C.[294] The time has now come for American conservatives, North, South, East, and West, to renounce timidity and boldly challenge the current political status quo. They must put aside their conservative persona and become revolutionaries after the order of the revolutionaries of 1776. Conservatives must initiate the movement for the radical restoration of constitutional government.

This is not a task for the mediocre, business-as-usual politician. This is not a task for the political pragmatist. Pragmatic politicians and timid conservatives will ask, "Can it be done?" This is not the question. The question revolutionaries ask is, "Should it be done?" If the answer to the second question is yes, then we will find the

---

294 For an explanation of this post-War Southern compromise with the Federal government, see Kennedy and Kennedy, 237-45.

honorable means to accomplish our goal! Pragmatic considerations will not allow for such a bold approach, but, to us, it is not a question of the next election but of the next constitutional government.

We have carefully detailed the participants in this struggle, we have demonstrated from historic records and contemporary news accounts that the Federal government has abused its powers, and we have demonstrated from the writings of the Founding Fathers and other historical records that, at one point in United States history, the sovereign state had and exercised the right and duty to defend its citizens from an oppressive Federal government. Whether the original cause of the loss of state sovereignty lies to the north or the south of the Mason-Dixon line is of little consequence for middle-class Americans today. Let the history buffs debate the cause while middle-class citizens all across this land work together to effect the cure. The discussion of the cure will assume the fact that it can be accomplished. In the next chapter, we will discuss the organizational efforts necessary to accomplish politically the enactment of the State Sovereignty Amendment. For now, we will limit the discussion to an explanation of the proposed amendment.

To re-establish the balance of power between the Federal and state governments envisioned by the Founding Fathers and the original thirteen ratifying sovereign states, it will be necessary for the sovereign states to ratify an amendment that clearly declares the sovereign authority of the state to act in defense of "We the people" when our rights and liberties are threatened by an unconstitutional act of the Federal government. This amendment will be explanatory and procedural in nature. It will outline the constitutional requirements for state interposition such as occurred in 1798 with the Kentucky and Virginia Resolutions.

The amendment will cover both nullification and secession. It is time that these major questions be put to rest and the Federal government placed on notice that its unwarranted intrusion into the reserved rights will be met by a vigorous and effectual challenge from "We the people" of the sovereign state. As John C. Calhoun and those who followed him knew, nullification of a Federal act by the state is a technique designed to preserve the Union. The Union is a government based upon the free and unfettered consent of its members. Force cannot be used to obtain consent. If, therefore, an act of the Federal government is so onerous that the people of the state object to the infringement of their liberty, without nullification their only recourse is submission in slavery to Federal authority or secession. Free men will not voluntarily submit to enslavement. But, they may not wish to remove themselves from the Federal Union. Nullification of an unconstitutional Federal act within the bounds of the state will allow the state to remain in the Union while awaiting the judgment of her sister states. The other states have a right to decide if they will allow the nullifying state to remain in the Union with them. If three-fourths of the states pass a resolution accepting the nullification, through their constitutional conventions, then the Federal act becomes null and void throughout the United States. If, on the other hand, three-fourths of the states reject the nullification, then, if the nullifying state wishes to remain in the Union with her sister states, she must accept the Federal act. If the nullifying state believes the Federal act is too onerous to the safety of that state and too costly to the liberties of the people thereof, then the state must pass an act of secession through her state convention and make arrangements to pay monies and debts owed the United States of America. One last contingency is possible. If there is not sufficient opinion to carry either side, then the state nullification stands only within the borders of that state and only until or unless a three-fourths vote is obtained either accepting or rejecting the initiating state's nullification.

Those who favor a dominant Federal government will argue that this amendment will destroy the United States. No, it will not destroy the United States, but it will return the United States to its original status as a Republic of Republics. The moral suasion of Federal bayonets cannot be substituted for the free and unfettered consent of "We the people" of the sovereign states. If the Sovereign Community within a state is convinced that to remain in a particular union would be destructive of their liberties, then no power on earth has the right to substitute military force in lieu of the free and unfettered consent of the people of the state. John Locke wrote that a people can not be free if they are denied the means of escaping tyranny. If a tyrant or a tyrannical government can issue oppressive edicts, court orders, guidelines, or unfunded mandates, and the people have no means to escape this onerous abuse of power, then the people are just as much a captive of an oppressive master as any slave.[295] The

295 See "Consent of the Governed—Key to Liberty" in the Addenda section.

notion that a combination of sovereign states has a constitutional right to force a weaker state to accept a government that would be destructive of its liberty should be unthinkable to all Americans who believe in the principle of "the consent of the governed." The excuse of maintaining the Federal Union is not a constitutional justification for violating the reserved rights of sovereign states. Horace Greely, editor of *The New York Times* and a loyal friend of the Union, declared, "I hope to never live in a Union pinned together by bayonets." Why? Because the Union is the political association of free men residing within their respective sovereign states. Force precludes freedom. A nation that must rely upon force to ensure compliance with its laws is, by definition, a tyranny.

Why is secession necessary for the protection of our liberties? Secession is necessary because it provides, as John Locke would describe it, an escape from tyranny. Protecting our liberty is its primary function, but secession has another important function. The general acceptance of the doctrine of secession would work for the preservation of the Union because it would encourage moderation in the passage of controversial Federal legislation. The Federal Congress would be reluctant to embrace extreme political positions that would have the effect of driving states out of the Union. Both the president and the Supreme Court would be similarly restrained. Before passing billions of dollars of unfunded Federal mandates, Congress would be forced to consider the reactions of "We the people" of the sovereign state. The same is true for federal gun control legislation, quota civil rights bills, and secret, midnight, Congressional pay raises. Secession is like Grandpa's shotgun; even though he never had to use it to defend his home, every criminal in town knew that Grandpa had it and, if necessary, would use it. The knowledge of the gun's existence made its use very unlikely. So it is with secession. It is always available if needed, ready to be appealed to if necessary, but, since all know of its existence, hopefully it will never be necessary to exercise this inalienable right. In our system of dual republics (state/Federal), secession is the ultimate defense for the liberties of "We the people."

Nullification, on the other hand, is another class of action. Its main purpose is to preserve the Union. When the people of Virginia and Kentucky were faced with the loss of the right of free speech and press in 1798, they had the alternative of (1) accepting the loss of free speech and press, (2) withdrawing from the Union and establishing a new government that would protect their liberty, or (3) interposing the sovereign authority of their state between an abusive Federal government and the people of their state. They chose the third option. Nullification bought time for other political actions to resolve the crises. Nullification is a transitional step. It is a warning issued by a Sovereign Community to the rest of the nation. It tells the other states that the people of a particular state believe that their dearest rights are being abused and that they appeal to their sister states and the people thereof for a decision favorable to their claim. As we have previously noted, if three fourths of the states agree with the nullifying state then the Federal act will be prohibited throughout the nation. But, if three-fourths of the states agree with the Federal action, then the nullifying state will not be allowed to hinder the acts of the Federal government. In our Republic of Republics, the three-fourths majority of the states (as opposed to the majority of the population) rules. The single state or the numerical minority must then decide if the benefits of the Union outweigh the loss or perceived loss of liberty. This is a decision that only the people within their Sovereign Community have a right to make.

Some who support a centralized national government will complain that nullification and secession will lead to the break-up of the Union. No state would hastily abandon our Republic of Republics because the benefits of Union are too many to leave for light or transient reasons. Judge Rawle, in *A View of the Constitution of the United States,* observed

> The seceding state, whatever might be its relative magnitude, would speedily and distinctly feel the loss of the aid and countenance of the Union. The Union losing a proportion of the national revenue, would be entitled to demand from it a proportion of the national debt. It would be entitled to treat the inhabitants and the commerce of the separated state, as appertaining to a foreign country. In public treaties already made, whether commercial or political, it could claim no participation, while foreign powers would unwilling calculate, and slowly transfer to it, any portion of the respect and confidence borne towards the United States.[296]

296 Rawle, 241.

The potential loss of commercial ties with other states would serve as protection against the flagrant misuse of nullification or secession. Only an abusive government actively oppressing the constitutional rights of the people could drive a people to consider the use of secession. But, if the Federal government enacted legislation "not pursuant" to the Constitution and attempted to violate the liberty of "We the people" of the sovereign state, then and only then would the exercise of our reserved rights of nullification and secession be necessary. Liberty cannot be evaluated on an accountant's ledger sheet. Regardless of how "commercially profitable" a system of government may be, if it does not provide for the safety of civil liberty, then the price of union is too high. Patrick Henry declared the purpose of the American Revolution was not to establish a great commercial empire but to gain the blessings of liberty for the people. "We the people" of the sovereign state must take those actions necessary to restore the original constitutional Federal/state co-ordinate governmental system and to assure the safety and security of their dearest rights and liberties. Instead of a big, tax-and-spend, abusive Federal government that recognizes no restraints on the exercise of its powers—Why Not Freedom?

This will happen only if "We the people" act together to pass an amendment declaring the right of the people of each sovereign state to judge for themselves if the actions of the Federal government are indeed "pursuant" to the Constitution. This is a judgment that must not be entrusted to some faraway, impersonal Federal agent or official. It belongs where authority originates; it belongs with the people of the Sovereign Community working through their respective state. To accomplish these ends, we propose the following constitutional amendment:

SOVEREIGN AUTHORITY AMENDMENT

The United States of America are a Republic of Republics deriving its authority from the consent of the governed residing within respective sovereign states. Each sovereign state is the agent of the people thereof. The Federal government formed by the compact of the Constitution is the agent of the sovereign states. Federal authority shall be supreme in all areas specifically delegated to it by the Constitution. All acts or legislation enacted pursuant to the Constitution shall be the supreme law of the land. The sovereign state reserves an equal right to judge for itself as to the constitutionality of any act of the Federal government.

Section. I. The sovereign state specifically reserves the right to interpose its sovereign authority between acts of the Federal government and the liberties, property, and interest of the citizens of the state, thereby nullifying Federal acts judged by the state to be an unwarranted infringement upon the reserved rights of the state and the people thereof.

1. State nullification of a Federal act must be approved by the convention of the state.

2. Upon passage of an act of nullification, all Federal authority for the enumerated and nullified act(s) shall be suspended.

3. Upon formal acceptance of nullification by three-fourths of the conventions of the states, including the original nullifying state, the enumerated Federal act(s) shall be prohibited anywhere in the United States or its territories.

4. Upon formal rejection of nullification by three-fourths of the conventions of the states, the enumerated Federal act(s) shall be declared constitutional, notwithstanding any judgment of any Federal or state court.

5. Until or unless there is a formal approval or rejection by the conventions of the states, the nullified Federal act(s) shall remain non-operative as to the original and any additional nullifying states. A state that in its convention ratifies a particular act of nullification shall be construed to have nullified the same act as enumerated in the initiating state's nullification.

6. No Federal elected official, agent, or branch of the Federal government may harass, intimidate, or threaten a sovereign state or the people thereof for exercising their rights under this amendment. No Federal elected official, agent, or branch of the Federal government shall attempt to influence or use his office to attempt to influence the deliberations of the people regarding the nullification of a Federal act, or the acceptance or rejection of a nullified Federal act.

7. Any United States military officer, non-commissioned officer, or Federal official or agent who carries out or attempts to carry out any order by a Federal official or agent to deny or hinder the people of the sovereign state from exercising their rights under this amendment shall be subject to the offended state's laws and may be tried

accordingly. Jurisdiction in such cases is specifically denied to all Federal courts, military courts, or any other court other than the courts of the offended state.

Section II. The government and people of these United States approve the principle that any people have a right to abolish the existing government and form a new one that suits them better. This principle illustrates the American idea that government rests on the consent of the governed, and that it is the right of the people to alter or abolish it at will whenever it becomes destructive of the ends for which it was established. Therefore, the right of a sovereign state to secede peacefully from the union created by the compact of the Constitution is hereby specifically reserved to each state.

1. An act of secession shall be executed by a convention of the people of the state.

2. The seceded state shall appoint representatives to negotiate settlement of all debts owed the Federal government, the purchase of Federal properties within the sovereign state, and the removal of Federal military installations and personnel.

3. Upon acceptable arrangement for the payment of sums owed the Federal government, the representatives may negotiate treaties of friendship, defense, and commercial relations. Said treaties are subject to the same constitutional ratification as other treaties.

4. Re-admission of a seceded state shall follow the same constitutional requirements as for any state.

5. No Federal elected official, agent, or branch of the Federal government shall attempt to influence the decision of the people of the sovereign state regarding their decision to secede from or to join this union.

6. Any United States military officer, non-commissioned officer, or Federal official or agent who carries out or attempts to carry out any order by a Federal official or agent to deny or hinder the people of the sovereign state their rights under this amendment shall be subject to the offended state's laws and may be tried accordingly. Jurisdiction in such cases is specifically denied to all Federal courts, military courts, or any other court other than the courts of the offended state.

7. The duty of the people of the sovereign states to exercise their

inalienable right to govern themselves, a right that existed before the formation of the Federal government, nothing in this amendment shall be interpreted in such a manner as to deem the Federal government to be the donor of the rights as exercised by the people of the states.

With the passage of the Sovereignty Amendment, "We the people" of the sovereign states will have the one sure means at our disposal to prevent future unconstitutional abuses of Federal powers. Yes, it will help to have conservatives elected to Federal offices, and conservative judges sitting on the Federal Supreme Court, but the local level is where the one and only sure method to prevent the destruction of our "dearest interests," our rights, and our liberties (not to mention the rights and liberties of generations of middle-class Americans yet to be born) will ultimately be protected. Many people are unable to overcome the impulses of the pragmatic politicians, and may be thinking, "Sure, its a great idea, but how can we convince three-fourths of the states to ratify such an amendment?" This is the job of an organized, middle-class, political revolution.

CHAPTER 28

Organizing for Freedom

As we have already pointed out, revolutionaries do not take a pragmatic political view. A revolutionary looks at what needs to be done and then determines a course of action required to bring it about. The typical business-as-usual politician will ask, "Can it be done?" He will then count the votes and decide whether he will support a particular political approach. The time for short-sighted, business-as-usual politics is over. If the middle class is to regain control of its political destiny, it must take charge of the political agenda. To do this, it must be organized. The middle class should not organize to elect a specific person to office; it should not organize to capture control of a political party; it should not organize to elect conservatives to control the various branches of the Federal government. All of these things and more will be a part of the movement, but the two most important points are (1) that it must organize to educate "We the people" of the sovereign states about our inalienable right to control the Federal government, and (2) it must conduct a campaign to encourage people to push the Sovereignty Amendment through Congress and their state legislatures.

This is more than a political campaign; it is a social movement. It is a crusade that transcends politics and brings diverse people from different sections of the country together to rebuild that once great Republic of Republics. It is a social movement that does not end when the last vote is counted. Yes, it is conducted during political campaigns, but it is also conducted during events such as county fairs, class reunions, and Sunday school parties. It taps into the living dynamics of middle-class society and incorporates it into the movement.

Every activity must be viewed as an opportunity to increase public awareness and acceptance of the necessity for passage of the Sovereignty Amendment. Once the majority of middle-class Americans understand the nature of our common political problem, our inalienable rights under the original Constitution, and the mechanism available to cure the disease of Big Government, then the people of America will apply the appropriate pressure to pass the Sovereignty Amendment. Once this Amendment is passed, then all the problems, insults, and attacks against the middle class by the liberal establishment will become moot. When "We the people" at the local level have in our hands the ability to checkmate the Washington establishment, power will then shift from the liberal establishment back to "We the people" of the sovereign state. At that point, we can say that the spirit of the American Revolution of 1776 once again resides in the people of America.

Many conservative activists have asked us, "What organization should we join in order to further this goal?" There is no one organization for any American to join to pursue the goals we are describing. There are many good groups of conservatives who can work to further the passage of the Sovereignty Amendment in their respective states. The important thing is to find like-minded conservative activists who are willing to put personality and ego aside and work together first to educate their local population and then to initiate the struggle to pass the Sovereignty Amendment. For Southerners, there are many good organizations that promote a positive view of a commonly held culture. One such outstanding organization that is pursuing these political objectives is The Southern League, Inc. It is dedicated to the restoration of constitutional government. It accepts members from any section of the United States and is willing to work with people and states outside of Dixie to further mutual goals. The authors of this book are charter members of The Southern League, Inc. and highly recommend it to you. The address is:

> Michael Hill, PhD, President
> The Southern League, Inc.
> P.O. Box 40910
> Tuscaloosa, AL 35404-0910
> Tel: (205) 553-0155

Other groups that are on the front line of the battle against Big Government are the Council of Conservative Citizens and the Ludwig von Mises Institute. Their respective addresses are listed in the

Addenda section. Also listed there is the Sons of Confederate Veterans, an organization dedicated to defending the history of Confederate veterans.

The organizing can begin as soon as you and a friend decide that you want to see a return to the principles of limited Federalism, State's Rights, and State Sovereignty. You should be prepared to form a Sovereignty Amendment group today. You can begin the task of educating your neighbors and fellow citizens about the abuse of power by the Federal government and what it will take to cure the disease of tax-and-spend Big Government. Don't let anyone sidetrack you; keep focused on the final solution to the problems facing us from an abusive Federal government. There are many issues that will present themselves. You must always decide whether the particular issue can be used by you to help educate the public about the need for passage of the Sovereignty Amendment and whether the particular issue can be used by you with your limited resources. We are not required to fight every battle that presents itself. We must carefully choose the issues as well as the time and places to confront our opponents. We must always be the ones who pick the battlefield upon which to engage the enemy of personal freedom in this country.

Remember that you are dealing with a public that does not understand how much of their freedom they have lost. You must be committed to the long run. It will take a considerable amount of effort to overcome the effects of years of viewing the left-wing media and the great socialist benefits conferred upon most Americans by our liberal education system. These are not insurmountable obstacles. Every day, middle-class Americans learn by hard experience that liberal welfare does not work, that taxes are too high, that the Federal government is attempting to control every aspect of our lives, and that reverse discrimination and quotas are cruel and unfair. In short, day by day Americans are learning from experience that the liberals have lied to them! It is our job to key in on these opportunities and offer an American solution to an un-American problem!

We are revolutionaries (a conservative revolutionary is somewhat of a contradiction of terms but nonetheless we are carrying forward the Revolution of 1776—therefore, we can justifiably claim the title of revolutionaries). We should keep in mind that we are asking men and women who are by nature very conservative to do something rather radical. It is our job to warm them up to the idea. A revolutionary's task has been described as similar to fish attempting to spawn. The fish represent the revolution. The water represents the population. If the water is too cold, the fish cannot spawn. In order for the fish to spawn, the water must be warmed. Once the temperature of the water is raised, then the water can support the fish, and spawning occurs. The revolution cannot occur if the population is cold to the principle of the revolution. Assuming the revolution is based upon sound principles, such as the American Revolution of 1776, then the revolution will succeed once the population understands the benefits they will derive from supporting the revolution.

How do we "warm the waters of revolution?" How do we take our fellow citizens who are not as politically active as we are and warm them up to the idea of restoring constitutional government? It must be done the only way it can be done in a free society—through public education. We must convert our fellow citizens from apathy to activism. This can only be accomplished at the local level. It cannot come down from the White House or the governor's mansion. It must originate, as does all legitimate power, at the grassroots. That is why it is so important to organize small groups at the local level and contest local elections with candidates who will make their support of the Sovereignty Amendment an integral part of their campaign platform and who will discuss the proposed amendment at every opportunity. In this scenario, there is no such thing as a lost election. Every election gives us an opportunity to reach more people with our message. Every election gives us an opportunity to demonstrate the failure of other political solutions and candidates. Every election gives us an opportunity to build a larger local network of members, followers, and supporters. The strength of this movement is the dedication of the individual members at the local level. No tyrant can destroy a people who know their rights and are dedicated to the principles of freedom.

You do not have to be a public relations expert to conduct this public education campaign, but you do need to understand some basic principles about public information campaigns. The task of our public information campaign is to convert fellow citizens into supporters of the Sovereignty Amendment. This is how we will "warm the waters." Once the people have been convinced that it is in their best interest to support the movement against their oppressors, they will then be receptive to the solution. A public education campaign is more than an advertising campaign. It is a social process whereby an entire people are persuaded that their current condition (economic, social, cultural, and political) is unfair and that this injustice is a direct result of the political status quo. The people must begin to identify the loss of freedoms with an overgrown, uncontrollable Federal government and the establishments that control and use the government for their own benefit. From this, the people must be persuaded that this movement offers the only alternative to remaining in their current subjugated condition. The people must be persuaded to support the concept of State Sovereignty as the only legitimate counterbalance to a Federal government that has abused its powers and oppressed "We the people" of the sovereign state.

The task of educating the public about the necessity for and the eventual victory of our resistance to Federal tyranny can be distilled into nine basic axioms:

1. The struggle for political freedom must be described in a manner so that the average person views the struggle as a life-or-death struggle, one that he cannot afford to lose. It should be suggested, intimated, and implied that the only alternative to victory for this movement is the continued destruction of the culture, the liberties, and the complete subjugation of "We the people" of middle-class America.

2. Most voters are too busy with their lives to be overly concerned with future ramifications of their day-to-day choices relative to political events. Therefore, they will not spend much time considering the philosophical rationale underlying their political beliefs or choice of candidates. Our public education efforts must be designed with this in mind. Slogans, ideas, and political concepts must be designed in a manner that catches the attention of busy individuals and then allows them to assimilate the message quickly. Our educational message, to be effective, must not be designed to lecture learned opponents, but to stimulate and inflame those who already have a deep-seated, though perhaps at the time unconscious, affinity for the values promoted by this movement.

3. Our task is not to make historians or philosophers out of the voters but to lead them to specific attitudes about their current condition, to direct their minds toward certain conclusions regarding how

best to correct their current political condition, and to lead them toward specific actions that all can take to liberate our people.

4. When dealing with the public, it must be remembered that the public's memory is exceedingly short. What was clearly stated yesterday is often forgotten today. Most people's minds are cluttered as a result of information overload. In the rush of making day-to-day decisions, people tend to make the quickest and easiest decision. Our educational messages must be limited to a few short items and must be repeated over and over until every American has heard and fully understands the message to the exclusion of the opposing message delivered by the liberal media.

5. This struggle is not a "gentleman's game." Our message must announce our movement as the only legitimate means by which the middle class may reclaim their political liberty. We must make sure that the American middle class understand that they are the only ones who can provide adequate safety and security for their liberties, whereas the opposition represents the liberal special-interest groups.

6. The purpose of our education efforts is to announce the principles of our movement. To do this, we must confine our efforts to simple, concise ideas and concepts. We must not fall prey to the temptation of the ego that would have us present a treatise on constitutional rights for public consumption. Such learned discussions have their place, but not as a method to educate the average person. Repetition of our message is the key to eventual success. Merely announcing the idea once or occasionally is not sufficient. The idea must be repeated again and again. Slowly over time, the great mass of the middle class will begin to assimilate the idea and will accept it as if it had been their conscious attitude all along. Actually, it has been an unconscious attitude or tendency. This attitude had been repressed by the overwhelming assault of liberal, anti-middle class propaganda and by the absence of our message. It will become a conscious attitude only after repeated exposure to our educational message.

7. The purpose of our educational efforts must be to convince American middle-class citizens that their rights have been destroyed, and that our movement is the only way they will regain their lost rights. This message, though varied in form, must never deviate from this central theme. The message must be repeated again and again. The form will vary, the instrument used to convey the message will

change, but the underlying theme of our educational effort must remain the same. The message must stress the fact that the middle class are being oppressed by the Federal government and that only by enacting the Sovereignty Amendment will the middle class be able to prevent current or future abuses of Federal powers.

8. The faithful members and supporters of this movement must be prepared for the struggle to come. They must be prepared to sacrifice money, time, and emotional energy for the movement. Victory will not come without a price. We must prove ourselves worthy of living in a constitutional Republic of Republics. Freedom is never free!

9. When discussing political concepts and philosophy, we must remember that the average person reacts more to emotion than to logic. Educational messages that concentrate upon theoretical concepts of government or historical justifications will not make an impression upon the greater mass of citizens. They will be reached by appeals to home, security, family, love of who they are and from whence they came (family and culture), and a desire to protect their loved ones from the attacks of those who would destroy their society. Our educational efforts must be linked to current events. Current events must be used to document the oppression suffered by the middle class, to demonstrate that the Federal government is the source of its oppression, and to assert that our movement offers the only viable and permanent solution to the excesses of unbridled Federalism.

The greatest strength of the Sovereignty Amendment movement is that it awakens the common man to the power that he has within him and the political power at his disposal; the power to restore the original constitutional Republic of Republics. It puts the common man in control of his political destiny. It arms him with a defensive weapon to shield himself from an abusive Federal government and, if necessary, a sword to slay the leviathan of Big Government. No longer must he wait patiently for the powerbrokers of Washington, D.C., to remember him. Once again, he is the equal of his elected leaders. With the passage of the Sovereignty Amendment, political power will not only originate at the local level, but it will also at last be controlled at the local level. Just like the liberty won in 1776, it will not come to us freely, as a grant from our benevolent master, but it will have been fought for and earned by modern-day minutemen—

men and women who, against all odds, struggled with Leviathan and
won!

SUMMARY OF SECTION III
Questions and Answers

*Q. Although I tend to agree with you in theory about the need to limit the
abuse of power by the Federal government, it appears to me to be gross overkill
to suggest secession as a way to do so. If we start reacting in this way to an
abuse of power by some government, how can we keep these movements from
continuing from state, to counties, to cities, and any other community even
smaller?*

A. It is obvious from the question you have asked that you understand that there is a need to control the abuse of power within our
Federal system of government, and also provide for some form of stability within the framework of our society. As we have pointed out
from the works of men such as John Milton and John Locke of England, and James Madison and Thomas Jefferson of America, at
some point in time a people must remove themselves from a form
of government that no longer respects their rights. Notice the words
of Jefferson in the Declaration of Independence: "[W]henever any
Form of Government becomes destructive of these Ends, it is the
Right of the People to alter or to abolish it." Secession is the act by
which "We the People" alter or abolish a form of government we
feel has become destructive of our rights. By the reinstitution of this
right, "We the People" of the states will have an effective check upon
the power of the Federal government. As Locke has demonstrated,
any people who do not have a way to escape tyranny can never be
free. As long as the Federal government remains the master of "We
the people" of the states, we will never be truly free.

The second part of your question touches upon one of the most
often expressed fears of a secession movement, i.e., that once a secession movement is initiated, it will continue until the smallest political
unit within a society has seceded from the rest of society. In other
words, our once great nation will increasingly fragment into smaller
and smaller units. We have often heard the historically misinformed
state that "if a state can withdraw from the Federal government, then
a county can withdraw from a state." There is one glaring fallacy in

this statement. Under our system of government, the states created the Federal government. Remember the principle of political relationships set forth in *Vindiciae Contra Tyrannos:* "Those who have powers to make, have powers to destroy." By the free and unfettered action of the people of the state, the states created the Federal government. A county or a city within a state exists because of a charter granted by the state. In other words, the state that created the Federal government also gives life to the county or city within a state. We therefore say that the creation cannot secede from the creator, any more than man, the object of God's creative will, can secede from God. In America, the colonies were given existence by charters granted from the sovereign of Great Britain. In 1776, the colonies declared themselves free and independent, and at the close of the War for American Independence, the sovereign of Great Britain had to recognize the independence of each of his former colonies. Throughout the formative years of the United States, it has always been the states that have created the governments we have lived under; therefore we say that "We the people" of the sovereign states are the sole repository of sovereign power in America. Secession is limited to the acts of a sovereign power, not to the ancillary departments of that authority. Only a sovereign community, i.e., in America, the states, can secede.

Q. Don't you think that the system of government that you propose, one that allows individual states to nullify acts of the Federal government or even to secede from the Federal government, would guarantee the break-up of this great nation into hostile camps?

A. First let me make sure that you understand that the system of government that we recommend was not dreamed up by us; it is the original Republic of Republics as handed down to Americans from our Founding Fathers. Opponents to limited Federalism, those who want a strong, all-powerful central government, usually attempt to argue the extremes when trying to prove that the original system of limited Federalism will not work. They do this by claiming the states will overuse the remedy of nullification and secession. They imply that, when the people of a state are not happy with a particular Federal action, the first reaction the people will adopt will be nullification or secession. In reality, these acts will be the last resort of prudent men and women. Only if no other way is left to defend the rights, liberty, and property of "We the people" will a state resort to nullification or secession. The very fact that these remedies are available will, in and of itself, cause the Federal government to attempt to avoid unconstitutional acts. Because these remedies are not currently available to "We the people" of the sovereign state, the Federal government is never hesitant to infringe upon our "dearest interests." Instead of destroying our American society, nullification and secession will cause a greater bond between the people as we attempt to harmonize our public policy to gain public approval and thereby avoid a call for state nullification or secession. *Nullification and secession force the Federal government to substitute diplomacy and mutual consideration in the place of the moral suasion of bloody bayonets.* The truth of the matter is that it is not those of us who desire a return to our original Republic of Republics who endanger the country. It is the liberal establishment who have been using the police power of the Federal government to force their left-wing social agenda upon an unwilling American middle class who are responsible for endangering the survival of our free American society.

SECTION IV

ADDENDA

INTRODUCTORY COMMENTS

One text can never answer all the questions about the issues we raised in *Why Not Freedom!* Nor can one author, or in our case, two authors, explain, in its totality, how this once free republic has devolved into the near tyranny of a centralized Big Government. It has been our desire in writing this book to point out the problems, and to offer a distinctly different approach in dealing with the problems, of an out-of-control Federal government. To assist you, the reader, in this effort, we have included the following addenda from articles written not only by us, the authors, but also by other Americans who are daily dealing with the problem of bringing Leviathan (Big Government) under control.

Bringing Leviathan under control will not be easy. Many have tried, and many have failed. Most failures are due to a lack of or appreciation for the nature of what is being fought. Most conservatives still cling to the illusion that by electing more conservatives at the Federal level, we will solve all the problems we are experiencing with Big Government. Surely this will help; but the underlying problem is still in place, that is, an all-powerful Big Government that is not answerable to "We the people." The right tools are necessary to do the right job. "Canst thou draw out leviathan with an hook?"[297] This question was asked of Job by God. God was trying to make Job understand a most important truth, that is, it takes more than a simple hook to land leviathan. "Get the right tools for the job," God was saying to Job. We also must always be aware that when we struggle with Big Government, which we refer to as Leviathan, we must have in our hands the proper tools to defend our "dearest interests." As our grandfather would say, "Only a fool would go bear hunting with a switch!"

The following articles are presented to you, the reader, with the hope that they will enlighten and encourage you to continue the struggle for true American liberty.

297 Job 41:1, *The Holy Bible.*

WHAT HAPPENED TO THE REVOLUTION OF NOVEMBER 8, 1994?

by Jeffrey Tucker[298]

The Republican leadership and their advisers are confirming Murray Rothbard's doubts. Writing in the *Washington Post,* Rothbard noted the vast ideological divide between the voters and those who control the Republican Congress. His prediction: the leadership will defend the old order of government control even as its legitimacy is unraveling. The revolution was betrayed, he said, even before the Republicans took control.

Since his article appeared, the Republican elites have thwarted the will of the newly elected backbenchers who campaigned against Washington. In only a few short months, the leadership has worked to sustain Leviathan and all its works, both foreign and domestic, under a new philosophical pretense.

Trade and Empire. The first bad sign appeared days after the election. Reeling from his party's defeat, Clinton—backed by the banking, media, and corporate establishment—demanded that Congress ratify the Gatt treaty establishing the World Trade Organization (WTO) to manage the international trading system. It was both economically unsound and extremely unpopular, facts which provided the political and economic reasons to say no.

Clinton had tried to force a vote before the election, but as part of their pre-election charade, the Republicans blocked it. To fool the voters, Newt Gingrich and Robert Dole even hinted that they opposed the WTO.

The election confirmed the voters' desire for an end to insider rackets like the WTO. But within days, the Republican elites—with ideological cover provided by D.C. think tanks dependent on political approval—told the administration they wanted the vote taken before the new Congress assembled. So in a lame-duck session, they shoved through the most unpopular trade treaty in several generations.

Expanding Civil Rights. The Congressional Accountability Act,

311

which applied all labor and business law to Congress, passed unanimously, which is a good sign that something was wrong. People have pointed out Congress's exemption from these laws for years. But the purpose was to highlight their hypocrisy and repeal bad laws. The Republicans reversed the logic and not only did not repeal them, but expanded them to apply to the entire legislative branch.

At the same time, no one pointed out the historic reason for the exemption: to preserve the separation of powers as conceived by the founders. These laws are enforced by the executive department. Think of how businessmen quake when they receive letters from the safety and labor authorities. Congress is now in a similar position, thus introducing the possibility of legislative blackmail by bureaucrats. Congress won't spend its own money on fines, thus lessening executive branch leverage somewhat, but the accusation of discrimination alone causes pressure groups to swing into action.

Welfare for Immigrants. After California's Proposition 187, which sought to cut off welfare to illegal aliens, passed by a two-to-one margin, many Republicans vowed to do the same at the national level. It was all set: Republican welfare legislation would eliminate handouts to non-citizens. Then Newt Gingrich and the Senate leadership popped up to declare this line of thought to be "anti-immigrant"—as if cutting off welfare subsidies is the same as hating people.

Whatever the final outcome, this incident is more important for what it tells us about the leadership's true commitments. What kind of conservative would pass out taxpayer largess to anyone stumbling across the border?

Balanced Budget. The first hundred days were supposed to be cut and slash time. No program would be spared. Instead, Gingrich led the party off on a wild goose chase to amend the U.S. Constitution. This sends the wrong message: it implies that the reason for high government spending and deficits is a defect in the Constitution. Moreover, if such an amendment worked to the disadvantage of the government, it would be ignored, just as the 2nd, 9th, and 10th amendments are swept aside. But if it became an excuse to raise taxes, it would become the most scrupulously followed part of the Constitution.

Taxes. The first item on the Republican agenda was supposed to be large cuts in income and capital-gains taxes, and an increase in the tax deduction for families with children. Clinton wised up after the humiliating election and proposed his own package to increase deductions for children and their college tuition.

For a brief moment, it appeared that a tax-cut bidding war was in progress. But Republican chairman Haley Barbour "outmaneuvered" the administration by calling off all discussion of tax cuts. The party would "pay for" future tax cuts with spending cuts now. Meanwhile, spending hasn't been cut, and thus tax cuts can't be "paid for."

Tenth Amendment. "States rights" are all the rage, but the Republican elite is attempting to co-opt the grass-roots movement to bring back the 10th Amendment. Instead of genuine federalism, where the people of the states answer to the feds only in rare cases, Congress gives us cosmetic changes in how governments themselves are regulated. And Dole's 10th amendment bill not only exempts all civil-rights laws and those involving "safety" and "health," it only slightly lessens regulatory burdens on governments, and not at all on businesses, colleges and universities, and individuals.

A related issue is "unfunded mandates" that the federal government (mostly under Republican administrations) has imposed on the states. Nobody is talking about repealing those mandates. The most "extreme" idea proposed by any leading Republican has been to fund the mandates through more spending.

Abolishing Agencies. No budget cut is permanent until: a) the agency goes out of business, b) its functions are not picked up by another agency, and c) the government stops spending money (including in the form of "vouchers" or subsidies to non-profits) to perpetuate the program. That means, for example, that if we want cuts in government spending on housing, we should abolish HUD, take its functions out of the government's hands, and forbid any agency from issuing, say, housing vouchers.

But the Republican elites are doing everything to avoid dealing with this truth. Their welfare reform gives money to the states, but does not spend substantially less at the federal level. All agencies would survive and the injustice of forced redistribution would continue. Some people have talked about getting rid of HUD, but dispersing its functions to other agencies. Meanwhile, Congressional elites permit no discussion of abolishing whole regulatory agencies.

Mexican Bailout. In the secret White House meeting following the collapse of the Mexican peso, Republicans and Democrats agreed to a $40 billion bailout. Clinton calls it "co-signing" a loan, but most people wouldn't do that for anyone but a family member, because the co-signer must be willing to be stuck with the entire tab. Plus, it's not the politicians' money at stake; they are co-signing a loan the taxpayers must pay.

It wasn't Al Gore or Bill Clinton who pushed hardest for the bailout. Paul Gigot of the *Wall Street Journal* says Newt Gingrich was Mr. Peso. Recall that he was also Mr. Nafta, and shoved through the treaty that first linked the two governments and currencies.

No issue better symbolizes the perfidy of the Republican elites and the reticence of the backbenchers to go along. Some freshmen assembled at a press conference to point out they did not get elected to bailout a corrupt, bankrupt, and socialist foreign regime. In doing so, they gave up any chance of favors from the leadership or advancement within the Congress. Good for them: they have less at stake.

Military and Technology. The Republican elites are pushing for a $200 billion boost in military spending to make up for Clinton's "gutting." Yet where are the threats? Surely the usefulness of more bombs has declined markedly with the Cold War over, if not for military contractors then certainly for the general population.

Military profligacy contradicts the views of the founders. The government is supposed to provide for the common defense and avoid entangling alliances. The budget should provide enough to defend our shores and no more. But if Republicans get their way, we will get spending increases that won't balance with cuts elsewhere. Average taxpayers will end up worse off and even more oppressed by the tax-and-spend state.

New projects on the wish list include a "reusable rocket" to replace the space shuttle and money for the "next generation" of nuclear power. Especially bad is the attempt to resurrect the far-flung "star wars" missile-blocking system (whose successes were rigged), not only for this country but for the *entire continent*. To think we were once told this program would use "off-the-shelf" technology.

Whitewashing History. Washington's game of governing requires the appearance of partisanship even when the reality is not there. The Democrats have to run against cruel-hearted Republicans who in turn have to run against profligate big spenders. This charade has continued for decades, because cooperation masquerading as conflict benefits both sides in a two-party democracy.

In the eighties, journalists praised or condemned Reagan's deep cuts in the welfare budget. Few writers mentioned welfare spending had more than doubled—and most of them wrote for this publication. So it is today. Liberals are portraying the Republicans as greedy and heartless budget cutters. And two journalist-historians—ex-Bushies Peggy Noonan and John Podhoretz—are writing of the first year, with Noonan being featured on tax-paid public television. If the model holds, they will proclaim cosmetic changes as revolutionary.

One of many injustices of the American political system is that the Congress is not run democratically. The longer you stay in Washington, the more likely you can control what the "process" produces, and the more perks, in power and prestige, you amass. (The freshmen who wanted to abolish plush Congressional pensions, which would solve the problem, were quickly shut up by Gingrich.) Yet as the elites blocked a backbench revolution, the system they attempt to preserve steadily collapses from below. Those creaking floorboards in the Capitol signal a lot of digging going on.

298 Originally published in *The Free Market*, the newsletter of the Ludwig von Mises Institute, March 1995. Jeffrey Tucker is the editor of *The Free Market*.

GAGGED BY CIVIL RIGHTS

By Justin Raimondo[299]

Is free speech still a constitutionally protected right? Like the right of private property, it is only allowed if and when the government approves of the outcome. Consider this case.

Alexandra White, Richard Graham, and Joseph Deringer of Berkeley, Cal., heard that the federal government planned to build a housing project for drug addicts in their neighborhood. They fought it for a year, publishing a newspaper, lobbying the city council and the state legislature, and filing lawsuits—all to no avail.

The city council, under pressure from federal bureaucrats, was deaf to their pleas. State lawmakers showed a similar lack of sympathy. Defeated, White, Graham, and Deringer reconciled themselves to the fact that they would soon be living next to a nest of dopers. Then the trouble *really* began.

Not content at having triumphed over the will of the neighborhood, a federally funded non-profit advocacy group called Housing Rights, Inc., filed a complaint with the Department of Housing and Urban Development (HUD). The residents then received a notice in the mail from the District Attorney's office. It warned that their activities—posting flyers, publishing a neighborhood newspaper, holding meetings and lobbying members of the city council—are illegal under the Americans With Disabilities Act, a civil-rights law that protects people with mental and physical disabilities from "discrimination."

Marianne Lawless of Housing Rights, Inc., argues that "statements made and actions taken by some neighbors violated the right of the disabled not to be discriminated against. They posted flyers, and they had their own little newspaper."

"If discrimination is likely to occur," Lawless told us, "the attempt to stop funding for such projects is illegal. If they had sent out flyers saying property sales would go down with Latinos, they wouldn't have gotten away with it." Lawless said she decided to go easy on them by

317

not asking for damages; what she wants is for them to "stop suing and stop making statements."

Working in tandem with Housing Rights, Inc., HUD has subpoenaed letters and articles written by opponents of the drug housing project, as well as tapes of public meetings held on the issue. Asked whether White, Graham, and Deringer deserve to be slapped with $50,000.00 fines for exercising their right to free speech, Lawless says "that's a hard question to answer."

This is the real face of the civil-rights revolution that has displaced and overthrown property rights in America. It wages an Orwellian crusade to wipe out thought-crime and to outlaw opposition to collectivism as "hate speech."

By labeling drug addicts "disabled," the federal government confers on them all the special rights and privileges that racial minorities now enjoy at others' expense. And along with drunks, child molesters, and psychopaths, Berkeley's drug addicts have a "right" to housing.

As HUD spokesman John Phillips has said, "advocating that housing not be provided to somebody because of attributes they have" is against the law. "Residents were saying 'We don't want people with disabilities in our neighborhood.'"

Those few left-liberals who still pay lip service to the idea of free speech should not be shocked. This is happening all over the country, and it's the logical outcome of the civil-rights principle, which, once established, is easily extended to every area of life: not just race but sex, sexual orientation, HIV status, and any other conceivable attribute, inherited or acquired. And this principle can easily be used to rein in free expression.

As Ms. Lawless postulates, "If a landlord says to somebody, 'we don't accept kids,' that is speech and we don't allow that. Just because these people are not the landlord, doesn't make any difference to me."

She reveals the not-so-hidden agenda of the egalitarians: to outlaw the opposition. If "discrimination against a dipsomaniacal HIV-carrier is illegal, then all opposition to the construction of tax-subsidized housing for such people is a conspiracy to deprive the 'differently abled' of their rights."

All this flows from the idea of outlawing "discrimination," a necessarily subjective concept which cannot be detected without mind reading or defined without coercion. This is why we have racial quotas and, now, limitations on speech. There is no other way to enforce the Jacobin schemes of the levelers.

The Berkeley incident illustrates one aspect of civil-rights legislation never discussed by its advocates—or even addressed by conservatives who seek to limit its effects while accepting it in principle. The purpose of civil rights is to hurt some—primarily, property owners—as much as it is to help others. Racial quotas do not uplift supposedly disadvantaged minorities so much as they damage those who are forced to comply.

The legal sanctions imposed by HUD's commissars and their enforcers in the non-profit sector are not designed to help homeless drug addicts. They are designed to hurt the middle class communities in which the dopers are forcibly implanted—to break them up, to shut them up, and to crush them politically. There are no "unintended consequences" in operation here; rather, the consequences are the predictable effects of malevolence combined with state power.

The pattern of attack is not limited to Berkeley. The same people who campaigned for civil-rights legislation in the fifties and sixties are now calling for the passage of "hate speech" laws, that would make it a crime to "denigrate" any member of an officially approved victim group.

Aside from encoding the pecking order under "multi-cultural" socialism, these laws criminalize speech, establish certain categories of prohibited (i.e. politically incorrect) organizations, and trample the Constitution: not only the First Amendment, but the equal protection clause, which, ironically, civil-rights advocates tout as the legal basis of their new social order.

There is only one way to stop outrageous attacks by federal agencies on ordinary citizens: we must roll back the civil-rights revolution. We must seek to repeal not just the Americans with Disabilities Act, which even the statist neo-conservatives want to amend, but all civil-rights legislation. Only then will we have destroyed the legal foundation of the modern statist project. As the Berkeley case shows, there can be no coexistence between individual rights and "civil-rights."

299 Originally published in *The Free Market*, the newsletter of the Ludwig von Mises Institute, October 1994. Justin Raimondo is a media fellow of the Mises Institute.

ECONOMIC INCENTIVES AND WELFARE

By Murray N. Rothbard[300]

Most people disagree with economists, who point out the important impact that monetary incentives can have on even seemingly "non-economic" behavior. When, for example, coffee prices rise due to a killing frost in Brazil, most people believe that the quantity purchased will not be affected, since people are "addicted" to coffee.

What they don't realize, and what economists are particularly equipped to point out, is that individual consumers vary in their behavior. Some, indeed, are hard core, and will only cut their purchases a little bit should the cost of a product or service rise. But others are "marginal" buyers, who will easily cut their coffee purchases, or shift to tea or cocoa.

People are shocked, too, when economists assert that monetary incentives can affect even such seemingly totally non-economic activity as producing babies. Economists are accused of being mechanistic and soulless, devoid of humanity, for even mentioning such a connection. And yet, while some people may have babies with little or no regard to economic inventive, I am willing to bet that if the government, for example, should offer a bounty of $100,000.00 for each new baby, considerably more babies would be produced.

Liberals are particularly shocked that economists, or anyone else, could believe that a close connection exists between the level of welfare payments and the number of welfare mothers with children. Baby-making, they declare, is the result of "love" (if that's the correct word), and not of any crass monetary considerations. And yet, if welfare payments are far higher than any sum an underclass teenager can make on the market, who can deny the powerful extra tug from the prospects of tax-subsidized moolah without any need to work?

The conservative organization Change-NY has recently issued a study of the economic incentives for going on, and staying on, welfare in New York. The "typical" welfare recipient is a single mother with two children. This "client" receives, in city, state, and federal benefits, the whopping annual sum of $32,500.00 in cash, Medicaid, housing assistance, food assistance, etc. Since these benefits are non-taxable, this sum is equivalent to a $45,000 annual salary before taxes.

Furthermore, this incredibly high figure is actually conservative, because it excludes the value of other benefits, including Head Start (also known as preschool day care), job training (often consisting of such hard-nosed subjects as "conversational skills"), child care, and the Special Supplemental Food program for Women, Infants, and Children (or WIC). Surely, including all this would push up the annual benefit close to the equivalent of $50,000. This also presumes that the mother is not cheating by getting more welfare than she is entitled to, which is often the case.

Not only is this far above any job available to our hypothetical teen-aged single mother, it is even far higher than a typical entry level job in the New York City government. Thus, *The New York Post* noted the following starting salaries at various municipal jobs: $18,000 for an office aid; $23,000 for a sanitation worker; $27,000 for a teacher, $27,000 for a police officer or fire fighter; $18,000 for a word processor—all of these with far more work skills than possessed by your typical welfare client.

Is it any wonder that 1.3 million mothers and children in New York are on welfare, and that this continues from one generation of girls to the next?

Economists, then, are particularly alert to the fact that, the more any product, service, or condition is subsidized, the more of it we are going to get. We can have as many people on welfare as we are willing to pay for. And if the state of being a single mother with kids is the fastest route to getting on welfare, that social condition is going to multiply.

Not, of course, that every woman will fall for the blandishments of welfare, but the more intense those subsidies and the greater the benefit compared to working, the more women and illegitimate children on welfare we are going to be stuck with.

Moreover, the longer this system remains in place, the worse will be the erosion in society of the work ethic and antipathy to the dole that used to be dominant in the United States.

Change-NY points out that it would be cheaper for the taxpayer to send welfare recipients to Harvard than to maintain the current system. In view of the decline of education standards generally and

Harvard's Political Correctness in particular, Harvard would probably be happy to enroll them.

300 Originally published in *The Free Market*, the newsletter of the Ludwig von Mises Institute, October 1994. Murray N. Rothbard (1926-1995) was the S.J. Hall distinguished professor of economics at UNLV and was the head of academic affairs at the Mises Institute.

PLEADING THE 10TH . . . AND WINNING!

By Llewellyn H. Rockwell, Jr.[301]

Law schools teach that the 10th Amendment is a relic. Yet a growing judicial and political movement is marching under its banner of state's rights. Federal imperialism may have reigned supreme since time out of mind, but at least one U.S. judge has now rolled it back.

The provocation was the Brady bill, the anti-gun law passed at the urging of the Clinton administration. The 50 states were ordered to enforce it with invasive and expensive background checks on customers. So sheriffs and police all over the country have tacitly and even openly defied it.

An example is Sheriff Jay Printz of Ravalli County, Montana. "I didn't have the time or the resources to run background checks on everybody," he says, adding, "We like our guns in Montana. . . . It's not unusual for a person to have 15 guns, or more."

His protest was heard in court by a courageous Montana federal judge, Charles C. Lovell, who promptly struck down a portion of the Brady law. His ruling was not based on the Second Amendment—which bars the federal government from violating our right to keep and bear arms—but on the Tenth Amendment.

Few Americans can even remember that part of the Constitution. Those who do usually deride and dismiss it. Yet it may be the most important passage in all the Bill of Rights. In plain words, it chains down the central government: "The powers not delegated to the United States by the Constitution nor prohibited by it to the States, are reserved to the States respectively, or to the people."

The framers saw the Tenth Amendment as a core principle of the American republic. As the final word of the original Constitution and the last amendment in the Bill of Rights, it was a protective seal against what Thomas Jefferson decried as "consolidation." And it emphasized that the republic was a compact among the states.

In *Federalist No. 39,* James Madison wrote, "Each State, in ratifying the Constitution, is considered a sovereign body, independent of others, and only to be bound by its own voluntary act. In this relation, then, the new Constitution, will, if established, be a federal, and not a national Constitution."

The powers of the federal government are "few and defined" Madison wrote in *Federalist No. 45*, whereas the powers of the state are "numerous and indefinite" extending "to all the objects" which "concern the lives, liberties, and properties of the people."

Even the consolidationist Alexander Hamilton admitted in *Federalist No. 32* that the states "would clearly retain all the rights of sovereignty which they before had, and which were not . . . exclusively delegated to the United States."

We have come so far from this idea that the "federal" government ought to be called the central government, or simply Leviathan. For it regards the states as mere subdivisions of its empire. And with the bulwark of state's rights pierced, robbing the people of their liberty and property has become ever easier.

The Tenth Amendment came under attack as early as 1828, when Northern industrialists swindled Southern planters with the protective tariff. Yet even after the aggression of the War Between the States, the crimes of Reconstruction, and the disputed ratification of the 14th amendment in 1867, the legal core of state's rights remained intact.

In the Progressive Era, however, state's rights took four heavy blows in seven years: the income tax, the direct election of senators, alcohol prohibition, and forced suffrage expansion (the Sixteenth through the Nineteenth Amendments). The New Deal and the mistaken judicial doctrine of "incorporation" then paved the way for the omnipotent central government of Hillary's dreams.

Trampling on the liberties once protected by federalism is the daily business of Congress, the executive branch, and the Supreme Court. These D.C. potentates socialize labor markets, impose taxes and business regulations, and subvert the freedoms of associations and contracts, from Arizona to Maine.

Virtually every state decision is subject to a centralized veto. The Justice Department tells Ovett, Mississippi, to embrace leftist cultural marauders. It tells Wedowee, Alabama, to fire its high-school principal. It tells Rockland County, New York, to repeal its recycling laws.

That's why Judge Lovell's ruling is so important: it begins to roll back consolidated government. And it's why we should expect a massive push to get the ruling reversed. The Left tolerates no attempt to turn back its progress toward unified, omnipotent government. But as much as the disarmament lobby may scream, the judge's ruling is more than reasonable, as well as historically and constitutionally appropriate.

"We're pretty independent in Montana," said William War, the chief of police in Helena. May all Americans, with the Constitution and state's rights restored, one day be able to say the same.

301 Llewellyn H. Rockwell, Jr., is president of the Ludwig von Mises Institute in Auburn, Alabama.

BURY OUR FREEDOM ON RUBY RIDGE

by Ron Kennedy[302]

The local farmers huddled together, nervously watching the approaching column of troops. Many were anxiously inspecting their assault weapons, anticipating a bloody clash with the approaching government agents. The powerful central government had dispatched its military agents with orders to confiscate an illegal cache of private weapons. Tyrants hate the thought of armed, law-abiding citizens. The year was 1776, the place was Lexington, Massachusetts. The assault weapons of that day would soon fire a shot that would be heard around the world and resound down to this day! The struggle of "little people" against the tyranny of a large central government is ageless.

Desperate times call forth the best and the worst in men and these were desperate times. Lawlessness was rampant, local government was unable to provide the necessary protection for private citizens. Jay-hawkers were roaming the countryside assaulting private citizens. An industrial empire had invaded an agricultural people. A valiant but hopeless struggle was being waged to protect their agricultural country. The private citizens soon learned that their only recourse was to organize themselves for self-defense. The St. Augustine Guards was one of many local militia units formed. The members brought their own private firearms. They drilled and when necessary they fought to protect their homes from both domestic criminals and the pillaging of an invading army. The members were all free black Southerners from the northwestern parishes of Louisiana. The date was 1863. The value of citizens with private arms protecting themselves and their society would be demonstrated many times during this tragic war.

The government tanks poured in and overwhelmed the private citizens defending their compound. The body count began even as the government was proclaiming victory over these dangerous extremists. The photograph of a burned corpse was smuggled out to document the atrocities committed by the government forces. A caption was placed on the photograph declaring, "Even death for freedom's sake is not defeat!" The date was 1956, the place was Budapest, Hungary.

In they came, tanks, fighter bombers, airborne troops fully equipped with the most sophisticated weapons available. On they came, overwhelming numbers, overwhelming technology, overwhelming logistical depth. All the world proclaimed them to be an unstoppable juggernaut, the irresistible force of tyranny. Yet, the little people of the invaded country refused to listen to those politically correct prophets of doom. When asked by a skeptical news reporter what good his muzzle-loading black-powder weapon was, the freedom fighter answered with confidence of one wedded to the ideal of liberty, "I can use it to shoot the invader in the face." With such pride and determination these gallant freedom fighters continued their resistance to tyranny until at last the invader "declared victory" and went home. The place was Afghanistan. Oh, the incomprehensible value of a private citizen armed and dedicated to the preservation of liberty.

Liberty, a word much used by Americans but little understood. Even less understood is the natural antagonism between a powerful central government and the private citizen's right to keep and bear arms. It should be no surprise to find out that the earliest attempts by the British to repress the call for American liberty were directed at the control and confiscation of firearms. Patrick Henry boldly warned his countrymen that it was foolish to wait because "when shall we be stronger—when we are totally disarmed?" His warning was followed by the often quoted, "Give me liberty or give me death." Henry knew only too well that liberty would not be "given" but it would be won—won by free men armed mostly with their own personal "assault weapons."

The politically correct crowd would have us to believe that this precious constitutional right to keep and bear arms did not apply to "We the people." Yet, in the published papers of the anti-Federalist (those Revolutionary War-era patriots who did not trust the proposed Federal government and who wanted to erect strict limits on its powers to infringe upon the liberties of the people of the sovereign states) we can see clear and concise evidence of their desire to protect the citizen's right to keep and bear arms. A group of Pennsylvania anti-Federalists on December 18, 1787, published a resolution demanding specific amendments to the proposed constitution to defend

Bury Our Freedom on Ruby Ridge

American liberty from an oppressive Federal government. Item seven of their resolution declared,

> That the people have a right to bear arms for the defence of themselves and their own state, or the United States, or for the purpose of killing game; and no law shall be passed for disarming the people or any of them. . . .

The Virginia Convention on June 27, 1788, proposed a Bill of Rights to be added to the constitution. The seventeenth item of their proposed Bill of Rights declared,

> That the people have a right to keep and bear arms; that a well-regulated militia, composed of the body of the people trained to arms, is the proper, natural, and safe defence of a free state. . . .

George Mason saw the potential for tyranny in the proposed Federal government better than any of his anti-Federalist contemporaries. He knew the danger posed by a strong centralized national government. He knew also that tyrants prefer their subjects to be disarmed. He declared, "To disarm the people [is] the best and most effectual way to enslave them."

The Federalists (those favoring a strong central Federal government) were no less ardent in their support of the citizen's right to keep and bear arms. James Madison in *The Federalist Number 46* attempted to appease the concerns of the anti-Federalists who warned of the day when the Federal government would grow abusive of its powers, become uncontrollable and oppress the people. Madison assured the anti-Federalists that the states

> . . . would still have the advantage in the means of defeating such encroachments. . . . the State governments, with the people on their side, would be able to repel the danger. . . . Besides the advantage of being armed, which the Americans possess over the people of almost every other nation . . . forms a barrier against the enterprises of ambition. . . .

But why all of this irrelevant verbiage and pretence of concern—after all we are Americans—such things can never happen here. This is a free country, a nation of laws, of the Constitution, such atrocities will never happen here—or so we are assured by our politically correct liberal establishment!

The door of her home swung open, the woman stood in the doorway clutching her infant to her breast, her face full of terror as she cried out to her husband. He had just been wounded by a government sharpshooter. Slowly the mother's face emerged in the government agent's telescopic sights. The cross hairs promised certain death to this enemy of the central government. Her face was so strained, the terrible picture of grief and terror. Only the day before she had watched as another government agent shot her fourteen-year-old son in the back as he fled from the stranger who had just shot the little boy's dog. Now she watched in horror her husband's struggle with these agents of death. She watched never realizing that her own short struggle with these agents of death would soon begin. With callous indifference the government agent held true the cross hairs of his assault weapon. Mother, child, wounded husband, the body of her dead son, her own face in the cross hairs, an eternity in a second. Slowly the government agent squeezed his cold finger around the steel trigger of his government supplied assault weapon. Her face erupted, as the government's hollow point bullet pierced the flesh of her face, crushed the bones of her cheek and exploded her skull. Thrown back by the force of her exploding face, she dropped her baby to the floor. Surely a sensation of nationalist pride must have warmed the government agent's cold heart as he watched this enemy of the central government receive from her government its answer to those who dare to challenge accepted ideology. The date was August 21, 1992, the place was Ruby Ridge, Idaho, U.S.A.

Months later a jury of twelve citizens listened to the charges made by the Federal government against Randy Weaver. The Federal government called fifty-six (56) witnesses who testified over the thirty-six days of the trial. Without calling any witnesses the defense rested. The jury found Randy Weaver not guilty on eight Federal felony charges. The judge had already thrown out two other Federal charges. The judge ordered the prosecution to pay for part of the defense expense. This is almost unheard of in a criminal case. One of the prosecutors was forced to apologize in open court because of "prosecutorial misconduct"!

The Federal government is expert at covering up its miscalculations and whitewashing its stained record. Even though Federal Judge Edward Lodge condemned the FBI and issued a lengthy list detailing the Justice Department's and FBI's misconduct, fabrication of evidence, and refusals to obey court orders and even though the Justice Department's own investigation recommended possible criminal prosecution of Federal officials and found that the rules of engagement contravened the Constitution of the United States; even in spite of all this evidence David Patrick, assistant attorney general for civil rights, rejected the findings and concluded that the Federal agents had not used excessive force. The Weaver case is by far the most important civil rights/civil liberties case the Clinton administration has yet resolved—and it resolved it in favor of granting unlimited deadly power to Federal agents.

Little by little our freedoms are being buried in places like Ruby Ridge. Little by little our liberties are being infringed upon by an all-powerful Federal government. One such place was Berkeley, California, where the Federal government's HUD agents brazenly assaulted freedom of speech. Three people were prosecuted by the Federal government for the high crime of publicly speaking out against a proposed housing development in their neighborhood. In Florida a man and his son were sentenced to two years in Federal prison for the high crime of dumping clean sand on a private lot they owned! Their high crime, according to the U.S. Army Corps of Engineers, was that they violated the Wet Lands Act. In California a property owner was fined $100,0000.00 when he cut a fire break around his home. His high crime—according the Federal government he may have destroyed a portion of a protected habitat of an endangered rat! No people, the rats are not endangered—they are working for the Federal government! The only thing really endangered is our erstwhile constitutional freedoms and liberties!

From the vantage point of time we can now safely state that the anti-Federalist, George Mason, was a better predictor of future events than the Federalist, James Madison. The question yet remains for all Americans—what are you doing to help defend and preserve our freedoms and liberties?

302 Originally published in *Southern Heritage Magazine*, P.O. Box 3181, Merrifield, VA 22116, John Cummings, editor.

BATF THUGS STRIKE AGAIN![303]

The lives of Harry and Theresa Lamplugh were turned upside down on the morning of May 25, 1994. Early that day, 15-to-20 armed men and women burst into their rural Pennsylvania home. Under the threat of violence, the Lamplughs cooperated completely with the intruders as they opened safes, locks and cabinets. In spite of their compliance, however, Harry and Theresa were treated with contempt. Throughout the ordeal, a fully automatic machine gun was intermittently thrust in both their faces.

The Lamplughs watched in horror as the thugs literally trashed their home. Furniture was overturned or smashed and papers were scattered everywhere. Three pet cats were ruthlessly killed—one literally stomped to death. The gang ransacked their home for more than six hours. When they finally left, Harry and Theresa stood confused and angry in the midst of their demolished home.

The brutal and inhumane events that you have just read about are not fiction. They were taken from the testimony of Harry and Theresa Lamplugh. Only the intruders were not some violent street gang members or foreign terrorists; they were agents of the Bureau of Alcohol, Tobacco and Firearms (BATF) and the Internal Revenue Service (IRS).

Why would two federal agencies send a small battalion of agents to terrorize this couple in the supposed safety of their home? What terrible crime did Harry and Theresa Lamplugh commit that prompted this brutal six-and-a-half hour ordeal? Shockingly there are no good answers to these questions.

Harry Lamplugh, however, is in the politically incorrect business of promoting gun shows. His organization, Borderline Gun Collectors Association, happens to be the largest gun show promoter in the Northeast. As anyone who has ever attended a gun show knows, there are more than firearms and accessories on display. A gun show is also a place where people of common interests meet to express their political views and share opinions. Not surprisingly criticism of the BATF runs deep at such a forum. And it is no secret that BATF spends considerable time and effort infiltrating these shows.

Since gun show infiltration is a massive undertaking that yields rel- ative small returns, the BATF has now honed in on a primary source, Harry Lamplugh. On May 23, 1994, the agents obtained a search war- rant authorizing both the BATF and the IRS to "search" the Lam- plugh home. Included in the list of items to be seized were any firearms, ammunition, holsters, cleaning kits, gun cases and firearms accessories. The Lamplughs' attorney points out that the warrant failed to name even one specific item. "Such warrants are vague, overboard and therefore unconstitutional," he said.

The agents also seized complete financial and business records of the Borderline Gun Collectors Association from 1988 to the pre- sent. This included all computer records and any other documents related to the sale and purchase of firearms. Obviously, the BATF was on some sort of "fishing expedition." But the most amazing aspect of the warrant is what was NOT on it. There was no reference to any crime by any person. The BATF appears to hold not only the Sec- ond Amendment in disdain, but the Fourth as well.

On Wednesday, May 25, 1994, the search warrant was executed. At about eight in the morning, Harry answered a knock on the front door and was instantly surrounded by agents. His wife was in the bathroom at the time. He had been sitting at the kitchen table in a pair of pajama bottoms having his morning coffee. "To this day I don't know exactly how many there were, but they had my house secured in seconds," Harry said.

According to Lamplugh, there were a total of six cars full of agents. They were not dressed in any uniform, and only two had the identifying AFT vests on. All firearms were drawn. An M-P5 machine gun was stuck in Harry's face. They did not announce who they were or why they were there, and no search warrants were displayed. "When asked if they had a search warrant, their first reply was 'shut the f— up mother f—er; do you want more trouble than you already have?,' with the machine gun stuck in my face," Harry said. "They then proceeded to tear my house apart."

The Lamplughs were not permitted to dress all day. "We couldn't even go to the bathroom without an armed guard, as if we were pris- oners in our own home," says Mrs. Lamplugh. Then, like a slap in the face, the agents stopped everything to eat lunch. "They gave no thought to what we were going through. Some agents went out for pizza, and they had a little party. It was like a room full of kinder-gartners with no chaperon.

They threw half-emptied soda cans, pizza and pizza boxes every-where. To some people, maybe it sounds like we're complaining about a small thing, but this is our home and they trashed it."

The agents' reckless conduct at the "pizza party" characterized their behavior throughout the raid. "Because I have cancer, I usu-ally have about 20 bottles of prescription drugs on the top of my bureau. For some unknown reason, they thought it necessary to open the bottles and scatter the contents all over the floor. Conse-quently, two of our cats got into the medication and died horrible deaths."

The agents continued their aimless search. "Where's the machine gun?" one of the agents asked. Finally, an indication they were look-ing for something in particular. "At first I didn't know what he meant," Harry said. "Then I recalled I once owned a Vietnam com-memorative Thompson, inlaid in 22 karat gold, but that was a semi-automatic." One of the agents then responded, "That must be what they're talking about." The agents were apparently looking for some-thing that wasn't even there, or illegal to possess.

However, they were very thorough in sifting through what was there. But for what reason did the agents take marriage and birth certificates, school records, insurance information, vehicle registra-tions and titles? Harry points out that "they were so thorough that for about two weeks we would have had a hard time proving who we were. They took all of our contacts with newspapers (over 600), all friends and family phone numbers, and even my medical records." There were 61 firearms and assorted ammo seized in the raid, valued at over $15,000. The agents took about 70,000 names and addresses of exhibitors and also gun show contracts through the year 2000. A stack of mail was opened, read and also confiscated.

Finally, at about three o'clock, the wrecking crew finished their destruction. In one final unconscionable act, female agent Donna Slusser deliberately stomped to death a cherished Manx kitten, and kicked it under a tree.

The affidavit in support of the warrant was made by BATF special agent Scott Endy. For reasons unknown to the Lamplughs, the affi-davits were sealed by a local federal judge. An Assistant United States

Attorney was asked by the Lamplughs' attorney to unseal the document, but he has steadfastly refused to do so.

The persecution Harry and Theresa have endured has been extremely harsh. At no time was this peaceful couple informed of any violation of the law, and to this day no charges have been brought against the Lamplughs. Yet, the BATF has refused to return any property, even medical records and other personal documents and possessions.

The actions of the men and women who entered the Lamplughs' home must not be ignored or forgotten. The Lamplughs are victims, not suspects, in this matter, and this is but one of the many examples of the BATF abuse of its power through the years. This government brutality must be stopped.

303 Originally published in *The Gun Owner,* December 1994, page six. *The Gun Owner* is published by Gun Owners of America, Inc., 8001 Forbes Place, Suite 102, Springfield, VA 22151.

CONSENT OF THE GOVERNED—KEY TO LIBERTY

By Walter D. Kennedy[304]

"Governments are instituted among men, deriving their just Powers from the Consent of the governed. . . ."

The unanimous declaration of the delegates of the thirteen United States in 1776 announced to the world the great American principle that free people have a right and a duty to give their consent to any form of government that exists over them. More to the point, a free people have the obligation to change any form of government radically which has proven itself to be destructive to their "Unalienable Rights."

Thomas Jefferson, in writing the Declaration of Independence, drew deeply from the writings of John Locke. Indeed, a reading of Locke's *Two Treatises of Government* will clearly demonstrate the relationship between it and Jefferson's ideas of "government by consent" and the obligation of a people to replace a tyrannical government with one that rules by the consent of the governed. Although Jefferson borrowed from Locke, it should be noted that Locke's theories of consent and the right of a free people to replace a tyrannical government are restatements of Rev. Samuel Rutherford's theories as taught in his book, *Lex Rex*.

These two principles of government, so nobly enunciated by the Founding Fathers of this Republic, have many worthy antecedents. Nevertheless, it was by the hands and efforts of the Patriots of 1776 that these two "Keys of Liberty" were boldly placed upon the political stage.

Locke points out that an institution of government is given power by a "community" of people for the exclusive reason of ". . . the Mutual Preservation of their Lives, Liberty, and Estates . . . Property." Locke notes that when these ends of government are no longer being met, the "community" retains the right to recall that trust given to government "[When trust] is Manifestly neglected . . . the trust must necessarily be forfeited." Here, Locke is describing the ultimate secession movement. When faced with a government that has overstepped its legitimately entrusted power, people of a Sovereign

Community have a duty to withdraw from that threatening institution. Liberty, not governmental institutions, is foremost in Locke's
theory of government, regardless of the type of institution, be it a
King, a President, a Congress, or a *Union*! During the great debate
which culminated in the adoption of the United States Constitution
and Bill of Rights, Patrick Henry echoed the same sentiments. Henry,
while advocating American Union, nevertheless, made it clear where
his first loyalty would remain when he stated "The first thing I have at
heart is American *liberty*; the second thing is American Union." Not
only did Patrick Henry, a leading Anti-Federalist, address the question of the relationship of a community and its government, but also
a leading Federalist defended the right of a people to abolish any
form of government that no longer served their needs. James Madison, in *Federalist Papers No. 43* states ". . . the safety and happiness of
society are the objects at which all political institutions must be sacrificed." Madison makes it clear that the safety and happiness of society are to take precedence over any institution of government or
even government itself.

Why does Locke, when considering the protection of man's freedom, place such emphasis upon the withdrawal of a people's consent to a government? The right of a people to withdraw from a
threatening government, i.e., to secede, is a simple act of self-protection and of self-preservation of unalienable rights. The individual rights of the people of a community to be secure in their right
of life, liberty, and property, along with their collective right as a
"community" (consent of the governed) will always take precedence over governmental institutions. As Locke declared, "Men can
never be secure from Tyranny, if there be no means to escape it."
Secession is the means by which a Sovereign Community escapes
from tyranny.

Now let us re-read Jefferson's famous Declaration where he states
"That whenever any form of government becomes destructive of
these ends [life, liberty, and the pursuit of happiness], it is the right
of the people to alter or to abolish it." When the King's government
refused to recognize the rights of British subjects in America, the
people of each colonial "community," in an act of self-defence and
self-protection, seceded from the British Union. They did so only
for the protection of their unalienable rights.

Now let us look at Jefferson Davis' Inaugural Address: "The right solemnly proclaimed at the birth of the United States . . . undeniably recognizes in the people the power to resume the authority delegated for the purposes of government." Note that in both 1776 and 1861 secession is viewed as a means of protecting liberty. Locke's theory of "consent" proved to be the foundation of two American secession movements and, no doubt, will always serve as a foundation for those who reject the tyrannical notion of an all-powerful government.

304 Originally published in *The Southern Review Newsletter.*

LONG MAY THE BATTLE FLAG WAVE

By Thomas DiLorenzo[305]

The NAACP is threatening to boycott South Carolina businesses unless the state permanently furls the Confederate battle flag in the state capital of Columbia. The threat has rallied passionate supporters of the flag who see it not as a salute to slavery, but as a symbol of other aspects of the Southern Heritage that all Americans should be proud of.

The average Confederate infantry soldier was not a slave owner and did not fight and die to preserve this institution. As Charles Adams points out in his book *For Good and Evil,* slavery is a most unlikely reason for the start of the War Between the States. In his first inaugural address Abraham Lincoln promised that he would not disturb slavery; abolition never appeared in the platform of any major political party; the Supreme Court upheld slavery in the 1857 Dred Scott decision.

In John C. Calhoun's famous response to Daniel Webster's defense of the union, Calhoun offered three rationales for secession: fear that the new territories would side with the North and out-vote the South on economic issues, fear of the unconstrained and unconstitutional growth of the federal government, and fear of oppressive taxation that the Northern numerical majority would force upon the agricultural economy of the South.

Slavery was not one of the rationales. "The institution of slavery," historians Charles and Mary Beard wrote in the 1929 classic, *The Rise of American Civilization,* "was not a fundamental issue during the epoch preceding the bombardment of Fort Sumter."

Evidence of what the average Southerner *did* fight for is found in historian James McPherson's new book, *What They Fought For, 1861-1865.* McPherson read more than 25,000 letters and 100 diaries of soldiers from both sides in the War Between the States to try to understand what, in their own words, these young men thought they were fighting for.

"These were the most literate armies in history to that time,"

McPherson writes. Their median age was 24; most of them had voted in the 1860 election, "the most heated and momentous election in American history." And they were voracious readers of newspapers who frequently engaged in ideological debates and expressed strong political opinions in their letters and diaries.

McPherson concludes that most Confederates "fought for liberty and independence from what they regarded as a tyrannical government." A young Virginia officer wrote his mother that the North's "war of subjugation against the South" was comparable to "England's war upon the colonies" and that he thought of the war as a "second War for American Independence."

An enlisted man in a Texas calvary regiment wrote his sister that just as their forefathers had rebelled against King George III to "establish liberty and freedom in this western world . . . so we dissolved our alliance with this oppressive foe and are now enlisted in 'The Holy Cause of Liberty and Independence' again."

An Alabama corporal who was taken prisoner at Gettysburg proclaimed he was fighting for "the same principles which fired the hearts of our ancestors in the revolutionary struggle." A soldier who was killed at Chancellorsville viewed the war as "a struggle between Liberty on one side, and Tyranny on the other." The letters of many Confederate soldiers "bristled with rhetoric of liberty and self government," McPherson found, coupled with "a willingness to die for the cause."

Confederate soldiers also believed they were defending their country against foreign invaders. In the words of a Union army officer from Illinois, "We are fighting for the Union . . . a high and noble sentiment, but . . . they are fighting for independence and are animated by passion and hatred against invaders."

And for good reason: although there were many atrocities committed by both sides in the war, it was the South whose civilians were pillaged and plundered by an invading army. During Sherman's march through South Carolina, "Columbia was . . . burning fiercely, in more than a dozen places simultaneously," writes Shelby Foote in his trilogy, *The Civil War*. "Cotton Town, a section of poorer homes" was "put to the torch" along with "stores and houses along the river front."

"One object of special wrath was the Baptist church where the South Carolina secession convention had first assembled," writes

Foote, "but the burners were foiled by a Negro they asked for directions." He was "the sexton of the church they sought and he pointed out a rival Methodist establishment . . . which soon was gushing flames from all its windows." Also gushing with flames was "the nearby Ursuline convent, whose Mother Superior was known to be the sister of . . . an outspoken secessionist."

Rampaging Union soldiers "hurried from block to block, carrying wads of turpentine-soaked cotton for setting fire to houses . . . while others used their rifles to bayonet hoses and cripple pumpers brought into play by the civilian fire department." When the sun finally rose on the morning of February 18, 1965, "two thirds of Columbia lay in ashes."

"Agonized mothers, seeking their children," were "rushing on all sides from the raging flames and falling houses" as "invalids had to be dragged from their beds, and lay exposed to the flames and smoke, " wrote E.A. Pollard in *The Lost Cause.*

In *Sherman's March,* Burke Davis writes that "black women of the city suffered terribly," many of them being "left in a condition little short of death" after regiments of Union troops subjected these women to "the tortures of their embraces." Southerners understood that the Confederate army—and its battle flag—was all that stood between them and debauchery and destruction.

Since the battle flag represents a fight against high taxes and centralized government, every freedom-loving American should honor it. South Carolina, don't tear it down!

305 Originally published in *The Free Market,* the newsletter of the Ludwig von Mises Institute, Auburn, Alabama. Thomas DiLorenzo is an adjunct scholar of the Mises Institute.

PUTTING SECESSION BACK INTO THE AMERICAN POLITICAL DEBATE

By George Kalas[306]

Hypocrisy is never a pretty sight, especially when practiced by governments. A case in point: since 1990, the United States has extended full diplomatic recognition to 20 secessionist republics which were formerly a part of the USSR, Yugoslavia, and Czechoslovakia. In doing so, the U.S. government recognized the legal right of Sovereign States to secede from their federal unions. This is the same Federal government which steadfastly denies the right of secession to American States! Indeed, any serious discussion of a modern-day secession by an American State is considered inflammatory, fanciful, and even taboo by many Americans. Why should this be so?

Many students of American history and government agree that secession is a right of the States. Apparently, the U.S. Government knows this too. In the late 1860's, the Radical Republicans were advised by the Chief Justice of the Supreme Court NOT to prosecute Confederate President Jefferson Davis for treason. Why? Because the U.S. government lacked firm legal grounds to do so.

This is especially clear to us when we consider that cadets at the United States Military Academy at West Point had for their use a textbook on the United States Constitution, written by a Northerner, that taught secession as a right of the States. Many cadets were taught Constitutional law from this textbook.

Lacking legal authority to prevent secession, the U.S. Government has always operated on the principle that it cares not if secession is legal or not; it simply will never be permitted. Southerners know how secession is to be prevented—through the use of military force. Today, we would call this a policy of "might makes right."

If military might were sufficient justification for denial of the Sovereign right of secession, then the Baltic States had no right to secede from the USSR, having been conquered fair and square by the Red Army, right? Of course not. Indeed, the U.S. Government

NEVER recognized the re-incorporation of the Baltic States into the Soviet Union. In fact, every administration from 1940-1991 regarded Latvia, Lithuania, and Estonia as "captive nations."

What did the term "captive nations" mean? In short, it meant that the Soviet re-incorporation of these States into its "Union" in 1940 was invalid because these States were united with the USSR by force. The United States viewed the Baltic States as nations whose legal governments had been usurped by the de facto military and political governance of a foreign power. Inherent in this concept was the recognition that these States never lost their right to be free and independent. In essence, the United States continued to recognize the Sovereignty of Latvia, Lithuania and Estonia.

Now, let's apply the United States Government's definition of a "captive nation" to the United States itself. Applying the concept in the most conservative manner possible, one can readily identify at least two "captive nations": the Kingdom of Hawaii and the Confederate States of America.

Hawaii, a self-governing, Sovereign monarchy was seized by the United States in 1893 when America declared Hawaii a "protectorate" and simply used the U.S. Navy to seize control of the islands—deposing the Hawaiian monarchy in the process.

In the American South, the story is all too familiar to most Americans. The Southern States seceded from the American Union and formed a new nation, the Confederate States of America. The United States refused to recognize the Confederacy and promptly invaded and conquered it. The States of the Confederacy were then compelled to rejoin the United States by military force.

The parallel to be drawn between the United States government's conquest of Hawaii and the Confederacy to the Soviet Union's conquests of the Baltic States is striking, to say the least. Given the similarities, it can reasonably be said that, by the U.S. Government's own standards, the Confederate States of America and the Kingdom of Hawaii still exist! (An astounding thought to many, but a logical one.) The peoples, cultures, and lands are still intact. Their right to self-government is perpetual. They are merely "captive nations" which retain the right to reassert their sovereignty as soon as they are able.

Recently, President Clinton and Congress have nudged the United States Government towards recognition of Hawaiian sovereignty with the passage and signing of the Hawaiian Apology Bill. This symbolic and important act was made possible largely as a result of the vocal and activist Hawaiian Independence movement, which counts among its members the Governor of Hawaii! This author believes that Confederate Americans should emulate the Hawaiian example and begin electing Confederate nationalists to their Governorships, State Houses and Congressional Delegations. In this way, the U.S. Government can be pressured to change its policy of threatening force to deny the right of secession to the States.

Now, some readers, like Pavlov's dog, will recoil from this idea—having been taught all their lives the Yankee propaganda that America is "one nation, indivisible." I would ask WHY this must be so? What is so SACRED about the American Union, or for that matter, ANY union. If union is such an inherently good thing, then wouldn't a worldwide union be even better? If so, then all nations should cede their sovereignty to the United Nations and be done with it. I can already hear the chorus of objections to that idea!

My point here is simple. If the American people truly believe it is the right of a free people to choose their own government, then we should not bar the discussion of secession from our political discourse in this country. State secession and the related right of nullification are the only true vertical checks on Federal power. Without these rights, the States are reduced to provinces and the people reduced to serfs—leaving the Federal Government our absolute masters.

But there is one psychological problem we must overcome. Even though we still have the right to secede, we have been terrified to assert it since 1865. Why? For fear that the United States Government will stage its own version of "Tiannamen Square" in Honolulu or Richmond. This fear MUST end. The spirit of our age favors secession. The age of empire is over. Americans should again begin to assert, publicly, the rights of State Sovereignty and secession. In doing this, we will reclaim the liberties endowed to us by our Forefathers, and in doing so, we will redeem the American experiment in freedom and self-government.

306 Originally published in *The Southern Review Newsletter.*

THE SOUTH

by Dr. Clyde N. Wilson[307]

The South, what to say in brief compass about the South?—a subject that is worthy of the complete works of a Homer, a Shakespeare, or a Faulkner. The South is a geographical/historical/cultural reality that has provided a crucial source of identity for millions of people for three centuries. Long before there was an entity known as "the United States of America," there was the South. Possibly, there will still be a Southern people long after the American Empire has collapsed upon its hollow shell.

One fine historian defined the South as "not quite a nation within the nation, but the next thing to it." The late M.E. Bradford, whose genial spirit watches over us even now, defined the South as a "vital and long-lasting bond, a corporate identity assumed by those who have contributed to it." This is, characteristically, a broad and generous definition. He proceeded to illustrate that when visualizing the South, he always thought "of Lee in the Wilderness that day when his men refused to let him assume a position in the line of fire and tugged at the bridle of Traveler until they had turned him aside." This was clearly a society at war, not a government military machine.

The South is larger and more salient in population, territory, historical import, distinctive folkways, music, and literature than many of the separate nations of the earth. Were the South independent today, it would be the fourth or fifth largest economy in the world. Citizens of Minneapolis consider themselves cultured because of their Japanese-conducted symphony that plays European music, and assume that the Nashville geniuses who create music all the world loves are rubes and hayseeds. New Yorkers pride themselves on their literacy culture. Yet in the second half of the twentieth century (if you subtract Southern writers) American literature would be on par with Denmark or Bulgaria and somewhere below Norway and Rumania.

Southerners are the most regionally loyal citizens of the United States. The South is the only part of the country that is potentially a nation. Southerners are also the most loyal to their States and their

351

localities of all Americans. But paradoxically—or perhaps not—they have traditionally been the most loyal to the country at large, ready to repel insult or injury without the need to be dragooned by any ridiculous folderol about saving Haiti or Somalia for democracy. Southerners have given freely to the Union and generally avoided the demands for entitlements that now characterize American life, But their loyalty has been severely tested, especially considering that all they have ever asked in return is to be left alone.

Southerners have less reason to be loyal to the collective enterprise of the United States than does any group of citizens. The South was invaded, laid waste, and conquered when it tried to uphold the original and correct understanding of the Declaration of Independence and the Constitution. It took twenty-two million Northerners, aided by the entire plutocracy and proletariat of the world, four years of the bloodiest warfare in American history and the most unparalleled terrorism against civilians, to subdue five million Southerners. This was followed by something even worse—the horror of Reconstruction. During this entire period, "the Northern conservatives" never opposed the smallest obstacle to the devastations of the radicals. In fact, the Northern "conservatives" have never, in the course of American history, conserved anything.

Since the war, the South has been a colonial possession, economically and culturally, to whatever sleazy elements have been able to exercise national power. A major theme of the American media and popular culture is ridicule and contempt for everything Southern. A major theme of American historical writing is the portrayal of the South as the unique repository of evil in a society that is otherwise shining and pure.

A severely condensed but essentially accurate interpretation of American history could be stated thusly: There are two kinds of Americans. There are those who want to be left alone to pursue their destiny, restrained only by tradition and religion; and those whose identity revolves around compelling others to submit to their own manufactured vision of the good society.

These two aspects of American culture were formed in the 17th century, by the Virginians and Yankees, respectively. The Virginians moved into the interior of America and carved their farms and plantations out of the wilderness. Their goal was to re-create the best of English rural society. They merged with even more vigorous and independent people, such as the Scots-Irish, to form what is still the better side of the American character.

The Yankees of Massachusetts lived in villages with preacher and teacher. They viewed themselves as a superior, chosen people, a City upon a Hill. As far as they were concerned, they were the true Americans and the only Americans that counted and they have always thought so down to this very day. Which means they ignored or slandered other Americans relentlessly. They still do. By Yankee I mean that peculiar group of ethnic New Englanders that has been described by Murray Rothbard as the great meddlers of American history, not all Americans beyond the South. The term "Yankee," in fact, was coined by the Dutch in New York in contempt for the shifty peddlers and canting hypocrites of New England.

Whenever the South has ruled—aided by good Northerners—America has been free and honorable, as in the days of Jefferson and Jackson. You know all you need to know by looking at the first decade or so of the federal government. During this period the Virginians gave away their vast Western empire for the joint enjoyment of all Americans, (thus making possible the Mid-west and West) and labored to erect a limited, responsible government.

The New Englanders, during the same periods, demanded a reserve of lands for themselves in Ohio; instituted a national bank and funding system by which their money-men profited off the blood of the Revolution; passed the Alien and Sedition laws to essentially enforce their own narrow ideological code on others; opposed the Louisiana Purchase; and demanded tariffs to protect their industries at others' expense. All of which was done in the name of "Americanism." (One of the first laws passed by Congress was a measure to continue the British imperial subsidy for New England fisheries.)

This profiteering through government, which John Taylor of Caroline called the "paper aristocracy," has always been accompanied by moral imperialism and assumptions of superiority that are even more offensive than the looting. It is from this that the South seceded. It is this combination of greed and moralism which constitutes the Yankee legacy, gives the American empire whatever legitimacy it can claim, and fuels the never-ending reconstruction of society. That is why we use Marines for social work, so that our leaders can congratulate themselves on their moral posture. That is why every town in the land is burdened with empty parking spaces bearing the symbol of the empire, so that the Connecticut Yankee George Bush can posture over his charity to the disabled. That is why, right now, wealthy Harvard University receives from the treasury a 200 percent overhead bonus on its immense federal grants, while the impoverished University of South Carolina receives only 50 percent of its much smaller bounty.

The term *American* is an abstraction without human content—it refers, at best, to a government, territory, standard of living, and a set of dubious and dubiously observed propositions. It refers to nothing akin to values or culture, nothing that represents the humanness of human beings. It could be reasonably argued that there is no such thing as an American people, although we have persuaded ourselves there was when shouldering the burdens of several wars. There was perhaps a time earlier in this century when an American nationality might have emerged naturally. But that time has passed with the onslaught of new immigrants.

Unlike the term *American*, when we say *Southern*, we know we imply a certain history, literature, music, and speech, sets of folkways, attitudes and manners; a certain set of political responses and pieties; and a view of the proper dividing line between the private and the public. Things which are unique, clear, easily observable, and continual over many generations.

The bloody St. Andrews cross of the Confederacy is a symbol throughout the world of heroic resistance to oppression—except in the U.S., where it is in the process of suppression. Southerners are democratic in spirit, but they have never made a fetish of democracy and certainly not of what Mel Bradford called "Equality." With T. S. Eliot, Southerners intuitively recognize that democracy is a procedure and not a goal, a content, or a substitute for an authentic social fabric. However free and equal we may be, we are nothing without a culture, and there is no culture without religion.

The South, many believe, still has a substantial authentic culture, both high and folk, and it still has a purchase on Christianity. That is, the South is a civilization reality in a sense which the United States is not, and it will last longer than the American Empire.

I have been speaking mostly about what the South has done for the United States, but this is to put things the wrong way around. A proper question to now ask is what can the United States do for the South? The Union is nothing except for its constituent parts. The

Union is good and just to the degree that it fosters its authentic parts. That is precisely why our forefathers made the Constitution and the Union and gave consent, voluntarily, to them—to enhance themselves, not the government.

As the Southern poet Allen Tate pointed out, the wrong turn was taken in the War Between the States when the United States ceased living by the Southern conception of a limited partnership and became instead a collection of buildings in Washington from which orders of self-justifying authority were issued. The great classical scholar and Confederate soldier Basil Gildersleeve remarked that the War was a conflict over grammar—whether the proper grammar "was the United States are" or "the United States is." We know which grammar is correct, but we have been using the wrong grammar for a long time now, and therefore can't expect to get anything right.

The South's lost political legacy was laid out by Rev. Robert Lewis Dabney, Presbyterian theologian and Stonewall Jackson's chief of staff, several years following the war. Echoing Calhoun he said:

> Government is not the creator but the creature of human society. The Government has no mission from God to make the community; on the contrary the community is determined by Providence, where it is happily determined for us by far other causes than the meddling of governments—by historical causes in the distant past, by vital ideas propagated by great individual minds—specially by the church and its doctrines. The only communities which have had their characters manufactured for them by governments have had a villainously bad character. Noble races make their governments. Ignoble ones are made by them.

The United States was created to serve the communities which make it up, not for the communities to serve the government. That is what the South and all authentic American communities need to recapture from a ruling class bent upon constantly remaking us. If we recapture that, we will again be citizens giving our consent to the necessary evil of a limited government, and not the serfs and cannon fodder of the American Empire.

307 Dr. Clyde N. Wilson is professor of history at the University of South Carolina. He is the author or editor of twenty books and the author of more than two hundred articles, essays, and reviews, as well as a contributing editor of *Chronicles: A Magazine of American Culture*. This article was originally published in *The Southern Patriot*, the newsletter of the Southern League, Inc.

THE WAR FOR STATE'S RIGHTS

By Ron Kennedy[308]

The struggle to defend State's Rights was the primary motivating factor leading to the War for Southern Independence. The struggle to defend State's Rights did not begin in 1860 but actually had its origin with the birth of the United States in 1776. The struggle for State's Rights is unique to the American experience. It was an American attempt to preserve individual liberties and protect the citizen's freedom from the tendency of all central governments to abuse their powers at the expense of the individual's civil liberties.

During Reconstruction, Supreme Court Chief Justice S.P. Chase (appointed by Lincoln) declared that "State Sovereignty died at Appomattox." According to this theory of constitutional law, General Lee surrendered not only his army at Appomattox but also the Tenth Amendment as well! Well, is the Tenth Amendment still a viable part of the Constitution? Does it still possess the moral authority necessary to protect the people of the states from an illegal, unconstitutional intrusion by the Federal government upon their reserved rights? Let us test the question—Does the Constitution grant to the Federal government the right to decide pupil assignments for local schools? No, it does not—yet, does the Tenth Amendment offer any protection from this abuse of Federal power? No, it does not. It is a mere paper barrier. Then I submit to you that the Tenth Amendment is an amendment in name only. In functional political reality, it does not exist. Our Confederate ancestors fought to preserve the American principles of limited government, State's Rights, and constitutional government but their generation was not the first to do battle in defense of these rights.

The first enemies of State's Rights were, strangely enough, monarchists. During the Constitutional Convention, when they attempted to centralize power in the newly proposed Federal government, they were referred to as consolidationists. Of course, this meant that power had to be taken away from the states, a proposal that met with universal disdain (remember, this was 1789). One of the leading consolidationists of the monarchy school was John Adams of Massachusetts.

357

He expressed the hope that the day would come when the people of America would have a hereditary chief magistrate and senate. Alexander Hamilton, one of the chief writers of the *Federalist Papers,* was also a monarchist. Thomas Jefferson declared of Hamilton that he "was not only a monarchist but a monarchist bottomed on corruption." In the introduction to Upshur's book, *The Federal Government Its Nature and Character,* C. C. Burr described the influence the monarchists exerted upon the development of constitutional law:

> In the convention which framed the Constitution . . . [the monarchists] exerted . . . [their] commanding influence to impart centralized, consolidated, or monarchical powers to the Federal Union. But . . . failing in this, in [their] subsequent interpretations of the constitution [they] did what [they] could to bend the instrument to suit [their] views. Judge Story, Chief Justice Kent, and, earlier, Chief Justice Jay, belonged to the same political party [as did Hamilton and John Adams]. They were Federalists, and so odious did this party become to the American people, that it was driven out of power at the expiration of old John Adams' single presidential term in 1800.

Judge Story, a Federalist, declared that the states were created pursuant to the instructions of the Continental Congress and, therefore, the states were not sovereign. According to Judge Story's view, the American people in the aggregate "We the people," formed the Federal government, giving it and not the states, final authority over questions relative to the Constitution. Daniel Webster and, later, Abraham Lincoln would follow Judge Story's erroneous philosophy. The contention that the Union, using Lincoln's own words, "preceded the state" can be dismissed with the simple reminder that, prior to the July 4th joint Declaration of Independence, Virginia had already established its own legislative authority, dismissed the Royal-appointed governor, and declared its independence in May of 1776!

Unable to force a king upon the American people, the monarchists turned their energies toward consolidating all power in the Federal government. To do this, they declared that the Supreme Court is the sole judge of questions relative to the Constitution. According to traditional Southern constitutional theory, the states, by ratifying the Constitution, created the Federal government to serve as collective agent and had delegated specific and limited authority to their mutual agent. The Federal government was created by a compact among sovereign states. According to the consolidationists, the agent would be the sole judge to the limits of its own power. The consolidationists viewed the Federal government as having authority over the states, whereas the bulk of Americans during colonial times and the South during the 1860s, viewed the states as the repository of sovereignty and therefore possessing the right to decide for themselves questions of whether or not an act of their agent, the Federal government, was constitutional. With such differing concepts of government, it was certain that conflict would soon erupt.

Many reasons have been advanced to explain why this struggle took place. In the final analysis, the primary motivating factor encouraging the consolidation of power was one of commercial greed—in a word, "money." Patrick Henry made it very clear that the purpose of the Revolutionary War was not to secure for Americans a great and mighty empire, but the blessings of liberty (often referred to in the South as the right to be left alone). This view was not shared by the writers of the *Federalist Papers* who declared it to be their intention to establish an American commercial empire. The attempt to give the Mississippi River to Spain is an example of how the agents of commercial influence attempted to act upon the development of the new union. The states of the Northeast, with its economy dependent upon commerce, desired to close the Mississippi River to commerce by giving control of it to Spain, thereby, forcing commercial trade eastward rather than down the river to the South. They were also fearful that an expanding West would draw off their labor supply and thereby increase their cost of labor. In short, the Northeastern mercantile interests feared a loss of their political and economic control of an expanding, and largely agricultural America. Gouverneur Morris of Pennsylvania wanted to give control of the Mississippi River to Spain because he thought this would allow the Eastern states to hold the population of the West under their control. Captain James De Wolf, one of Rhode Island's most prosperous and infamous slave traders, realized the potential in developing manufacturing in the United States. He transferred capital from his slave enterprises and built one of the earliest cotton mills in the New England states. He sensed that the new industry needed political influence to protect its supply of raw materials and markets. In 1821, he was elected to the United States Senate where he, a man who had grown rich in the African slave-trade, was a strong advocate of protectionist tariffs and opposed the extension of slavery to Missouri. His interest was no longer in the African slave but in the white mill worker. Slowly, political philosophy of limited versus centralized government began to take on a commercial character as the Northern states turned to the Federal government as a source of money for internal improvements and a source of protection for their emerging commercial empire. The money for internal improvements in the North was derived, to a greater extent, from the Southern states. In the words of Virginia's Senator Grayson, the South had become the "Milch cow of the Union." Despite loud and forceful protest from the Southern states, the numerical majority of the North continued to use the Federal government to transfer Southern wealth to the North. Senator Benton in 1828 declared that the states of Virginia, Georgia, North Carolina, and South Carolina provided 75% of the revenue to support the Federal government.

A basic principle of sovereignty is that the sovereign power cannot be compelled to submit to the jurisdiction of a court. The states were reluctant to ratify the Constitution because they feared the power proposed for the Supreme Court. The monarchist Alexander Hamilton attempted to calm their fear when he stated that immunity from suit was "inherent in the nature of sovereignty." John Marshall, a Federalist, who would later work so hard to consolidate the power of the Federal government, assured the hesitant states with this statement: "I hope that no gentlemen will think that a state will be called at the bar of the Federal Court. . . . [I]t is not rational to suppose that the sovereign power should be dragged before a court."

In *Chisholm v. Georgia,* an individual attempted to sue the state of Georgia in Federal court. The Supreme Court ordered the sovereign state of Georgia to appear and defend itself. The states were shocked—not exactly what they had been led to believe! The Georgia legislature passed a bill ordering that any Federal agent attempting to execute the Federal court's order should "suffer death, without benefit of clergy, by being hanged." In record-setting time, eleven of the thirteen states ratified the Eleventh Amendment declaring that the Supreme Court had no judicial power to hear a suit brought by an individual against a state.

The Virginia anti-Federalist Grayson, while debating the proposed constitution, warned Americans of the danger to state sovereignty inherent in the proposed Supreme Court when he declared: "This court has more power than any court under heaven. What has it in view, unless to subvert the state government?"

Another Virginia anti-Federalist George Mason's words border upon prophecy: "When we consider the nature of these courts, we must conclude that their effect and operation will be utterly to destroy the state government. . . . There are many gentlemen in the United States who think it right that we should have one great, national, consolidated government, and that it was better to bring it about slowly and imperceptibly rather than all at once. . . . To those who think that one national consolidated government is best for America, this extensive judicial authority will be agreeable."

In 1798, Congress demonstrated its ability to infringe unconstitutionally upon the liberties of the American people when it passed the Alien and Sedition Acts. Essentially, these acts made it a Federal crime to oppose any measure or measures of the government of the United States. If any person should write, print, utter, or publish anything that might be interpreted as opposition to the official policy of the government, that person could be arrested for sedition. The purpose of these acts, passed while the Federalist John Adams of Massachusetts was president, was to stifle political opposition to Adams and his monarchist consolidationist party. Without any doubt, these acts violated the Bill of Rights. According to the consolidationist (monarchists, Federalists, Radical Republicans, or liberals) theory of government, the Supreme Court is the sole judge of whether an act of the Federal government is constitutional. Here was an early and clear opportunity for the Federal Supreme Court to demonstrate its ability to dispense justice by declaring these acts in violation of the constitutional provisions we refer to as our Bill of Rights. Instead of moving to protect American civil liberties, the United States Supreme Court actually participated in the enforcement of these acts! Using these acts,

* Federal Supreme Court Justice Chase (Justice S. Chase, Federalist, served 1796-1810) was instrumental in having James Calendar, editor of the *Richmond Examiner,* indicted for sedition. He was tried and found guilty.

* Federal Supreme Court Justice Bushrod Washington tried Charles Holt, editor of a New Haven newspaper, for sedition.

* Federal Supreme Court Justice Patterson tried Vermont Congressman Matthew Lynon. Lynon had published an article in the *Vermont Journal* critical of Adams. Lyon was indicted for sedition, tried, found guilty, and sentenced to four months in jail.

*Federal Supreme Court Justice Chase ordered David Brown to divulge the names of his friends who shared his anti-Federalist views. Mr. Brown refused to betray his friends. Federal Justice Chase was so enraged that he fined Brown \$450.00 and sentenced him to jail for eighteen months.

Barely a decade had passed since the writing of the Bill of Rights and those who desired a strong centralized Federal government (call them monarchists, Federalists, or consolidationists) had made a mockery of American civil liberties; this was done with the aid and active participation of the United States Supreme Court, the Congress, and the president. The Constitution became a mere paper barrier; no obstacle at all, to the forces of Federal tyranny. Those who controlled the Federal government decided to ignore the Constitution. The only bulwark left between the tyranny of an abusive Federal government and the civil liberties of "We the people" was the sovereign states. Those who desired the establishment of a strong centralized Federal government realized that State's Rights had to be destroyed. To destroy the doctrine of State Sovereignty, i.e., State's Rights, Federalist Supreme Court Justice Story asserted that (1) the people of the thirteen colonies were one people during the colonial period, (2) the people of America formed a nation declaring independence July 4th, 1776, (3) the state governments were organized pursuant to the instructions of the Continental Congress, (4) the Preamble of the Constitution proved that "We the people" formed a national Federal government with absolute supremacy, and therefore, (5) sovereign authority resides in the Federal government to the exclusion of the states. Justice Story's erroneous logic proved to be the primary source of consolidationists such as Daniel Webster and eventually Abraham Lincoln. Lincoln's astounding pronouncement that "The Union preceded the states" is rooted in the erroneous logic of Federalist Justice Story.

An equally radical and absurd "constitutional" theory was advanced by Senator William H. Seward, Republican of New York.

Seward advanced the notion that the Constitution must be sub-servient to "higher law," especially those ideas expressed in the Dec-laration of Independence. According to this view, the Declaration of Independence was THE founding document, established by the sovereign people of America as opposed to being an act of sover-eign states. Thus, the Declaration supersedes the Articles of Confed-eration, the state constitutions, and the United States Constitution as fundamental law. The significance of Seward's novel utilization of the Declaration of Independence is that it struck at the core of constitu-tional government by attacking the concept of State Sovereignty. The idea of "Higher Law" is rooted in a natural law tradition—a tradi-tion full of ambiguity and subject to various interpretations. A polit-ical movement that articulates a reasonable political ideology forms a natural law basis that would possess the theoretical wherewithal to challenge effectively conflicting positive laws embodied in a written constitution. Such natural law theory was rejected by John C. Cal-houn.

Seward's logic served the consolidationist dreams perfectly. Here, at last, was a method to circumvent the strict reservation of rights so plainly written into the Constitution. This transformed the Union from a compact among consenting sovereign states into a national compact of individual American citizens, a compact that could be controlled by the numerical majority of the North. The South rec-ognized the danger posed by this new school of radical consolida-tionism. Senator Clay of Alabama declared, "When they get control of the federal government . . . the Southern States must elect between independence out of the Union or subordination within it."

> Earlier, John C. Calhoun had foreseen this danger: That the gov-ernment claims and practically maintains the right to decide in the last report as to the extent of its powers, will scarcely be denied. . . . It follows that the character of the government, has been changed, from a Federal Republic, as it originally came from the hands of the framers, and that it has been changed into a great national consolidated democracy.

The struggle between the proponents of State's Rights and those favoring centralized Federalism would continue until the numerical majority of the North at last seized complete control of the Federal government. The South was faced with the choice of surrendering its legitimate rights under the Constitution or securing those rights by seceding and forming a new government dedicated to the principles of the original Constitution. When the Southern states seceded, the commercial interests of the North saw its "Milch cow" escaping and waged an aggressive war against the South to maintain its commercial empire. The South was at last conquered, her right to self-determination denied, and she was turned into a colonial province of the Northern commercial empire. In America today, far too few citizens understand that State Sovereignty and State's Rights are the bedrock principles upon which the constitutional Federal Republic was established. Our liberties and freedoms as Americans cannot be guaranteed and protected without this essential principle of State Sovereignty. Recall Federal Judge Chase's words, "State Sovereignty died at Appomattox." He was right; State Sovereignty died with the Confederate States of America—slain by the commercial and political interests of the Northern numerical majority.

Professor Hoar of Maine, author of *The South's Last Boys in Gray,* said that Americans have lived long enough to see the Confederate soldiers' worst nightmare come true—a Federal government completely out of control! Look at what has happened to our country as a result of consolidating all power into one Big Government:

* In 1948, the typical family of four paid only 2% of its income to the Federal government in taxes. Today, a typical family of four pays 24% of its income to the Federal government and an additional 10% to local and state government. In 1948, the personal exemption shielded about 80% of the family's income from Federal taxes. To receive similar protection today, the standard exemption would have to be raised from the current level of $2,300 to $8,200. The result of this difference in tax load paid by families is that parents are working longer hours just to stay even. We have become a nation of indentured servants—sharecroppers, growing tax revenues for the government!

* To further its busing decision, a Federal court imposed a doubling of the local property taxes in Kansas City. Recall the American battle cry during the American revolution "No Taxation without Representation?" Obviously, the Federal judiciary feels that such old-fashioned principles no longer apply.

* There is a new "constitutional" theory being promoted by the movers and shakers of the liberal establishment. It is called "Critical Race Theory." In a nutshell, this constitutional theory insists upon equality of results, challenges employment testing, and supports strict racial quotas.

* The current administration has new legislation pending in Congress establishing national job qualifications standards designed to assure compliance with civil rights laws. The bill is an innovative form of race norming. The national standards would be set so low that the least skilled could qualify. Thus, an employer would be forced to hire by the numbers (quotas) to avoid the accusation of intentional discrimination.

Yes, the War for State's Rights continues even today. The principles for which our Confederate ancestors fought represent the ideal antidote of this sick society. That is why it is so important for us to know and articulate those honorable principles—to rise to their defense—and to be ever desirous to tell the world that our Confederate ancestors did not fight for a lost cause—they were fighting for the Right Cause!

Southerners now are faced with a challenging question. The question is, Shall we rise to the challenge? Shall we rise to the challenge of the cultural bigots who are attempting to destroy our heritage? Shall we rise to the challenge of the media that are daily slandering our culture and heroes? Shall we rise to the challenge of the political establishment that continues to use the force of government to deprive us of our liberties? Shall we accept the challenge to begin electing Confederate Freedom Fighters to office and announce to the world that State's Rights, State Sovereignty, and constitutional government—just like our conquered nation—SHALL RISE AGAIN!

308 Originally published in *Southern Heritage Magazine*, P.O. Box 3181, Merrifield, VA 22116, John Cummings, editor.

DRIVING DIXIE DOWN
THE DESTRUCTION OF SOUTHERN CULTURE

By Ron Kennedy[309]

The relentless attack upon Southern Heritage reached its judicial height in 1990 when the NAACP failed to convince a Federal court to order the state of Alabama to remove the Confederate battle flag from the state capitol. This failure was only a minor setback for the liberal establishment. In 1991, *The Yale Law Journal* carried a legal treatise in which the author outlines and recommends newer and better judicial tactics designed to outlaw the display of Southern symbols.

The article, entitled "Driving Dixie Down: Removing the Confederate Flag from Southern State Capitols," typifies the virulent hatred of those who are determined to destroy America's Southern Heritage. The appearance of specific guidelines for the removal of Confederate flags in a prominent New England law school journal demonstrates that the liberal campaign of anti-Southern cultural genocide is endorsed and approved by the liberal establishment. Earlier in 1991, Harvard University demonstrated its anti-Southern intolerance by harassing and deriding Miss Briget Kerrigan when she displayed pride in her Southern Heritage by flying a Confederate flag from her dorm room window.

Hatred of the South is not new, and examples of it are legion. Ralph Waldo Emerson declared, "If it costs ten years, and ten to recover the general prosperity, the destruction of the South is worth so much." Prior to the War for Southern Independence, an Englishman stated that there was nothing Northerners "hate with so deep a hatred" as Southerners. In 1862, Gen. Benjamin "Beast" Butler of Massachusetts added the lynch rope to the arsenal of weapons used against the South. A Southern youth made the mistake of removing the invader's flag from a building in occupied New Orleans. He paid dearly for his patriotic enthusiasm. General Butler, commanding officer of the occupation forces in New Orleans, ordered the young Southerner hung by the neck until dead! Such is the tradition of

367

anti-Southern hatred, a tradition inherited and perpetuated by the liberal establishment.

Liberalism is the logical outgrowth of nineteenth-century imperialism. Liberals are in fact latter-day manifest destiny, *e pluribus unum,* imperialists. These imperialists created numerous historical myths to justify their invasion, conquest, and occupation of the Southern nation and the destruction of the original constitutional republic of these United States. These myths of history are accepted and used by the liberal establishment to justify the unconstitutional growth in the power of the central government.

Modern-day liberals depend upon these myths to sustain the alliance between Northern liberals, black militants, and Southern scalawags. This unholy trinity of political power provides the very power base necessary to maintain the liberal establishment's control over education, media, and the government.

To perpetuate this liberal myth of history, the liberal establishment, like any other empire, requires a monopoly in the marketplace of ideas. When was the last time you heard a public educator explain the War for Southern Independence from the Southern point of view? Similar monopolies have developed around the world. After the English invaded and conquered Scotland, laws were enacted to ban aspects of Scottish culture, such as the wearing of kilts, the playing of bag pipes, and other social customs. The English imperialists knew that, if the Scottish people were allowed to preserve their heritage, their pride would serve as a catalyst for the resurgence of Scottish nationalism and would encourage the Scots to demand the right of self-government. The USSR reacted in a similar manner after it invaded and occupied Lithuania. Liberals understand that, if Southerners are allowed to view our heritage with pride we may become too uppity and begin to threaten their power base.

The author of *The Yale Law Journal* article relies upon an unquestioned adherence to the liberal myth of history. He mounts his faithful steed, "False Premise," and rides southward to do battle with the windmills of his liberal imagination. Unfortunately for us, he is destroying not windmills but the cultural heritage of our conquered nation. The following is an example of the article's flawed reasoning:

> The flag's force as a symbol stems from its history. The flag was
> initially designed as a rallying symbol for Confederate troops
> heading into battle. The rebels were fighting for territory, for

economic control, and—it goes without saying—for slavery. The way of life for which the South fought reduced blacks to chattel and left them with 'no rights which the white man was bound to respect.' For blacks, this way of life meant being torn from their homes in Africa, transported like animals across the ocean, bought and sold at auctions, forced to work in inhuman conditions, and raped, burned, and beaten by their masters. The Confederate flag glorifies and moralizes this brutal regime.

If this assessment were correct, then all the evils of the world could be symbolized by one Confederate battle flag. The author of this article offers no concrete evidence to support his slanderous and false allegations against the Southern people. He merely announces his liberal-sanctioned, politically correct version of liberal propaganda, and we are left with only one option, accepting his views. This blind faith in the liberal myth of history is the essence of imperialist propaganda which allows no opposing ideas. The myth has a monopoly in the marketplace of ideas. It controls freedom of access to the media. The use of the myth allows the liberal establishment to condition, as liberal propagandists see it, the gullible masses. The liberal propagandist rings the bell "slavery" and the masses respond with an outpouring of anti-Southern venom. By controlling access to the media and education, the liberal establishment has removed certain embarrassing facts and consigned them to an Orwellian memory hole. Imagine how embarrassing it would be for the liberal establishment if there were general knowledge that Massachusetts was the first colony to engage in the slave trade, that much of the capital used to build the industrial Northeast was amassed from profits of the New England slave trade, that it was primarily the Northern colonies which refused to allow a section in the United States Constitution outlawing the slave trade, or that the thirteen stripes on the United States flag represent thirteen slave-holding colonies, the majority of which were Northern colonies! What would happen to the politically correct arguments against the South if the PC crowd were confronted with the words of one of President Jefferson Davis' former slaves who, when asked by a liberal what he thought about Jefferson Davis, declared, "That I loved him, and I can say that every colored man he ever owned loved him"? The author of this anti-Southern article "Driving Dixie Down" would be hard pressed if he had to compete with the words of a black Mississippi state representative who, in 1890, declared his support for the erection of a monument honoring Confederate soldiers: "I too wore the gray, the same color my master wore. We stayed four long years, and if that war had gone on till now I would have been there yet." It is certainly convenient for the cultural bigots to have a powerful liberal establishment to assure the flow of politically correct propaganda.

The law journal article, "Driving Dixie Down," has an unarticulated but emphatically implied theme that can best be summarized as, "Crackers ain't got no rights." The entire article is a series of attempts to find new and better ways to suppress the symbols of Dixie. No consideration is given to the First Amendment rights of Southerners to express our opinions freely and to participate equally in the "marketplace of ideas." Accordingly, liberals extend First Amendment rights only to those who engage in politically correct speech and expression. It is important to note that the author of the law journal article is not attacking the Confederate battle flag exclusively. He attacks all symbols of the Old South. Those Southerners who are so eager to rush to appease the liberal establishment by substituting the Stars and Bars for the Confederate battle flag need to read Yale's law journal's diatribe of cultural bigotry. Its author is an equal opportunity cultural bigot—he hates all symbols of the South equally! Southerners should consider that the attacks against flying a Confederate flag at the state capitol in Raleigh, North Carolina, centered around the flying of the first national flag (Stars and Bars), not the Confederate battle flag. Southerners should also recall that there have been numerous demands to remove Confederate monuments which had no flags associated with them. Representative Holmes in Montgomery, Alabama, recently declared that it was "time to discard all Confederate symbols." Southern schools, using "Colonels" as a name for their mascots, have been forced to rename their mascots because "Colonels" was proclaimed to be offensive, i.e., too Southern. In this era of multi-culturalism, Southern culture is not politically correct, and, therefore, Southerners have, according to the liberal "PC" police, no right to express pride in their heritage. The lesson for closet Confederates is that there is no place to run and hide; compromise and appeasement is no substitute for standing up and defending our heritage. *The Yale Law Journal* article advances a theory that symbols once used by people engaging in evil activities, when used at a later time by governments, have a chilling effect upon the free speech of certain people. For the purpose of discussion, let us examine this theory and carry it to its logical conclusion. Assuming, for the sake of discussion, that symbols chill free speech, we could logically deduce that certain books have a chilling effect on free speech and, therefore, should be banned from public schools and libraries. According to the "chilling" theory, the South was fighting for slavery and repression. To allow citizens to read Davis' *Rise and Fall of the Confederate Government* would encourage otherwise "normal" people to resist racial equality and black liberation. Further, access to Davis' book would be a direct attempt by the state to encourage politically incorrect ideas dangerous to the free speech of blacks. According to the "chilling" theory, anything that "chills" free speech is unconstitutional. The logical conclusion then would be to remove all such books from the public domain. The problem is that, once the PC crowd starts down the path of cultural cleansing, where will they stop? For instance, if they visit the Peabody Museum in Salem, Massachusetts, they would find a lithograph of the infamous Yankee slaver, the *Nightingale*. What flag would they find flying on that ship? The same flag that flew on her while she was an active participant in the nefarious slave trade—the United States flag! What a chilling effect the sight of this flag must have for some people. I suppose the politically correct thing to do is to ban the United States flag!

The article offers the argument that a state flying the Confederate flag is engaging in government speech. According to this theory, such speech is not protected by the First Amendment, and, therefore, the Federal courts have a duty to ban government speech that chills individual free speech. Implicit in this allegation is that the mere sight of any Southern symbol casts a pall of fear and intimidation over vast segments of the black community, causing them to refrain from freely participating in the "marketplace of ideas." The article's author must have a rather low estimation of the manhood and womanhood of black Southerners if he thinks that the mere sight of a Southern symbol will create such paralyzing fear. He also ignores the fact that, according to a poll by the *Atlanta Constitution,* February 16, 1991, 68% of all Southerners, 76% of whites, and 31% of blacks viewed the Confederate flag as a symbol of Southern Heritage, not as a symbol of racism.

The article's author also ignored the government speech engaged in by the Federal government that not only chilled free speech in the South but also violently denied the Southern people their right of self-determination. Is the author suggesting that the right to live under a government established by the consent of the governed is less important than the vague possibility that a historical symbol may chill someone's desire to express freely themselves? But, as Southerners know only all too well, vassals of an empire have no rights except those few grudgingly sanctioned and enjoyed only at the pleasure of our masters. Masters who have and will again suspend any right when it becomes politically expedient.

The article alleges that the use of Southern symbols by "white supremacy" Southern state governments years ago taints those symbols so thoroughly that, even though current leaders no longer espouse such views, the symbols remain tainted. Therefore, according to the article, the use of those symbols must be judged in light of the original intent, not current usage. The article's author is, in fact, espousing a judicial endorsement of a concept that evil intent is passed from one generation to the next! This theory attempts to punish the current generation for the alleged sins of prior generations. But, again, notice how selective this politically correct theory operates. It would punish Southerners, but what about liberals such as Lincoln who endorsed white supremacy, the Northern states who enacted exclusion laws forbidding free blacks from moving into their fair states, the Northern states who voted to deny the franchise to blacks and to forbid interracial marriages, or the New England states who earned fortunes through the African slave trade? The logical conclusion would be to ban all historical symbols associated with policies no longer accepted by the politically correct liberal establishment. But liberal hypocrisy ignores its own odious past and, with self-righteous complacency, points to the mortal decadence it ascribes to the South.

This article is a typical example of how a liberal using a false premise can argue for the destruction of America's Southern Heritage. While making this vicious and slanderous attack upon Southern Heritage, the article's author has wrapped himself in the robes of righteousness by claiming that he is really inveighing for the rights and liberation of oppressed blacks—sound familiar? Glory, glory, hallelujah; the liberal Empire goes marching on!

The Yale Law Journal article should serve as a warning to all Southerners. Southerners must arise from their complacency and recognize the seriousness of their plight. The South is not an equal partner in this nation. This nation, the United States, today, is not the legitimate and natural outgrowth of the constitutional union the Southern states voluntarily joined in 1787. Southerners were the victims of armed aggression, invasion, and foreign occupation. Our former, prosperous economic and influential political status was destroyed, and the constitutional republic of sovereign states was replaced by a centralized Federal tyranny. Southerners are the children of a conquered nation. They must realize and confront this harsh fact. Once they recognize their position as an oppressed people, they can then continue the struggle begun by their Confederate ancestors to regain their lost estate of constitutional government and liberty. To ignore the condition of the defeated South merely gives the liberal establishment more time to complete their campaign of cultural genocide. Driving Dixie Down or The South Shall Rise Again—the choice is ours!

309 Originally published in *Southern Heritage Magazine,* P.O. Box 3181, Merrifield, VA 22116, John Cummings, editor.

CULTURAL GENOCIDE

By Ron Kennedy[310]

It was a crowded meeting, unusual for a local school board committee meeting, but this meeting was different. We were not here to discuss education of our children: we were here to engage in an ongoing battle with those who are conducting a hate-filled, anti-Southern campaign of cultural genocide! I made my way through the crowded room and found a seat. As a stranger to that area, I had the advantage of being able to observe the players without knowing which side they were on. You could tell from the expressions on the faces of the school board members that they were not looking forward to this meeting. The room buzzed with nervous anticipation. Both sides appeared anxious about what the other side would do or say.

While waiting for the meeting to begin, I recalled the numerous previous battles Southerners and other conquered people have fought to defend their proud heritage. This meeting, after all, really was not so unusual, although I am sure several school board members would have argued that point. But, in reality, the attempt to destroy the heritage of the South was in full force after Lee's surrender at Appomattox. Many returning veterans were forced to remove the buttons from their military coats. Henry K. Douglas, a former staff officer for "Stonewall" Jackson, was arrested for wearing his Confederate uniform in public, and the United States Army stationed armed guards at Arlington Cemetery to prevent Southern ladies from placing flowers upon the graves of their loved ones! No, the attempt to deny the Southern people our right to honor and display the symbols of our heritage is not new. The modern-day cultural bigot is the spiritual descendent of an army of invasion, conquest, occupation, and oppression. Same song, different verse.

Nor is it something unique to the Northern invader and modern-day, politically correct, liberal. When England finally completed its conquest of Scotland, one of the first things it did was to outlaw symbols of Scottish heritage. The invader made himself master of a conquered people and immediately set about destroying the symbols of Scottish nationalism. Why? Did the English Empire really feel threatened by kilts, bag pipes, and other symbols of Scottish culture? As a matter of fact, they did! They knew, just like the liberal invader and the contemporary left-wing cultural bigot know, that anything that might serve to remind the conquered population of their former glory and freedom tends to encourage "unhealthy" disrespect for foreign domination. It tends to encourage anti-imperialist notions of self-determination and archaic ideas that the local people have a right to a government formed upon the consent of the governed! So, for the greater good of the Empire, it is best to destroy or, at least, repress these quaint local customs. The Communist imperialists did the same thing when they invaded and conquered the Baltic states. Stalin had no use for Confederate (oops), I mean Lithuanian flags, except maybe in some dusty old museum exhibit. Yes, the modern-day liberal is following a well-trodden path of tyranny, when he demands the removal of "offensive" Southern symbols. The history of tyranny demonstrates that a conquered people have no rights even though they make up the democratic majority within their defeated nation.

At last the meeting began. It was easy to see that the school board president had conducted difficult meetings before. He was diplomatic but firm. Everyone would have an opportunity, but there was no doubt about who was running this meeting. The issue revolved around the mascots of two schools, one the "Rebels" and the other the "Colonels." Several speakers thought these names were offensive and encouraged racism. "Good," "bad," "evil," "virtuous," these are mortal attributes—can inanimate objects possess moral attributes? The more I listened, the more I wanted to cry out, "What's your real purpose? What are you really trying to do? What or whom are you really trying to punish—symbols or people?" My mind raced back to Senator McGovern's failed presidential campaign when he told Southerners that busing was a penalty we would have to pay to make up for the sins of our past! I also recalled the statement of a black political leader in Baton Rouge, Louisiana, who responded to a question about why the majority should be forced to endure busing by stating, in effect, that they (the minority) now had the power and it was our (white citizens) turn to suffer. Yes, there were several speakers who appeared to want to turn the political process into a Hatfield,

McCoy blood feud. So now, we see spite and hatred as witnesses arrayed against our Southern Heritage.

Other speakers followed, each in their turn sounding more and more ridiculous. One gentleman honestly thought that the fuss over the Confederacy was much overrated because Louisiana was "in the Confederacy for only one year." One year! Tell that to the men and comrades of the Twelfth Louisiana Infantry who marched away in 1861, fought four long and dangerous years, surrendered in 1865 in Greensboro, North Carolina, and then walked back to Louisiana! One year indeed! Add misinformation to the list of witnesses arrayed against our Southern Heritage.

Then, there appeared a lady of no small weight in the community who declared that her ancestors had suffered under Nazism in Europe. She declared that, even though she hated the symbol of Nazism, the swastika, she still would not want to deny someone the right to display one. But she did not think it would be right for the school board to use public money to place a swastika on a public school. Therefore, she thought the use of "Rebels" and "Colonels" was wrong "since it was offensive to some shouldn't we change those names, sort of like a sacrifice to prove that we are sorry?" or words to that effect. Let it be written, let it be done. Without even presenting the slightest evidence, this lady equates our Southern Heritage with Nazism! In addition, she decides to dispense with the democratic process of majority rule and to allow the dictatorship of the minority, just because a few people decide that a historical symbol is offensive! The big lie and the rule of the few are more appropriate for Nazism than an American school board. Add stupidity to the list of witnesses arrayed against our Southern Heritage.

Next, there arose a white United Methodist minister. No Bible-thumper he; no, this man surely must belong to the modern school of liberation theology. He had personally attended a local football game where the mere presence of a "Rebel" flag was sufficient to deny black people the right to sit in the bleachers wherever they pleased. He was mortified at this gross example of insensitivity and virulent racism. My, my, I have heard Greenpeace tree huggers who made better sense! I must have a higher appreciation for the manhood and womanhood of black Southerners than this liberation theologian because I cannot imagine a modern-day black Southerner being intimidated by an individual much less by an inanimate object!

The liberation theologian would not countenance the idea that, to the majority of Southerners, the Confederate flag represents heritage, not racism! This was not the first time he had spoken out demanding the removal of that hated flag! He was driven, nay, consumed by a self-righteous fury against that hated banner of the Confederate South. No need to remind him of the rights of the majority! Don't bother him with facts and arguments about constitutional rights of free expression; his mind was already made up! It would be well if he would heed Thomas Paine's admonition: "He that would make his own liberty secure must guard even his enemy from oppression." But, no matter, he was prepared to use the police power of government to deny Southerners the right to express their love freely for their Southern Heritage. Now comes intolerance to the list of those witnesses arrayed against our Southern Heritage.

Several people spoke on behalf of keeping the Southern symbols and mascots for the schools. A Baptist minister, a local GOP committee member, re-enactors, a representative of the Sons of Confederate Veterans, and numerous other private citizens. No one made a plea for or defense of racism. All denied any linkage between the Southern mascots and racism. The only negative witnesses appearing on our side were "lack of courtesy" and "lack of respect." These two did not come boldly before the board and defend their opinions but, instead, cowardly hissed and booed from the back of the room. I was embarrassed to be linked with such rude behavior. Somebody's mama would have whipped them if she had seen their behavior that night! Yes, even the children of the conquered nation can also be guilty of intolerance. Thomas Paine's recommendation applies to us, just like it does to the liberation theologian. Not only is it right to respect those who you disagree with but also it is dumb not to be respectful because, in our situation, it plays into their hands if we act in a disrespectful manner.

Shortly after the failure of the liberal establishment to remove the Confederate flag from the Georgia state flag, the "civil rights" establishment decided upon a new tactic. They took their campaign to a small Georgia town where the largest Klan group in the state just happened to be located. Now the intention was to provoke a reaction similar to the one they provoked in Forsyth County. What happened? Nothing! The local Sons of Confederate Veterans and other concerned citizens met with the appropriate individuals and convinced them not to react. The liberal press was eagerly awaiting the expected fray. It did not happen, and the cultural bigots lost again. Being a Southern gentleman or lady is not only the right thing to do but also the smartest thing to do. Even though we are the victims of intolerance, this does not justify intolerance on our part.

At last, the meeting was over. We had seen an array of witnesses speaking against our Southern Heritage; spite and hatred, misinformation, stupidity, and intolerance were all there. Unfortunately, "lack of respect" and "lack of courtesy" booed and hissed from our corner. Like pesky mosquitos late at night, though they be small in size and few in number, their sound filled up the room.

The committee of the school board decided to put the decision off until the following night when they voted eleven to four to keep the Southern mascots. Good for our side, but the opposition vowed to take the matter to Federal court. Yes, believe it or not, back in 1969 a Federal court ruled that all symbols of the South must be removed from the schools because, according to the Federal judge, they tended to promote segregation. Without the benefit of due process, the heritage of the majority was branded by a Federal judge as "racist" and was censored. We must now look to the same Federal government that gave us invasion, conquest, occupation, and oppression to dispense justice! Perhaps secession, Lithuania style, isn't such a bad idea after all!

310 Originally published in *Southern Heritage Magazine,* P.O. Box 3181, Merrifield, VA 22116, John Cummings, editor.

RECOMMENDED ORGANIZATIONS

The following is a list of a few of many organizations that are currently working to restore our original constitutional government or fighting to preserve our American Heritage. If you would like to take an active part in this ongoing struggle, then we invite you to check into these organizations. Each organization is different. One may concentrate on fighting busing and reverse discrimination, whereas another may be fighting to preserve Southern Heritage, and another may be engaged in the political struggle to re-establish the authority of the Tenth Amendment, nullification, and secession. As with any organization, we encourage you to make sure that the organization's goals are goals that you will proudly support. *Caveat Emptor!*

1. The Southern League, Inc., P.O. Box 40910, Tuscaloosa, AL 35404-0910; tel: 205-553-0155; Dr. Michael Hill, president; board of directors, Dr. Clyde Wilson, Dr. Grady McWhiney, Dr. Thomas Fleming, and Rev. J. Steven Wilkins. The Southern League is dedicated to putting secession back into the American political debate. Its goal is to secure the economic, social, and political independence of the South and any other American state that desires to resurrect our original constitutional Republic of Republics.

2. The Ludwig von Mises Institute, Auburn, AL 36849-5301; tel: 344-844-2500. The von Mises Institute is a world-renowned conservative "think tank" located in Auburn, Alabama. Its scholars have been in the vanguard of the struggle to dethrone Big Government and restore local control, State's Rights, and limited Federalism.

3. The Sons of Confederate Veterans (SCV), Box 59, Columbia, TN 38402-0059; tel: 1-800-My-Dixie or 1-800-My-South. The SCV is composed of male descendants of Confederate veterans. It is dedicated to preserving and promoting the legacy of America's

Confederate heroes. The SCV has been in the forefront of the battle to maintain the public display of Confederate battle flags and monuments and the celebration of Confederate holidays. The SCV has led the fight to correct the "politically correct" history of the War for Southern Independence. The Confederate Rose is sponsored by the SCV and is a society for ladies who wish to help promote and preserve America's Confederate Heritage.

4. The Council of Conservative Citizens (CCC), P.O. Box 9683, St. Louis, MO 63122. The CCC has been actively engaged in the fight against busing and reverse discrimination. The CCC has local chapters in states throughout the country.

RECOMMENDED BOOKS

1. *The South Was Right!* James Ronald Kennedy and Walter Donald Kennedy, Pelican Publishing Company, 1101 Monroe St., Gretna, LA 70053, 2nd edition, 1994. The authors maintain, through rigorous research, that the South had a legal precedent to secede and a right to defend its borders. Even today it has just as much reason to reclaim its liberty as the people of Poland and the Baltic states. This book gives the invaded nation's view of the War for Southern Independence.

2. *A View of the Constitution: Secession as Taught at West Point,* William Rawle, edited and annotated by Walter Donald Kennedy and James Ronald Kennedy, originally published in 1825, republished in 1993 by Old South Books, P.O. Box 46, Simsboro, LA 70251. One of the first texts on the United States Constitution. Judge Rawle, a Northern abolitionist, unequivocally stated in this work that the states have a right to secede from the Union.

3. *Abandoned: The Betrayal of the American Middle Class Since World War II,* William J. Quirk and Randall Bridwell, Madison Books, New York, NY, 1992. The authors demonstrate how liberalism's experiment with non-democratic government created a fatal schism between the government and the majority of Americans.

4. *Guns, Crime, and Freedom,* Wayne LaPierre, Regnery Publishing, Inc., Washington, D.C., 1994. The best single source for those who wish to defend their right to keep and bear arms. The author explores issues such as crime, gun control, and media bias.

5. *Lost Rights: The Destruction of American Liberty,* James Bovard, St. Martin's Press, New York, NY, 1994. The author provides documentation of a government out of control. From Justice Department officials seizing people's homes to the perpetrators of the Waco siege, government officials are tearing the Bill of Rights to pieces and this book gives you the details.

6. *The News Manipulators: Why You Can't Trust the News,* Reed Irvine, Joseph C. Goulden, and Cliff Kincaid, Book Distributors, Inc., Smithtown, NY, 1993. Reed Irvine has performed yeoman's work in the struggle against the biased left-wing news media. Read this book and you will never trust the media again. See for yourself that national left-wing media such as *Time* have admitted to "tailoring" the news to push causes that they believe in.

7. *A Constitutional History of the United States,* Dr. Forrest McDonald, Robert E. Krieger Publishing Company, Malabar, FL, 1986. In the preface of his book this noted authority wrote that for the better part of the first century of American history under the Constitution the Supreme Court made no claim to being the sole or final arbiter of what the Constitution meant: "I share Jefferson's belief that it is the right and duty of all branches of the federal government and of the states as well—and not just of the federal judiciary—to guard the Constitution against encroachments."

8. *Original Intentions: On the Making and Ratification of the United States Constitution,* Dr. M. E. Bradford, The University of Georgia Press, Athens, GA, 1993. The author reveals a Constitution notably short on abstract principles and modest in any goal beyond limiting the powers of the government it authorizes.

9. *Founding Fathers,* Dr. M. E. Bradford, University Press of Kansas, Lawrence, KS, 1994. Bradford complied biographical sketches for all fifty-five Framers who attended the Philadelphia Convention. He examined their constitutional theories, their visions for the newly founded union, and their opinions on ratification of the Constitution.

10. *The Confederate Constitution of 1861,* Dr. Marshall L. DeRosa, University of Missouri Press, Columbia, MO, 1991. The constitutional principles reaffirmed by the Confederate Constitution are relevant not only to the history of the War for Southern Independence, but to fundamental issues currently confronting the American republic. DeRosa's insights into the nature of American Federalism will fuel contemporary debate on civil rights and liberties, presidential line-item veto power, and fiscal responsibility.

11. *Principles of Confederacy,* John Remington Graham, Northwest Publishing, Inc., Salt Lake City, UT, 1994. The author, a Northerner, explains the original meaning of every clause of the American Constitution as framed by the Philadelphia Convention of 1787 and the First Congress in 1789. Here is the fundamental law of a confederacy of free, sovereign, and independent states whose root precepts were used to dispel injustice and induce peace. The rejection of these principles led to the American Civil War and the establishment of Big Government in Washington, D.C.

12. *Time on the Cross: The Economics of American Negro Slavery,* Robert William Fogel and Stanley L. Engerman, W. W. Norton and Company, New York, NY, 1989. This study of the economics of American Negro slavery was denounced by the politically correct crowd. But, to the dismay of liberals, in 1993 Dr. Fogel was named the Nobel Laureate in Economic Science as a result of this work! Proof that truth, though crushed to the earth, shall rise again!

13. *The Federal Government: Its True Nature and Character,* Abel P. Upshur, St. Thomas Press, Houston, TX, 1977, reprint of 1868 text. Judge Upshur refutes those of the Story and Webster school who believe that the Constitution made the Federal government the supreme ruler of the people of the United States.

14. *Free To Choose,* Milton Friedman, Harcourt Brace Jovanovich, New York, NY, 1980. Friedman explains why it is necessary to protect individual freedom and its importance to economic prosperity.

15. *Civil Rights: Rhetoric or Reality?,* Thomas Sowell, William Morrow and Company, Inc., New York, NY, 1984. The author is a Senior Fellow at the Hoover Institution, Stanford University. He dares to raise questions that others would not admit to thinking: ". . . something that needs to be said—and because other people have better sense than to say it."

16. *The Law,* Frederic Bastiat (1801-1850), The Foundation for Economic Education, Inc., Irvington-On-Hudson, NY, 1994. This little book warns all who will read it that government has within it the propensity to abuse the rights and property of the people. The

author describes the legitimate function of government and warns against any government that attempts to deprive its citizens of their property by way of taxation.

17. *For a New Liberty: The Libertarian Manifesto,* Murray N. Rothbard, Macmillan Publishing Company, Inc., New York, NY, 1973. Murray Rothbard (1926-1995) was one of America's leading advocates of limited Federalism, individual responsibility, and local control of government.

18. *Judicial Dictatorship,* William J. Quirk and R. Randall Bridwell, Transaction Publishers, 1995. The authors of *Abandoned: The Betrayal of the American Middle Class Since World War II* turn their guns on the Federal Supreme Court. They discuss such issues as who will decide if government has gone beyond its proper powers.

Bibliography

BOOKS

Bastiat, Frederic, *The Law,* reprint of 1850 edition, The Foundation For Economic Education, Inc., Irvington-On-Hudson, New York, 1994.

Bledsoe, Albert T., *Is Davis a Traitor?,* The Advocate House, St. Louis, Missouri, 1879.

Bradford, M.E., *Founding Fathers,* University of Kansas Press, Lawrence, Kansas, 1994.

Bradford, M.E., *Original Intentions: On the Making and Ratification of the United States Constitution,* The University of Georgia Press, Athens, Georgia, 1993.

Brutus, Junius, *Vindiciae Contra Tyrannos,* reprint of 1689 translation, Still Waters Revival Books, Edmonton, Canada, 1989.

Burnham, James, *Suicide of the West,* The John Day Company, New York, New York, 1964.

Calhoun, John C., *The Works of John C. Calhoun,* D. Appleton and Company, New York, New York, 1844.

Carey, George W. and McClellan, James, *The Federalist: Student Edition,* Kendall/Hunt Publishing Company, Dubuque, Iowa, 1990.

Curtis, George M. III and Thompson, James J. Jr., Eds., *The Southern Essays of Richard M. Weaver,* Liberty Press, Indianapolis, Indiana, 1987.

DeRosa, Marshall L., *The Confederate Constitution of 1861,* University of Missouri Press, Columbia, Missouri, London, 1991.

de Tocqueville, Alexis, *Democracy in America,* Mayer and Lerner, Eds., Harper and Row, New York, New York, 1966.

Ely, James, *The Guardian of Every Other Right: A Constitutional History of Property Rights,* Oxford University Press, New York, New York, 1992.

Fischer, Louis, *The Life of Mahatma Gandhi,* Harper and Row, New York, New York, 1983.

Fogel, R. W. and Engerman, S. L., *Time on the Cross,* Little, Brown and Company, Boston, Massachusetts, 1974.

Friedman, Milton, *Free to Choose,* Harcourt Brace Jovanovich, New York, New York, 1980.

Graham, John Remington, *Principles of Confederacy,* Northwest Publishing, Inc., Salt Lake City, Utah, 1994.

Henry, William Wirt, Ed. *Patrick Henry: Life, Correspondence, and Speeches,* reprint of 1891 edition, Sprinkle Publications, Harrisonburg, Virginia, 1993.

Herrnstein, Richard J., and Murray, Charles, *The Bell Curve: Intelligence and Class Structure in American Life,* The Free Press, New York, London, Toronto, Sydney, Tokyo, Singapore, 1994.

Hutchins, Maynard, Ed., *Great Books of the Western World,* Encyclopedia Britannica, Chicago, Illinois, 1952.

Irvine, Reed, Goulden, Joseph C., and Kincaid, Cliff, *The News Manipulators: Why You Can't Trust the News,* Book Distributors, Inc., Smithtown, New York, 1993.

Kennedy, James R. and Kennedy, Walter D., *The South Was Right!,* Pelican Publishing Company, Gretna, Louisiana, 1994.

Kent, James, *Commentaries on American Laws,* Da Capo Press, New York, New York, 1971.

LaPierre, Wayne, *Guns, Crime, and Freedom,* Regnery Publishing, Inc., Washington, D.C., 1994.

McDonald, Forrest, *A Constitutional History of the United States,* Robert E. Krieger Publishing Company, Malabar, Florida, 1982.

O'Brien, David M., *Constitutional Law and Politics,* W. W. Norton and Company, New York, New York, 1982.

Pole, J. R., Ed., *The American Constitution for and against The Federalist and Anti-Federalist Papers,* Hill and Wang, New York, New York, 1987.

Quirk, William J. and Bridwell, R. Randall, *Abandoned: The Betrayal of the American Middle Class Since World War II,* Madison Books, Lanham, Maryland, New York, London, 1992.

Rawle, William, *A View of the Constitution: Secession as Taught at West Point,* reprint of 1825 edition, Walter D. Kennedy and James R.

Kennedy, Eds., Old South Books, Simsboro, Louisiana, 1993.

Rothbard, Murray N., *For a New Liberty: The Liberterian Manifesto,* MacMillan Publishing Company, New York, New York, 1973.

Rutherford, Samuel, *Lex Rex,* reprint of 1644 edition, Sprinkle Publications, Harrisonburg, Virginia, 1982.

Semmes, Raphael, *Memoirs of Service Afloat,* reprint of 1868 edition, The Blue and Gray Press, Secaucus, New Jersey, 1987.

Sowell, Thomas, *Civil Rights: Rhetoric or Reality?,* William Morrow and Company, New York, New York, 1984.

Storing, H., Ed., *The Anti-Federalist,* The University of Chicago Press, Chicago, Illinois, 1985.

Upshur, Abel P., *The Federal Government: Its True Nature and Character,* reprint of 1868 edition, St. Thomas Press, Houston, Texas, 1977.

Weaver, Richard M., *The Southern Tradition at Bay,* Arlington House, New Rochelle, New York, 1968.

Whitaker, Robert W., *A Plague on Both Your Houses,* Robert B. Luce, Inc., Washington, New York, 1976.

Winters, John D., *The Civil War in Louisiana,* Louisiana State University Press, Baton Rouge, Louisiana, 1963.

NEWSPAPERS

Detroit News, 12/10/91

The Hattiesburg (MS) *American,* 7/11/93

The (New Orleans, LA) *Times Picayune,* 3/18/94

The (New Orleans, LA) *Times Picayune,* 10/10/94

The (New Orleans, LA) *Times Picayune,* 12/14/94

The (New Orleans, LA) *Times Picayune,* 1/1/95

The (New Orleans, LA) *Times Picayune,* 1/3/95

The USA Today, 12/21/93

The USA Today, 1/20/95

The Wall Street Journal, 5/28/93

The Wall Street Journal, 6/1/93

The Wall Street Journal, 6/22/93

The Wall Street Journal, 6/27/93

The Wall Street Journal, 9/27/93

The Wall Street Journal, 9/29/93
The Wall Street Journal, 9/30/93
The Wall Street Journal, 10/13/93
The Wall Street Journal, 11/2/93
The Wall Street Journal, 11/10/93
The Wall Street Journal, 12/9/93
The Wall Street Journal, 12/13/93
The Wall Street Journal, 12/15/93
The Wall Street Journal, 12/27/93
The Wall Street Journal, 12/29/93
The Wall Street Journal, 12/31/93
The Wall Street Journal, 1/31/94
The Wall Street Journal, 2/3/94
The Wall Street Journal, 2/8/94
The Wall Street Journal, 2/25/94
The Wall Street Journal, 4/19/94
The Wall Street Journal, 4/26/94
The Wall Street Journal, 5/4/94
The Wall Street Journal, 5/18/94
The Wall Street Journal, 6/6/94
The Wall Street Journal, 7/11/94
The Wall Street Journal, 8/23/94
The Wall Street Journal, 8/31/94
The Wall Street Journal, 9/7/94
The Wall Street Journal, 9/12/94
The Wall Street Journal, 9/14/94
The Wall Street Journal, 9/20/94
The Wall Street Journal, 9/29/94
The Wall Street Journal, 10/4/94
The Wall Street Journal, 10/12/94
The Wall Street Journal, 10/19/94
The Wall Street Journal, 10/20/94
The Wall Street Journal, 10/23/94
The Wall Street Journal, 12/21/94

The Wall Street Journal, 1/4/95
The Washington Times, 7/4/94
The Washington Times, 9/28/92

MAGAZINES AND JOURNALS

American Spectator, August 1994
Congressional Record, March 8, 1991
Congressional Record, June 12, 1991
82 Michigan Law Review, 1983
Insight, August 22, 1994
Southern Partisan, 2nd Quarter, 1994
Urban Lawyer, Summer 1988
Washington Legal Foundation, October 23, 1992
World, August 13, 1994

COURT CASES

Barrow v. Baltimore, 77 Peters 234 (1833)
Brown v. Board of Education of Topeka, 347 U.S. 482 (1954)
Chisholm v. Georgia, 2 U.S. 419 (1793)
Marbury v. Madison, 1 Cranch 137 (1803)
Minnick v. Mississippi, 498 U.S. 146 (1990)
Plessy v. Ferguson, 163 U.S. 537 (1896)
Wickard v. Filburn, 317 U.S. 111 (1942)

Index